The Process of Creative Writing

THE PROCESS

OF CREATIVE

WRITING

Revised Edition

1236

PEARL HOGREFE

Professor of English, Iowa State College

Harper & Brothers: Publishers: New York

CONTENTS

PREFACE

The author of *The Process of Creative Writing* (first published in 1947) hopes that this revised edition will be useful to two groups of people: first, those who are interested primarily in the techniques of writing; second, those who have also a philosophy of creative writing.

Being among those who do have a definite philosophy, the author is willing to state that philosophy explicitly. First, the best material for creative writing is the stuff of experience, especially inner experience, or outer experience interpreted by inner feeling. Part of this idea was stated by Sir Philip Sidney more than three hundred fifty years ago: "Fool!" said my muse to me, "look in thy heart, and write." Another part of the same idea, perhaps, is that one must explore and discover significant experience and must use his mind also to shape it into created form. Second, creative writing is communication. The term does not mean the use of simple words that would make any child understand, or the distortion of the complex and intangible to make it seem simple, or the violation of the writer's individuality. It does mean that a writer must have in mind an audience (even if it is a limited, select one) and must make an honest effort to convey something significant to him, instead of taking shelter in obscurity. Third, honest writing, for the writer himself, is an education, a growth, a release of tensions, and a discovery of powers. If you do not agree with this philosophy, perhaps you have one of your own, or at least a no-philosophy.

The term *process* in the title is closely related to a philosophy of writing. It implies that the writer is like a miner, refiner, and goldsmith combined. He digs out nuggets of truth from the stores of his experience, separates gold from dross, finds techniques and patterns, and then shapes the gold into artistic units. (The term *process* as used in Chapter 15 and some of the other chapters in Part II, has a more limited and conventional meaning. It is used for the kind of exposition that tells how things are done, for general principles explained in time order. In this sense *process* is an accepted term used in most of the textbooks that deal with exposition.)

Some important changes have been made in this edition of *The Process of Creative Writing*. First, Part I now emphasizes specific narrative, from the moment of experience to the developed short story. Second, Part II, which has been added, emphasizes personalized exposition—all generalized information, subjective or objective, whether it uses time, space, space and time, or logical patterns. The assignments concern only personalized material (material made vivid and interesting by descriptive and narrative details, by the writer's attitudes, and by consideration of the reader's interest). But those who wish to write impersonal exposition or to ask their students to write it may find that the discussions of analyzing and outlining are applicable to either type.

The emphasis on overlapping throughout the book is no accident. It is deliberate and intentional, to bring out the profound truth that, although there are differences, there are no rigid lines between narration and exposition, narration and description, exposition and argument, or between incident and short story, personal and impersonal essay. We do make definitions which are useful for teaching and for handling pieces of writing that approach the norm. But the more individual and artistic a unit of writing is, the more difficult it is to define or classify. Definitions and principles are not laws or strait jackets.

In this edition of the book questions on reading have been added at the end of all the chapters that have readings of any length. Anyone who wishes may, of course, ignore these questions. Their chief purpose is to guide students away from reading only for the facts, and toward reading for the details which make writing effective. Compositions written by other students offer more contrast between success and failure in achieving effects; professional examples, though they are not always perfect, furnish a stimulus to aspirations.

Teachers, and students as well, have raised questions which have no visible effect on this edition. First, why aren't there longer assignments earlier? The real answers to this question is that almost any assignment may be as long as the writer chooses, or at least long in proportion to his skill and the complexity of his material. If a student can write a short story for his assignment in Chapter 3, probably no one will wish to stop him. Another form of the same question is this: Why don't we get at a short story earlier? One answer to it has just been given. Another answer is that the assignments in Chapters 11, 12, and 13 are essentially short stories. For each of them the mature student may write a story as long and complex as his powers permit. But time is fleet-footed; human flesh is frail enough to crave food, sleep, and recreation; and each unit of human flesh has other courses in college or other duties in life; hence the assignments are phrased below the maximum. Second, why isn't there more reading, or why aren't there more short stories? To include large numbers would increase the size of the book beyond practical limits. For writing models, too, the stories should mainly illustrate contemporary techniques; and professional writers often ask large fees for the privilege of reprinting whole stories. Thus the price of the book might be doubled. Perhaps those who wish more reading can supplement by using some of the excellent anthologies already in print. Third, why is narration placed first in the book? A minor reason is that chapters on narration composed most of the first edition; thus it was natural to add a Part II. But a major reason is that this author, though believing that either exposition or narrative could be taught better *after* the other, considers the sensory details of narrative especially important to personalized exposition. A teacher who wishes to use Part II first might ask his students to read Chapters 1, 2, and 3 as background for personalized exposition.

Since the first edition of this book appeared I have enjoyed hearing (by letter, telephone, and in person) from many individual readers not connected with college classes. Whether you are interested in techniques only or in your development through writing, I have had you also in mind during this revision. May I hope that you will find this second edition useful?

PEARL HOGREFE

ACKNOWLEDGMENTS

As I complete the revised edition of *The Process of Creative Writing* I am grateful still to those people whom I thanked in the earlier edition, including the administrators who have made possible a program of creative writing at Iowa State College. I wish to thank also the teachers in other colleges and universities who have found the book useful and have told me so. Some teachers have given detailed comments. Chief among these are Roxy Lafforge, Executive Dean, Philippine Christian Colleges, who sent me the comments of her students; and Cecil B. Williams, Oklahoma A. and M. College, who prepared a questionnaire on the book and sent me a complete set of student answers. I am grateful also to the individuals, college students and others, who have written me directly about the book.

Two members of my own department, Leonard Feinberg and Albert L. Walker, have used the book enough to have definite opinions. Both have given a critical reading to some parts of my new discussions, made other detailed comments, and suggested some new readings. To both I am sincerely grateful.

PEARL HOGREFE

October, 1955

Any idea that ignores the necessary role of intelligence in production of works of art is based upon identification of thinking with use of one special kind of material, verbal signs and words. To think effectively in terms of relations of qualities is as severe a demand upon thought as to think in terms of symbols, verbal and mathematical. Indeed, since words are easily manipulated in mechanical ways, the production of a work of genuine art probably demands more intelligence than does most of the so-called thinking that goes on among those who pride themselves on being "intellectuals." . . . Only the psychology that has separated things which in reality belong together holds that scientists and philosophers think, while poets and painters follow their feelings. In both, and to the same extent in the degree to which they are of comparable rank, there is emotionalized thinking . . . artists have for their subject matter the qualities of things of direct experience; "intellectual" inquirers deal with these qualities at one remove, through the medium of symbols that stand for qualities but are not significant in their immediate presence. . . . But there is no difference as far as dependence on emotionalized ideas and subconscious maturing are concerned.

From *Art as Experience* by John Dewey
Courtesy of G. P. Putnam's Sons.

PART I

Narration, Short Story

1

Introduction

If you wish to write well, what are the bases for your development?

Your first basis is originality. If you are a complete conformist you cannot do good writing. If you strain to be different you may only distort your growth and become eccentric. You cannot be completely different, of course, but you can be reasonably original. How? Your inner life and even your combinations of outer experience are entirely your own: your meeting with another person is never twice alike; you never see twice exactly the same sky or the same pattern of weather; you cannot, in two separate moments of time, repeat the same details in your stream of consciousness. "What is called 'originality' in a writer—if it is rightly so-called— is nothing but the complete absence of duplicity." [1] That is, you can be original, within the limits of your own personality, by being yourself.

Your second basis of good writing is honesty. How can you achieve honesty, and what does it mean in writing? You must have something to say, whether it is large or small, and you must mean what you say, instead of trying to fool your reader or yourself or playing a guessing game with him when you do not know the answer. You do not need always to have a "message"; certainly you should not sound like a preacher or a teacher. But when you say what you feel as honestly as you can, you have a large scope; you

[1] Phyllis Bottome, "The Responsibilities of a Writer," in Dale Warren (ed.), *What Is a Book?* Houghton Mifflin Company, 1935.

3

may communicate the feel of a moment of experience or suggest social significance with deft individuality.

But suppose, to take an extreme or improbable case, that you are not trying to shock people, and that your honest attitudes are unsocial or immoral when judged by conventional standards. Should you still write honestly? Yes, even then you need to say as much as you can of what you mean and to mean something in all you write.

Whether you are social or antisocial, you can write about trifles without being superficial or trifling, if your muscles and nerves believe what you say and if you find fresh, individual words. In suggesting that trifles are amusing or tiresome or refreshing or beautiful or ugly, you can write well.

Your third basis for development is the discovery and use of your best subjects. To find these you need to explore the world of your outer experience—your surroundings, the people you know, the events you watched or shaped; but even more you need to explore your world of inner reality which is built from your own thoughts and feelings. Your outer experience is unimportant when it is not shaped by your inner experience. Your better subjects are those which move you to amusement, dislike, or admiration; your best subjects are those which involve your psychological needs—your dreams and hopes and fears—though you may need to create action or characters to give them tangible form.[2]

How will you find good subjects? If you are in a college class, your teacher's questions and suggestions may help—especially the suggestions made in conferences—your fellow students may stimulate you, or you may use the questions in the Appendix of this book.

You may find ideas also by doing spadework in the soil of your experience. Begin by trying to recall your earliest memories, especially pictures and sensory details, asking yourself not only what you recall but why, and whether memory has any importance for you in the present. Analyze your environments and their effects on you. List the people who have had an influence, good or bad, on you; try to understand their traits and your attitudes to them. Find

[2] Bernard De Voto, "The Threshold of Fiction," *Harper's Magazine*, January, 1940. This article states well a view that many other writers support.

the ideas which have become emotionalized for you from life, including the principles held by your family, your friends, and your community, your own agreement or disagreement with these principles, and your code of conduct or personal philosophy. Name your frustrations, satisfactions, loves, hates, fears, prejudices, so far as you can penetrate that complex jungle of yourself.

You may use the results of this spadework to start a creative diary. This diary will not be a mere record of facts, but jottings to recall people, events, scenes, attitudes, or ideas so that you will be ready to use them in the future; it will not be creative writing but the raw material for future writing. If you work at it consistently, a few minutes each day, you will have a wealth of material. But do not assume that you ever have enough subjects; adding five or ten more, even if you never use them, may give you extra dividends in using your one best subject.

Fourth, your willingness to communicate your attitudes to your readers in some way, either subjective or objective, is an important foundation for your writing. You cannot interest readers by giving them a mere collection of facts. If you have unusual skill, you may *seem* to write objectively. But you will neither develop nor learn techniques by arranging mere facts and then leaving the reader to make up his own mind about your meaning.

Fifth, you will try to learn how to control or to create your own inspiration. Of course you can work better at some times than others, whether you are repairing a car, playing football, washing dishes, singing, giving a piano recital, or writing. But in life you meet deadlines—when the game is called, or the concert begins. Few poems or stories spring full-grown from the brain of an unsuspecting Zeus; some poems which seem spontaneous, like those by Poe and Swinburne, exist in early drafts that are quite different from the familiar versions. Your stories which rely on a last-minute burst of inspiration will usually be failures, though an occasional story which develops without conscious effort may come from years of unconscious creation. Your complex stories which are successful will probably come from a growing ability to use your mind for planning and your emotions for the final creation without having them interfere with each other. Nothing hinders a writer's growth as much as an illusion that he may wait instead of sweat for an inspiration—unless it is a willingness to stagnate in chaotic academic writing.

How can you create or control your inspiration? First, you will have regular times for writing, when you are not abnormally tired. Second, through spadework in your experience and a creative diary, you will have on hand a good supply of subjects. Third, you will read stimulating material, even read it aloud, to stir your senses, attitudes, and imagination. Fourth, you will use all your senses on your own subject. Fifth, when you are learning a new technique, you will have the patience to practice, as if you were learning a new method of welding or a new stroke in tennis. Your techniques become useful as you learn to use them without conscious struggle.

You will find some of these ideas developed more fully in later chapters. But your ideas about originality, honesty, finding and using your best subjects, communicating your attitudes, and learning to create and control inspiration will be the foundation of your development.

PROGRESSIVE DEVELOPMENT

You will probably develop your powers best, unless you are an unusual student, if you begin with simple assignments and emphasize each time a new technique or closely related techniques. But even at the start you should feel free to use any methods at your command and to write units as complex as you can manage. Always you will use techniques to express living material. You will not do exercises to prepare you for writing; instead you will write.

ASSUMPTIONS

Certain assumptions have been made in this chapter without comment; certain others will be made later. All of these have been tested by the experience of many students and all have been helpful to some students. None of them are dogma but they all have support in the practice or the theory of effective writers. You may try them for yourself. But unless your effort is to be wasted, you must try them thoroughly. Here are the most important of these assumptions or working hypotheses:

1. Artistic writing is experience, the communication in words of a living impulse.

2. A living impulse involves the mind, the emotion, and the body.

3. The senses are the means by which human beings experience a living impulse, re-create it for others, or perceive it aesthetically in the artistic creation of other people.

4. "An experience" is specific. Hence, the emphasis in the assignments which follow will be placed upon using a specific time, place, mood, and situation. (Those who do excellent work with less specific details have earned their right to use their own methods.)

5. Creation is activity.

6. Moments of change and growth are the best parts of subjects to use in conveying experience.

7. Plot, if it is an organic growth from material, helps a writer express himself with ease and power.

8. Any method or technique is bad if it thwarts, and good if it helps, the communication of the living material.

2

The Feel of Experience

The material for your creative writing, as you noticed in Chapter 1, comes from your attitudes to experience. You cannot use bare experience free of attitudes any more than you can make silk purses from blackberry briars. Usually in a unit of creative work you express one attitude or emotion which is its center, its reason for existence. Often, especially in longer units, you express other, subordinate emotions which are essential to your artistic aim. But always you express attitudes—whether you communicate your enjoyment of swimming, your pleasure in a beautiful scene, or your admiration, irritation, amusement as you respond to a person. When you describe, characterize, narrate, when you write a sketch, a poem, a short story, a novel, or even an article which is not pure information, you are expressing attitudes. In this chapter you are beginning with simple activities; then you will progress to more complex units, until you are writing a well-developed story or even a novel. In all these things the use of your mind is important, too; but wherever you succeed, you will express attitudes or emotions.

You may be accustomed to other terms for the same thing: flavor, personal slant, individuality, emotional coloring, an inner feeling, a value judgment or a sense of values. But no matter what term you use, your individual reaction makes your writing creative.

If you wish to write without having any attitude to bring out you might write scientific facts, reports of testimony in a court of law, or news stories, though many news stories have personal slanting, more or less concealed, for the reader's interest. But you should not try descriptive and narrative writing as it is discussed in these chapters.

If you wish to leave a reader to find a meaning of his own because you do not have one, you have given up all the methods you might use to create a real interest in your reader. You have also given up the values you might get from writing—such values as finding your meaning, your attitudes and perceptions, and selecting and arranging to bring order from chaos. You have already reached a dead end. For your job as a writer is to communicate something and to know the kind of audience you wish to reach. You cannot hope to reach morons, children, and sophisticated adults all at the same time; often your best audience will be people with your own tastes and interests. But you must have your own artistic aim.

HOW TO EXPRESS YOUR ATTITUDES

How will you express your attitudes with the greatest power? You will not *tell* us in general terms, using exposition; you will *show* us your experience. An amateur writer is *telling* us, for example, when he says: "Dick found it very hard to make a decision." But in the passage which follows he is *showing* us:

Dick shifted in his chair. He looked down at his feet, curled nervously around the legs of his chair. Shaking his head, he tried to clear the smoke from his brain. "I'd better say something," he thought. He bit his cheek, swallowed, and put on his most engaging smile.

When *showing* is effective, a writer tends to use specific details with suggestion. What is *suggestion*? It is connotation, a hint, an implication of a second and an emotional meaning along with the literal meaning of the words. Sometimes individual words carry a suggestion or a connotation, as the word *house* carries a factual meaning, but the word *home* carries the same factual meaning with emotional overtones. More often whole phrases, sentences, or paragraphs carry suggestion; and to the good writer or the good reader, the closing sentence of a long story may carry a suggestion which has been building up through the complete story. The details you use in your writing will not automatically carry suggestion, of course; but if you have an attitude to express and if you imply this attitude through your details, you are using *suggestion.*

When a weather bulletin reads: "Weather clear, 25° to 28° below zero, with little or no wind," the statement is a mere exposition of fact, with no suggestion of personal attitude unless the reader puts it in for himself. But suppose a person says about the same weather:

Twenty-five below! Air as clear as a bell and the sun shining. That lake is hard as steel and smooth as a mirror. Where are my skates?

He *suggests* his enthusiasm better than he would if he explained: "The weather is right for skating; I'll try it." Suppose someone else says of the same weather:

Twenty-five below! My fingers are numb and my face aches. Two more blocks to go—they're like two miles to me.

He *suggests* his dislike by specific details. The person who says, "Ugh! I hate this cold weather," merely *explains* his personal attitude. The one who says, "Well, you know it's not exactly a summer day outside, is it?" uses understatement with some suggestion. The one who says, "Wow, it's cold enough to freeze the ears right off a brass monkey," uses trite exaggeration with some suggestion. Two people may talk satirically about the same cold weather, seeming to state one attitude but suggesting the opposite attitude:

"Balmy weather all right, isn't it?"
"Oh—yeah, fine. Like to go with me on a picnic?"
"Oh—ah—sure. Perfect picnic weather! Just perfect. Where'll we go?"
"How about Lakeside Park? Not more than five feet of snow there. We can shovel that off in no time."

Of the methods which have just been illustrated, you will need most the simple ability to use *suggestion* for your approval or disapproval. But for those who can use them well, understatement, overstatement, and the satirical tone are powerful weapons.

What are specific details? They are sensory perceptions—things that you see, hear, touch, taste, or smell. *Touch,* of course, includes muscular reactions and response to heat or cold. Your use of these perceptions is perhaps your easiest and most effective way of communicating your attitudes.

Of course you realize that your sensory perceptions are not an end in themselves but only a means to an end. The end is to stimulate you to discover the heights and the depths of your own thinking and feeling—the only way for you to improve your subject matter—and to bring your subject to *life* for you before you begin putting it on paper. If you wish to write, then, your senses are ready to be good servants to your emotion and your mind.[1]

IMPORTANCE OF SPECIFIC DETAILS

You can find evidence for the importance of specific details in the remarks of those who write about language. The authors of *The Control of Language* state:

In point of fact, the most successful way of describing our feelings, when we are thinking directly about them is to stop thinking about them directly, and to begin thinking about the things to which they are attached. By describing these things, coloured by our feelings, we shall communicate our feelings.[2]

When Dewey says that art is the communication of *an experience* he emphasizes the specific.[3] When Conrad explains the writer's work in his Preface to *The Nigger of the Narcissus*, he emphasizes specific details:

Fiction—if it at all aspires to be art—appeals to temperament . . . and creates the moral, the emotional atmosphere of the place and time. Such an appeal, to be effective, must be an impression conveyed through the senses; and, in fact, it cannot be made in any other way, because temperament, whether individual or collective, is not amenable to persuasion. All art, therefore, appeals primarily to the senses, and the artistic aim when expressing itself in written words must also make its appeal through the senses, if its high desire is to reach the secret spring of responsive emotions.[4]

Your senses are important in writing because they are important

[1] Alec King and Martin Ketley, *The Control of Language*, Longmans, Green & Co., Inc., 1939.
[2] *Ibid.*
[3] John Dewey, *Art as Experience*, G. P. Putnam's Sons, 1934.
[4] Joseph Conrad, *The Nigger of the Narcissus*, Doubleday & Co., Inc., 1914.

in living. You are usually unmoved when you hear general statistics about the number of people killed in an accident; but you suffer when you hear the screams of a person who is struck by a car or see his mangled body. Your emotion grows with contact when you are fond of a person. When you relive an experience in memory, anticipate events by sensory creation, or remake them in a more satisfying form, your emotions renew themselves. These processes—recall, anticipation, and glorified recall—are forms of creation.

Try these working hypotheses, then, in your writing: First, your power to communicate grows when you use authentic sensory details; second, as you use your senses sharply on significant material, your control over your creative power increases.

KINDS OF SPECIFIC DETAIL

The usual sensory perceptions have been mentioned as sources of specific detail. You may clarify your own practice by realizing that all details, whether sensory or not, are either *subjective* or *objective,* and that writers usually blend the two in good writing.

Objective details are those which normal observers tend to experience in the same way, or those we find ourselves in agreement about when we check them with one another. For example, we can agree on the number of trees in an area; we may agree that one tree is large and others are smaller. If our senses are normal, we will probably agree that we hear certain sounds and that certain objects feel rough or smooth. But when we try to tell others exactly *what* a sound is like—that it is hollow, that it chills us, or that it is like a nervous foghorn—our details become subjective. And when we try to say just *how* the smoothness *or* roughness of an object affects us, we use details that are even more subjective.

Your specific thoughts, emotions, desires, your memories, your pictures of the future are all subjective; you may blend them into your unit of composition by words or express them in talk and thus make them objective. Your unobtrusive physical reactions—muscular tension, tightness of the throat, sweat in closed hands, a slight trembling, the beat of your pulse—are subjective. But they may increase until they become apparent to others; then they have become objective.

You will not profit by splitting hairs over the subjective *or* objective quality, but it may help you to realize that writers combine them, often in one of these ways (though a writer seldom uses one way exclusively through a whole unit): first, objective details, with no aim except to report the facts; second, subjective details mainly, used to *explain* an attitude; third, subjective details, used mainly to *show* an attitude; fourth, objective details (at least details which seem objective when examined separately), used to build toward a significant attitude or meaning; fifth, subjective and objective details combined, according to the need of the moment, to bring out a significant attitude.

The first kind of writing is not worth while unless it has a practical aim which puts it outside the scope of creative work. It is the kind of writing a freshman does when he puts down everything he vaguely remembers about a fishing trip without being himself interested in anything:

We wanted to get an early start on our fishing trip, so we set the alarm for five o'clock. As soon as it went off, we got up. Then we got some breakfast ready and ate it. Next we packed our supplies, including our fishing tackle, in the car, and started driving. By this time the sun was almost up. For two hours we drove along Highway 30. . . .

But let us leave our freshman still traveling—and never arriving so far as writing is concerned. He writes badly because he has no desire to tell his reader anything, because he does not use his senses, and because he does not know himself what he thinks and feels.

The second kind of writing, a mere explaining of attitudes, has already been illustrated. You have been warned against it as a main method at this stage; but later you may need to use bits of such explaining in longer narrative. If your reader does not find that it takes his mind off your aim, it may be harmless, useful, or even necessary.

The fourth sort of writing, the use of details which seem objective but which build toward a significant attitude, is excellent if you can achieve this mature style. It is certainly worth trying. A story by Jerome Weidman, "The Explorers," is usually considered objective in method. In it three young men notice a pretty girl on a park bench and try to make her talk. She ignores them successfully until they prolong their torment of a small boy while they try to get him to ask her questions for them. The story closes in this way:

> The girl rustled the paper in her lap and glared at him. She was breathing quickly and her lips were pressed thin.
> "A poor little kid like that," she said.
> "Girlie," Flassy said, "a girl with eyes like yours, you shouldn't never —"
> Lou reached over and touched Flassy's knee. He pointed to the clock on the boathouse. "Flassy," he said, "it's late. We better get going. Johnny'll be waiting."
> All three of them looked at the clock.
> "That's right," Flassy said.
> He stood up at once and the three of them walked away briskly. They buttoned their tight coats and adjusted their hats as they went, but they did not look back at the girl on the bench.[5]

The third way of writing, using subjective details to show an attitude, and the fifth way, combining subjective and objective details at need to suggest an attitude, will probably be the most effective ones for you. You may use either in almost any descriptive-narrative assignment, and you will find examples of them in the reading at the end of the chapter.

So far the assumption has been that you are using specific details. But some writers, professional or amateur, are able to use general details with suggestion and power, telling us how they usually felt in certain situations:

> I remember the 'coon and 'possum hunts, nights, with the Negroes, and the long marches through the black gloom of the woods, and the excitement which fired everybody when the distant baying of an experienced dog announced that the game was treed; then the wild scramblings and stumblings through briars and bushes and over roots to get to the spot; then the lighting of a fire and the felling of the tree, the joyful frenzy of the dogs and the Negroes, and the weird picture it all made in the red glare—I remember it all well, and the delight that everyone got out of it, except the 'coon.[6]

[5] Jerome Weidman, "The Explorers," from *The Horse That Could Whistle Dixie*, copyright 1939 by Jerome Weidman, published by Simon & Schuster, Inc.

[6] Mark Twain, *Autobiography*, Harper & Brothers, 1924.

Perhaps the ability to use general details with power takes more maturity than the ability to use specific ones. You may wish to experiment to see whether you can use either kind according to your preference.

COMPARISONS, LITERAL AND FIGURATIVE

Thinking in comparisons, literal or figurative, will help you find much effective detail. Comparisons contribute to conversations, to public speeches, to all forms of fiction; a comparison is often the foundation of a whole poem or the basis of some powerful phrase in the poem. Writers who think quickly in comparisons increase their vividness and power, whether they inform farmers about feeding cattle or express a cosmic sorrow in a sonnet. In literal comparisons you notice that one object is like another similar object—that John, whom you are describing, resembles Henry, whom your listener already knows; both have the same stocky build, broad face, and brown hair. Next, you begin to see likenesses in two objects which are quite different: John's walk reminds you of your grandmother's fat duck at Thanksgiving time, or music is like the sound of a waterfall in the mountains. Thus you begin using figures of speech instead of literal comparisons.

The origin of good figures of speech, or imaginative comparisons, is much the same whether you hear them in daily life, use them in your writing, or find them in books. They grow from a desire to communicate something and to make it vivid and powerful. In daily life you are so hungry, for example, that your plain statement, "I am hungry," seems quite inadequate. So you say, "I'm as hungry as a bear," or "as ravenous as Susie at the Zoo." In any comparisons you will tend to follow your interests, your deeply embedded experience, or your recent impressions. If you are interested in machinery you may say, "My mind was hitting on all six cylinders," or "What he needs is a mental self-starter." Or you will find your own comparisons. If you are an imitative person you will tend to use conventional comparisons: "hot as fire, cold as ice, soft as silk." If you have sharpened perceptions and sensitivity you will use individual comparisons—whether you are educated or uneducated. But if you borrow and repeat the comparisons which other people use you will find that they are worn down, like used coins; they will not convey the warmth of your discovery. You can be original, in both literal and figurative comparisons, by discovering and expressing yourself.

Good comparisons, then, and all good figures of speech, grow from your observation of life. They are not a mere decoration. They are not bookish and imitative. They are so individual that they are colored with your emotion. The best figures use objects or means of expression which are simpler, clearer, more tangible, or more charged with the power of suggestion than any literal statements. When you use comparisons or figures of speech well, you have something to say, your literal words are inadequate, and you find a comparison to make your expression stronger or clearer. Thus you use them as a help in effective communication.[7]

VISUALIZING

Probably you have the ability to relive experience, either by recall or by glorified recall, or to anticipate experience in a vivid, rosy light. Then you can probably re-create experience in order to write about it.

First, choose a subject that appeals to your mind, emotions, and senses, about experience you have had or would like to have.

Second, try to discover what the subject means to you, why it interests you, and what attitude you wish to emphasize.

Third, using all your senses on it, create an imaginative unit which is real. Do not merely recall past sensory experience in a

---

[7] Simile, metaphor, personification are the figures of likeness or of comparison between objects which have some fundamental differences. A simile is an expressed comparison between two objects of entirely different classes; the comparison, if effective, causes one likeness between them to stand out more sharply because of difference. Words such as *like* or *as* express the comparison. A metaphor is merely a condensed simile; the likeness is implied or suggested; one thing is called the other. *Simile*: The man fought like a tiger. *Metaphor*: The tiger of Mentone led his men to victory. A personification results from describing something inanimate as if it had human life. Figures of substitution, *synecdoche, metonymy*, result from rejecting a vague term and finding instead a specific, vivid detail which is closely associated with it. Common instances are the use of the whole for a part, a part for the whole, a definite term for the indefinite, a proper name for an abstract quality it suggests, the container for the thing contained, the cause for the effect: ten sails in the harbor, the cattle on a thousand hills, a Judas, the bitter cup, the bright death quivering at his throat.

passive way; do not use only your mind and do not let trite, general words interfere. Instead, try to experience *sensory perceptions in your imagination*. Keep on until you can remember your created unit as you remember experience. Why? You may realize both the experience and your attitudes more sharply; for the use of the senses, according to some psychologists, involves the use of that part of the brain which controls the emotions. And you will find exact words for fresh, individual details. Thus you may write so that your reader will realize your experience as if it were his own.

Fourth, as you write, select only the best details from those in your consciousness, instead of emptying your mind, like a scrapbag, on paper. If you have visualized well, you may experience a dozen details for each one you write. Use the ones that are interesting to you, instead of deciding, "This detail is real to me, but nobody else would be interested in it." People who know little and tell us all produce thin, lifeless writing. People who know many details and tell us all drown us in words. People who experience much and select the best produce rich, stimulating writing. When you plan, then, and when you write, use selection.

If you already understand your own thoughts and feelings and if your senses are already alert, you may write quite spontaneously. If so, you are fortunate. But if you must work more slowly, do not become discouraged; instead, practice using your senses in daily life until they are ready to help you write.

YOUR STYLE IN SIMPLE NARRATIVE

If you ask the average student who tries to write description and narration why he has trouble saying what he means, he will probably answer, "I just don't have a big vocabulary. I could write if I knew more words." He is probably wrong. He knows enough words. His trouble is in dulled perceptions and in his ignorance about what he thinks and feels. The writers of significant modern fiction do not necessarily have big vocabularies, nor do they tend to large and bookish words. They avoid heavy connectives—*however, whereas, notwithstanding, nevertheless*—because such words sound like bookish exposition. They use simple, tangible, and suggestive words, often a large number of one-syllable words. They merely know what they mean to do with these words.

While you are using simple words, try to use combinations of words that seem fresh and individual—not trite, conventional combinations which we call clichés. Do not talk about "the beauty and peace of nature, fresh from the hand of God," or "the scene which no artist could paint," or the "tall pines which stood like sentinels"; do not tell us that your "heart stood still" or that the words fell "with a dull thud" or that you "felt terrible." But do not limit yourself to the negative method of avoiding trite expressions. Instead, go back to find the individual experience under the concealment. Just what did you see, hear, or touch? What were your physical reactions? Get interested in your discoveries; find words for them. Then your writing will not be trite.

As simple but suggestive diction will serve your purpose, so you will probably do better to use simple sentences, not formally balanced clauses and not extremes of periodic sentences. Sentences with many *which* clauses sound like formal exposition, not simple narrative. You may find that impressionistic phrases will sometimes convey attitudes better than formal sentences, since the struggle to find a formal verb for every sentence can call attention to itself in subjective narrative. Sometimes, then, try mere phrases, verbs, or nouns, instead of formal sentences, as they are used here:

Stark days these. Stark nights too. In the parks the trees stand firm, the bare boughs creaking in the wind. The gravel paths, clean from many rains, are neat against the dead brown of faded grass. The wind blows, the leaves fall, and smoke rolls up from factories.

Through the South Side the trains come in at night, long gray metal monsters, racing from off the plains, thundering over viaducts, small squares of light glittering from their windowed steel bodies.

And mist hangs over the lake, drifting to the shore. Tugs creep up the river like water beetles, blunt-nosed, going under bridges, chugging. Fog hangs over the Loop all night. The empty iron streets are gray and dead. . . .

A sprawl of shacks nibbling at the prairie, then came the smokestacks and the noise. A blare, a crash, and the hum of turbines all day long.[8]

At least avoid all expository heaviness. When you are writing narra-

[8] Albert Halper, "Young Writer Remembering Chicago," *On the Shore,* Viking Press, 1934.

tives of action you will use vivid verbs, either as main verbs or in participial constructions. Where a vivid verb will serve, it is better than a weaker verb with adverb modifiers. And a vivid noun is better than a vague noun with several adjective modifiers, if the one vivid noun will do the same work.

In general, train yourself to be suspicious of many adjectives and many adverbs, as you might be suspicious of subversives. Trim them ruthlessly; do not let adjectives come in pairs, like the animals going into the ark; consider whether one adverb is better than two or three; trim out vague adverbs like *very*, which seldom pay for their lodging in narrative.

When you are writing about personal experience, personalize in some way; use *I, me, my, mine,* or *we, us, our, ours* freely, without fear of natural repeating. If you are afraid of the first person, give yourself a name—*Alan* or *Joan* perhaps—and then use *he, his, him,* or *she, her, hers,* and so on. Your readers will be drawn into experience more easily if you let them follow the actions and the attitude of one character.

If you are a student with training in artistic theories, you may wonder why you have not yet been told to write with restraint, the great principle of classic art. Restraint implies that you have power, or even an excess or extravagance of feeling to control. Probably you do not need a curb at the start. Instead, you might do better to seek out the hidden springs of feeling, wherever you can find them, clear away the rubbish of fear and conventionality, coax the drops into a trickle and finally into a stream. If the stream threatens to become a torrent, try restraint.

WRITING YOUR COMPOSITION

Communicate briefly the feel of a moment or a few moments of experience. Develop only the most significant part, without explaining the background of your attitude and without writing a whole story. Try to use details in the order you experienced them; that is, use a simple time pattern. Suggest your dominant attitude; show us instead of explaining to us; thus you will achieve a "oneness" of effect by "keeping your eye on the ball" and persuading your reader to keep his eye on the ball. Your method of achieving this dominant attitude is repetition and more repetition and then still more repetition with subtle variations. As for length, perhaps you will need only a well-developed paragraph or, if you need to quote talk, several brief paragraphs.

When you are ready to begin writing, forget directions and techniques, so far as your conscious mind is concerned, and write. Most techniques become really useful after you learn to use them subconsciously; but you may need to stumble through conscious stages first, just as you learned to play the piano or drive a car.

TESTING AND REVISING

After your work has cooled, read it critically. Read it aloud. Prune unessential words. Are the remaining words vivid wherever vivid words are desirable? Are they simple and suggestive? Do you need more active verbs and concrete nouns? Do you find trite phrases? If so, relive your sensory details, discover what you saw or heard or touched or felt; then find the words for your individual experience. Have you used unnecessary passives or other indirect phrasing? Have you personalized, possibly with the second person if you can use it consistently, or with the first or third person?

Test yourself also by these more specific questions:

1. Have you observed sharply? Have you seen, heard, tasted, smelled, touched, or responded with your muscles, until you have found a freshness of experience?

2. Has your thought response to your subject been better than your expression of that response?

3. Have you written with power—with the ability to call out a response in your reader?

If your work needs much revising, do not be satisfied with mechanical tinkering. Revisualize until it becomes an imagined experience. Then rewrite.

READING

STUDENT PASSAGES

The room was too small for us that night. Four white walls pressed in about us and strangled the breeze ruffling at the windows. The glaring white light made the room seem hot and dead.

I tossed my coat on the bed and went to sit with Ginny on the window sill. We sat quietly, our faces in our hands, staring at the night. Presently Jeannie left her desk and stood behind us.

The cool, clean breeze carried away all sounds of the night, but we could hear shuffling footsteps in the halls and occasionally the slamming of a door.

"It's beautiful . . ."

"Makes you wish you could be part of it . . ."

Jeannie sighed. "I've got to get back to work."

"Work! I can't—not if I flunk out."

We saw the soft rustling fingers swaying in the darkness, the few bright stars that had escaped from the misty clouds, the timid lightning glimmering in the distance, the dark humps of trees beyond the lake, and the nearer trees silhouetted by the street light.

That night was like some horrible dream. I can't think of it now without shuddering. The billetman signaled that the rod pass was clear, so John Tomara, our foreman, stepped out in it to examine the dies for flaws. Suddenly a long white rod of high carbon steel shot out of the die, striking him high on the thigh. He just stood there in shocked amazement till somebody hit the safety stop and plunged the whole mill into silence. Then, with a gasping scream, he crumpled to the floor. The reeking stench of seared human flesh made me retch and grow deathly sick as I helped cut the glowing metal away from his leg. We carried him out to the gate and took him to the hospital.

Work the rest of the night was mental torture. I could stare at those red rods as I passed them through the dies, and see his blood on the floor.

I had heard the cat scratching and crying at the door, but I only pulled the covers more tightly over my sleep-befuddled head. Then mother let her in, with a sympathizing, "Won't that old hag let you into her room? You just go right in." Now the cat is tiptoeing around my pillow, standing first on one foot and then the other, ceaselessly walking around and around. With little kneading paws she digs into the defiant flesh of my forehead and neck if she can reach it. She pushes her cold, wet nose into one crack in the wall of blankets and rubs it against my face. With little purrs and cries of delight, she at last finds a weak spot in the covers I am protecting myself with; and she settles down happily across my neck, making breathing almost impossible. Too sleepy and cold to move her away, I hear in the distance my mother saying, "Now leave her alone. Remember, she's YOUR cat."

The girls stumbled over ruts in the barnyard as they hurried toward the small square of light from the barn.

A cold little hand touched a warm one. "Dorothy, is milk from a cow clean? Does it taste good?"

"Sure. Wait and see. Got your cup?"

The touch of the cool cup to Thelma's lips was reassuring. Then a big swallow of warm milk made its way down her small esophagus.

"Gwan. Drink it. 'S good."

Dorothy's noisy gulping only added to Thelma's feeling of illness. Bravely she tried another swallow. The tasteless, foamy, fuzzy stuff lay in her mouth until she could stand it no longer. With a great effort she swallowed the spineless liquid.

"Want some more?"

"No—no, thanks. —No, *thank* you."

Grandpa lay like a shriveled doll under the old patchwork quilt that Grandma had made when Mama was small. The old man's blue-veined hands restlessly roamed the coverlet, picking at little invisibilities; but the eyes were sunken and closed; empty now of the life that had burned within them once. The color had gone from his face, and the skin over his tight sharp features was waxen and transparent, like the thin shells of paraffin on Mama's currant jelly. The room was silent except for the ticking of the clock and Grandpa's ragged breathing. He lay still and shrunken, picking away at nothing on his coverlet, just picking and fussing with nothing.

A sudden beam of light shows the black forest of double-decker beds, crowded in rows on the right and the left. A drowsy, shiny-faced girl closes the door behind her and gropes her way down the narrow lane between beds. Bumps a metal bed corner. Shoves a mateless slipper under a cot. Blackness turns gray and objects take form. She moves to the second upper berth on the left.

The sleepy groper pulls back the blankets. Hoists herself by placing a foot on the bed below and swinging upward. Drops one slipper, then the other, from her high counterpane plateau. Slides down between sheets. Bed springs protest their new burden. Then quiet.

Quiet? A clock beats time, monotonously, imperatively. From the Girl who Snores comes a slow purr. A cougher down the aisle wearily rises to seek a drink of water and carries out of the room the nose-tickling scent of mentholatum. The shaft of hall light thrusts its path into the darkness, then is snuffed out with a sharp door-slam.

A cool breath of wind draws aside the curtain, slips over the sill to brush cold-creamed cheeks, to raise corners of blankets, to gather lotion and sleep smells, and then hurries out the far window.

Criss-cross patterns of branches mark up squares on the wall. Bundled humps of bedclothes hide unaware forms. The clock ticks on and on, and the Girl still snores, breathing slowly in and out, in and out.

PROFESSIONAL EXCERPTS

Timidly, he lifted the latch on the gate and walked to the steps. He paused, waiting for someone to challenge him. Nothing happened. Maybe nobody was home? He went to the door and saw a dim light burning in a shaded niche above a doorbell. He pushed it and was startled to hear a soft gong sound within. Maybe he had pushed it too hard? Aw, what the hell! He had to do better than this; he relaxed his taut muscles and stood at ease, waiting. The doorknob turned. The door opened. He saw a white face. It was a woman.

"Hello!"

"Yessum," he said.

"You want to see somebody?"

"Er . . . Er . . . I want to see Mr. Dalton."

"Are you the Thomas boy?"

"Yessum."

"Come in."

He edged through the door slowly, then stopped halfway. The woman was so close to him that he could see a tiny mole at the corner of her mouth. He held his breath. It seemed that there was not room enough for him to pass without actually touching her.

"Come on in," the woman said.

"Yessum," he whispered.

He squeezed through and stood uncertainly in a softly lighted hallway.

"Follow me," she said.

With cap in hand and shoulders sloped, he followed, walking over a rug so soft and deep that it seemed he was going to fall at each step he took. He went into a dimly lit room.

"Take a seat," she said. "I'll tell Mr. Dalton that you're here and he'll be out in a moment."

"Yessum." [9]

At first there was nothing. There was the faint, cold, steady rain, the gray and constant light of the late November dawn, with the voices of the hounds converging somewhere in it and toward them. Then Sam Fathers, standing just behind the boy as he had been standing when the boy shot his first running rabbit with his first gun and almost with the first load it ever carried, touched his shoulder and he began to shake, not with any cold. Then the buck was there. He did not come into sight; he was just there, looking not like a ghost but as if all of light were condensed in him and he were the source of it, not only moving in it but disseminating it, already running, seen first as you always see the deer, in the split second after he has already seen you, already slanting away in that first soaring bound, the antlers even in that dim light looking like a small rocking-chair balanced on his head.

"Now," Sam Fathers said, "shoot quick, and slow."

The boy did not remember that shot at all. . . . He didn't even remember what he did with the gun afterward. He was running. Then he was standing over the buck where it lay on the wet earth still in the attitude of speed and not looking at all dead, standing over it shaking and jerking. . . . [10]

[9] Richard Wright, *Native Son*, Harper & Brothers, 1940.
[10] William Faulkner, "The Old People," *Go Down, Moses*, Random House, Inc., 1942.

QUESTIONS

Which, if any, of the six student selections have the feel of reality? Which ones also suggest a definite attitude of the writer? Which ones, if any, do not succeed in doing either? What details in each passage are ineffective or effective?

In the selection from *Native Son*, which character gives tenseness to the moment of experience? What emotion is he experiencing? Is the feel of experience brought out by his specific thoughts, his talk, his actions, or by all of these details?

In the selection from "The Old People," whose experience is emphasized? What emotion is he feeling? Again, do his specific thoughts, his talk, or his action do most to bring out the feel of the experience?

ADDITIONAL HELPS

1. If your senses are sluggish give yourself special practice in using them on life, in the odd moments when you walk alone, wait, or ride on trains and buses. Experiment with one sense at a time: identify fabrics by touch; determine with the help of your nose what shops you are passing; learn from your ears what is happening in the room with you or on the street outside. When you wait, perhaps in a classroom, close your eyes and listen. Analyze, compare: when you notice that one auto horn is deep, resonant, slow, prolonged; that another is shrill, high, intermittent; that the same horn is different in fog and in clear weather; that one person's face is a delicate oval; that another person's face is a bulky rectangle, you are making progress. Good writing comes from capturing individuality, finding the quality which makes a thing different from others of its class. If your eyes are keen to nature but dull to people, watch people. If your ears are indifferent, analyze sounds. If you are unconscious about bodily movements, find out how your muscles express your desires and aversions.

2. Make specific the method of observing life by sitting for a half-hour or more at some place where sensory details will interest you. Observe and analyze:

Two or three sounds.
Two or three objects (form, color, texture).
Two or three touch sensations.
Two or three odors.
Two or three sensations of taste.

3. Find comparisons to help you communicate two or three of the sensory discoveries which interested you most in the preceding experiment.

4. Select one of your most interesting discoveries from the preceding experiment, and think it through in the time order of your discovery, so that you can communicate it step by step in the same way.

5. Explore your experience in each of the following situations:

Standing dangerously near the edge of a cliff.

Smelling a cellar, an attic, a kitchen, a factory, a doctor's office, grass, earth.

Tasting two kinds of apples, two kinds of oranges, orange and grapefruit, green plums, ripe tomatoes when you are thirsty after hoeing them.

Hearing food frying, food boiling, two different auto horns, sawing wood, a crowd cheering, skating, walking in wet snow, a dog or cat expressing anger.

Touching chewing gum, velvet, plush, clean sheets, cat's fur.

Experiencing the power of machines; the keen edge of a knife; the feel of a good gun; the motions of skating, bowling, airplane travel, hunting; the sound or odor of factories; muscular response to work, or hitchhiking, dancing, canoeing.

Seeing the face of a person in bewilderment, in anger, in sorrow.

Feeling the handshake of timid, of old, of thoughtful people.

6. Do sensory experiences of touch, taste, odor ever appear in your writing? Perhaps they are primitive and utilitarian, but their use at times may make your work three-dimensional and authentic.

7. Use your senses sharply when you read. In a passage like this find out whether you think vaguely about mere words, as *orchards, grass,* or whether you smell apple blossoms and grass, feel the air, touch, hear the bird's song, and blend these perceptions into a unit of imagined experience with your own addition of sunshine and sky:

"Apple orchards blossom there, and the air's like wine.
There is cool green grass there, where men may lie at rest,
And the thrushes are in song there, fluting from the nest." [11]

Take a favorite novel or a collection of short stories. Select four or five passages which attempt to convey the attitude of some character to simple, rather objective experience. Is the attitude in each passage well or badly conveyed? Why? If all these passages convey the intended attitude well, look in some other source, perhaps one where you do not expect to find good writing, for passages which convey attitudes less well. Serial stories in newspapers offer possibilities.

[11] "The West Wind" from *Poems* by John Masefield, 1915, 1928. By permission of The Macmillan Company, publishers.

3

An Activity

Your writing assignment suggested at the close of this chapter is an activity based upon personal experience. Your individual topic may be subjective or objective, but if it is subjective you will try to make it tangible by talk, action, and specific thoughts which seem to belong to one moment of experience and no other. That is, you will try to write a simple, significant narrative limited to one time and one place. Again you will use sensory details, draw your reader into the experience so that it has emotional reality, and secure unity of effect by repetition with variations. Your details will thus "add up" to a simple meaning or attitude.

WHAT NARRATIVE IS

Whenever you write of actions or events that have happened in space or time you are writing factual narrative. Of course you do not have to report them in exactly the same time order in which they happened. Factual narrative includes incidents which you have experienced and later report to your friends, news stories, some history, some biography or autobiography, and testimony in court when a witness is asked to "tell the court exactly what happened."

When you write creative narrative you use events as if they had happened in time and space. But since your aim is not merely to report facts but to interpret them, you seldom try to photograph mere facts. You may do so in exceptional cases, when you try to recall some strange event by asking yourself *what* really happened and *why* it happened. Even when you use a framework of events as they happened, you will enlarge the background with details that emphasize your attitude. But more often you will rearrange or even create a set of events to bring out better, not the facts but the significance of an experience. For example, you are trying to express your boredom in a special situation, but you have known boredom in similar situations and in different situations many times. Though your narrative is a one-time, one-place unit, it may blend details from other times and places or use details which seem to be created from nothing but which fit into your whole artistic aim. Thus you can express your truth with more power. From this time on, you will be dealing with creative narrative; and though some statements may be true of factual narrative also, the term *narrative* will be used without qualification.

You will aid your own progress if you remember that narrative is not sharply separated from exposition in all pieces of writing, just as people are not all "good" or "bad." Like professional writers you do not try merely to write narrative or exposition; instead, you have something to say, and as soon as you write with enough skill you may interweave bits of exposition with narrative. But for the present you will gain by writing units of specific narrative and by weeding out explaining in general terms. Though some history, some biography, and some autobiography may be narrative, when the writer of these forms moves from events to explain causes or results in general terms, he moves from narrative to exposition. And when a writer of fiction stops his action to explain events which must be mentioned but are not important enough to be developed by talk and action, or to explain the motives of his characters, he is probably writing exposition. Or he may be writing one kind of general narrative.

GENERAL AND SPECIFIC NARRATIVE

You will find it useful to distinguish between *specific* and *general* narrative now, though you will for the present be using specific narrative. General narrative is sometimes exposition in its aim, when it is used to explain processes, or a way of life, or the customary behavior of people. But general narrative can be used to communicate the feel of life, without any intent to give practical information. When it is used for the latter purpose the writer frequently but not invariably uses the present tense, as in Mark Twain's account of the arrival of a steamboat. After telling us about the quiet of the place, with the town drunkard asleep by the wharves, the writer continues:

Presently a film of dark smoke appears above one of these remote "points"; instantly a negro drayman, famous for his quick eye and prodigious voice, lifts the cry, "S-t-e-a-m-boat a-comin'!" and the scene changes. Drays, carts, men, boys, all go hurrying from many quarters to a common center, the wharf. Assembled there, the people fasten their eyes upon the coming boat as upon a wonder they are seeing for the first time. And the boat *is* rather a handsome sight, too. She is long and sharp and trim and pretty . . . there is a flag gallantly flying from the jack-staff; the furnace doors are open and the fires glaring bravely; the upper decks are black with passengers; the captain stands by the big bell, calm, imposing, the envy of all; great volumes of the blackest smoke are rolling and tumbling out of the chimneys—a husbanded grandeur created with a bit of pitch-pine just before arriving at a town; the crew are grouped on the fore-castle; the broad stage is run out far over the port bow, and an envied deck-hand stands picturesquely on the end of it with a coil of rope in his hand; the pent steam is screaming through the gauge-cocks; the captain lifts his hand, a bell rings, the wheels stop; then they turn back, churning the water to foam, and the steamer is at rest. Then such a scramble as there is to get aboard and to get ashore, and to take in freight and to discharge freight, all at one and the same time . . . Ten minutes later the steamer is under way again, with no flag on the jack-staff and no black smoke issuing from the chimneys. After ten more minutes the town is dead again, and the town drunkard asleep by the skids once more.[1]

Probably Mark Twain, as a boy on shore, had watched the arrival of steamboats a thousand times, and later, as a pilot, had looked as many times from the boat at small towns on the river. Hence he is able to tell us what usually happened but to make it so vivid that we participate as the town wakens, lives for a few moments, and then falls asleep again. But his aim is not to explain ideas or processes; instead, he keeps suggesting, "This is the feel of the experience," or perhaps, "This is the feel of any

[1] Mark Twain, *Life on the Mississippi*, Harper & Brothers, 1923.

such experience as I remember it through the nostalgia of the past."

As a contrast, here is specific narrative as a student used it in a one-time, one-place pattern, with events which happened only once:

> I caught the gleam of the gold filling in her tooth as she smiled at me over the amber crown of her Coke. "Did you know?—Bill's at the formal with Marjorie tonight."
>
> I felt the bottom drop out of my stomach. My throat was suddenly dry and tight. The voice that lied back was much calmer than I should have thought possible. "Sure, I knew it. It's all right." She had her mouth open to say more, but I interrupted. " 'Scuse me, Alice, but there's the girl I'm meeting—I've got to dash."
>
> Bill! Another girl. Good old faithful Bill. Why, only the other night —I moved between the oak tables and sat down with my friend Joyce. The green napkin slid across the table from the waiter's hand. "What'll it be?"
>
> "Small lime." Funny, there was that calm voice again. Funny, how a throat with that drum-like tightness could produce that voice.

The preceding narrative brings out its significance by a pattern of subjective details contrasted with objective details of talk and action.

TRANSITIONAL NARRATIVE

When you need to pass over time intervals in longer narratives because nothing important is happening, you will sometimes need only a word or a phrase, such as *Later . . . Next day . . . After two hours of steady pounding. . . .* You will sometimes need a paragraph or more, to build a bridge from one important scene to another in your story; and if you were writing a novel, you might even need a short chapter. When you use a paragraph or more of such material you are using general narrative, or summarizing narrative, as a mere transition from one important scene to another important scene. For example, in a story of a flood, you might begin with one or more tense and specific scenes in which your characters learn about their danger and the danger grows. Then you might build a general bridge like this:

> In the hours that followed we moved our belongings upstairs—

pictures, clothing, dishes, silver, records, everything that the two of us alone could move. We took turns measuring the water on the gauge in the back yard. We listened to endless broadcasts repeating the same warnings, the same directions to follow if we needed help.

Then you might return to a tense and specific scene again:

At five in the evening Alex came back from a tenth or maybe a twentieth check of the water gauge. He stood there a moment like a statue in the middle of the bare living room.

"We're getting out of here," he said calmly, "while the phone's still working and we can call them. —It is still working, isn't it?"

"Yes, but are you sure we need to—" Something in his complete control, his lack of all expression stopped me.

Of course you will not need all these techniques in the simple one-time, one-place narrative which is your objective in this chapter. But you may work with more confidence on simple narrative now because you have looked at variations of the pattern, and you will also be ready to use any variation which your individual subject demands.

TECHNIQUES FOR GOOD NARRATIVE

If you write a first-class narrative about some activity you will not be making a mere report of events in time order. You will be applying to a longer unit the techniques discussed in Chapter 2, giving throughout the feel of experience and suggesting your attitude. You may need to bring out a character, to emphasize a mood or an idea, just as you would do in a longer story. If so, go ahead. Tell your incident or simple story as well as you can. Again, you will need to say something you really mean—whether it is a trifle or something larger than a trifle.

Here are some techniques which may be helpful at this stage of your writing. First, quote actual talk verbatim instead of reporting indirectly to us what characters said. Probably the readings at the end of the chapter will furnish all the illustrations you need for this skill.

Second, learn to limit by choosing a few significant moments, instead of ranging vaguely over hours or days of time. Then enlarge your few moments from within, with an effect of rich detail. For example, suppose the activity centers around a young man fresh from college who takes a job with a section crew on a railroad, between his freshman and sophomore years, to earn money for future college work. Suppose he is testing his own determination and his manhood, at least his physical manhood. He may actually go through days of conflict. But select a few moments of active intense conflict by asking yourself questions like these: What part of his first day is hardest? The first half-hour? The last half-hour when he is trying to stick to work until quitting time? Or the time after lunch when food has made him sluggish, his muscles have begun to stiffen, he is hot and thirsty, but he can't stop yet for water? Or is the beginning of his second day worse, when his muscles are sore? Or are the last thirty minutes of the last day of the first week hardest, when he looks forward to a bath, a good dinner with longer relaxation, and wonders whether he will come back Monday morning or whether he will say at five o'clock that he is quitting? Probably most subjects will offer you a chance to reject a long period of time and to choose a few moments of decisive experience.

Third, learn to begin within your active situation or, as some writer on the short story once said, "to pick up your puppy a little in front of the middle." When you begin within the situation you will need to learn how to weave in gradually explanation of various kinds: to clarify the situation, to give some setting, to introduce one or more characters. Or, to say the same thing another way, you need to tell *who, where, when, what,* and *why* and to do this by narrative so easily and gradually that we as readers are scarcely conscious of the process. If you are an amateur, you may tend to tell us nothing or to start with a paragraph of general explanation which will seem out of place in a vivid one-time, one-place narrative. Probably your best means of explaining to your readers are talk, thoughts of a chief character, memories of a chief character but not formal memories called flashbacks, and bits of author comment. As for the use of talk, try from the start to use it in small bits, to combine it with bits of action, and to manage action and details so that you can avoid the "he-saids" and "she-saids." Try also to use thoughts without saying "he thought" and "he remembered."

This beginning illustrates an effective way of bringing in essential information. It is from a student narrative called "Drilling In."

Mary Ellen braced herself against the dashboard as the old coupé bounced to a standstill; then she relaxed unconsciously as Father said, "Guess we're here on time. No signs of great activity yet."

She looked up at him. His face had the same excited-but-trying-to-be-calm look he had had at lunch when he asked her, "Like to see the well drilled this afternoon?" And he had grinned as he took another bite of cornbread.

Now Father and Mary Ellen got out of the car and walked across the large clearing surrounded by mesquites and post oaks, except where the twisting road led out to the highway. White-faced cattle looked out from the brush, gazed indifferently at the activity around the well, and then returned to their grazing.

"We began to get gas this morning. By four o'clock we should hit the pool. Maybe we'll get a gusher." For a moment Father seemed to be talking to himself.

When they reached the wooden platform with the high, wooden derrick above it and the long sloping shed behind it, Father cupped his hands under Mary Ellen's elbows and swung her up onto the oily floor. For an instant the noise of the engine suffocated her; the wide, swift belt made a sinister flapping as it sped round and round on its endless journey; and above her head great pipes and cables seemed ready to fall on her. Then Father was standing behind her, giving her shoulders a friendly squeeze. At once the engine was a friend, the belt was a silly, monotonous ribbon, and the pipes and cables were as firm as the stars.

In the preceding passage what does the writer tell us about the time, the place, the general setting, the specific situation, and the attitude between father and daughter? Is the past used at all? How? Is talk used well? Does the writer avoid the "he-said," "she-said" technique? Use the readings at the close of the chapter to study other beginnings.

Fourth, learn to use unity of focus. If you personalized consistently in your first composition you probably used a rudimentary kind of unity of focus, even though you did not call it by that name. When you use the senses, the mind, and the attitude of one character to tell us everything in the story; when you present other characters to us only through this one character; when you use setting only as seen through his eyes, and action only as he acts, observes action, or tries to use it for his purpose, you have unity of focus. Your one character is a microscope through which we realize the whole story. This technique has some limitations, of course; it will not help you with material which calls for different points of view. But it is like life; each of us, willy-nilly, experiences life through his own mind and senses, his personal unity of focus. None of us can do otherwise. If you learn to use unity of focus well, you will have a powerful weapon to strengthen your writing.

Fifth, when you use unity of focus, you have a natural suspense through your main character's efforts, hopes, and fears.

Sixth, let your main character struggle toward some definite small thing if your material permits; let him make some small decision or accomplish something else equally small. Thus unity of focus and your suspense will probably be more effective. In an activity, for instance, your main character may try to last till quitting time, land the big fish, find the screech-owl's nest, or win the point in basketball. If your material does not permit a small conflict so definite, and if your main character is putting up hay, selling shoes, or working on the assembly line, you may use a few moments of action to build a mood of continuing action—on and on, never ending.

Seventh, if you are using either a small conflict which comes to an end or a mood which suggests an unending struggle, you have an organic unit, one that grows out of your meaning; you also have a beginning, a body or a middle, and a conclusion or even a climax and a conclusion. If you have a small conflict which will grow to a climax or conclusion you may even be conscious of a simple narrative question: *Will John win the point in basketball?* By having a good beginning which brings out special reasons why John wishes to win this particular game, by developing the body with hope and fear, by leading us to the climax—the moment when he wins or loses the point—by showing us his reaction to his own hope or failure, you may make a small incident effective. That is, you may do so if you tell it in fresh, individual language which make it seem like a new experience.

SUBJECTS

The term activity includes all labor, all sports whether organized or unorganized, all efforts to develop manual skill, all creative effort, and even psychological situations in which you try to persuade another person to take some action or make a decision.

Some of these tangible subjects may help you find your best topic: adjusting to the strain of factory work, hating its monotony or enjoying its precision, plowing with a tractor, detasseling hybrid corn, beginning a ski race, skating, playing polo, making a strike at bowling or a free throw in basketball or a tackle in football, breaking the tape in a mile run, shooting a buck, landing a trout, winning or losing in tennis, playing golf, wrestling, auto racing, taking a plane up on a first solo flight, struggling against flood or blizzard, climbing a mountain, finding a hawk's nest. Such simple subjects as dusting, icing a birthday cake, or making a block print may be significant when they involve a clash of personalities or a desire to please another person. If you prefer a psychological subject you might choose one in which you try to persuade another person to do something: to give you a job, to make a contribution to a community fund, to buy a ticket, to buy advertising, to accept a committee appointment, to lend you five dollars or a car or a formal dress.

A subject which has physical action or offers a chance to use conversation will be easier to handle. A psychological subject (one in which the important action is within your own mind) will probably be harder but it may be worth the effort. Any activity which has brought you maturity, self-reliance, group approval, the discovery that you enjoy creation and are exhausted by monotony is a significant subject. So is any subject that leads you to discover your own strength and weakness. Above all, consider the subjects in which you have failed. When you analyze the cause of your failure you can decide whether to treat the failure seriously, humorously, or satirically.

WRITING YOUR COMPOSITION

Write a simple narrative about an activity which is important to you. Select a few important moments and expand those moments from within. Use any potential conflict within yourself or between you and other people. Visualize. Plan to use talk unless your individual subject does not permit its use. Plan unity of focus, using either the first or the third person, according to your skill. Create a unit of experience. Write with as much vividness and power as you can find in yourself and in your subject.

TESTING AND REVISING

1. What has your artistic aim been in this composition? That is, what unity or oneness have you planned to bring out—a unity of idea, or a unity of attitude only, or both?

2. Have you achieved that aim? Is your result excellent, average, or poor?

3. Is the unit worth while for you the writer? Is it worth while for a reader?

4. What techniques or details have you used well or badly?

5. Does your material seem authentic?

6. Have you personalized? Used unity of focus?

7. Have you pruned all trite, conventional words?

8. Is your diction fresh and individual?

9. Does your unit have power—the ability to make your reader respond?

READING

TRANSLATION* [2]

Doris Plagge

Around the whitewashed sculpture studio several students worked, whistling, bending, squinting at their studies on the square work table, now and then pausing to brush away the curious flies that hovered over the glistening clay. Sunlight poured in at the high windows, and Jean heard the swish of water far down the corridor outside as the janitor played his hose on the cement bricks.

"Unity—that is what we must work for! We must have that *feeling* for the composition."

The soft voice of the instructor ran through Jean's head again

[2] An asterisk after a title denotes a student composition.

and again. She blinked her tired eyes rapidly in a determined effort to rub out the image of the lumpy, shapeless clay figure before her. Somehow her new piece of sculpture lacked all character, she decided. It was dull—it was meaningless, without feeling. Absently she dug her clay-smeared hand into her smock pocket and stared again at the crumpled paper she found there. The feeling was there—on paper. In two dimensions she could do it. Her sketch of the puckish boy and girl holding a Christmas candle had all the life and vitality she was trying to translate in the clay—there it lay in their round arms and bodies, their active legs and fresh smiles. It was alive. The lump of clay was static. A real problem, to combine a boy, a girl, and a candle into a unit with mass, strength, and one-ness. . . .

She turned suddenly back to her bench and looked through narrowed eyes at the crude shapes of arms and legs and bodies. Turning the board she squinted again, her eye traveling along the rhythmical lines of the form and weighing the masses one against the other as the instructor had done.

Ah—why, of course! That's it! Her square, bony fingers attacked the clay and prodded the shapes up and tight together, accenting each curve and bend of the arm and leg, tipping the head and curving the back so that the round chests of the children pressed against their load in the earnestness of childish delight.

Behind her the instructor watched, chuckling at her exuberant fingers, and noted that her blue eyes sparkled with a fire that would not fail her now.

"That's it—now it's beginning to *live!*" he said. "You have to put the lift and up-swing into it— Now, here—and here—keep that arm round; keep that freshness of the children there. And fill it in here, and here—make it one mass. Unity is what we must work for! We must have that feeling for the composition."

Jean laughed to herself in the silent but excited way she knew so well. She always felt it coming when something important happened; it was just as though her whole happiness went to live deep in her throat, and kept all sound from coming out.

"I've got it now," she thought. "It's alive."

BROWN BOXES*

Pat Minear

"Helluva life, isn't it? Pick 'em up, set 'em down, but they keep coming down that damn chute." Slim picked up another box from the long chute that fell from the top floor of the factory down to the box car where we were working.

"Yeah, pick 'em up, set 'em down, then stack 'em up again. A fine job they said, good working conditions, friendly fellow-workers, modern conveniences. Well, they can shove it." I lifted another box off the rollers on the chute and carried it into the box car. I let it drop on the row that Slim had started.

"Whatta you want—funny stories or handshakes every ten minutes?" Slim threw the ammunition box on top of the one I had just dropped and pulled out a sweat-stained pack of cigarettes. He extracted two, threw me one and lighted his.

"That's pretty good stuff they hand out." He touched the flame from the match to his cigarette and offered the light to me. Blowing out a fine stream of smoke he went on. "Yeah, good stuff. They gave it to me about six months ago."

"You been throwing these boxes that long?" I asked.

"It's good for the arms." He looked at his dirt-streaked arms.

I looked at my own bare, dirty arms. "Maybe I'll fight Joe Louis next week."

"Another one coming down," Slim said.

I could hear the thin, whirling sound the rollers on the chute made as the box moved over them. "Maybe the damn thing will fall off," I offered.

"That's what they got engineers for, to see that they don't. The boxes go just right, ever'thing goes right. They add two and two and get four. You're two, I'm two, together we make four. It's simple."

"Real simple," I said. I felt licked.

Slim pulled up a box and sat down. His sweaty "T" shirt hung loose in front as he put his elbows on his knees. I sat down on the floor and let my back rest against the side of the box car.

"They're workin' slow in the sweat shop this morning," I said.

"Yeah."

"Tired?" I asked. "Big night, huh."

"I'm mighty tired." His voice was even and low. "I'm tired of watching these brown boxes comin' down that chute and listenin' to the wail they make. 'Minds me of a bunch of bawling kids in a nursery asking for attention, pressin' a guy in, always crowdin' yuh."

Another box started to sing as it sped over the iron rollers. It stopped with a short thud as it struck the other box on the rack at the end.

"When were you ever in a nursery?" I asked. "The closest you ever got was when you walked by one." I hoped he'd come back on that one. I'd worked with Slim for about a month now, and we kept a good argument going to break the monotony. He didn't snap back, just looked at the floor, and his voice was easy and quiet.

"These damn boxes start a man thinking. I musta put ten thousand of 'em in box cars. They come down that chute one after another, all the same, brown and warm and heavy. You pick 'em up and stack 'em and send 'em down the track. They don't know where they're going or why. Boxes don't hafta think."

"Where'd you work, 'fore you come here, Slim?"

"On a farm in Kansas," he answered. "Raised wheat, lotta wheat, lotta wheat in Kansas."

"How'd you like farming, Slim? I ain't never been on a farm. Hard work, is it?"

"Yeah, it's hard work," he said. " 'Cept in the winter when the snow lies on the ground. It ain't like city snow. It's white and clean and crunches when you walk on it. Farm's a nice place in the winter."

Two more boxes came down. You can tell there's two 'cause you get two thuds when they hit.

"How'd you come to work on a farm?" I asked.

"I was born on a farm. Seem funny, me being born on a farm?"

"You don't remind me of a farm, not the smooth way you handle that waitress at Pete's."

Another box whirled down and Slim waited for it to hit.

"You must be sick," I said. "You ain't acting right at all. If you wanta lay off, go ahead. I can handle this for . . ."

"I ain't sick." He lifted his head, and I could see his eyes. He looked like a man who was thinking hard. "No, I ain't sick. I just keep thinkin' of that farm and the way the hills roll over each other. It gets lonely on a farm, but it gets lonely even when you got all the people in the world right around you. 'Cept it's a different kind of lonely feeling on a farm—a man gets lonely 'cause he wants to share his feelings. You feel alive, even if the dust is chokin' yuh and yuh can't hold a straight furrow 'cause yuh can't see the ground. A man feels alive on a farm."

He stopped talking and a drop of sweat rolled down his nose and dropped off into the dust on the floor.

"A man could get to feelin' like one of those brown boxes after a while. I'd hate to begin to feel like . . ."

"What the hell do you think this is, the noon hour?" The voice boomed into the car and I jumped up. I knew who it was. The flat, dark face of Carl, the foreman, appeared, as he pulled himself up into the box car.

"Well," he said. "You guys on a strike or sumpthing? There's enough boxes piled up on that rack to start a small ammunition dump." He waved a hand at the chute. "If you jokers haven't got enough to do I could hook another chute onto this car." He directed his words at Slim, who sat looking up at him.

"Well," he said to Slim.

"I was thinking," Slim said.

"Oh, you were thinking. We pay you for thinking, all right. Look, we got lotsa guys that think—you stack boxes. What the hell were you thinking about? It's late for spring fever."

"You go to hell."

"What did you say?" I could see the blood rush to Carl's face.

"I said, you go to hell." Slim got up off the box.

"Why, damn you, who do you think you are? You've been loafing for the last week. This is no old people's home. Here you work or else."

"I just quit. Now you got your 'or else.' Is there anything else you want?"

"Why, you damn loafer, I'll . . ." Carl shut his mouth tight, as he caught the movement of Slim's right shoulder. He backed up fast.

"You're fired, though. Get your money and get out. If it's trouble you want I got some boys outside who can . . ."

"Shut up, I'm leaving now." Slim turned to me and stuck out his big right paw. I could feel its roughness and strength as he gripped mine.

"So long," he said. "Too bad you ain't never been on a farm."

He walked past Carl who carefully watched him but said nothing. Slim dropped out of the door of the car and headed for the main office. Carl turned toward me.

"Well," he said. "You wanta quit too?"

I wanted to say the words Slim had used but they stuck in my throat.

"No," I said. "I'll get those boxes off the rack. I've never been on a farm."

ARCHER PILGRIM [3]

Don Jackson

It was decided to do the vaccinating in the hog house, the low brick building behind the barn. Dave and Arch were out there getting things ready after breakfast, when the veterinarian came. They had driven the hogs inside and had crowded them into a corner by means of two gatelike partitions that formed a square pen in the corner.

Doc Brown drove into the yard in a battered car and eased himself out onto the ground. He was fat. The car seemed to rise back to normal position on its springs as the doctor removed his weight. He dragged a pair of overalls from the back seat, hung them over his arm, and looked down toward the hog house.

"Anybody home?" he yelled jovially.

Dave and Arch appeared in the doorway.

"Sure!" Dave called. "We'll be right up."

When they reached the car, Doc Brown had pulled out his paraphernalia and was assembling it. He looked up.

"Well, Dave, bring on those hogs."

"We've got 'em cornered for you, Doc."

[3] Reprinted by permission of Dodd, Mead & Company from *Archer Pilgrim* by Don Jackson. Copyright, 1942, by Dodd, Mead & Company, Inc.

Arch's attention turned to the equipment which the doctor had laid on the running board of his car—brown bottles with rubber caps, and a bag of gleaming instruments. There was a smell of antiseptic about the veterinarian, a strong odor that never left him. He was attaching needles to syringes, puttering about in the bag as he chatted with Dave.

"Guess we'd better have some water," he said.

Dave turned to Arch. "Run up to the house and ask for some hot water," he said.

Arch hurried to the back porch and yelled to his mother, and she handed him a pail with steaming water in it. He went back to Doc Brown and Dave as fast as he could without slopping water out of the pail.

The doctor was pulling his overalls on over his dark woolen trousers, having some difficulty because the trouser legs had a tendency to slip up and bulge when he tried to pull the overalls over them. He sat down on the running board of the car and wrestled with his clothing.

"Got to get myself on a diet, I guess," he laughed. His hair was white and tousled, and his face burned red from the sun. He would not wear a hat.

He fastened the suspenders of his overalls, put his hands on his knees, and looked at Arch.

"Are you going to help, Charley?" he asked.

"My name isn't Charley," Arch objected shyly.

Dave said, "I thought maybe he could dab on the iodine, or something, Doc."

Doc Brown got up and poured some hot water into a shallow pan which he had taken from the cluttered back seat of his car. "Well, Sir, I guess maybe we can fix that up," he said. "I usually do it myself, but if Charley wants to do it, he can." He dumped a couple of large blue-green tablets, from a dirty pillbox, into the pan of water.

Arch felt relieved, now that the doctor had assented to his help, and became suddenly talkative. He took a couple of steps toward the car.

"What are those pills?" he said, pointing to the tablets dissolving rapidly and coloring the pan of water.

"Antiseptic," Doc said. "Bichloride of mercury. Kills germs." The doctor had laid his two syringes in the solution and was pouring iodine into a tin cup from a large bottle. Arch watched intently, because that cup was to become his instrument—his excuse for being so near the fascinating doctor and his curious tools. Doc Brown made a swab by wrapping cotton around a stick, plunged it into the can of iodine, and handed the can to Arch.

"There she is, Charley," he said. "Don't drop the stuff."

Arch held the can tightly with both hands. What if he couldn't do it right? What if the men would get disgusted with him and send him off to play? The thought worried him.

Another car came roaring into the driveway then, scattering chickens into the grass on either side and rousing Pete, who had been reclining under the doctor's car.

"What's all this?" Doc asked.

"The Horton boys," Dave said. "They're helping this morning." Dave yelled at Pete, who was barking at fever pitch, and the dog crawled back under the doctor's car.

The Horton boys were in their early twenties, just out of high school a year or two and ready to begin farming for themselves. They were tall, laughing young men, past the rash boisterousness of adolescence but far from the grimness of middle age. Bill had always wanted to be a cowboy, and he wore a wide belt in his blue denim trousers, studded with bits of colored glass and gleaming metal. A wide-brimmed black hat covered his blond hair. George was a mechanic at heart; a pair of pliers bulged in the hip pocket of his overalls. He wore an engineer's cap of blue denim, pushed far back on his head, revealing hair as blond as Bill's. Both boys were tanned deeply, and they wore their sleeves turned far up into a tight roll as high above their elbows as they could twist the fabric.

They had rolled out of the car like a detachment of police leaving a patrol wagon to engage a rioting mob. Bill and George did everything in surprise attacks, and usually did whatever they started in a thorough manner. Farming, fighting, courting the young women of the neighborhood, each was a job to be done correctly and enthusiastically.

"Well, what are we waitin' for?" Bill said, sliding his hands into his tight pockets and striding up to the doctor's car.

"Middle of the morning already," George complained. He bent down and patted Pete, who had reappeared.

"Easy there, boys," Dave said. "Ol' Doc here's too hefty for all this rushing around. Gotta let him take his own time."

Doc chuckled. "Yes, Sir, that's a fact." He started picking up his equipment. "Well, let's get at this."

The Horton boys, in the pen, caught the hogs and carried them, squealing and squirming, to a V-shaped trough, one end of which was propped against the pen at the top, the other resting on the ground. It was a feeding trough that Dave had brought from the barn lot for the purpose. When Bill or George Horton struggled to the edge of the pen with a violently obstinate hog, he lifted the animal over the fence and deposited it in the trough, without care or tenderness. A leather strap passed over the animal's lower jaw to aid in holding it firmly.

Then the carrier held the hog's forelegs, and Dave, at the lower end of the trough, held the hind legs. Arch's share of the work came next, to step up with a dripping iodine swab and paint a spot about two inches square at the base of each foreleg and on the inside of the left hind leg, in the fleshy portion of the ham.

At first he was hesitant about applying the iodine. Doc Brown grabbed the swab and painted the first hog himself, when Arch seemed too slow.

"You see, Charley, you slap it on like this," Doc said, deftly handling the swab. "You're too darned pokey."

Right then Arch wanted to quit. What was he doing here anyway, working with these big guys? They couldn't expect him to do right the first time.

But when the next hog was stretched out in the trough, Arch managed to do his job without help, and Doc Brown said, "That's the stuff, Charley."

He felt better then. And by the time the fifth or sixth hog had been dumped out of the trough he was a veteran iodine swabber.

Each time Arch stepped back triumphantly, the doctor moved

in to finish the operation. He used two hypodermic syringes, which he kept in the pan of disinfectant near by. With the large one he made an injection in each foreleg. That was the serum to immunize the animal against cholera. With a smaller syringe, containing the potent virus, he made a similar injection in the hind leg. The hog was then turned loose and placed on the ground outside the pen, to wander, stiff and bewildered, off to join its fellows.

The Horton boys perspired, got dirty, and had a good time. Bill had a smudge across his face where a hog had tossed its head and smeared a mixture of dust and saliva on his cheek. George had taken off his shirt, and the dust and contact with the hogs had already made his white undershirt a dirty gray.

"What'll she weigh?" Dave asked, as the men quieted a hog on the trough and waited for Doc to wield his syringes.

The Horton boys appraised the animal.

"Looks bigger when she's upside down like this," George said. "How about sixty pounds?"

"Sixty!" Dave shouted. "Why, these hogs'll average more'n that. And this is one of the biggest ones."

"Okay," George said. "What's your guess?"

Dave thought a moment. "She'll hit eighty."

The Horton boys laughed loudly, and said nothing, as if the very thought that the hog weighed eighty pounds was beyond consideration.

"I'd say seventy," Arch put in, but nobody heard him. He had no idea of what the animal would weigh; it always mystified him when someone was able to tell the weight of a hog or cow by just looking at it.

Doc Brown vaccinated the hog and said, "Never yet seen a case where the guy that owns a hog don't say she weighs more'n she does, and the other feller says she weighs less."

"Okay, you tell us what she weighs," Bill demanded.

Doc filled his syringes from the brown bottles of serum and virus, punching the needles through the red rubber caps of the bottles and drawing the fluid into the glass tubes.

"Well, say seventy pounds," he said.

Seventy! Arch could have floated into the air and soared about the rafters. He had said it exactly right. He tried not to seem overly delighted, and said, "Guess I'm the one that said seventy pounds."

Bill grinned at him as he flopped another hog into the trough "Looks like you're a born farmer," he said.

Wonderful, magical, hypnotizing words. To be pronounced a born farmer by a tall, brown, laughing fellow like Bill Horton was almost more than he could stand. He swallowed hard a couple of times. There was energy in him that needed spending. He wanted to grab the door of the hog house and wrench it off its hinges. Or push down the side of the building and stride out into the open air. Instead, he painted iodine on another hog.

"Don't be getting ideas into the boy's head," Dave said to Bill. "We're trying to persuade him he ought to amount to something."

"No, Sir," Arch declared. "I'm going to be a farmer."

"Sure," Bill said. "That's the stuff. Nothing wrong with farming."

Dave turned to lift a hog off the trough. He lowered the animal to the ground more slowly than usual and stood watching it wander away. Arch was afraid the subject was going to change, so he repeated, "I sure am going to be a farmer."

George Horton grinned at the boy.

"Ask your Dad what he's got against farming," he told Arch.

"Now wait, boys," Dave spoke quickly. "I'm not saying there's anything wrong with farming. Let's forget it." He laughed.

Doc Brown brought their attention back to vaccinating with a sharp: "Hey, you monkeys. Let's tend to business."

The Horton boys charged into the diminishing group of unvaccinated hogs, and the dust rose in greater billows. Arch felt that his father had been beaten. Yes, the Horton boys had overshadowed his father, and he wanted to be like them.

He looked at Dave, working there in his dirty clothes, with sweat soaking through his shirt. There were little dark places in the corners of his eyes, where dust had collected. His face was bristly with whiskers. For an instant, Arch didn't like his father.

The vaccinating didn't last all morning. The last hog squealed his opposition to modern medicine at eleven o'clock. But by the time the pen had been torn down, and Doc had his instruments packed, it was half past eleven.

"Well," Dave said. "Dinner'll be on in a little while."

"No, I'd better run on into town," Doc protested, according to custom.

"Can't do that. You got to stay," Dave insisted, also according to custom.

"We can just run on home, too," the Horton boys said.

"Now, look, men. We've got a lot of steak and fresh cherry pie in there. Want us to throw it out?" Dave said.

The men ceased their protesting, and it was silently understood that everyone would stay to dinner. The conversation swung around to other matters.

QUESTIONS

Has the writer of "Translation" chosen an easy or a difficult subject for her narrative about an activity? In specific terms, what is her artistic aim? Is her achievement of this aim excellent, average, or poor? Does she draw all readers into her experience, or only those already interested in art? Does she limit her time well? Does she use unity of focus? Partly or entirely? What are her best details? Is this unit a sample of what *you* might expect to do now, or is it limited too much in its development?

In "Brown Boxes" what are the likenesses between Slim and the writer, or the character represented by the first person? The differences? Are these likenesses and differences well planned for the writer's aim? What is the artistic aim? Is there unity of idea or of attitude or both? How many conflicts are either implied or developed in the narrative? How much information is brought in after the talk starts? Is there unity of focus? Is the conclusion well shaped for the writer's aim?

If this excerpt from *Archer Pilgrim* were a complete unit, what things, if any, would need explanation? Would Dave and Arch need to be introduced to us, at least their relationship to each other? Why is Arch anxious to help in the vaccination? Does he succeed or fail in this effort? What larger conflict is implied between him and his father? Which of the two, Arch or his father, do the other characters support in this conflict? How do they give this support, and is it given consciously or unconsciously? What is the relationship in Arch's mind between the vaccination, estimating the weight of the hog, and getting agreement from the others about his being a farmer? Are subjective and objective details both important? How are the subjective details brought out? Is there unity of focus?

4

Setting; Environment

The term environment will be used in this chapter
to include all that is usually meant by two terms: first, *setting*,
in motion pictures or the theater, "the scenic environment, either
indoor or out, including all the physical surroundings, properties,
furniture, buildings, etc., within which a scene is enacted"; second,
environment, "all the external conditions and influences affecting
the life and development of an organism." (Usually environment
will refer to the development of a human organism, though there
is no reason why a writer with enough background should not
write a story with animals as characters.) It seems convenient to
discuss setting and environment together, and the discussion
which follows will illustrate some ways of using them in narrative.
Then you may choose one of several composition assignments and
perhaps analyze some subjects for future stories.

In most early literature, setting or environment tended to be
simple. Writers named essential objects or places without describing them, as the writer who told the story of Ruth and Boaz in the
Old Testament mentioned the fields of wheat and barley, the
gleaning, the threshing floor, the city gate, and other details. And
in Ali Baba's adventure with the forty thieves the narrator used
the forest, the cloud of dust, and the tree with a vividness which
contributes not to character or to psychological attitudes but to
simple suspense:

48

One day, when Ali Baba was in the forest, and had just cut wood enough to load his asses, he saw at a distance a great cloud of dust, which seemed to be driven toward him; he observed it very attentively, and distinguished soon after a body of horsemen. Though there had been no rumor of robbers in that country, Ali Baba began to think that they might prove such, and without considering what might become of his asses, resolved to save himself. He climbed up a large, thick tree, whose branches, at a little distance from the ground, were so close to one another that there was but little space between them. He placed himself in the middle, from whence he could see all that passed without being discovered, and the tree stood at the base of a rock, so steep and craggy that nobody could climb it.[1]

Gradually setting was used more, but often as a mere backdrop for human action, like an arrangement of flowers or pictures to make a room attractive. It was not an intimate part of the action, or a help in the interpretation of feeling, or a means of revealing character, or a causal force exerted upon human beings. Like the landscape in early paintings or old-fashioned sets in the theater, it was decoration.

With the evolution of the nineteenth-century novel, novelists tended to use huge blocks of objective, impersonal description of both places and people. For example, Scott began *Ivanhoe* with one paragraph of geographical background, added four paragraphs of historical material about Normans and Saxons in the reign of Richard I, a sixth paragraph about a local scene at sunset, and three paragraphs in which Gurth the swineherd and Wamba the jester were described and contrasted. All this description had scarcely a suggestion of action and hence was impersonal. Only in the tenth paragraph did the two, Gurth and Wamba, start talking. Chapter II used the same methods in introducing a churchman and his party; Chapter III repeated the methods in describing a hall and Cedric the Saxon, who lived there. Finally the groups of people in the three chapters met at the home of Cedric, and situations began to appear. Of course *Ivanhoe* is a historical novel; but the writer of good historical fiction now is likely to begin with a specific character or situation.

[1] *The Arabian Nights*, edited with introduction by W. H. D. Rouse, E. P. Dutton & Co., 1907.

If you wish to interest readers, you will not imitate old-fashioned methods and use huge blocks of static, objective material. Instead, you will use setting and general environment in active, subjective ways and learn to weave small bits of it into an artistic unit; you will not describe things for their own sake but use them as parts of a whole communication. Like professional writers, you may need background in brief narratives, poems, perhaps novels, and short stories. Such poems as Sandburg's "Chicago" and Frost's "Mending Wall" use setting in essential ways. One novel, *Shadows on the Rock*, begins by letting us see the raw settlement of early Quebec through the eyes of Auclair as the last ship for the season is putting out to sea; and throughout the book the characters are concerned with conflicts between the old civilization and the new, between sharply contrasted environments. In short stories, especially where you cannot use space recklessly, you will need to use setting in small bits which are active and subjective.

When setting is essential for your work you may have to deal with varied materials: places, scenes, objects, including landscapes, valleys, houses from inside or outside, rooms, cities as seen from hills or from airplanes or with the bird's-eye view of imagination. You may also find it necessary to analyze the effects of geographical background or of the environments which people have created for you.

SELECTION AND ARRANGEMENT

In using places, scenes, and objects you may have a complex problem. Your purpose is usually twofold: first, to let your reader experience with his senses; second, to communicate to him your attitude. Your problem is more complex when your material is static, without any action, but occasionally you may need to use brief bits without action.

Your difficulty often arises because you are confronted with so many details. You must select. But before you can select you must observe and discover the essentials—perhaps the shape, size, color, such a dominant impression as harmony, peace and quiet, cluttered disorder, noise. Perhaps the essentials are objective, and yet the objective and the subjective may be closely related. For example, if you look at farming country, you may choose to emphasize its peaceful quiet; another person, its opulence; another, its unbearable solitude. Each of these qualities is suggested by the scene, but each person chooses from the scene according to his preference. But every writer who uses objective reality has an obligation to use it honestly, without distortion. Finding the essential quality or the essentials in the subject is one form of selection; deciding on your attitude is another. Both are forms of your personal truth. Hence, every subject is its own problem, both subjective and objective, and no specific rules will completely solve these problems.

After you have found the essential quality of your scene and have realized your attitude, your problem of selection appears in a new form. You cannot give your reader an unarranged catalogue, you cannot give him a chaotic mass of relevant detail; either will block communication.

With nearly any subject you need to select, arrange, and infuse the details with your attitude almost as one process. For example, if you begin describing a room as "a long, sunny room, with groups of broad windows overlooking the garden," you have selected details of the room, arranged them so that we grasp the broad outlines, and infused the phrases with the *suggestion* of your enjoyment. Giving us the broad outlines of arrangement at the first is often helpful, as one who sketches outlines his picture and then fills in the details.

If your subject is static, certain principles may be helpful. First, give a general view, add details, and return to emphasize the general view. Second, proceed from the near at hand to the far away; or reverse, starting with the distant and coming to details near at hand. Third, describe in the order of discovery, giving first the striking details and adding others as you notice them. Fourth, find a center of interest in the physical details and then tell of other things as they are grouped about this center. Fifth, progress from the least to the most important; that is, arrange details in the order of climax. Used alone, this last method may be difficult; used with some physical framework or pattern of action, it may be effective communication.

If your subject is active instead of static, it will probably be easier to handle. You may find a pattern of activity in a subject which at first seems static. You may make your subject even more active by considering what some character, probably yourself, would do in the place or scene you are picturing. For example, suppose that your favorite camping spot is a small valley beside a mountain lake. You may let us see this place as entirely static. You may make it semiactive by letting us see it when dawn comes or twilight gathers. You may make it more active by describing it when you are arriving, perhaps in the evening, and making camp. Whether you are acting or watching other people act, your details will naturally fall into a time pattern. With a time pattern, you will become more specific in situation and circumstances. Your activity will tend to simplify your problems of *selection* and *arrangement*.

Whether your plan is active or static, you will write more clearly and easily if you know *who* is seeing the place, scene, or object, *where* he is, and whether he stays in one spot or moves about. If your character remains in one spot you will tell us only what he can perceive from that spot, unless you make clear that he is thinking of other things which he cannot see. If your character moves about, you will warn us by transitional words and phrases. In this assignment, too, you may secure unity of focus through the mind of your chief character.

Suppose, for example, that your subject is your home town. You need to make many decisions about specific details as you create your experience. First, do you prefer to suggest your early affection for the place, your later indifference, or your pleasure in getting back after you thought that you had ceased to care? Second, what time will you prefer for your purpose—summer or winter, a rainy day or a snowstorm, morning or evening? Third, from what place will you show us your town—the hill above or the corner of Main Street? Fourth, if you are coming back to the town, how are you coming? By train or bus or on foot? With whom—your father, an older brother who has been away and will understand, or a younger brother who will wonder at your attitude and ask you to explain? Will you stop on a hilltop overlooking the town? Will you compare the valley to a green bowl with the gray and white town at the bottom? Will you show us the tiny lake at the other side of the town first, because it catches your eye, and then the wide gray street bisecting the town and leading to the lake? Will you show us your house by relating it to the whole street, and to a lake which is your center of interest? Will you use your talk with your brother to lead us to your discovery— that it is good to be back? No one else can answer these questions for you. No matter how you answer them, your mind will serve as a focus through which we see and share your attitude. You may bring a composition like this to a close as you leave the hilltop, making it a well-rounded unit of experience; or you may use this scene later as the introduction to a story.

USING PLACES, SCENES, OBJECTS

You will often need to let your characters handle objects, just as actors handle properties on the stage. If these objects have an emotional significance or if they are unfamiliar to most readers you may need to select, arrange, and infuse them with a character's attitude but in an active situation. For example, an American woman and the chief of a tribe in Liberia come to an understanding without words as they examine each other's creative work:

The visitor was old Chief Kondea and the thing he had brought was a wooden rice bowl. It was oval at one end and pointed at the other, with flared sides so that it resembled the hull of a toy ship. The white wild-rubber wood had been rubbed to a high gloss and the rim was decorated with a geometric design burned with a hot wire. It was as large as an ordinary vegetable serving dish, which is just the right size for an individual serving of country chop.[2]

In another situation the same writer describes a kind of house which is unfamiliar to most of her readers; and though this description, considered alone, is not active, it does contribute to an active relationship.

The house they gave me was so new the thatch smelled like damp hay. The door, a single slab cut from the buttress root of a bombax tree, had been intricately carved in bas-relief. The forward surfaces were stained with turmeric, the wood showing through the golden dye in silvery streaks. The recessed areas were charcoal black.

Everything about the house evidenced skill and care. I had long ago

[2] Esther Warner, *New Song in a Strange Land,* Houghton Mifflin Company, 1948.

succumbed to the charm of a clean mud house; this was the nicest I had ever seen. The bed which Johnny was preparing to "dress" was a raised clay slab about twelve inches above the floor. The head and foot were high clay partitions, back of which dry firewood was neatly corded. Both bed and floor were carpeted with new pandanus mats the color of ripe wheat.

In the center of the floor was a raised cube of clay on which a little fire had burned down to rubescent twinklings. Above the fire, supported on a three-legged black iron ring, was an egg-shaped pottery jar which contained my heated bath water. There was nothing else in the room except my cases, which seemed in these surroundings a clutter amongst perfection.[3]

This concise description of a city as the writer comes into port tends to be active, with details arranged from the near at hand to the far away, and with emphasis on color:

The first port of call was Genoa. It rose out of the sea in the early morning, an amphitheater of pearl-gray, yellow, and rose, against a background of treeless green hills with crumbling forts on their crests.[4]

Moods or attitudes of characters are often stressed through setting. In a biography of young Galileo, for example, when the boy thought of suicide, the writer used impressionistic memories, freed from exact place and time patterns, to contrast with his earlier happiness:

His thoughts moved to the friendly village of Vallombrosa: the pealing of an organ in the monastery, with its stone flags and white-washed wall—a fairy-tale world of music and incense, ruled by the fat, eternally smiling abbot, Don Orazio Morandi, whose favorite pupil he was . . .[5]

The attitude of Studs is emphasized by setting when he is waiting to escort a girl whose background is above his own level:

Studs observed that the Scanlans had a lamp in every corner, floor-lamps, table-lamps, and lamps on the piano. The parlor contained so much furniture that it seemed overcrowded. He wanted to light a cigarette but restrained himself for fear he might spill ashes. He looked

[3] Esther Warner, *Seven Days to Lomaland*, Houghton Mifflin Company, 1954.

[4] Jan Valtin, *Out of the Night*, Alliance Book Corporation, 1941.

[5] Zsolt de Harsanyi, *The Star-Gazer*, G. P. Putnam's Sons, 1939.

at a rose-green pottery lamp set on the table near the heavy blue velvet drapes. He moved to sit on a large overstuffed davenport that was upholstered in dark blue velour. He touched it, studied it.[6]

Specific objects may be used to emphasize the mood of a character, as the bridge is used at the beginning of this story:

When she opened her eyes the next time she saw that day was coming, for the air beyond the hospital window had lightened into a deep, shadowless blue-violet, so newly begun that the lights along the bridge had not yet been turned out. At this moment, balanced between night and day, the bridge itself was a surprise. She had been too preoccupied to notice it, when she came here, hours ago. How many hours? She did not know.

"What time is it?" she asked.

"Nearly seven," her husband said. "I'll have to leave in a few minutes."

The bridge was wonderfully beautiful. In the cold winter air, its many lights trembled and quivered like stars; it was as if all the constellations of the sky, with their different-sized stars, had come down and arranged themselves in this great, horned, scintillating arc. Its brilliant, glittering beauty was one more thing—a crown for all her happiness. . . .[7]

Setting, used actively, may introduce a story, especially one which depends largely on setting for its development:

He was rolling in the first early dark down a snowy road, his headlights pinched between dark walls of trees, when the engine coughed, recovered, coughed again, and died. Down a slight hill he coasted in compression, working the choke, but at the bottom he had to pull over against the three-foot wall of plowed snow. Snow creaked under the tires as the car eased to a stop. The heater fan unwound with a final tinny sigh.

Here in its middle age this hitherto dependable mechanism had betrayed him, but he refused to admit immediately that he was betrayed.[8]

---

[6] James T. Farrell, *Studs Lonigan*, Vanguard Press, 1935.

[7] Elizabeth Enright, "The First Face," *The New Yorker*, December 15, 1951.

[8] Wallace Stegner, "The Traveler," *Harper's Magazine*, February, 1951.

An object or some part of a setting may become a symbol—a tangible sign of intangible attitudes or of changing emotions, as a boat becomes a symbol in the story which opens thus:

She was a duckboat, you know, like the kind you've seen and hungered after in the catalogues you look through during winter nights when the river's frozen hard and black like granite, and the wind is moaning to come in, and the train whistles are howling like souls come out of Chippahanock Cemetery. Only in the catalogue, her lightness and smoothness don't show, and you can't feel her turn in her own length or guess how fast she'll go upstream against an east wind and the waves chopping at her.

She was made of thin lath, her bow decked over, and she was painted light green—the color of maple leaves in early spring, and varnished with clear varnish and sanded and varnished and sanded again, and worked on with steel wool until the bottom was as smooth as the granite ice in winter that froze without wind. She was swift and light, like a kingfisher, and she seemed blonde in her greenness.

We would come down to her by the river early in the morning— the three of us, Carl, his sister Helen, and me—and she would be waiting for us there on the sand that had been left by the June rise of the river, and her greenness and the dry gold sand and Helen's hair all seemed blonde and light and lovely at once.[9]

Descriptions of place may be used to point up character. You have probably looked sometimes at an empty stage, before the entrance of a character, and formed a sound idea of the character for whom the setting was created. You may sometime have waited in a house, a room, or an office to meet a stranger, and you formed impressions of his character before he entered; your own room or apartment, if it is in its typical condition now, would reveal you to a stranger. So a writer may describe a place and either forecast or emphasize character:

The negroes were aware of the house. It stood a few hundred yards away, hidden behind two live oaks, isolated and remote in a patch of hammock. It was a tall square two-stories. The woman who gave them water from her well when the nearby branch was dry looked to them

[9] Bill Berge, "That Lovely Green Boat," *Furioso*, Fall, 1951. Winner of the Knopf-Furioso Fiction Contest for 1951.

like the house, tall and bare and lonely, weathered gray, like its un-painted cypress.[10]

The situation which develops is made possible by this setting.

USING LARGER ENVIRONMENT: ITS EFFECTS

You may also be concerned at this stage with the effect of your environments on you. Much modern fiction, both novels and short stories, grows from conflicts deeply rooted in environment. For example, *The Grapes of Wrath* pictures people who struggle against a threefold environment: drought, caused by natural forces; depression, caused by complex and unconscious acts of men; mechanistic farming, evolved by men skilled in machinery and profit taking. Against these triple forces, the "Oakies" are helpless but not entirely defeated.

Short stories and sketches often grow from conflicting environ-ments. The college student who once worked in a steel mill where men beside him were burned to death in accidents, the student writing about a boy who comes to college but longs for the placid animals on the farm who never give him assignments, the fresh-man girl who tries to act sophisticated—all these people are strug-gling with contrasting environments. Stories of men in army train-ing camps or in battle are often records of adjusting to new environments.

Environment, in this large sense, means physical surroundings first of all. Physical environment includes climate and geography (which are beyond human control), some details which can be changed by man, and also buildings, parks, and physical arrange-ments which have been created by man. What physical and geo-graphical surroundings have you known? Have you lived by the ocean, by lakes, rivers, mountains, on the prairies, in the country, small towns, cities? In different parts of the United States? In foreign countries? What experiences and what conflicts have grown from these environments? What tastes, habits, and attitudes toward the future have been influenced by these physical surroundings?

But your environment means much that is not physical. It in-

[10] Marjorie Kinnan Rawlings, "Gal Young Un," *When the Whippoorwill,* Charles Scribner's Sons, 1940.

cludes your economic, educational, occupational, social, religious, ethical, political, emotional, and psychological background—all that is suggested by any of these terms. It even includes attitudes which you have because your ancestors were certain types of people and you despise or revere them.

What class of society do you belong to, according to your own estimate? Why do you place yourself in this class? What criteria do you use in separating it from other classes? What are your attitudes to the other classes? What economic level do you know first-hand? Do you know one level only, or have you at some time lived on a different level? What occupational or professional backgrounds do you know well? Has your background given you mechanical or nonmechanical, social or nonsocial attitudes, feelings of superiority or inferiority? Have you felt pride in your background? Have you ever resented it? Do you think that the sons and daughters of bankers, merchants, doctors, teachers, lawyers, and laborers develop the same or different attitudes to themselves and other people?

What educational environments do you know well? Have they impelled you to thoroughness or carelessness, to original thinking or to accepting authority, to narrowness or to breadth and tolerance? What social, religious, and ethical backgrounds have you known? What racial or religious conflicts have been part of these patterns?

Some of the environments already mentioned have been created for you by people. It is possible that your most important environments have been shaped for you by the people in your community —by such individuals in the community as a doctor, a minister, a teacher, a policeman, an athletic coach—or by relatives, friends, parents, brothers and sisters. Which of the environments made for you by people have been important? Is your community tolerant or intolerant, kind or unkind? Does it demand conformity, and is its demand desirable or undesirable? Or does it give you freedom to grow? Has some teacher created an environment in which you became resentful or in which you were stimulated to develop? Have your parents given you security, affection, and a chance to make your own decisions? Or have you been insecure, lacked affection, and been too rigidly controlled? Have your brothers and sisters hindered or helped your development? Have you hindered or helped them?

Has any special part of your environment helped or hindered you? Has it given you new tastes and interests, desires or aversions? Determined your future profession or your philosophy of life? Given you emotional security or insecurity? Created needs, fears, frustrations? Affected your relationship with other people in the past, present, or future?

Has any part of your environment created conflicts or led to situations because you wished to break away from some pattern of belief or conduct?

What effect is your present environment having on you?

What specific situations do you recall in connection with any of these ideas which are important to you? Which are so complex that they might be jotted down now and mulled over for future stories?

If you wish to develop, learn now to begin with your experience. As one playwright and screen writer has said about the problem:

> I have talked about this sort of thing frequently with other professional writers, and almost always they have felt they wasted many years going in wrong directions. I know I have. And we always agreed that the best writing, particularly in our formative years, is writing based on our own lives. I don't mean factual autobiography. I mean characters, experiences, emotions, backgrounds with which we are familiar. Writing must ring true, and especially for the beginning writer, you can make a character you know more authentic than a character you invent.[11]

The same writer went on to say that everyone does better if he can approach his experience objectively or even if he can think of himself unfavorably. For example, he once tried to write a narrative based on himself as a boy but as a sensitive, superior fellow. His effort was a failure. Then he looked at his boyhood faults: he hated to get up in the morning or to do any work, and he hoped for wealth without effort. When he wrote about himself in this way, he had a real character and, he adds, one more like himself than he cared to admit.

[11] Samson Raphaelson, *The Human Nature of Playwriting*, The Macmillan Company, 1949.

WRITING YOUR COMPOSITION

A. Find some part of your environment which has had a significant effect on you. Consider the surroundings of your home, your community, places where you have worked for pay, places where you have been in military training or service, and environments that have been created for you by nature, by social or industrial forces, or by individual people. Find something which stirs your senses and your imagination. Then communicate, through a few moments of active experience, your attitude to the environment. Do not *explain* the effects; *suggest* in a descriptive-narrative pattern.

B. Choose a place, a scene, or an object which has significance for you. Write about it so that your readers will realize it with all their senses and at the same time realize your attitude. Probably you will find it desirable to use a simple situation with a specific time of day and year, and a special kind of weather. At least use a descriptive-narrative pattern.

READING

NURSES' HOME *

Dorothy Dunkelberg

We eighteen new probationers were herded up to the third floor of the nurses' home and deposited two at a time at each consecutive door on the right side of the long, narrow, drafty hall. At the end of this corridor the tall thin window spread just enough light to show worn spots on the dull green, coarsely woven carpet, and to emphasize the gloom of dark-stained woodwork and a high, box-like ceiling. The nurses-to-be, coupled down the aisle, faced the squat, expressionless superintendent—a post of white starch in the center of the hall. The monotone of her thick voice never varied from its I've-said-this-a-hundred-times-before pitch. "Chapel is at 5:30 every morning. No one is excused——Line up for breakfast at the first bell——Lights out at 9:30." Having concluded her instructions, she left.

As her padded steps faded out down the stairs, I pushed open "our" door and looked in. The short, white half-curtain twitched at the window opposite and pulled a cold gray draft through.

Beside the window were two flat-topped, stained gumwood dressers. Backed to the wall opposite them were two iron cots, covered with white cotton spreads. Between the dressers and cots against the left wall two straight chairs sat stiffly, and across from them, between us and the window, were a long dark desk and two closet doors.

Hesitant, we stepped in, and the door blew shut behind us with a metallic click.

THE BEST CONCRETE IN THE DAM *

Tom Vernon

"There it is, just over the Pedroes." Cobb pointed to the sky. A droning speck above the mountains grew into an airplane which angled down to the landing strip.

"They better hurry up, or Blackie's liable to die before they get him to town, like that carpenter last winter." Al squinted against the dust raised by the desert wind. All over the camp men watched in the direction of the air strip.

"He ain't hurt bad enough to die, but he ain't ever gonna be the same again," said Cobb.

"Lucky the weather's good enough for the plane to come out. When Bobby Jack got his knee smashed he had to ride the sixty miles over that damn mountain road. The nurse shot him full of morphine, but the driver said Bobby Jack screamed every time he hit a bump, and that road is pure bumps," said Al.

"Talk about screams, you shoulda heard Blackie today while he was fallin'. I reckon any man would make a racket fallin' eighty-five feet," said Cobb.

"Was that how far it was?" Al spat out his quid of Brown's Mule Cut Plug.

"That's what the surveyor fellas said. He started up a rope by the stiffleg pier up on the side of the cliff. The rope he was tied by had some slack up at the top, and when he put his weight on it the slack played out sudden like and when it stopped it snapped him off the end like crackin' a whip. He fell eighty-five feet into that open space behind the power-house. I guess we been averagin' about one bad fall a week on this here dam. I ain't afraid of workin'

high, but when men start fallin' like rain I get a little skittery."
Cobb watched the plane as it took off and headed back over the mountains.

"The company oughta have a doctor out here. That nurse is gettin' so old she don't even come out of her house anymore. You ever hear about that high-scaler that almost died from loss of blood when he got his face smashed in?" said Al.

"Never heard about him," said Cobb.

"Well, when they first started preparin' the site for the dam they had to do a lot of blastin' up on the cliffs. One day, after blastin' a big chunk off, the high-scalers went back up and started drillin' again. This one fool guy sees a hole already started so he sticks his jack-hammer in the hole and turns it on. Well, there was a stick of dynamite in that hole that hadn't gone off, and it blew that seventy-pound jack-hammer right into his face. There he was, out cold, hangin' at the end of a hundred-foot safety rope. They had a hell of a time gettin' him down, and by the time they got him to the nurse he was soaked with his own blood. And don't ya know, that nurse wouldn't give him any plasma until she called town and got permission from some doctor." Al turned as another sheet of dust blew toward them.

"Ya know," said Al, "they say the best concrete in the dam is that what's got plenty of tobacker juice in it. I guess they gotta have plenty of blood too."

EVENING IN BROOKLYN [12]

Thomas Wolfe

For suddenly you remember how the tragic light of evening falls even on the huge and rusty jungle of the earth that is known as Brooklyn and on the faces of all the men with dead eyes and with flesh of tallow gray, and of how even in Brooklyn they lean upon the sills of evening in that sad hushed light. And you remember how you lay one evening on your couch in your cool cellar depth in Brooklyn, and listened to the sounds of evening and to the dying

[12] Excerpted from "No Door" in the collection *From Death to Morning* by Thomas Wolfe; copyright, 1932, 1935 by Charles Scribner's Sons; used by permission of the publishers.

birdsong in your tree; and you remember how two windows were thrown up, and you heard two voices—a woman's and a man's— begin to speak in that soft tragic light. And the memory of their words came back to you, like the haunting refrain of some old song—as it was heard and lost in Brooklyn.

"Yuh musta been away," said one, in that sad light.

"Yeah, I been away. I just got back," the other said.

"Yeah? Dat's just what I was t'inkin'," said the other. "I'd been t'inkin' dat yuh musta been away."

"Yeah, I been away on my vacation. I just got back."

"Oh, yeah? Dat's what I t'ought meself. I was t'inkin' just duh oddeh day dat I hadn't seen yuh f'r some time. 'I guess she's gone away,' I says."

And then for seconds there was silence—save for the dying bird-song, voices in the street, faint sounds and shouts and broken calls, and something hushed in evening, far, immense, and murmurous in the air.

"Well, wat's t' noos sinct I been gone?" the voice went out in quietness in soft soft tragic light. "Has anyt'ing happened sinct I was away?"

"Nah! Nuttin's happened," the other made reply. "About duh same as usual—*you* know?" it said with difficult constraint, inviting intuitions for the spare painfulness of barren tongues.

"Yeah, I know," the other answered with a tranquil resignation— and there was silence then in Brooklyn.

"I guess Fatheh Grogan died sinct you was gone," a voice began.

"Oh, yeah?" the other voice replied with tranquil interest.

"Yeah."

And for a waiting moment there was silence.

"Say, dat's too bad, isn't it?" the quiet voice then said with comfortless regret.

"Yeah. He died on Sattiday. When he went home on Friday night, he was O. K."

"Oh, yeah?"

"Yeah."

And for a moment they were balanced in strong silence.

"Gee, dat was tough, wasn't it?"

"Yeah. Dey didn't find him till duh next day at ten o'clock.

When dey went to look for him he was lyin' stretched out on duh bat' room floeh."

"Oh, yeah?"

"Yeah. Dey found him lyin' deh," it said.

And for a moment more the voices hung in balanced silence.

"Gee, dat's too bad. . . . I guess I was away when all dat happened."

"Yeah. Yuh musta been away."

"Yeah, dat was it, I guess. I musta been away. Oddehwise I woulda hoid. I was away."

"Well, so long, kid. . . . I'll be seein' yuh."

"Well, so long!"

A window closed, and there was silence; evening and far sounds and broken cries in Brooklyn, Brooklyn, in the formless, rusty, and unnumbered wilderness of life.

And now the red light fades swiftly from the old red brick of rusty houses, and there are voices in the air, and somewhere music, and we are lying there, blind atoms in our cellar-depths, gray voice-less atoms in the manswarm desolation of the earth, and our fame is lost, our names forgotten, our powers are wasting from us like mined earth, while we lie here at evening and the river flows . . . and dark time is feeding like a vulture on our entrails, and we know that we are lost, and cannot stir . . . and there are ships there! there are ships! . . . and Christ! we are all dying in the darkness! . . . and yuh musta been away . . . yuh musta been away . . .

And that is a moment of dark time, that is one of strange mil-lion-visaged time's dark faces.

QUESTIONS

Whose viewpoint is used through the sketch called "Nurses' Home"? What attitude is emphasized? What words in the first sentence imply this attitude? Is the implication carried through the sketch? Does the writer accomplish the simple artistic aim? At this stage will you gain most by doing something simple like this unit, where you repeat im-plication with variety, or should you try something more difficult?

Is "The Best Concrete in the Dam" a comment on environment? Is the environment geographical? Is it created partly by people like the nurse? Is it created by the hazards of the job itself? Or is it a combination of these factors? Whose view is presented? What situation is used? Has the writer chosen an effective situation or could he do better? What is the effect of the comment at the end?

In the excerpt called "Evening in Brooklyn" what attitude does Wolfe imply about nature? About the man-made city? About the people he uses? Just what does he think is wrong with these people? What contrast does he suggest between human possibilities and aspirations, when compared with human achievement? What does he mean by the term *ships* in the latter part? Is the term a symbol? Is the repetition in the talk effective or ineffective? Why? What is the writer's aim in using the talk? Is Wolfe concerned only with people who live in Brooklyn or with humanity?

5

Human Relationships

Most good fiction deals with human relationships. Some writers use these relationships for the complex patterns of whole novels, with only minor emphasis on setting; others picture the struggle of people against the social and industrial forces which men create and use; a few, like Jack London in *The Call of the Wild* and Herman Melville in *Moby Dick*, pit their people against vast forces of nature. But usually the writers are concerned in some way with the tensions between people. Whenever you write narrative, then, you are likely to need all possible skills for bringing out these tensions. In significant fiction you cannot do without these skills; in radio or TV drama you can use them to good advantage; in murder mysteries, or space stories or other science fiction, where the plots and the gimmicks are soon exhausted, you would find them an asset.

Human relationships are difficult compared with objects and landscapes; they are subtle and intangible, they must be brought out by suggestion. But if you wish to gain skill in writing, you will find them good problems. You can use them now because you will express them in simple units, not in novels or complex stories, and because you experience them yourself almost every moment of your waking life.

A brief narrative by William Carlos Williams, "The Use of Force," is a good example of the moment-of-experience pattern used to bring out human relationships. A doctor is called to see a little girl with a high fever. The girl says that her throat is not sore, but she refuses to let the doctor examine it, and he suspects that she has diphtheria. After she has splintered his wooden spatula, he uses a metal spoon and forces her to reveal her membrane-covered tonsils. Of course he could tell himself that he has noble motives, but if he did, the author would have a commonplace story. Instead, as soon as the doctor wins, he knows that he has gone "beyond reason"; his influences have been "a blind fury, a feeling of adult shame, bred of a longing for muscular release. . . ." He regrets the motives of his victory. This regret, the author's real theme, makes the incident unusual.

A brief narrative, "Do You Like It Here?" by John O'Hara makes use of human relationships. A teacher in a boys' boarding school accuses a boy of theft. Though the teacher's motives are ignoble and he lacks evidence, he assumes noble motives. The incident ends without resolution or development to tell us "how it comes out." Thus it is not a fully developed short story. But the author knows his characters and their background well enough to suggest sympathy for the boy against unscrupulous adult authority.

Perhaps you can make human relationships interesting with a similar brief development. You need not try to carry a problem to its final solution nor to write a character sketch. Of course your people may be as individual as you wish, and sometimes they may need to be different. Only one kind of child would resist a doctor as the child resisted in "The Use of Force"; but the major aim is not to bring out her character, only to emphasize the doctor's attitude to his motives. And so you will need to have an attitude, or an attitude plus an idea, and to develop it vividly with talk and action.

SUBJECTS

Where will you find subjects about human relationships? As a human being you have many areas to explore and many ideas which will help you in understanding yourself and other people. You are a son or a daughter, perhaps a brother or a sister, a brother-in-law or a sister-in-law, a nephew or a niece, a grandchild, a friend, a classmate, a sweetheart, an uncle or an aunt, a husband or a wife, a father or a mother. In your community you have been the student of certain teachers, the patient of some doctor, a member of some church group, perhaps the client of a lawyer, a customer of various businesses, a member of social organizations or of theater groups, athletic teams, debate clubs.

What has been your experience in a specific one of these relations? What problems have you tried to solve? What conflicting loyalties have you met? What changes in outer circumstances or inner feelings? Perhaps you visit a member of your family who is dangerously ill; you are shocked at the change but try to conceal your knowledge and your feelings. You are introduced to future relatives-in-law; your fear congeals or thaws into friendliness. Your favorite brother or sister marries and moves far away. You and a friend part to attend different colleges; your friend changes or you both change according to the inevitable laws of separation and growth. You discover that your friend or your sister learns easily something that you have tried without success; you try to resolve the conflict between affection and jealousy. You are sure that a supposed friend is lying to you when you have a right to know the truth. If you are a mature person you may find a whole area of subjects in your changing attitudes to your parents: an early need for security, a resentment of control, a belief that they knew little, a discovery that they were wiser than you thought, a recent realization that you are beginning to protect them. Any ordinary situation, like one of these, may be made significant by the way you bring out its implications.

You may find something individual to say in less intimate relationships. You are asked to lend a book you prize, to tell when another person came in last night, to respond to an effusive greeting, to admire someone's hat or suit. You smile to yourself at the person who suddenly becomes friendly in the hope of getting something from you, the person who boasts, the naïve girl who tries to act sophisticated.

You may be interested in the minority groups of your community—the people who are different in nationality, speech habits, race, politics, or religion; the intelligent, well-behaved young people who happen to live on the wrong side of the tracks. If you have ever belonged to a minority yourself because you supported an unpopular cause, traveled in an alien land, or became lost in a city where you found yourself the only person of your race, you have a rather individual approach to the minority problem. In handling minority problems which begin with general attitudes you will need to select individuals to represent your large idea, to choose or create a specific situation, and if possible, to give your topic freshness by your attitude and your diction.

You may be interested too in individuals who refuse to conform to a community either in dress, in other habits, or in beliefs—the modern equivalents of the village atheist. Or you may know some recluse who is credited with a romantic legendary past; your interest is not in that past, though, but in a present relationship to so-called normal people.

But whether you are interested in more or less intimate personal relationships, minority groups, or individual nonconformists, you do not need to restrict yourself to solemn topics. Happiness, laughter, satire, and comedy, as well as tragedy, grow from contacts between people. Death, loss, sorrow, misunderstanding, frustration, restraint, immaturity, arrested development, ill will, hate, and destruction exist; but even today they are not the whole of life. If your experience gives you something authentic to say, write about life rather than death—about marriage, birth, understanding, fulfillment, freedom, maturity, growth, good will, love, and creative living. Explore both sides of all your human coins.

USING SITUATIONS

The term situation is used here for almost any position, condition, or set of circumstances in which you find yourself; here it refers to human relations. Mere trifles are often sufficient to show how one person reacts to another, just as trifles may reveal character. A man shows his attitude to a waitress while he orders a cup of coffee. A woman reveals her attitude to a person outside her class by a glance, a tone of voice, a few words. You may make small encounters significant through talk, action, specific thought and feeling. That is, you may succeed if you know exactly what attitude you wish to suggest.

Situations are subjective or objective. Crises which go on inside you without betraying themselves to others (as crises in human relations often do) are subjective. Crises which reveal themselves in words, actions, gestures, facial expressions have become objective. Your need in writing about human relationships is first to realize the significance of inner experience and then to communicate this significance by subjective and objective details.

Situations are static (fixed, lifeless, inactive) or dynamic (active). A static situation is often uninteresting, especially if the character involved is apathetic or unconscious of his position. But with a certain kind of character, a static situation may come to life like a smoldering volcano. For example, you may be unconscious of your emotional security until you are threatened with its loss. Then your static situation becomes active.

Dynamic situations will probably have a greater impact on your readers than static ones, and you will develop them more easily. If they cause you to grow in emotional awareness they are good subjects. If they make you or your character act or decide swiftly because they promise rewards or penalties, they are truly dynamic.

Sometimes when you start with a static situation, you prefer to make it more dynamic. You may do so by asking yourself what action would be reasonable or natural for you in these circumstances; that is, if life does not furnish you activity, create it. For example, you feel keenly the loss of a friend; but in real life you learned about your loss slowly through the events of days or weeks. Instead of photographing life, create a dynamic situation, one-time and one-place, developed by talk and action: you extend an invitation or make a request of a friend, but he wriggles his way out and refuses you. Your invitation or request may be a trifle, but the attitude in refusing can be made significant. You may find dynamic situations, as well as subjects, by looking within or by observing other people. Suppose that at some specific moment you have a sharp feeling of anger, sorrow, pleasure, or embarrassment. Look for its cause. Or start with situations: you are asked to lend a car or a formal dress to a careless acquaintance whom you do not wish to offend. What are your inner feelings? What do you do or say? Why? What other things could you do or say? What do you wish afterward that you had said and done?

DEVELOPING A SITUATION

An active situation usually has a conflict, though it may be simple and implied, not fully developed. A conflict is a struggle between opposing forces; it *begins, develops,* and comes to a *climax* in which one force succeeds or gives up the struggle. The conflict may come from desires or urges within you or your chief character. It may come from your effort to persuade another person to decide or to do something, or from your resistance to his efforts to persuade you. Usually you will need to develop your active situation rather fully in the middle or the body, that is, between the point where the conflict begins and the point where we realize what the result will be.

TECHNIQUES

For a situation which brings out human relationships you will need again some techniques discussed in preceding chapters; and whatever you write, you will use the full visualizing which makes good servants of your senses.

You will need again certain other techniques already discussed, but for different reasons or in new forms. When you wrote about activities, environment, places, scenes, objects, you could begin by looking at tangible things outside yourself. Here you may often need to begin with subjective feelings and then find tangible ways of expressing them. Hence your own physical reactions may be more essential. Under emotion you breathe rapidly, your eyelids widen or narrow, your lips tighten or relax; your muscles contract at the approach of a person you dislike or fear or hold in awe, and they relax at the approach of a person you like; you act mechanically in certain states of fatigue or grief. Though these are general statements, your experience each time is specific. Your fresh discoveries, in yourself and then in others, will give you effective help. Keen senses tend to become keener at moments of emotional tension, sometimes etching into the memory details which, unemotionalized, would be trivial.

You will need unity of focus perhaps much more than you did in earlier assignments. If you deal with two characters you will need to emphasize one more than the other, perhaps by playing up one character at the beginning, in the close, throughout your composition, and even in the title. *You* may be the mind which gives us unity of focus, either because your attitude is the center or because you are watching another person who is the center. Or someone else, if you have mature skill in working with character, may furnish you the mind, the senses, and the emotion to use as a microscope for the whole scene.

Your immediate surroundings or those of your character may furnish the objective details. Again your problem will be much greater because you are not merely reacting to outer details; you are starting with inner feeling and using outer details to express this feeling. But as a human being you have a tendency to relate yourself and your surroundings. Even time seems swift or slow as you experience joy or sorrow. You can find infinite patterns of likeness or contrast in a room, an apartment, a house, nature, the details of a city. For instance, a small apartment with inexpensive furnishings can provide you with objective details for expressing boredom, aesthetic distaste, or high adventure because it is the setting for a new home. The details are nothing in themselves; they have power as they become a framework for your attitude. For it is not in your stars but in yourself that you find the flavor of good writing.

You may find that some new techniques are useful. You may need to describe people in some detail, even though character work is not yet your major aim. But you may need to *hear* human voices; to *see* people until you have observed something different about their eyes, mouths, faces, hair, hands, and gestures; to use these discoveries to illuminate the attitude of a moment. But unless your subject demands these details, do not strain to use them now; if you do need them, you may anticipate the chapters on character.

You will probably need to use the talk of people, unless you have an unusual subject. If you use talk well it will sound like talk, not formal, bookish language, and it will be suited to the person, his mood, the situation, and the listener. You will also need to blend the talk of people with their thoughts and actions and to show the ball of conversation, as it is served and returned, between two people.

You may have a real need for pictures of the past or of a possible future. Or your character may picture present events in another place where he wishes to be or is happy not to be now. For example, the person who is away from home but longs to be there may see and hear in his imagination what people are doing there at this time of year and day; the person who is glad to escape may experience similar events in his imagination, but with the suggestion of entirely different attitudes. With many subjects, the past, the future, and present events which are happening in another place are more effective when they are used in small bits and deftly woven into the present, without repetitions of "he thought" or "he remembered." The readings at the close of this chapter will give you some examples of these techniques.

You may need to realize and use repetition as an effective device in narrative. You will find repetition invaluable for all subtle feelings as well as for human relationships. Try to express your attitude in your title and in the skillful repetition of words, phrases, and ideas through your whole narrative. If your character begins to feel lost and alone and if the development of this aloneness is your major aim, tell us not once but forty times, but tell us with subtle variety.

TONE COLOR: RHYTHM

If you have maturity of feeling and sureness of purpose you may be ready to think about tone color with your more complex experience; at least you may begin to study it in the writing of others. When your language suggests its emotion by its sound, you have tone color. It is suggestion carried to the *n*th degree, so that we might realize your emotion if we could hear the tune without the words—if the language were coming over a radio turned so low that meaning escaped us, or if we were foreigners listening with no knowledge of English. Perhaps you are already familiar with the term *tone color* in poetry; the same quality appears in emotional prose. It is not limited to melancholy attitudes in either prose or poetry—though you may well suppose that some writers and teachers think it is. You will find it just as useful in expressing vigor, speed, happiness.

Tone color is influenced by many elements of style. First, the length of words is important. If you use many short words you tend to suggest activity, vigor, speed; if you use long, flowing words you are likely to suggest lassitude, restfulness, melancholy. Second, falling and rising rhythm may contribute to tone color. The use of long words accented at the beginning probably increases the effect of melancholy or lassitude: *silently, monotonous, oppressive.* One-syllable words or words accented on the final syllable tend toward vigor and speed. Third, consonant and vowel sounds influence tone color. If you use many consonants like *j, k,* hard *ch, r,* you tend to harshness or vigor; using *m, n, l* often, contributes to a flowing melody. If you choose words with many fronted vowels, made with the teeth and the tip of the tongue, you tend to gaiety and lightness. Words that are heavy with vowels, formed at the back of the mouth suggest sorrow or solemnity. Fourth, tone color is heightened by certain words which sound like the action they describe, such as *cracking, buzzing.* Fifth, certain words, as individual words, have the power to suggest a certain emotional tone, as you may see from comparing *house, home,* or *weep, cry, bawl.* Sixth, certain words or phrases take a power of suggestion from their use in well-known literature as the phrase *green pastures* borrows implications from the Twenty-third Psalm. Seventh, broad prose rhythms influence tone color, just as regular rhythm deepens the mood of poetry.

How can you learn to suggest emotion by the sound of your words? First, notice in your reading the methods which other writers use. Of course you cannot really write better because you resolve to use long or short words and because you keep your mind on your resolution as you write. But you can absorb certain techniques until they are at home in your thinking and finally become a part of your spontaneous writing. Second, read aloud both prose and poetry—any passages which seem to you perfection—to increase your sensitivity to the sound of language. Third, memorize poems and prose passages from the Bible, Shakespeare, Milton (or from Steinbeck and Thomas Wolfe, if their writing seems to you the best of its kind). These three methods are merely ways of looking intensively at other writers to see how they have worked. Then as you find significant subjects and realize your attitudes, you may begin to express your attitudes by the sound of your words; thus your writing may develop its own tone color. Of course you do not wish to work mechanically to secure mere sound. If you achieve a tone color which is individual you will not do so because you have memorized certain technical details but because your own feeling is finding its expression in the sound of your language.

WRITING YOUR COMPOSITION

A. Write a narrative in which you say something significant to you about a human relationship that is intimate or at least personal. Know the attitude or the full meaning you wish to bring out. Choose or create a situation as dynamic as you can make it in view of your aim; know whether a character discovers, changes, succeeds, or fails in his particular desire—even if he is merely trying to feed his own ego. Create an experience in which you live sensory details instead of thinking vaguely about mental concepts. Hear talk and see action.

Then forget about a conscious strain to use techniques. Write your narrative.

B. Write a narrative in which you say something significant to you about some group or minority relationship. Use the other suggestions given above.

C. Write a narrative in which you say something that is significant to you about human relationships involving a nonconformist in your community. Use the other suggestions given above under A.

TESTING AND REVISING

After you have written your narrative and have let it cool, test it with these questions:

1. Have you communicated to readers your chosen attitude to a human relationship?

2. Have you expressed it with as much power as you can command at this stage of your work and with this subject?

3. Does your unit seem authentic and individual?

4. Have you used talk, action, or even the hesitations and silences of a character; the past, future, or the present time in another place; and other specific details, so far as they will serve your subject?

5. Have you achieved an emotional awareness, a suggestion that gives your work unity? Have you used repetition to achieve this unity?

6. If you wish, add this question: Have you achieved tone color? (But do not be severe with yourself about mere sound.)

READING

IRON MAN *

George Thomson

"Come on, come on! Speed it up, Dope! How'm I ever gonna make a musician outa you?" My brother's voice came crackling down the stairs and, as usual, ruffled my temper the wrong way.

"If being a musician means being like you, I'm not so sure I want'a be one," I muttered. Then to myself I added grimly, "This is gonna be one sweet session."

The telephone jangled irritably and I jumped to answer it.

"Hello!"

"Hello!—Hello, is this Tom?"

"No, this is Gee. Shall I call him?" The voice fumbled uncertainly as I put down the receiver and called up the stairs, "Phone for you, Wingy. Whiteman wants to sign you up."

For no good reason I started up the stairs just as Tom started down. I had some vague hope that I might trip him, but I took a cuff in the ear for my pains and was pushed back downstairs. I finished the climb swearing to myself.

From the floor below Tom's voice drifted upward; at first sharp and brittle, then drifting off into silence. "Maybe it IS Whiteman," I thought hopefully. The receiver clicked dully and for a moment there was quiet; then footsteps came slowly up the stairs until Tom's prematurely grey hair appeared at floor level—gradually followed by the six-foot and 180 pounds of bone, flesh and sarcasm that made my brother such a menace.

"Who was it, Champ?"

"Hunh? Oh—nobody, nobody." His voice was flat and colorless but he looked no different than usual. Somehow the suggestion of trouble clung to me.

"Aw, come on! Get it off your chest. Did your girl drop you? Did Williams give you the sack? Did somebody hock your hor—?"

"Go to hell, will you?" He turned on me savagely and for the first time in years I was really afraid of him. Then his hands dropped and his shoulders slumped. The pain and fight went out of his eyes, and we both tried to act as if nothing had happened.

"Listen, Gee." His voice was almost soft but it was still miles off and it didn't sound like it wanted me for company. "You remember Spud Jackson?"

This was familiar ground and I regained some of my ebbing confidence. "Sure. He's the best swing and legit bass fiddler in the business and probably the only guy that'll put up with your guff for two weeks in a row."

"Yeah, that's the guy. He killed himself tonight." Cold and precise the words rattled together like death's-heads in the quiet of the room.

"What!" My voice cracked with the shock and surprise. "Not Spud! He wouldn't! You're kiddin'!"

"Oh, sure." His voice was a sword edge dulled on the grit of pain. "I'm always kiddin' about things like that. Come on, pick up your horn. If you're gonna play in my outfit, you've gotta be good."

"But Tom, not tonight! Not after Spud—"

"Whose friend was he—yours or mine? Now pick up that horn!"

We stuck to it for ninety long minutes. Once he said, "Keep it up, you're almost as good a trumpeter as Goodman already." And there I slipped. "But Goodman plays clarinet!" I protested.

"Oh, does he now?" Heavy with sarcasm the answer came back and I marked up one more mental cross that I swore I'd avenge.

At last it was over. I put my horn away sulkily and clumped downstairs for a glass of milk. Tom just stood with the gleaming trumpet resting lightly on his fingers—I always held mine like it might blow up—his eyes followed me down. Before I reached the bottom he lifted the horn to his lips and began to play softly.

I was just finishing my milk and pie when I noticed that the room was no longer pulsing to the gentle silvery rhythm. The sound had become louder, note by note, until now a strange melody—twisting and screaming—battered my mind and carried it off into a cacophony of emotion.

My first sense of pride in having a brother who could make music like that changed almost at once to disgust and shame. "How can he play jazz when his best friend just killed himself? How can he think of music—music like that—at a time like this? What sort of a brute is he? Doesn't he hold anything in respect?" I was mad and shocked and with no clear plan in mind I raced for the stairs.

Abruptly the mad, flashing horn stopped. There was complete and deafening silence. A second later something fragile and metallic shattered into the wall and fell to the floor with a dull and broken clanging. I crept quietly up the stairs and stopped—my fingers biting into the plaster until green paint gritted under my nails. One look was enough.

Almost even with my eyes the golden trumpet lay grotesquely twisted—the bell split in half and folded back into a senseless jumble of tubes and valves. Tom was sprawled at the desk, his face buried in his arms, wide shoulders retching in the misery of his sobs. On the floor, at his feet, lay a snap-shot of a homely, smiling young man—leaning on a bass fiddle.

I turned and stumbled downstairs—a stranger.

SISTER CECILIA *

Margaret Mattison

I stood outside her door in the music building, the same place I had stood once a week since the fifth grade. Funny that I should feel the same strain that I always felt before I met her. This time there weren't any neglected arpeggios or any measures I hadn't quite memorized. This was simply a social call, the annual call before I went back to school in the fall. Still, I was afraid to push back the door.

The old clock across the hall jumped to three o'clock. My signal. I slid the door back and stepped in. Just one step and wait for her to see you. That had been my rule for eleven years. That was my rule now.

There she was. Officially, Sister Mary Cecilia, Professor of Music.

The first day I had called her "The Lady in the Black Mail Box" because I had never seen a nun before. I couldn't figure out whose sister she was. Finally I decided she was Jesus's sister. Later she was "Slave-driver" and "Old Bat" and finally "Dear Sister Cecilia." To her face she had always been "Sister."

She stood on a folding chair, watering her African violets. There were rows and rows of them now, all direct descendants of the plant her brother had sent her from the Chilean Embassy. She gave each plant its daily allotment, peeked under its leaves and cooed to the blossoms. I remember once I said, "My mama can't raise flowers like that." "Your mother raises children," was all she said.

When she came to the end of the row, she saw me.

"Little Margaret," she cried and she flew down from her perch. I was surprised that she was so little. Not over five foot two. She had seemed taller than that when she sat next to me at the piano with her red-blue pencil ready to rap my knuckles. Still "Little Margaret!" I guess she didn't want me to grow up. I was the only child she had been near since her days on the fruit farm in Michigan. There she had been the second mother to thirteen younger brothers and sisters. There were no children in the cloister in Alma. There were no children in the novitiates' residence. I was the only child she had known at the school.

Suddenly she kissed my cheek. The rest of her body seemed to pull away, but she kissed my cheek. It was as though she was stealing something. She hurried over to her chair, sat down stiffly, and began twisting her rosary around her square fingers.

I was afraid to choose the topic of conversation because I knew she would ask me a question I couldn't answer. If I mentioned school she would ask me if I were taking piano lessons. If I said something about the family she would ask when my sister was coming home. How could I explain that she didn't come to visit because she was still afraid of Sister Cecilia? Afraid to talk. I just sat there.

"Margaret, you've had your hair cut. I liked your braids. And the plaid ribbons."

Listen, woman, I'm twenty years old. And I'm not a Chippewa princess. Short hair has come into its own. Or haven't you noticed.

"I used to have long braids when I was a girl. I lived on a fruit farm in eastern Michigan. I was the oldest girl and we used to . . ."

The story of the fruit farm. I should have known! This was the fifth time I had heard the story of the mincemeat, head cheese, and the apple bin. In fact every time I paid my social call, she told it to me. I didn't even have to listen anymore. Instinct told me when to smile and when to say "How nice." If she talked about her life, why didn't she tell about her forty-dollar music lessons in Europe or her good friend José Iturbi? José called her by her given name, and he came down to see her whenever he was in Minneapolis. She admired him as a person, but she scolded him because he tried to play boogie-woogie. It would spoil his technique.

"In those days we older girls did all the house work so that Mother could spend all of her time in the kitchen. Every fall she would get the stone crocks out of the cellar and make mincemeat. I never got her recipe, but I can remember . . ."

Yes, Sister Cecilia, and I can remember when you taught me my fractions . . .

"This note gets half as many counts as this half note. What kind of note is it?"

I didn't say a word. I just sat and stared at the black spot with the tail.

"Now, honey (She always called me "Honey" when she was losing her patience.), what is half of a half?"

I glanced up at the clock on top of the piano. Fifteen minutes more of this.

"It isn't written on the face of the clock. What is half of a half? What is half of half a dollar?"

I was saved. I knew an answer.

"Twenty-five cents," I lisped through my braces.

That was the beginning of a long slow process, but she finally taught me my fractions. . . .

"Mother would boil the pig's head in spices for two days on the back of the range. Then she peeled the meat off the bone and put it into a press. Father always had to run the press, and that was the only time during the year that he was in the kitchen. After it was pressed . . ."

What was it about this little woman that was so mighty? The

girl who had her lesson before mine would run out of the room in tears almost every week. But the next Monday she was always back for more. We slaved all week for just a simple "That's better" or "Some improvement." When I was a senior in high school, I was supposed to give my last recital. Sunday evening, a new formal, and baskets of lilacs on the stage! I got strep throat ten days before. Saturday morning the doctor told Dad that I wouldn't be able to give it. That afternoon I had to get out of bed to answer the phone.

"This is Sister Cecilia over at the college. I just wondered if Little Margaret would like to start the program a little later because of her illness? Say eight-thirty instead of eight o'clock."

Something in that voice! I said that eight-thirty would be fine and that I would tell Margaret. I practiced the Gershwin the rest of that afternoon. And I gave the recital at eight-thirty with a temperature of 102. It was worth it. Sister Cecilia said I had done well.

"We didn't have pressure cookers like they have today, so we dried the fruit and stored it in the apple bin. We used to keep six barrels of apples for ourselves. Six different kinds of apples. In a good year we could have apple pie at Christmas time."

That was almost the end of the story. I had to think of some way to get out of there. Forty-five minutes was a nice respectable time to stay. Dentist appointment? Help Mother? Help Mother. That always touched her.

"Well, Sister, I think I'd better be going. I have to go help Mother. A man brought her a bushel of beans to can, and she wants me to snap beans."

"Your mother cans! How wonderful! Not many women do now, you know." She stood up and pulled her outer sleeve over the patch in her dark brown blouse.

"I have something for you, Little Margaret."

Just the same. That first year she always saved her breakfast fruit for me. Five grapes in a piece of tissue paper or half a brown banana. One lesson, *The Happy Farmer,* Sister Cecilia and I put in an especially bad hour. The notes were blurred and tears were dropping onto the keys. When I left she said, "Here is an orange for you, honey." I ran out to Mom in the car, threw the orange in the back seat and said, "Take your old garbage."

Now Sister Cecilia pulled open her bottom drawer and brought out a bundle of tissue paper.

"It has been in the family for years. Grandmother got it from Great-grandmother. Mother got it from Grandmother. As oldest girl I got it from Mother."

She held it out to me. "It has been on my altar. It prays for me. Now I want you to have it."

I took her treasure and started peeling away the tissue paper. An ivory madonna. Slender and graceful. With heavy lids and a gentle smile on her face.

I looked into the little woman's face. For the first time the woman was separated from the black habit. She was no longer professor of music. She was more like the lady next door or like my own mother. I felt as if I could tell her anything. I could tell her that I didn't take piano lessons at college. I could even tell her that I had been afraid of her.

"Sister Cecilia."

She smiled slowly but her eyes were wet. She put her hands over mine as I held the madonna.

"Now I want you to have it, Little Margaret."

She reached up—was she going to kiss me again? She stepped back. As if some authority had whispered in her ear. Reminded her that she was a Franciscan sister, married to the church and serving God.

"You'd better get home to those beans," she said. I slid the door back. "Goodbye, Sister Cecilia."

"May God bless you, Little Margaret."

LIFE OF MA PARKER [1]

Katherine Mansfield

When the literary gentleman, whose flat old Ma Parker cleaned every Tuesday, opened the door to her that morning, he asked after her grandson. Ma Parker stood on the doormat inside the dark little hall, and she stretched out her hand to help her gentleman

---

[1] Reprinted from *The Short Stories of Katherine Mansfield* by Katherine Mansfield, by permission of Alfred A. Knopf, Inc. Copyright 1922, 1937, by Alfred A. Knopf, Inc.

shut the door before she replied. "We buried 'im yesterday, sir," she said quietly.

"Oh, dear me! I'm sorry to hear that," said the literary gentleman in a shocked tone. He was in the middle of his breakfast. He wore a very shabby dressing-gown and carried a crumpled newspaper in one hand. But he felt awkward. He could hardly go back to the warm sitting-room without saying something—something more. Then because these people set such store by funerals he said kindly, "I hope the funeral went off all right."

"Beg parding, sir?" said old Ma Parker huskily.

Poor old bird! She did look dashed. "I hope the funeral was a—a—success," said he. Ma Parker gave no answer. She bent her head and hobbled off to the kitchen, clasping the old fish bag that held her cleaning things and an apron and a pair of felt shoes. The literary gentleman raised his eyebrows and went back to his breakfast.

"Overcome, I suppose," he said aloud, helping himself to the marmalade.

Ma Parker drew the two jetty spears out of her toque and hung it behind the door. She unhooked her worn jacket and hung that up too. Then she tied her apron and sat down to take off her boots. To take off her boots or to put them on was an agony to her, but it had been an agony for years. In fact, she was so accustomed to the pain that her face was drawn and screwed up ready for the twinge before she'd so much as untied the laces. That over, she sat back with a sigh and softly rubbed her knees. . . .

"Gran! Gran!" Her little grandson stood on her lap in his button boots. He'd just come in from playing in the street.

"Look what a state you've made your gran's skirt into—you wicked boy!"

But he put his arms round her neck and rubbed his cheek against hers.

"Gran, gi' us a penny!" he coaxed.

"Be off with you; Gran ain't got no pennies."

"Yes, you 'ave."

"No, I ain't."

"Yes, you 'ave. Gi' us one!"

Already she was feeling for the old, squashed, black leather purse.
"Well, what'll you give your gran?"

He gave a shy little laugh and pressed closer. She felt his eyelid
quivering against her cheek. "I ain't got nothing," he murmured. . . .

The old woman sprang up, seized the iron kettle off the gas
stove and took it over to the sink. The noise of the water drum-
ming in the kettle deadened her pain, it seemed. She filled the pail,
too, and the washing-up bowl.

It would take a whole book to describe the state of that kitchen.
During the week the literary gentleman "did" for himself. That is
to say, he emptied the tea leaves now and again into a jam jar set
aside for that purpose, and if he ran out of clean forks he wiped
over one or two on the roller towel. Otherwise, as he explained to
his friends, his "system" was quite simple, and he couldn't understand why people made all this fuss about housekeeping.

"You simply dirty everything you've got, get a hag in once a
week to clean up, and the thing's done."

The result looked like a gigantic dustbin. Even the floor was
littered with toast crusts, envelopes, cigarette ends. But Ma Parker
bore him no grudge. She pitied the poor young gentleman for
having no one to look after him. Out of the smudgy little window
you could see an immense expanse of sad-looking sky, and whenever there were clouds they looked very worn, old clouds, frayed
at the edges, with holes in them, or dark stains like tea.

While the water was heating, Ma Parker began sweeping the
floor. "Yes," she thought, as the broom knocked, "what with one
thing and another I've had my share. I've had a hard life."

Even the neighbours said that of her. Many a time, hobbling
home with her fish bag she heard them, waiting at the corner, or
leaning over the area railings, say among themselves, "She's had a
hard life, has Ma Parker." And it was so true she wasn't in the
least proud of it. It was just as if you were to say she lived in the
basement-back at Number 27. A hard life! . . .

At sixteen she'd left Stratford and come up to London as
kitching-maid. Yes, she was born in Stratford-on-Avon. Shakespeare,

sir? No, people were always arsking her about him. But she'd never heard his name until she saw it on the theatres.

Nothing remained of Stratford except that "sitting in the fire-place of a evening you could see the stars through the chimley," and "Mother always 'ad 'er side of bacon 'anging from the ceiling." And there was something—a bush, there was—at the front door, that smelt ever so nice. But the bush was very vague. She'd only remembered it once or twice in the hospital, when she'd been taken bad.

That was a dreadful place—her first place. She was never allowed out. She never went upstairs except for prayers morning and evening. It was a fair cellar. And the cook was a cruel woman. She used to snatch away her letters from home before she'd read them, and throw them in the range because they made her dreamy. . . . And the beedles! Would you believe it?—until she came to London she'd never seen a black beedle. Here Ma always gave a little laugh, as though—not to have seen a black beedle! Well! It was as if to say you'd never seen your own feet.

When that family was sold up she went as "help" to a doctor's house, and after two years there, on the run from morning till night, she married her husband. He was a baker.

"A baker, Mrs. Parker!" the literary gentleman would say. For occasionally he laid aside his tomes and lent an ear, at least, to this product called Life. "It must be rather nice to be married to a baker!"

Mrs. Parker didn't look so sure.

"Such a clean trade," said the gentleman.

Mrs. Parker didn't look convinced.

"And didn't you like handing the new loaves to the customers?"

"Well, sir," said Mrs. Parker, "I wasn't in the shop above a great deal. We had thirteen little ones and buried seven of them. If it wasn't the 'ospital it was the infirmary, you might say!"

"You might, *indeed*, Mrs. Parker!" said the gentleman, shuddering, and taking up his pen again.

Yes, seven had gone, and while the six were still small her husband was taken ill with consumption. It was flour on the lungs, the doctor told her at the time. . . . Her husband sat up in bed with his shirt pulled over his head, and the doctor's finger drew a circle on his back.

"Now, if we were to cut him open *here*, Mrs. Parker," said the doctor, "you'd find his lungs chock-a-block with white powder. Breathe, my good fellow!" And Mrs. Parker never knew for certain whether she saw or whether she fancied she saw a great fan of white dust come out of her poor dead husband's lips. . . .

But the struggle she'd had to bring up those six little children and keep herself to herself. Terrible it had been! Then, just when they were old enough to go to school her husband's sister came to stop with them to help things along, and she hadn't been there more than two months when she fell down a flight of steps and hurt her spine. And for five years Ma Parker had another baby— and such a one for crying!—to look after. Then young Maudie went wrong and took her sister Alice with her; the two boys emigrimated, and young Jim went to India with the army, and Ethel, the youngest, married a good-for-nothing little waiter who died of ulcers the year little Lennie was born. And now little Lennie—my grandson. . . .

The piles of dirty cups, dirty dishes, were washed and dried. The ink-black knives were cleaned with a piece of potato and finished off with a piece of cork. The table was scrubbed, and the dresser and the sink that had sardine tails swimming in it. . . .

He'd never been a strong child—never from the first. He'd been one of those fair babies that everybody took for a girl. Silvery fair curls he had, blue eyes, and a little freckle like a diamond on one side of his nose. The trouble she and Ethel had had to rear that child! The things out of the newspapers they tried him with! Every Sunday morning Ethel would read aloud while Ma Parker did her washing.

"Dear Sir,—Just a line to let you know my little Myrtil was laid out for dead. . . . After four bottils . . . gained 8 lbs. in 9 weeks, *and is still putting it on.*"

And then the egg-cup of ink would come off the dresser and the letter would be written, and Ma would buy a postal order on her way to work next morning. But it was no use. Nothing made little Lennie put it on. Taking him to the cemetery, even, never gave him a colour; a nice shake-up in the bus never improved his appetite.

But he was gran's boy from the first. . . .

"Whose boy are you?" said old Ma Parker, straightening up from the stove and going over to the smudgy window. And a little voice, so warm, so close, it half stifled her—it seemed to be in her breast under her heart—laughed out, and said, "I'm gran's boy!"

At that moment there was a sound of steps, and the literary gentleman appeared, dressed for walking.

"Oh, Mrs. Parker, I'm going out."

"Very good, sir."

"And you'll find your half-crown in the tray of the inkstand."

"Thank you, sir."

"Oh, by the way, Mrs. Parker," said the literary gentleman quickly, "you didn't throw away any cocoa last time you were here—did you?"

"No, sir."

"*Very* strange. I could have sworn I left a teaspoonful of cocoa in the tin." He broke off. He said softly and firmly, "You'll always tell me when you throw things away—won't you, Mrs. Parker?" And he walked off very well pleased with himself, convinced, in fact, he'd shown Mrs. Parker that under his apparent carelessness he was as vigilant as a woman.

The door banged. She took her brushes and cloths into the bedroom. But when she began to make the bed, smoothing, tucking, patting, the thought of little Lennie was unbearable. Why did he have to suffer so? That's what she couldn't understand. Why should a little angel child have to arsk for his breath and fight for it? There was no sense in making a child suffer like that.

. . . From Lennie's little box of a chest there came a sound as though something was boiling. There was a great lump of something bubbling in his chest that he couldn't get rid of. When he coughed the sweat sprang out on his head; his eyes bulged, his hands waved, and the great lump bubbled as a potato knocks in a saucepan. But what was more awful than all was when he didn't cough he sat against the pillow and never spoke or answered, or even made as if he heard. Only he looked offended.

"It's not your poor old gran's doing it, my lovey," said old Ma Parker, patting back the damp hair from his little scarlet ears. But Lennie moved his head and edged away. Dreadfully offended with her he looked—and solemn. He bent his head and looked at her sideways as though he couldn't have believed it of his gran.

But at the last . . . Ma Parker threw the counterpane over the bed. No, she simply couldn't think about it. It was too much— she'd had too much in her life to bear. She'd borne it up till now, she'd kept herself to herself, and never once had she been seen to cry. Never by a living soul. Not even her own children had seen Ma break down. She'd kept a proud face always. But now! Lennie gone—what had she? She had nothing. He was all she'd got from life, and now he was took too. Why must it all have happened to me? she wondered. "What have I done?" said old Ma Parker. "What have I done?"

As she said those words she suddenly let fall her brush. She found herself in the kitchen. Her misery was so terrible that she pinned on her hat, put on her jacket and walked out of the flat like a person in a dream. She did not know what she was doing. She was like a person so dazed by the horror of what has happened that he walks away—anywhere, as though by walking away he could escape. . . .

It was cold in the street. There was a wind like ice. People went flitting by, very fast; the men walked like scissors; the women trod like cats. And nobody knew—nobody cared. Even if she broke down, if at last, after all these years, she were to cry, she'd find herself in the lock-up as like as not.

But at the thought of crying it was as though little Lennie leapt in his gran's arms. Ah, that's what she wants to do, my dove. Gran wants to cry. If she could only cry now, cry for a long time, over everything, beginning with her first place and the cruel cook, going on to the doctor's, and then the seven little ones, death of her husband, the children's leaving her, and all the years of misery that led up to Lennie. But to have a proper cry over all these things would take a long time. All the same, the time for it had come. She must do it. She couldn't put it off any longer; she couldn't wait any more. . . . Where could she go?

"She's had a hard life, has Ma Parker." Yes, a hard life, indeed! Her chin began to tremble; there was no time to lose. But where? Where?

She couldn't go home; Ethel was there. It would frighten Ethel out of her life. She couldn't sit on a bench anywhere; people would come arsking her questions. She couldn't possibly go back to the gentleman's flat; she had no right to cry in strangers' houses. If she sat on some steps a policeman would speak to her.

Oh, wasn't there anywhere where she could hide and keep herself to herself and stay as long as she liked, not disturbing anybody, and nobody worrying her? Wasn't there anywhere in the world where she could have her cry out—at last?

Ma Parker stood, looking up and down. The icy wind blew out her apron into a balloon. And now it began to rain. There was nowhere.

QUESTIONS

Which is the writer of "Iron Man" more concerned with, the relationship between him and his brother, or between his brother and Spud Jackson? Do both contribute to one artistic aim? What is the artistic aim? Is the title effective? Is there unity of focus? Is the past relationship of the brothers implied, and if so, does the past contribute to this incident? Is the situation developed through the whole narrative? Is the talk natural? Is subjective or objective material more important? Are the details used in the last sentences melodramatic or effective?

Is "Sister Cecilia" developed as a one-time, one-place narrative? How much is the past used and what is the writer's chief method of bringing it in? Flashbacks—that is, whole incidents? Thoughts of the writer? Details in time order? Memories brought back by the things Sister Cecilia says and does now? What had Sister Cecilia's attitude to the writer been in the past? What is the attitude in the present? What had been the writer's attitude to Sister Cecilia in the past? In the present? Does the attitude change or remain static? What simple conflict is carried through the whole unit? Is that conflict resolved by an outer event or an objective climax? By a subjective climax?

In the "Life of Ma Parker" how is the past used? Is there plan or accident in using memories mainly in this order: a happy memory of Lennie begging a penny, a survey of Ma Parker's past life, the suffering and death of Lennie? What is the artistic aim of the story? Why does the writer begin after the funeral? What is the climax of the story? Is the whole unit sharply finished or left unfinished? Is the ending effective? Is the Literary Gentleman effective in the story? How and why? Does the story emphasize the attitude of Ma Parker only to the Literary Gentleman, or to all her employers, or to people in general? How does the writer use spaces and dots?

6

Ideas in Short Narrative:

VARIED TECHNIQUES

In Chapter 5 you considered the problem of narrative used to express human relationships. It is possible, of course, to use brief narrative units also to develop ideas drawn from experience or to characterize people. While you are doing either of these things, it is possible to give the units your mood or feeling or that of a character, or it is possible to develop a unit which emphasizes a mood above everything else. That is, you may use short narratives to emphasize either mood, character, or idea, just as writers emphasize these elements in fully developed short stories.

In this chapter your aim is the development, in a short narrative, of an idea, a general conclusion, which you have drawn from specific experience. For example, you comment one day because of things which have just happened to you, "Big brothers *can* be understanding and helpful at times," or "Parents seem to have forgotten the problems they had when they were twenty," or "It's easy to forget campaign promises after election, in the community or on campus." When you have chosen your idea you are ready to choose or to create the time, place, and situation which will give your idea flesh and blood.

Several kinds of techniques or patterns may be useful to you at this stage and in later assignments: contrast patterns, envelope patterns, both of which may be subjective or objective; subjective patterns, including unity of focus with variations, a controlled stream of consciousness, and symbolism; and also objective narrative.

CONTRAST AND ENVELOPE PATTERNS

Contrast patterns are useful for you in presenting different slants on ideas or on human relations. You may use such a pattern when a character pretends to have one attitude to a person but has another which he is concealing, when two or more characters have entirely different opinions about an idea, when characters who talk have a certain belief but another person who keeps silent knows that they are wrong.

You have seen the envelope pattern used in movies or in drama, sometimes, as in *Brigadoon*, with fantasy, and sometimes with realism. A conventional pattern is something like this: A grandfather, in the opening scene of a play, objects to a grandson's proposed course of action; but reminded by his grandson's attitudes, he relives a story of his own youth forty years earlier; in the closing scene he returns to his grandson's problem in the present, either changed or unchanged. The opening and the closing scenes, often the same scene split into two parts, envelop the rest of the play; that is, they form an envelope pattern. Usually but not invariably this pattern is used for contrast. You may wish to try it now in a brief narrative and then, if your material makes it desirable, use it again in a longer story later.

UNITY OF FOCUS

In earlier chapters you met the terms *subjective* and *objective*. You are familiar with *unity of focus*, the technique by which a writer lets us experience everything in a story through the attitude, mind, and senses of one character. *Everything* includes our knowledge of other characters, setting, and action; even the suspense is built from the hopes and fears of this one person.

Unity of focus tends to be subjective. Though it has its limitations and though you may need self-discipline if you learn to use it well, it is perhaps the most effective single technique you can learn to use. Even if your reader does not notice how you are getting your effect, you can give him psychological reality, character, and suspense; you can persuade him to respond to your created experience.

You may find that some variants of unity of focus also are useful. Some writers use it effectively for a major character at a specific time and place but give in addition a suggestion that his actions are typical:

His greatest pleasure in life came always at dusk. Its prelude was the reading of the evening paper in the train that took him out of the city. By long association the very unfolding of the grimy ink-smelling sheets was part of the ritual: his dark eyes dilated, he felt himself begin to "grin," the staggering load of business detail, under which he had struggled all day in the office, was instantly forgotten. He read rapidly, devoured with rapacious eyes column after column—New York, London, Paris, Lisbon—wars, revolutions, bargains in umbrellas, exhibitions of water colors. This consumed three-quarters of the journey. After that he watched the procession of houses, walls, trees, reeling past in the mellow slant light, and began already to feel his garden about him. He observed the flight of the train unconsciously, and it was almost automatically, at the unrealized sight of a certain group of trees, oddly leaning away from each other, like a group of ballet dancers expressing an extravagance of horror, that he rose and approached the door.[1]

Some writers apparently use unity of focus, but they blend in details which the character does not realize himself; this might be considered a skillful kind of author comment:

She is not at home in the world. Every day she teaches children who remain strangers to her, though she loves their tender round hands and their charming opportunist savagery. She knocks at unfamiliar doors not knowing whether a friend or a stranger shall answer, and even if a known face emerges from the sour gloom of that unknown interior, still it is the face of a stranger. No matter what this stranger says to her, nor what her message to him, the very cells of her flesh reject knowledge and kinship in one monotonous word. No. No. No. She draws her strength from this one holy talismanic word which does not suffer her to be led into evil. Denying everything, she may walk anywhere in safety, she looks at everything without amazement.[2]

[1] Conrad Aiken, "The Dark City," *Bring, Bring, and Other Stories*, Boni & Liveright, 1925.

[2] Katherine Anne Porter, *Flowering Judas*, Harcourt, Brace & Company, 1940.

Other writers who use unity of focus deftly enlarge with details which suggest a satirical attitude of the writer:

Mrs. Willoughby could see it as clearly as if it had appeared in type. There would be a small advertisement in the Sunday *New York Times* some day, seeking letters written by Mrs. Peter Willoughby, especially those written in her teens, when she was Janet Tucker. "Letters sent for use in the forthcoming volume will be carefully returned," the advertisement would say. "The Blake correspondence is of particular interest." Then the heirs of Henry Blake would send a packet of her letters to New York, and it would all come out, like the correspondence of Tschaikovsky and Mme. von Meck.

Just what she would have done, in the meantime, to have catapulted her to fame and brought public demand for her correspondence, still was unrevealed to Mrs. Willoughby; but sometimes, she reflected, mere events, over which one has no control, lift one into the limelight.[3]

You may find unity of focus useful also when used for minor characters. For example, a child may be made a mental and emotional microscope to show us events; and though he is unconscious of the real meaning in what he sees, he suggests the meaning for us. "Innocence" by Rose Wilder Lane, which is reprinted in many collections of short stories, is an example. Or the minor character may be an adult who has seen and heard certain events but does not understand their implications. In Ring Lardner's "Haircut," for instance, the barber who tells the story thinks that Jim Kendall was "certainly a card," but the reader comes to know him for a sadist who caused tragedy and murder. Such characters, well used, give power to a story by subtle contrast. The minor character used for unity of focus may be an understanding and sympathetic observer, effective because of his ability to watch the main character and other characters and to combine detachment with sympathy:

When at last I awoke, the Sunday morning sun was high and hot over the garden. Looking out the window, I could see Dad and Steve leaning against the fence and staring off into the woods. . . . I was about to go down to join them when I caught a glimpse of a letter drooping from Steve's fingers. This was a man-to-man affair that I wasn't going to sit in on.

[3] Mary Elizabeth Plummer, "Mrs. Willoughby's Letters," *Atlantic Monthly*, September, 1942.

Their voices had been pitched too low for me to hear, but suddenly Steve whirled from the fence and faced his father. I could hear the rising tension in his voice as he fought for self-control. "But I tell you, Dad, I'd rather do anything else in the world than hang up my horn. . . . Me—a banker!"

Dad's face was sad and worried, but his voice was still calm as he tamped more tobacco into his pipe. "How good a musician are you, son?"

For a moment Steve was taken back in surprise, but he recovered enough to say slowly, in a voice that I could scarcely hear, "Well, I'm probably the best cornet man in this end of Illinois." [4]

Professional writers sometimes succeed in letting us realize the thoughts of several characters at once, but it is hard for inexperienced writers to use this technique succesfully:

"Let us return thanks," said Jess, and the four heads bowed in silent prayer.

Jess meditated on God but asked for nothing. Eliza talked with her Father of gifts and wants alike. Emanuela floated wordless before a blazing throne. Jane prayed, "Take away my fever blister, take away my fever blister." Then being of a reasonable and conciliatory nature, "or if Thee'd rather just make it invisible. Thee has the power, O Lord," she reminded Him. "Make it invisible for the Illumination." [5]

Writers who use unity of focus with specific narrative often allow the main character to hope, to remember, and even to generalize about previous experiences. If the character seems to be thinking at a specific instant, the general memory will blend with the narrative, as it does in this example:

Mrs. McNary paused at the door. "Your husband already paid the rent."

Statement of fact. Not another way of saying: You can't escape now. A long time ago Elizabeth had heard the triumphant drawing of a bolt in those six words. Now she only looked hopefully at the bed. "Your husband fixed it all up for you," Mrs. McNary said. "It's a Murphy, and comes down."

Yes, Elizabeth thought. Struggling with it at night, it reminded her often of a vast, impersonal avalanche, a two-ton sheeted polar bear,

[4] George Thomson, "Cornucopia," an unpublished story.

[5] Jessamyn West, *The Friendly Persuasion*, Harcourt, Brace & Company, 1945

upright, with crushing arms, descending suddenly or descending not at all.[6]

STREAM-OF-CONSCIOUSNESS PATTERNS

Psychological tendencies in life and in writing have led to unity of focus and also to the stream-of-consciousness techniques. If you examine your own mind at any waking moment you experience a constant, rapid flux of sensory details and thoughts from the past, present, and future, from reading and from life. The whole seems an incoherent mass of hopes, regrets, hates, loves, fears, though one detail often leads to another by associations which are conscious or unconscious. When writers try to capture all this flow, they have an uncontrolled stream, interesting perhaps, but lacking in the selection of artistic communication; or they have chaotic literary associations which make parts of James Joyce's *Ulysses* a kind of crossword puzzle. But you may get something from watching psychological details in literature and from using impressionistic details yourself in a controlled stream of consciousness—that is, you may select and arrange them to intensify an attitude or feeling. In the passage which follows, impressionistic details are used to bring out the confusion in the mind of Stephen Kumalo, a small-town minister, as he travels to the wicked city of Johannesburg:

The journey had begun. And now the fear back again, the fear of the unknown, the fear of the great city where boys were killed crossing the street, the fear of Gertrude's sickness. Deep down the fear for his son. Deep down the fear of a man who lives in a world not made for him, whose own world is slipping away, dying, being destroyed, beyond any recall.[7]

In *Mrs. Dalloway*, one of the early, effective stream-of-consciousness novels, Virginia Woolf devoted a whole book to the life of the mind of her main character for a single day, beginning with these passages:

Mrs. Dalloway said she would buy the flowers herself.
For Lucy had her work cut out for her. The doors would be taken off their hinges; Rumpelmayer's men were coming. And then, thought

[6] Josephine W. Johnson, "The Rented Room," *Harper's Bazaar*, June, 1943.
[7] Alan Paton, *Cry, the Beloved Country*, Charles Scribner's Sons, 1948.

Clarissa Dalloway, what a morning—fresh as if issued to children on a beach.

What a lark! What a plunge! For so it had always seemed to her, when, with a little squeak of the hinges, which she could hear now, she had burst open the French windows and plunged at Bourton into the open air. How fresh, how calm, stiller than this of course, the air was in the early morning; like the flap of a wave; the kiss of a wave; chill and sharp and yet (for a girl of eighteen as she then was) solemn, feeling as she did, standing there at the open window, that something awful was about to happen; looking at the flowers, at the trees with the smoke winding off them and the rooks rising, falling; standing and looking until Peter Walsh said, "Musing among the vegetables?"—was that it?—"I prefer men to cauliflowers"—was that it? He must have said it at breakfast one morning when she had gone out on the terrace—Peter Walsh. He would be back from India one of these days, June or July, she forgot which. . . .

For having lived in Westminster—how many years now? over twenty—one feels even in the midst of the traffic, or waking at night, Clarissa was positive, a particular hush, or solemnity; an indescribable pause; a suspense (but that might be her heart, affected, they said, by influenza) before Big Ben strikes. There! Out it boomed. First, a warning, musical; then the hour, irrevocable. The leaden circles dissolved in the air. Such fools we are, she thought, crossing Victoria Street. For Heaven only knows why one loves it so, how one sees it so, making it up, building it around one, tumbling it, creating it every moment afresh. . . .[8]

In the opening paragraphs of *The Track of the Cat*, the author uses a single person who is still asleep to create a fine suspense in his story of adventure and character:

Arthur was the first in the Bridges' ranch house to hear the far-away crying, like muted horns a little out of tune. The wind turned and came down over the shoulder of the Sierra against the house, shaking the log wall beside his bunk and hurling the snow across the window above him. It let go and slid away south wailing under the eaves. The house relaxed and the snow whispered twice by itself, and then the faint, melancholy blowing came from the north.

Arthur rolled over to lie with his back to the wall, and curled his arm up over his head, as if to protect himself from an attack he couldn't fight against. The sound like horns sank away; the gale surged

[8] Virginia Woolf, *Mrs. Dalloway*, Harcourt, Brace & Company, 1925.

back over it, roaring through the pines on the mountain, and he didn't wake. In the shallower sleep that followed, however, the sound became a human voice crying out in despair.[9]

A long dream sequence follows, in which his brother Curt, Joe Sam, Joe Sam's black panther, and a threat of danger are blended. Then the dream is over, and Arthur is trying to waken:

His bare left hand was touching something cold and smooth, but it wasn't ice. Extending his fingers, he moved them along the surface, and found it curved. He cupped his hand over the smooth curve, uncertainly mocking the remnants of the fear that still made him breathe like a man who has been running hard. It was an old test with him, this touching something real. He was awake now. His fingertips, exploring gently in above the peeled log, touched the flat, clay caulking. He felt the powdery surface of the clay rub off on his fingertips, soft as the dust off a moth's wing.[10]

In the preceding passages there is an expert blending of the sounds of the weather outside and the setting, as if they are in Arthur's consciousness, with the cry of the mountain cat. Through a main character we feel the suspense which will animate much of the story, and we have realized the quality of Arthur's mind. Such a skillful blending of elements in unity of focus and stream of consciousness is a fine pattern for imitation—so long as one uses imitation to find and not to stunt his own powers.

SYMBOLISM

You may be interested in using symbolism as a part of subjective techniques. As the term is used here, symbolism means the use of some tangible object to suggest intangible attitudes or relationships. For instance, one story uses a white peacock in the snow to suggest a wife's indifference to her husband, and the symbolism is continued through his efforts to kill the peacock. If you wish to read an entire story which uses it effectively, try "The Snows of Kilimanjaro" by Ernest Hemingway. Symbolism is a tricky business for less experienced writers. At its vague, fuzzy worst it is intolerable; at its best it is more difficult than realism but it may also be powerful. If you are not ready to try symbolism at this stage, notice

[9] Walter Van Tilburg Clark, *The Track of the Cat*, Random House, 1949.
[10] *Ibid.*

how physical objects, used without any apparent symbolism, can lend reality and feeling to stories. For instance, in "Iron Man" (Chapter 5) the horn is a stage property used to show Tom's attitudes; in "Sister Cecilia" the gift of the ivory madonna crystallizes the writer's feeling for the music teacher she has known eleven years. Watch tangible objects in your reading, and use them whenever you can in your writing.

OBJECTIVE NARRATIVE

Objective narrative, in a pure form which seldom exists, is the kind of writing in which the writer seems to express no attitude at all to the events he records. Theoretically, there is no author comment (neither the essayical comment of nineteenth-century writers nor the deft details used by writers now), there are no memories or hopes of characters unless they become objective in talk, and there is little subjective description of any kind. Actually, a close examination of most so-called objective narrative reveals some subjective details. In the best objective narrative the writer is so skillful in using techniques that, without seeming to suggest attitudes, he builds unobtrusively to a cumulative power at the close; or he is mature and sure of his own feelings, so that he can create a total effect without apparent effort. Thus he uses the high art which conceals art.

Though you may not succeed now with objective writing, you may learn much by trying it and even by trying to write the same narrative with objective and then with subjective techniques. "The Rock," a student selection at the end of this chapter, may help you find out what you can do with objective techniques.

WRITING YOUR COMPOSITION

A. Choose a personalized idea that has been drawn from your experience and is simple enough to be brought out in a brief narrative. Perhaps it will be similar to one of these: My relationship with my parents has been changing; I have done several things in the last few years to help me control my own destiny; I admire the nonconformist. Or it may be entirely different if it challenges your interest. Develop your idea by a specific situation, in a one-time, one-place pattern.

B. Choose an idea or an attitude which you can develop by contrast. Use any of the techniques discussed in this chapter, try an envelope pattern if it seems appropriate to your material, or experiment with any subjective techniques you wish to try. Use specific narrative or description for some part of your unit.

C. Write a narrative by objective methods or mainly by objective methods. Be sure that you do more than write events in a time order. That is, let your facts suggest an attitude, possibly a cumulative effect at the end.

D. Using the same material for both, write one sketch using subjective techniques and another using objective techniques.

READING

THE WHEEL *
Margret Wallace

There were three Coke glasses on the table, two of them empty. Mary's long slim fingers wound nervously around the third one, rhythmically, monotonously swishing the ice around. Her dark eyelashes hung against her cheek, emphasizing the shadows around her eyes and the cleft above her nose.

She heard Jan say, "Was he smiling at you or at me, Liz?" and laughed inside herself—a funny short laugh that left her tight and sick. She had looked up when he went by, had smiled back, and flinched at his impersonal glance, had wished again —

Liz was saying, "Isn't he cute?" and Mary remembered. Yes, he was cute. His hair was blonde and curly and his shoulders were broad. His mouth was just the right size for an easy smile and his hands were square and clean.

But then you saw his eyes.

Well, no—maybe you wouldn't. They weren't particularly large, and they were no browner than brown eyes usually were and his lashes were short and stubby and inconspicuous. No, Jan and Liz wouldn't notice them. Neither would any of the girls back at the dorm. The ones who raved so about him. The ones who'd "give anything for just one date with that darling Davie Shepard." Well, that was all right. She had said it herself once. The only difference was, she had *had* a date with him.

She looked up suddenly at Jan and Liz. They didn't know about that date—or the dates that followed. She hadn't told them. It would have led to complications.

"—I bet he'd be loads of fun."

"Well, quit betting. They say he's going steady."

"Yeah, I heard that, too."

"Wonder what she's like."

"Some big drip, no doubt—not nearly good enough for him."

"Naturally not."

Mary's mind winced. "O.K., maybe I am a big drip," she thought. "Maybe I am crazy. I wish I were."

She took a sip of the Coke, letting it burn slowly down her throat, stinging away the tightness. He was gone now, out the door, surrounded by laughing boys.

"I never see him with a girl."

Of course not. No, Davie. Girls were for dark corners where you could talk to them if you wanted to, or kiss them if you wanted to, or just ignore them and think about yourself.

"Well, he probably hasn't much time for girls. He's a pretty big wheel, you know."

Sure—big wheel. Editor, chairman, publicity director, business manager, president. Davie was good at that—a "great guy"—a "natural executive." He had a theory about that. If you got enough people working for you, and forgot about it hard enough, things would come out all right.

What about the time he had been general chairman for his fraternity house dance. The huge paper rose that hung from the ceiling had blown itself down in the middle of the dance, and Mary had seen Davie's easy smile become thin hardness. Why couldn't he have laughed it off, or propped it up in a corner as if it were supposed to be there? But Davie couldn't. Davie had to throw the rose away with a hopeless shrug and heap insults and demerits on the pledges in the committee and look sad and lost all evening so that people said, "It's too bad that had to happen after David did such a beautiful job."

A beautiful job.

David had other theories, too. They were all good. Like the one about his folks. "They'll worry anyhow," he'd say, "so why knock yourself out to do what they want."

Or the one about studying. "What's the use of breaking your neck trying to get through in four years when your folks have the money to keep you in six?" So Davie took it easy. He knew all the tricks and all the professors and all the tests—he knew the right people.

And then there was his theory about politics. "Someone has to be—well, diplomatic. It might just as well be a good guy like me!"

Mary looked down at the ice in her Coke. The ice bobbed gently up and down, as if it were drowning. The Coke tasted watery by now. Suddenly she pushed it away.

"Come on, kids. Let's go." She had to move, put on her bandana, pick up her books. She was dying inside.

Davie was no good.

That was tough wasn't it, Mary. How many times had she gone over and over it, telling herself, knowing it, believing it, accepting it, gritting her teeth against the thought of him.

Once after he had called her half an hour before a formal to say he couldn't make it, she had locked her roommate out and had spent hours telling him off in the darkness of her mind. But when she saw him, and felt the slow warmth of his smile seep into her, she knew she couldn't ever say it.

Sometimes, when she let herself, Mary wondered how many more days—weeks maybe—or months, she'd go on telling herself how worthless he was.

And melting inside instead.

People had called it a purple cloud, a blue haze, a whirlpool, a dreamy heaven. They were wrong. Mary knew they were. It was a dull gray-green, with red sparks in it that clutched and choked and whispered to her at night, and wouldn't let her eat, and blurred the pages of her chem book. That was for Mary. That was life. That was Hell.

Jan said, "Davie's a good guy. He'll go places some day."

PURGATORY *

Robert J. Avey

The blazing sun shouldered aside streamers of mist as it blossomed inexorably from the sea. Higher and higher it rose and pursued the gloom. Deeper and deeper it drove the lingering shadows into the indifferent water, but one shadow remained.

As the sun mounted higher above the waves it revealed the impertinent shadow to be man-made. Not only was the shadow man-made, it also contained man. At least they might have been men at one time. Now there was little left but skin, bone and souls. Perhaps these were not men at all, but only souls. Certainly they did not look or act like men, but if they were souls, they were not beautiful souls. Perhaps a soul is only beautiful when it can hide behind a glib tongue and a full belly.

Three souls, partitioned between death from too much water and death from too little water, by a fragile shell of plank, saw the sun and cried out, mistaking it for the face of God.

"God forgive me for my sins, for I have always loved You and spread Your gospel," said one.

"God let me live and I will shout Your glory to the world," said another.

And "Damn you, sink back in the sea, and let our fires burn out in the dark," said the third.

The sun burned on toward the meridian and eventually the souls cried out again.

"God let me live and I will shout Your glory to the world," cried the first.

"God, take care of my wife and child," cried the second.

And "Damn you, give me strength to use my knife, and I will drink their blood," cried the third. The frail craft rose and fell sluggishly with the greasy swell. The sun burned its way toward the western horizon, and the souls cried out for the last time.

"God save me," cried the first.

"God save my family," cried the second.

And, "Damn you, search for me in Hell," cried the third.

A far-flying gull spied the lonely coffin and swooped to investigate. There was no motion to frighten him away, so he landed and stared impassively at the three things who had been cast in the image of God, born free and equal, and masters of their environment. He pecked curiously at a protruding eyeball. The lid did not flutter.

The sun moved on toward the west and sank into the jagged

horizon. As the sun sank there was no steam . . . Only fire behind the man-made mountains.

THE ROCK *

Tom Vernon

"I'm tellin' ya he's got the hardest head ya ever seen," said Windy, patting the small boy's tow head. "What ya think we call him Rodney the Rockhead for?"

The small boy beamed at the three older boys gathered around him and wiggled like a puppy being scratched behind the ear. He was a grubby seven-year-old, small for his age.

"Nuts, nobody's got a head as hard as you say his is." Red came from across town. He was skeptical of everyone outside his own neighborhood.

"The hell he ain't," exploded Virgil, Windy's overgrown side-kick. "Last year when he fell out of ole man Talmage's garage's rafters, it didn't even draw blood when he lit on his head. Just made him kind of goofy for awhile. And besides you ain't never seen him butt into a tree, have ya?"

"Nah, and I bet you ain't neither," said Red.

"You callin' me a liar?" Virgil threw down his school books and stepped toward Red.

"Cut it out, Virge." Windy grabbed Virgil by the shoulder. "I wouldn't believe it either if I hadn't already seen it. Show him, Rock." Rock shook his head. "Why not?"

"Mom told me not to anymore," the Rock said in a small voice.

"Look, Rock. We went and told Red about how tough you are. We know you got the hardest head of anybody, but Red won't believe us until he sees ya do it. This ain't like the schoolyard. Won't no teachers ketch ya like last week." Again Rock shook his head. "Ah, come on, you ain't gonna let down the reputation of the neighborhood, are ya?"

The Rock looked at the ground and kicked at a grasshopper. He raised his head and said, "Okay, oney don't tell my brother, cause he'll tell mom."

The Rock ran full speed at a tree twelve feet away, lowered his head in the last instant, and rammed it against the tree trunk. He bounced off and fell to his knees.

"Gawd!" yelled Red. "I ain't never seen nothin' like that before. Tell him to do it again."

"That was pretty good, Rock, but let's see you do it real hard, like the time you knocked the bark off that hickory tree," said Windy.

The Rock took a longer run and smashed into the tree with doubled force. Again he fell to his knees.

"Cheeeerist, ain't that somethin'! You ought to charge admission for this," said Red.

"Do it again," Windy said, "and show Red your bank shot."

The small boy again charged the tree, caromed off, ran at another tree, and rammed it. He staggered back to the older boys and, somehow, managed a lopsided grin as he looked up into Windy's face.

"That was real fine, Rock. 'Bout the best you ever done. I guess Red sure knows you ain't no chicken." Windy laid his arm across the Rock's thin shoulders.

"You see now, Red, why we call him the Rock?" Virgil said triumphantly.

WHERE DID YESTERDAY GO? [11]

Charles Angoff

"Where did yesterday go, Daddy?" Anne asked her father.

He was a bit startled by the question. His two-year-old daughter had asked him puzzling questions before, and he had somehow answered them, as fathers learn to answer the strange, beautiful, philosophical questions of their children. But this time he was at a loss. Not so much because an answer did not occur to him but because the question seemed to bring into being a world of almost unbearable sadness. Where, indeed, did yesterday go?

"Tell me, Daddy," insisted Anne.

Her father kissed her in tribute to her loveliness which she had just innocently enhanced with her carefree profundity.

[11] *The Best American Short Stories, 1950*, edited by Martha Foley. Published first in *The University of Kansas City Review.*

She extricated herself from his embrace. "Please tell me, Daddy, where yesterday went."

Her father answered, "Anne, yesterday had to go home to have his dinner and then have a bath and then go to bed."

"Why, Daddy?"

"So that in the morning he could get up early to meet tomorrow."

"Is tomorrow, Daddy, pretty like yesterday?"

"Yes. Sometimes not so pretty, sometimes prettier."

"Oh."

"Yes, Anne."

"I'm glad, Daddy."

She smiled at him, and ran off in a hop, skip and jump.

David watched his little daughter and marveled at her power. More than anyone else in his life she had made him acutely conscious of time—its impersonality, its deep sorrow, its healing softness, its sudden cruelty. His mind began to leap backward in his own life, and he became taut and mellow, filled with both a sweet confusion and a fierce yearning that seemed to attract mighty musical tunes, as it hopped from one planet of memory to another.

The earliest recollections of his life appeared more real to him at the moment than the very chair he was sitting on. . . . It was in a little Russian village in a one-room apartment, really little more than a hut. There was a big oven in the corner, way off. A brick oven. It was Saturday, the Holy Sabbath. His mother and grandmother were reading a holy book near the oven. They were saying a prayer for the late afternoon, *minchah*. It was deep winter. There was snow on the sills of the three huge windows not far from the oven. It felt pleasantly warm in the room. The room seemed more huge than ever before, neater, perhaps because of the Holy Sabbath atmosphere.

David was about three. He was sitting on a large bed, playing with an aunt, Chashel. A warm and pleasant odor was coming from her. David touched her on her neck, her face, her breasts, her waist, her arms, over and over again, and Chashel smiled and laughed and hugged him. And it was getting darker and warmer and lovelier. David buried his head in Chashel's soft neck.

Then David's mother, David himself, the cow, and the stick his mother was carrying. David was probably four and a half or five then. Mother said, "Only a little bit more, darling, and if we don't find it, we'll just go back and the cow will return by herself. A bad cow."

David cried because he was tired from all the walking and crying and because he resented the slur on the cow's reputation.

"A good cow, darling," said Mother. "I guess we better go back." She lifted David and carried him home. He held on to his mother's neck tight with both his arms. And it got darker and warmer and lovelier.

Then there were the apple trees on top of the hill, not far from the church of the Russian Greek Orthodox Church. David had been warned to stay away from it all the time. "You are Jewish and they are different," his father had told him by way of explanation. David couldn't follow the logic of this argument, but he already sensed that the logic of grown-ups was a mysterious thing and not to be questioned.

David didn't always obey. The apple trees near the church looked so nice. So David and two other Jewish boys took turns climbing to the first branch of one of the trees and tearing off a few apples. They hid them in their blouses . . . and ran and ran to the nearby stream. Many yards away an old man was splashing his naked feet in the stream. His shoes and stockings were near him. He was talking to himself and as he did so, his beard moved forward and back, forward and back. David was fascinated by the movement of the beard. . . . But there were the apples. He felt them, each of them, in his little hands. The apples were round and green and just a little sticky . . . And again it became dark and mysteriously warm . . . and somehow the stream and the old man and his splashing feet and the other boys and the apples and the cow and the stick and the aunt came together and made one big ball . . . and David left the stream and walked homeward with a leaping heart.

Die Gesalzene Bobe, the Salty Grandmother. She was David's paternal grandmother. Always she was referred to as the Salty Grandmother, apparently because she was inclined to be a bit mean. David was taken on a visit to her home, in a village some ten miles from his own home. It was raining outside and David somehow felt that it was also raining inside. It was smoky and there were so many men with beards and women with *fatchailes*, scarfs, and everybody was talking . . . and David's father kept on telling him to kiss the Salty Grandmother. David was about four, or perhaps less, and he tried to oblige his father, but he somehow had great difficulty. He was lonesome for his mother, too. She had to remain at home for some reason that made no sense to him. Suddenly David kissed the Salty Grandmother. Everybody else burst into laughter, but David burst into tears . . . And in the big wagon home, his father's overcoat smelled as if it were filled with rain . . . and father patted him on the back. . . . "Sleep, my Davidel, sleep, a great scholar you will be, a great scholar, sleep, my child, a light of Israel you will be . . . sleep . . . sleep . . . sleep."

A great scholar . . . Always and everywhere David heard this in his youth in the little village where he was born. . . . A great scholar . . . a joy to your parents . . . a glory to Israel . . .

Torrents of words and scenes of years far back.. . . . So clear . . . so very much alive . . . and yet they are of the past, thought David. But are they?

Why do they make the breast heave so? Why, because of them, these things of the past, do the trees and the grass and the people passing by there, and all else, why do they all seem so much more vivid? Can dead things be the cause of so much greater living?

"Daddy, Daddy!" Anne was pulling at his trouser leg.

"Anne!"

"I am back."

"You are back, darling." David lifted her on his lap and looked deep into her eyes. She smiled and pinched his nose and made a grab for his glasses. He evaded her grasp, and kissed her.

"You're a funny daddy," she said.

He squeezed her arm.

She became solemn. "Daddy, you forgot something."

"What did I forget, Anne?"

"You forgot to tell me where yesterday went."

"I did tell you, darling. Remember?"

"Tell me again."

"1 will a little later, Anne. It's a long story. I think your mother wants you now."

"You promise, Daddy?"

"I promise."

"All right."

QUESTIONS

What contrasts are emphasized in "The Wheel"? Which character is used for unity of focus? How and why has this character's opinion of Dave Shepard changed? How does it differ from the opinion of the other two girls? What is the artistic aim of the whole unit? How important is subjective material in bringing out the clash of views? How is the subjective material handled? Has the writer made a wise choice of situation, time, and place? Is the situation brought to a definite or an indefinite ending? What is the relation of this ending to the writer's artistic aim? Is the writer's paragraphing usual or unusual? What is the writer trying to do with it, and is she successful in her aim?

In "Purgatory" what idea is the basic aim of the writer? Are the three men alike or different? Are they consistently alike or different? What ironic contrasts does the writer use? Why does he use these words or phrases: "impertinent shadow," "a glib tongue and a full belly," and "three things who had been cast in the image of God, born free and equal, and masters of their environment ? Are the sun and the mist used at the beginning and the end partly as symbols or only as stark realism?

What is the writer's artistic aim in "The Rock"? Does he achieve his aim? Is his method entirely objective or are there subjective details? How does he use events from the past? What are the motives of the characters? Is Windy cruel, or ignorant and immature? Does the sketch have understatement or restraint? What reasons do you have for your answer? What is the effect on the reader, and is this effect foreseen early in the narrative or is it cumulative?

What idea is emphasized in the sketch entitled "Where Did Yesterday Go"? What emotional attitude becomes a fundamental part of the idea? Is the envelope pattern effective for this material? What contrasts does it help the writer bring out? Does the writer pass easily from the opening scene to the memories and back to the closing scene? Are the memories descriptions, incidents, character sketches, or combinations of all these? Are they vivid and emotionalized? Which one makes the most complete use of subjective techniques?

7

Character:

GENERAL AND SPECIFIC DETAILS

If you wish to write well, you need to make your characters seem like individual people, not stereotypes. Acquiring this skill is difficult. You may be hampered partly because you know so much about real people, partly because you do not know enough about them, and partly because you have so many possibilities when you consider the methods of characterizing them.

First, among the methods, you may perhaps use direct explanation, with the writer explaining his own views of a character, the views of others, or the character's views of himself. In theory this method is likely to be dull. But it is sometimes effective when used by a sharp observer, useful in long fiction when a writer introduces a character or explains his attitude in new situations, and possible in short narrative when deftly used in small bits. Second, you may describe a character; you have large choices between general, passive details and specific, active ones, or between mere clothing and obvious features against a shrewd selection of details to suggest character. Of course the specific, active description and details that imply character are usually more effective. Third, you may use the surroundings of a person to show us what he is like—habitual surroundings which he creates himself, or an alien environment which he accepts, dislikes, fears. Fourth, you may use the thoughts of a character about anything, either the stream-of-consciousness flux or conscious controlled thoughts in specific situations. Fifth, you may show us how your character reacts to other people. Sixth, you may let him talk. Seventh, you may use his actions, including little mannerisms which are habitual, specific movements in one-time, one-place situations, or the patterns of action in a whole narrative. If any general conclusion is sound, perhaps talk and action are your most effective methods of developing a character.

You may already realize that there is overlapping in this list of methods, but some of it cannot be avoided. For instance, when a writer wishes to tell us how his character feels about another character, he may explain, use the character's specific thoughts, or let him talk or act so as to imply his attitude. Or he may combine these methods. When you examine good narrative you are likely to find several methods skillfully combined.

EXAMPLES OF EXPLAINING CHARACTERS

Since you are not yet an experienced professional, you may need to escape confusion by isolating some methods and working chiefly on them. Hence it is suggested in this chapter that you use generalizations but combine them with certain specific details. You do not need the long, all-inclusive explanations or generalizations which some novelists use, but they make a good starting point for your thinking. In *Arrowsmith*, Sinclair Lewis used much explaining in presenting such characters as Angus Duer, Madeline Fox, the Tozers, and Dr. DeWitt Tubbs. In this paragraph he was explaining Duer as his chief character saw him:

Duer was one of the few among Martin's classmates in the academic course who had gone on with him to the Winnemac medical school. Duer had been the valedictorian. He was a silent, sharp-faced, curly-headed, rather handsome young man, and he never squandered an hour or a good impulse. So brilliant was his work in biology and chemistry that a Chicago surgeon had promised him a place in his clinic. Martin compared Angus Duer to a razor blade on a January morning; he hated him, was uncomfortable with him, and envied him. He knew that in biology Duer had been too busy passing examinations to ponder, to get any concept of biology as a whole. He knew that Duer was a tricky chemist, who neatly and swiftly completed the experiments demanded by the course, and never ventured on original experiments which, leading him into a confused land of wondering, might bring him to glory or disaster. He was sure that Duer cultivated his manner of chill efficiency to impress instructors. Yet the man stood out so bleakly from a mass of students who could neither complete their experiments nor ponder nor do anything save smoke pipes and watch football-practice that Martin loved him while he hated him, and almost meekly he followed him into Digamma Pi.[1]

He summed up Madeline Fox in this way:

Madeline was a handsome, high-colored, high-spirited, opinionated girl whom Martin had known in college. She was staying on, ostensibly to take a graduate course in English, actually to avoid going back home. She considered herself a superb tennis player; she played it with energy and voluble swoopings and large lack of direction. She believed herself to be a connoisseur of literature; the fortunates to whom she gave her approval were Hardy, Meredith, Howells, and Thackeray, none of whom she had read for five years. She had often reproved Martin for his inappreciation of Howells, for wearing flannel shirts, and for his failure to hand her down from street-cars in the manner of a fiction hero. In college they had gone to dances together, though as a dancer Martin was more spirited than accurate, and his partners sometimes had difficulty in deciding just what he was trying to dance. He liked Madeline's tall comeliness and her vigor; he felt that with her energetic culture she was somehow "good for him." [2]

At the beginning of Chapter 12 Lewis gave an interesting sketch of Max Gottlieb, but it is too long to reprint here. Some of the single-sentence character sketches are interesting:

Mr. Tozer was as thin and undistinguished and sun-worn as his wife, and like her he peered, he kept silence and fretted.[3]

Other writers of fiction find these explanations of character useful. Thomas Hardy in *The Return of the Native* uses a chapter called "Queen of Night" to explain the character of Eustacia Vye. Even writers of short stories sometimes use effectively general sketches of their characters, as John Steinbeck introduces Elisa Allen:

[1] Sinclair Lewis, *Arrowsmith*, Harcourt, Brace & Company, 1925.
[2] *Ibid.*
[3] *Ibid.*

She was thirty-five. Her face was lean and strong and her eyes were as clear as water. Her figure looked blocked and heavy in her gardener's costume, a man's black hat pulled low down over her eyes, clodhopper shoes, a figured print dress almost completely covered by a big corduroy apron . . .

. . . Her face was eager and mature and handsome; even her work with the scissors was over-eager, over-powerful.[4]

Often in short stories a writer uses a small bit of explanation woven deftly into a narrative scene:

She turned quickly. Miss Kitty Preston, her face curiously flustered, stood facing us.

"Ailie Calhoun, I didn't think it of you to go out and delib'ately try to take a man away from another girl."—An expression of distress at the impending scene flitted over Ailie's face—"I thought you considered yourself above anything like that."

Miss Preston's voice was low, but it held that tensity that can be felt farther than it can be heard, and I saw Ailie's clear eyes glance about in panic. Luckily Earl himself was ambling cheerfully and innocently toward us.

"If you care for him you certainly oughtn't to belittle yourself in front of him," said Ailie in a flash, her head high.

It was her acquaintance with the traditional way of behaving against Kitty Preston's naïve and fierce possessiveness; or if you prefer it, Ailie's "breeding" against the other's "commonness."

"Wait a minute, kid!" cried Earl Schoen. "How about your address? Maybe I'd like to give you a ring on the phone."

She looked at him in a way that should have indicated to Kitty her entire lack of interest.

"I'm very busy at the Red Cross this month," she said, her voice as cool as her slicked-back blond hair. "Goodby." [5]

Later, in a brief narrative of character, you may need to use an occasional sentence of explanation; and later still, in short stories, several sentences. At any time the test is your ability to use the explaining smoothly, so that it seems a natural part of the narrative.

[4] John Steinbeck, "The Chrysanthemums," *The Long Valley,* Viking Press, 1938.
[5] F. Scott Fitzgerald, "The Last of the Belles," *Taps at Reveille,* Charles Scribner's Sons, 1935.

FINDING YOUR SUBJECT

A well-known example of the specific-general pattern recommended in this chapter is William Allen White's comment on his daughter, "Mary White." The author wrote at the crisis of her death; he wished to explain that she did not "fall" from her horse, that she had never fallen from a horse in all her sixteen years, and that she had been knocked off by the branch of a tree as she turned to wave at a high-school friend. Thus he implied her zest for life and people; he continued analyzing that zest in comments on her riding in the past, her friends, her books, her art, her use of her car, her zeal for helping others. He closed with a vivid account of her funeral. The sketch has unity because the writer wished to correct a rumor; because he used a central idea, the girl's zest for living; and because he fused these details into an emotional unity by his attitude to her death.

Like the author of "Mary White," you may find the method effective for characters you are estimating in a crisis: your friend graduates, moves away, dies, marries, receives some honor, is elected to an office, is accused of a social blunder, a sin, or a crime. You approve, regret, or defend, at least by implication. You think, "Yes, that's like Joe to win that honor," or "He's been lucky, but maybe he deserves it, too," or "He was always trying to see if he could get by with things against the rules, but I never thought he'd get into serious trouble." You can present a character who has developed, one who has failed to develop, one made of strange contrasts, one who has puzzled you or justified your hopes. Considering him in a crisis, you are impelled to think over all you know about him, select things which have a bearing on the crisis, and find an attitude of regret or approval which grows from the crisis. Thus your method gives you at the same time freedom and restraint: freedom to analyze a whole character and to use memories as specific incidents with talk and action, as impressionistic details, or as emotionalized generalizations; restraint because you are choosing a pattern when you select scenes for the beginning and the end. Begin the search for a subject by listing the people you might write about some time, preferring those you have known for months or years. Eliminate or put aside for future compositions the people who seem unadapted to the methods suggested here or those you might develop with some creation. For this first character sketch it is assumed that you will not only be using a real person but also analyzing facts from experience. If several of the people brought into focus for you by events seem good subjects, take your preference or choose one arbitrarily.

USING YOUR CHARACTER

Analyze your chosen character rather fully. What makes him tick? When and where is he most himself? When and where is he unhappy or ill at ease? What are his customary actions? What causes him to do certain things and what are the results of these actions? Is the recent event or crisis one that you expected, or were you surprised by it? Is he a person who seems to change, or is some quality in him a constant? Has your attitude to him changed or remained the same? What one quality of his is most important? If you cannot decide, list informally all the qualities which come into your mind. Does unity appear in these qualities? For instance, you may have jotted down "generosity," "thoughtfulness of older people," and "forgetfulness of self." Are the three really one quality? If the qualities on your list are really distinct, do you wish to say something like this: "Joe is such a contradictory character that I've never known what he would do next—and recent events bear me out." Or can you choose from your list the one quality you value, or the one which led to the recent event? For instance, if he has always been reckless, in spite of good traits, and if he has recently caused a bad accident, you may decide to emphasize his recklessness.

You may begin with a specific scene, use any combination of generalizations or of specific incidents and generalizations, and close with a specific scene. Or you may vary the pattern, as some writers do, by beginning with a specific scene, using some generalizations, using a long incident with some general statements, and ending with a specific scene which shows the change in a character. Your scene at the end may be a return to and a completion of the scene at the beginning; if so, you are using a form of the envelope pattern discussed in Chapter 6. For contrast and change in a character, you may need a new scene at the end. Try to use a specific scene or description at the beginning and the end; then combine specific scenes or generalizations as you wish in the remainder of your unit.

WRITING YOUR COMPOSITION

Choose and analyze the character you wish to write about, using the suggestions in the preceding discussion. Plan one or more situations for the beginning and the end. Jot down all sorts of memories —ideas, impressions, incidents, or possibly the incident which brought about a change in him—for the middle of your unit. As you recall, let your senses have free play with your memories. Create a unit which is fused into one emotionalized experience. Then write your composition.

TESTING AND REVISING

1. Whether you have used one trait of your character or several traits, have you achieved a unity of idea in your work?

2. Have you emphasized a unity of attitude?

3. Have you used talk and sensory details wherever they might be effective?

4. Will your reader care about your character?

5. Have you written about him as if you care yourself?

ANNE *

Dick Campbell

I leaped over the three front steps and jabbed nervously at the doorbell, hoping that Anne would be ready this time. She sometimes seemed to delight in the late entrances that we made at most of the parties we attended. I planted my thumb on the button and held it there. Anne's voice rang with excitement through the upstairs window. "Come in, Ran, and make yourself at home. I'll be down in two jiffs. The evening *Trib* is on the radio. Oh, I'm so excited I hardly know which way to turn!"

I heard her from the inside now. The living room, small and modestly furnished, gave one a sense of home and rest. "Oh, Ranny," Anne called from the head of the stairs, "Ranny, don't you think it is wonderful that we were invited to Mrs. Van Ouster's party for her niece? I am just dying to get inside that house. It looks just like a palace, up on that great big hill. You have to climb a lot of stairs before you even get to the front porch, only I guess you call theirs a veranda. Mother said it is so luxurious inside—big oozy chairs with velvet on them, a winding stairway, and a grand piano, and carpets all over the floor. I wonder what Mrs. Van's niece is really like. I was talking to Sybil today, and she said that she and Joe weren't invited and that the niece was just a snobby little snip. My, won't the rest of the gang be burned up when they read the write-up the *Bugle* is sure to have. O-oh, Ranny, aren't you thrilled?—Ranny?—— Aren't you thrilled?——"

"What?—Oh, yes—yes, it will be fun." I often wondered why I liked Anne. Sometimes she was almost as disgusting as my baby sister. Why did she always have to be late? We were late to Jordan's party just because she wasn't ready. She said she had worked hard that day, and when I asked her what she had done, she started to cry and said, "You think I don't know how to do a thing, don't you?" We had just made up when Jack had his dance. We were the last ones to arrive, and Anne insisted that we be the last ones to leave after the refreshments. She had acted so silly with Jack's cousin during the evening. Then she threw him a kiss when I finally did get her started out the door. She never did that to me.

She always handed me her books on the way to and from school. She even had me tie her shoestring on Main Street once, and then laughed at me, accusing me of turning red. She danced very gracefully, though, and could say just the right word no matter what happened, but either Virginia or Peggy could do that too. Would she be that puzzling even next year when she was eighteen?

"Ranny, I'm just about ready now." Folding the newspaper that I had leafed through, but hadn't read a word of, I stood up and looked toward the stairs. She was already descending.

Her brown hair lay in crisp waves which became curls at the ends. Her dark eyes flashed in young excitement. The long peach-colored dress and high-heeled pumps made her look grown-up—that look which all young girls strive for. In her hand she carried the golden compact I had so proudly given her on her last birthday. She said nothing; I too was silent. We only smiled. After I helped her with her wrap we started down the front walk to another party, late—as usual. But I did not care, for she had slipped her little hand through my arm.

THE SISSY *

Donald W. Hendrickson

I remember the first time I saw Harper. The ship had just put out to sea from Frisco and the steward had sent him up to clean up the radio shack. He was eighteen years old, tall and skinny, and his long legs were a little bowed. He wore very thick glasses. His eyes were pale blue and looked at you steadily enough but always shyly and submissively. His shoulders hunched a little, and his movements were hesitant and awkward. He was already seasick. He was suddenly finding himself on a ship bound for the other side of the world, miserable with the brutal pitching of the ship, taking part in a life of which he knew very little, and disliking and fearing what he knew.

He was lonely and eager to talk. I found that he came from a small town in New York. He had been in college for six months before he had enlisted. He had liked college and it was easy to picture him among stacks of books, studying diligently.

It was a long trip. Only seven months, really, but seven months of the worst sort of monotony. We were one of thousands of ships that had been sent to the Pacific to support the invasion of Japan. The war had ended and we had been caught out there. We were sent from island to island trying to discharge a cargo that no one had any need for. Eniwetok, Ulithi, Saipan, Guam, Okinawa, months of swinging idly and forgotten at anchor, a useless ship on a useless voyage. A man could eat and sleep and work a little. He could go slowly insane. It got to all of us, once in a while, and we'd walk back and forth on the deck with that great feeling of restlessness ripping our minds apart. We wanted and we cursed the wanting but there was nothing.

Harper never fitted in. Gradually, he became the butt of jokes and a scapegoat for the crew's discontent. He withdrew even more into himself and spent most of his time in his room, reading. He must have read the small store of books on the ship over and over again. He hardly ever spoke to anyone, and then shyly and defensively. I think he hated all of us. I know he hated his petty, menial job.

The source of most of Harper's persecution was a man called "Rivets." He was big and loud. That's about all I remember about him. I don't think there was much else to remember. You find his kind everywhere. There are a lot of explanations for that kind of a man but it must have been something pretty degrading that caused "Rivets." He baited Harper unmercifully. He played jokes on him and made him look like a fool. The jokes were little nasty things, constantly repeated with an almost maniac perseverance. Although most of the crew weren't bad men and disliked "Rivets," they were intensely contemptuous of Harper. Harper must have become a fixation with him. He poured out all his frustrations in tormenting Harper. He looked happy while he was doing it. Harper took it all. He never resisted or tried to get even. It would have been hard to do so.

I was a little sorry for Harper. Several of us were, even though it's hard to be sorry for a man you think is a coward. I used to drop in his room from time to time. One day, about the fifth month of the trip, I was sitting in his room talking with him. We were at Okinawa, at anchor as usual, about a mile out from the flat pile of rubble that had been the city of Naha. It was raining dismally, as it had been for a week. While we were talking, "Rivets" wandered in. I could see Harper stiffen. "Rivets" sat down on Harper's bunk, rumpling it. He grinned contemptuously. "Hi-ya, Tiger. How's my boy, today?"

Harper squirmed and said nothing.

"Did you sleep well, last night, old buddy?"

Harper hesitated, then said, "Yes."

"I heard some low character threw a bucket of water in your porthole."

"I didn't notice."

"Rivets" laughed in Harper's face and looked around the room. The door to Harper's locker had swung open. There were several pictures inside, mostly of Harper's family. He must have been horribly homesick. There was one picture, larger than the rest, that could only have been Harper's mother. She was benevolently ugly and wore thick glasses over eyes that must have been a bashful pale blue. "Rivets" pointed at the picture and laughed coarsely. "Hey, Harper, what do you keep that thing for? To scare the rats away?"

Harper jumped. "That's my mother."

"Rivets" kept laughing, irritatingly. "She looks like a barmaid I picked up on the Liverpool waterfront. She married?"

I was disgusted. Disgusted with Harper for being a fool and a coward, and disgusted at "Rivets" for being what he was.

"Rivets" persevered. "What's the matter, buddy? Isn't your Mamma got a husband?"

Harper sat with his head bowed as if in intense concentration, then he seemed to decide something, something irrevocable and of mortal importance. He rose awkwardly from his chair and stood completely relaxed. He spoke flatly, "Get up, 'Rivets.'"

"Rivets" had been about to say something, and his mouth was open. It stayed that way. For just a moment, he was lost, then he struck an exaggerated attitude of mock fear. "Why, what for, buddy? You aren't going to hurt me, are you?" It didn't sound quite convincing.

Harper stood waiting. He wasn't even breathing hard. His face held no expression nor did his eyes, except that they weren't shy anymore. He spoke quietly and with conviction, "If I can, I'm going to kill you."

"Rivets" sat motionless. He didn't seem to be able to say anything. I think I know what he was thinking. He was thinking, as I was, that Harper had gone mad. Maybe he had. He was pretty sure that he could take Harper, but he was even more sure that if he made one mistake, if he should happen to slip, or misjudge the roll of the ship and stumble, or any one of a hundred possibilities, Harper would kill him without mercy. He was also pretty certain that Harper would die trying. His eyes shifted uneasily to me. I think that he wanted me to try to break it up. I don't think that I could have produced anything more in the way of argument than a gurgle, right then, and somehow, I didn't want to. I could see "Rivets" figuring the odds and I could see his decision start to set within him. Gradually, his face started to flush. He, too, had decided something.

Harper spoke insistently, "Get up, you yellow louse." His voice was still steady.

"Rivets" didn't get up. He breathed quickly in the silence of the room. Harper waited a long time, then spoke again, suddenly. This time his voice held contempt. "Get out."

"Rivets" got up and left without looking at either of us. Harper sat down and there was a long silence. He looked at me, his eyes bashful and self-conscious. He was trembling a little. He started talking about whatever it was we had been discussing before "Rivets" had come in. I got out of there as soon as I could.

"Rivets" told everyone that Harper had gone crazy. The crew admitted the possibility and, fascinated, demanded all the details. "Rivets" was rather evasive but I managed to fill in the little details that he might have overlooked. Harper didn't show any more symptoms of insanity, though, and one day I passed by the mess room and saw Harper playing poker with some of the men. A cigarette dangled out of his mouth and he studied the cards shrewdly. He had never been invited to play, before. It must have been a great day for him.

QUESTIONS

Is the sketch called "Anne" effective or is it too superficial in its present form to be worth while? Could the writer have given the same topic more significance? Is the young man's attitude characteristic or natural? Does the writer split one incident or use two incidents for the beginning and the close? Does his own attitude change or remain constant? Does he use enough material from the past to justify and support his idea?

Does the author of "The Sissy" use one scene or two different scenes for the beginning and the end? Why? What bearing do paragraphs two, three, and four have? Is their inclusion justified? Are the generalizations about "Rivets" in the fifth paragraph justified? Does this unit, from paragraph six through the next to the last paragraph, use mostly narrative or mostly generalizations? Is the amount of each justified by the subject, or is it not? Where are the writer's sympathies, with Harper or with "Rivets"? Does the reader tend to agree with the writer in sympathies or not? Why?

8

Character:

PHYSICAL DETAILS

Writing about people, as it is discussed in this chapter, may be harder for you than either your earlier assignments or your character work in Chapter 7. In that chapter you were asked merely to analyze a person you had known for some time. Here you are asked to do more complex things. If writing about people seems difficult, you are probably asking yourself questions like these: How can I know people well enough to write about them? How can I be fair? How can I emphasize a basic trait, as this chapter assumes that I am to do, when people are complex?

Your problem is no greater in writing than in living. How can you know people well enough to offer a job to one applicant out of fifty? To choose a friend? To risk marriage? To confront the qualities that may appear in your own child? In life or in writing you can search for information and then act on your available knowledge at the time. In writing you can quiet scruples by suggesting that your knowledge is incomplete, by realizing that the subject of your sketch is not exactly the flesh-and-blood person but your creation based on him, and that you may some time change your mind.

In writing and sometimes in life you will need to search for a basic trait, or a quality that is fundamental, constant, and significant. If you are picking a personnel man, you may feel that shrewd-

122

ness about judging people is basic; if you are considering marriage, you may believe that an enduring loyalty is basic. In preparing to write, you may think that a fondness for perfume is constant but neither fundamental nor significant. If you are an aesthetic person, not an average one, you may think that indifference to beauty is fundamental. To most of us, indifference to human suffering seems more important. Also to most of us generosity, stinginess, kindness, cruelty, honesty or dishonesty in some form, courage or cowardice seem significant. As all creative writing is an expression of individual values, your selection of a basic trait is your honest individual choice. Sometimes you may choose a trait so important that it will lead your character to success or ruin; sometimes you may select merely the little foible that amuses you where others see an unreal perfection. You have nothing worth telling about people except your own discoveries; each discovery comes from your own growth and is a stage on the way to an ultimate truth you will never reach. But it is not a scientific conclusion.

Why do you need to emphasize a basic trait? You might answer the question by asking yourself another question: Why do you need to aim at a bull's-eye, instead of the side of a barn, when you are developing skill in shooting? You narrow your target to gain skill. But when you write about a person you need not be so rigid that he is stiff, like a dry skeleton; at your pleasure he may say other little things which do not contradict his basic trait. If you need a basic trait for your own guidance you also need it for your reader. To tell him all that you visualize would probably do nothing but confuse him. Your composition would thus lack the essential oneness which comes from selection and arrangement, a oneness which is intensified by repetition and subtle implication. For instance, if your character is insolent, do not tell us or show us once only; let him swagger and speak with contempt through your whole unit. Repeat and repeat, with variations and by implication.

BRINGING YOUR CHARACTER TO LIFE

Whenever you write about people in narrative, your ability to make your major character seem like flesh and blood is the real test of your skill. You would like to present not a puppet, an automaton, a generalized abstraction, a flat, one-dimensional figure, but a rounded, individual, three-dimensional figure. When you are reading narrative written by other people, you sometimes find yourself responding to a character: you see him enter a room, hear his voice or his breathing, strain your muscles with his; you hope and fear for him if you sympathize, and if you do not sympathize you hope and fear for others; you understand his motives and his mind. You have the feel of his experience as you read. That is, a character seems alive for you as a reader when you realize him with your *senses*, react to him with your *emotions*, follow him with your *mind*. Can you bring your characters to life for your readers?

KNOWING YOUR CHARACTER

Perhaps no one can tell you fully how to breathe life into your characters. Certainly there is no magic formula, or more characters in literature would give us readers the illusion of flesh and blood. Knowing your character is your best approach. Here are two working hypotheses. First, your chances for bringing to life your own character grow as you understand him with your *mind*, your *senses*, and your *emotions*. Second, you can do something to know your character by *your conscious effort*. Then you can hope to fuse your details into a created experience that will give him the spark of life.

Professional writers take great pains to know their major characters. A man who had his fourth novel under way was asked by a group of students about his methods. "Oh, *no!* No outlines." As he spoke he was pulling from his brief case a sketch of his village with its chief trees and houses, a summary of his central idea, plot scenarios, the wording of his closing paragraphs, and biographical sketches of his characters. For his main character he had a synopsis covering ancestry, past life, environmental influences, occupations, future aims, physical appearance, emotional drives, and a basic trait. He had built his main characters from years of unconscious incubation, using the problems of his own family and the people in the community where he spent his childhood. He was using conscious incubation also, trying to "get inside the skin" of his chief character, to know him with mind, emotions, and senses. Since experienced writers take so much trouble before they write a narrative, perhaps you may need to try knowing your characters before you begin to write.

How can you know a character? You can begin by watching people. Some of these questions may help you:

What is the person's face really like? What is individual about his eyes, mouth, nose? Does his expression change easily? (Observe him in different situations—when he talks to a girl he likes, to a man he likes, to a man he distrusts, when he feels inadequate, when he is happy, anxious to please, ready to drive a bargain, asleep, adjusted to a formal social affair.) What is his hair like, in color, in texture, in arrangement? How does he manage his hands and feet? What gestures does he use? How does he walk—does he stride, wobble, saunter, sneak, lurch, march? Are his muscular movements free and spontaneous? Do they reveal his urges and aversions? What mannerisms does he have? Does he narrow his eyes when he thinks? Does he snap his fingers when he is perplexed? How does he shake hands? Does his bodily position or his expression change when he is with inferiors, superiors, when he is asked to use his mind or his hands, when he is caught off guard? Can you realize his inner feeling when his face takes on a certain expression? Could you describe him, selecting the physical details to make him seem an *individual*?

How does your character speak? Does he drawl? Does he clip off his words? Is he precise or slovenly in his pronunciation? Is his voice high or low, thin or rich and resonant, easy or strained? What are his pet expressions, bywords, expletives? Is his language informal or bookish? Is it idiomatic and picturesque, or flat, conventional? When you close your eyes and listen to his talk, do you hear an individual speech rhythm? When he is absent, after you have observed him carefully, can you hear his voice in your imagination? Can you make other people hear his voice?

How does he laugh? Does he express honest amusement, or is he covering up other feelings? If you heard this type of laugh from an unseen stranger, what would you think of him?

As you study any character, you will observe more shrewdly when you notice that physical details have their constant and their changing elements. For example, your character's eyes are always blue, but they may look a lighter blue when he is happy and a steel blue when he is angry. His voice, too, is always the same in some ways, yet it changes in other ways to reveal his moods. Then your character is one person when he is static and another when he is active—or perhaps he is a dozen different persons as he takes part in different activities. He will probably interest you and us more when he is active. Then be sure to observe him in at least one activity.

As you observe physical details, using your senses, you are also learning to understand your character with your mind. What do you know about his inclinations, tastes, interests, favorite sports, reading habits, ambitions? If his ambitions are strong, are they controlled by scruples? Is his vanity strong? What are his fixed ideas? His prejudices? His dominant motives? What does he desire most or value most? What does he think about when he is most himself? What thoughts does he have which he would be unwilling to tell his best friend? Would he tell any of these thoughts to a stranger? How does he treat equals, superiors, children, servants? (Although you probably cannot know all these things about one actual person, the questions may help you sort out what you do know. But when you create a character, from the dust of your experience, you can know these things and more.) What is his basic trait? Why does he have this trait?

As you use your senses and your mind, learn your own emotional attitude to your character. Do you reverence, admire, love him? Do you envy or pity him? Do you feel dislike, aversion, disgust? Does he make you angry? Is your feeling so complex that you have trouble analyzing it? How do your own muscles behave when your character approaches?

Try to realize what emotions your character is feeling and then suffer or enjoy with him if you can. If your sympathies are narrow, begin with characters like yourself. Then enlarge your powers; for example, imagine yourself "inside the skin" of a small boy with a fishing pole, three small fish, and an interest in snakes. Can you hear the faint squish of dust under his bare feet, feel the fishing pole growing heavy on his shoulder? Can you identify yourself with a boy watching a fire truck—hear the truck, feel his tense muscles, see the firemen as they adjust their bodies to speed, and also feel a longing to ride on that fire truck? Can you at least sympathize with the characters you choose to write about?

Sometimes "to know all is to forgive all"; sometimes your sense of values, as you understand a character, keeps you from sympathy and even gives you a positive aversion. If you find yourself neutral or lukewarm after you have observed your character, do not waste time writing about him. If your interest was genuine to begin with, your attempt to grasp him with your mind and your senses has probably clarified and strengthened your attitude.

CHOOSING CHARACTERS FOR YOUR WRITING

How and where will you find characters to use in short narratives?

First, you may observe a real person, trying some of the suggestions and questions given above, discovering a basic trait, and realizing your attitude to him. Though this method may seem like photography, it is not quite photographic. You may observe the person in different situations before you choose your time, place, and situation; and when you have chosen where to show him in action, you need to select and arrange to stress the basic trait and your attitude.

Second, you may observe a real person but add conscious or unconscious creation to the observation. For instance, his basic trait is shyness; and having known other shy people, you create a situation for him and use actions or gestures which come from other people at other times and other places. Of course you fuse all these details into a created experience.

Third, instead of beginning objectively, you may try to present a character who has your thoughts and feelings, a trait in you which seems basic, and a situation you have experienced. Thus you will have reality in the inner life of your character. You may give yourself another name and use the third person. But you may have a problem about his physical appearance. Either try to give him the physical exterior you do have so far as you can tell, or the one you would like to have, or the one your worst enemy would assume in describing you, or the one you observe in another person whose thoughts and feelings are like yours.

You will probably make combinations of the three approaches to character which have just been discussed. And even if you try the second or the third approach, you will necessarily use your thoughts and feelings as an approach to others.

Fourth, after you have enlarged or discovered your sympathies and mastered some techniques, you may use characters who seem to be entirely your own creation. There is no reason why you should not use them if you can make them seem authentic and individual. Probably they will not come from pure creation but will be fused from things your conscious mind has forgotten.

Which of the four methods should you use now? Use the one you can manage best as a start; then you can experiment with the other methods. But if you are ready to create characters now, continue to observe real people. Even if you are not using them consciously, your observation of them will keep you from drifting toward bloodless abstractions. And no matter where you begin, your intellectual, emotional, and sensory information must be fused at last into an imagined and emotionalized experience. If your full visualizing helped you in earlier assignments, try it as a working hypothesis here, both for surroundings and for the characters themselves.

USING SPECIFIC DETAILS

Your most effective way of presenting character, as well as other experience, is by specific details developed with suggestion. You may use many different kinds of details, and, as you remember from Chapter 7, there are many ways to show character. When you show us a person's attitude to an activity, an environment, situations, human relations, you imply character. When you show us his attitude to a news broadcast, a painting, a prize fight, a piece of good music, a good dinner, you are, in a limited way perhaps, implying character.

There are four main kinds of specific detail which come direct from a study of people: *talk, actions, thoughts,* and *details of physical appearance* used with suggestion. This chapter will deal with details of physical appearance, the next chapter with talk; in both chapters and in all narrative writing about people, you will be using actions, thoughts, and other methods as you need them.

Details of physical appearance, when well used, usually suggest one or more of these: first, a mere *type*; second, an *individual*; third, a *basic trait*; fourth, your *attitude* to the character.

The person who wrote these details gave us only a vague type, and hence ineffective details:

> He was a large man with heavy features. He was neatly dressed in a black suit, with black shoes, a blue shirt, and a splash of brightness in his tie.

In the description which follows, the writer used highly individual details but implied little about a basic trait or an attitude:

> He wore a low loose collar that left the most of his neck exposed at all times, but more of it could come out of some place beneath if he were startled. His skin was pink and brown and was lumped somewhat like the skin of an old chicken cock. He always smelt of moist shoe leather. The rims of his eyelids were nervous and red and they twitched continually. He would cross to Journeyman's orchard for so trivial a thing as to report the first housefly of the spring or a large warm-weather ant that crawled over his wife's bottle stoppers.[1]

In this passage the writer approves of Nancy as a "nice" or a "good" girl, but the whole effect is vague and unreal:

> Slanting rays of the sun illuminated the face of Nancy Graves and gave a reddish glow to her auburn hair. It made her fine features stand out as clearly as though they were chiseled from rosy stone. Yet with all the strange light, there was no hint of harshness about the lovely deep eyes and the soft lips.

Here is a passage which combines details to make a character seem individual as well as typical, to emphasize a basic trait and the writer's attitude:

> Kurt was sitting popeyed near the stove when he entered. Aunt Phrena, fat and bulging as dough in a pan, peeped at him through wobbly lids and cried, "Kurt, get me the Comfort Book." She flung her apron over her head, howling into the crocheted edges, "The poor sweet dove, sweet as my sister, my poor dead sister. Come in, Johnny, come in. Ach, the Lord giveth and the Lord taketh away."

[1] Elizabeth Madox Roberts, *Black Is My Truelove's Hair,* Viking Press, 1938.

Uncle Herm, pulling his whiskers, tried to interfere. "Bull wheels of Moses Almighty, Phrena! He ain't no dove. He's cold, that's what he is; pinched blue." Then he shouted, "Get me the lantern, Kurt. The team is waiting to be unhooked."

Johnny had milk and mush that night mixed with Aunt Phrena's reading; " 'He feedeth his sheep like a gentle shepherd.' Eat your mush, Johnny. 'Yea, like a gentle shepherd' "; on and on. Once she interrupted herself to say, "Kurt, you go outside now first, before you fall asleep and wet your pants." Then she continued, " 'Like a good shepherd he watcheth over his flock.' You hear that, Johnny?"

He nodded, choking over a spoonful.

Uncle Herm hitched about as if nettle-stung. "Almighty, Phrena! Give the boy a chance. His stomach's empty; let him eat. Talk later."

Aunt Phrena replied with bitterness, "That's right, Herm Barewolf. Stuff his miserable, sinful body; stuff it full of corruptible food and forget his poor starving soul—his poor, skinny soul." For a moment her round, chubby face was rigid; then it crinkled into grief and she wept gulpily. "I try so hard to be good, and you're all against me; all of you." She lumbered from her chair and into the bedroom, closing the door squeakily. Uncle Herm muttered in his whiskers. All at once he went out of the house. But Johnny sat scared and hardly breathing, until Kurt's heavy lips folded back in a grin. "Let's go to bed," he yawned.[2]

SELECTION AND ARRANGEMENT

You will need to use all your skill in the selection and arrangement of details if you are to present your characters effectively. First, you must know your characters. Your choice of a basic trait and your consciousness of an attitude are the foundations for both selection and arrangement. If you use too many details you will submerge your artistic aim in a flood of words. If you do not arrange well, your reader will not be able to build a unified picture. Your arrangement is likely to be effective when you give your reader a general outline first, like an artist when he begins sketching; then you can add gradually the specific details which complete the outline. Sometimes the added details will seem to result naturally from continued observation. In this description Conrad starts with a general outline:

He was an inch, perhaps two, under six feet, powerfully built, and he advanced straight at you with a slight stoop of the shoulders, head

[2] Herbert Krause, *The Thresher*, The Bobbs-Merrill Company, 1946.

forward, and a fixed, from-under stare which made you think of a charging bull.[3]

If Conrad should continue with more detail about Jim's eyes, mouth, or hands, you, as a reader, would be ready to attach these to the general impression. But when a writer begins with small details, such as eyes or hands, he must manage with unusual deftness or he will leave you bewildered by details in empty space.

Sometimes your arrangement of details may be determined for you by a certain pattern of action. You are in a small-town basement office waiting to see Mr. Smith; you hear heavy feet pounding down the steps in a slightly uneven rhythm, and a pleasant rumbling as Mr. Smith answers a greeting; when the door opens, you see Mr. Smith in general and then in particular, hear him at close range, feel his handshake, and see his movements as he turns to you. Arrangement, then, is an individual problem, determined by *you*, your purpose, your subject, your choice of a time, place, and circumstances.

WRITING YOUR COMPOSITION

A. Write a "thumbnail" sketch of a person; that is, write a few sentences about him as he looks, acts, and perhaps talks, in a one-time and one-place situation. Know the basic quality of this person and the attitude you wish to bring out. Choose a person in whom physical details do something to emphasize his character, but be sure that you are interested in something more fundamental than queer features or queer clothing.

B. Write a "thumbnail" sketch of another person, unifying by your choice of a basic trait and your attitude to him, but do not restrict yourself to a specific time, place, or situation. Be sure that you do more than make flat statements of fact; let your general statements carry suggestiveness and power.

C. Write a longer character sketch, a narrative, with one time, one place, and one situation, in which you bring to life a character of your own choosing. Use one who stimulates your mind, your senses, and your emotions until you make discoveries. It does not matter whether your attitude is amusement, aversion, admiration, or affection. Choose a character whose physical appearance interests

[3] Joseph Conrad, *Lord Jim*, Doubleday & Co., 1900.

you, but again be sure that you are interested in something more fundamental than features or clothing.

Before you begin to write, know your character; select a basic trait; become conscious of your attitude; choose a simple situation in which your character tries to do, decide, or get something which will reveal him, or one in which he refuses to act. Decide on another person, perhaps yourself, for unity of focus. Then create an experience. Use hope and memory; do not restrict yourself to the details you observe at one time and place.

TESTING AND REVISING

After your first draft has cooled, test your work by these questions:

1. Has your character come to life? Does he seem like an *individual* of flesh and blood?

2. By selection and arrangement, have you emphasized a *basic trait* of your character?

3. Have you communicated by suggestion your *attitude* to your character?

4. Does your work progress and grow, as a satisfying, artistic unit?

5. Have you used the skills from previous assignments that might aid you in this composition?

READING

Specific "Thumbnail" Sketches

MAE *

Red hair brown at the roots frizzed about her plump, brightly made-up face. A tight purple dress accentuated her enormous bosom and uncontrolled hips. Her chuckles came from deep within as she chewed on a cold chicken leg and finished her bottle of beer at three in the morning before going fishing.

DEFEAT *

Slowly she fished a spoon out of the greasy dishwater and dried it on a gray towel. Her hair hung unevenly behind her ears. A faded print dress sagged around her bony shoulders but was strained tight across her swollen middle. The split seams of her worn shoes revealed bony, dirty feet. Her coarse complexion had been pretty once and her eyes an eager blue. Now a squalid, barefoot child with uncombed hair hung tightly to her leg.

LECTURER *

A lithe prize-fighter figure in a blue suit bounded up on the platform. He lectured vigorously, punctuating his words with scrawled chalk drawings on the board. His details about penicillin and antibiotics interested a would-be scientist; but his face fascinated the artist. His high cheek bones left deep triangular hollows below, his high forehead swept back to bushy waves of hair, and the smooth tan leather of his skin was accented only by two penetrating blue eyes.

LITTLE GOSSIP *

A carroty streak flashed by our window; and we heard the back screen door slam shut.

"Are you ready for Sunday school yet?" piped a high, thin voice.

Then a trim little mite trotted primly into the living room, her orange hair severely braided in two long plaits. Looking around with her sharp greenish eyes, she offered the information with gossipy relish, "My Papa came home late last night and broke a window."

A RIDE? *

"Want a ride, sailor?"

"Sure."

The girl sitting beside me seemed to fit into the sleek convertible as if she were a part of its modern design. The look of youth was stamped on her sunburned face, and her yellow hair streamed back in the wind with a jaunty air of freedom.

"Mom would have fits," she was saying, "if she knew I was picking up strange men, but you'd just missed your bus, and it's a long wait for the next one. My brother's in the navy too . . . he's an ensign."

She wasn't the kind of girl you would call beautiful . . . she had too many freckles, and her nose was a bit too small and flat, but there was something about the way she talked. . . .

"I say, would you mind lighting me a cigarette? It's too damn windy for me to attempt it."

She winked coyly as she took the lighted cigarette, and turned to wave at someone in a passing car. She drove too fast.

BANKER *

Too late to dodge him, I recognized the approaching thin figure as Mr. Rye, the banker. He came ladling out his steps with deliberate recklessness in an effort to appear youthful and agile. At speaking distance, he touched his hat and hauled up his professional smile, which exaggerated his long, one-sided chin and gave his face the appearance of having been carelessly cut on the bias. Dark-rimmed glasses curtained his small eyes, which were crowded close against a nose jutting at forty-five degrees.

FOUR CHARACTERS [4]

Lew Barchi: "He was a short, slight man with putty-colored hair and skin and a limp that favored his right leg. Bluish grey eyes burned feverishly in the long rectangle of his face, an ugly face dominated by a mouth full of narrow teeth, crowded and yellow. His lips, though very long, splayed apart when he was excited, and froth gathered at their corners. There was froth there now."

Bill Bevis: "a burly man with no neck and a funny, grinning, perfectly round head set between his shoulders like a pea in a spoon."

Charlie Dann: "Charlie hadn't moved; but his pointed fox face had gone as grey as the stiff, high pompadour above it, and a pulse beat in his temple. Roxy was suddenly afraid."

Mr. Purdy of Eastern Dairies: "A purring butter ball of a man emerged, and behind him swaggered the manager."

General "Thumbnail" Sketches

DOC *

His graying hair was worn a little thin on top. Confidante to

[4] All four of these passages are from Josiah E. Greene, *Not in Our Stars,* The Macmillan Company, 1945.

hundreds of country folk, his shoulders were beginning to droop. Often he sat after office hours, his head buried in his hands.

HOUSEMOTHER *

The others call her Mother Holliday, probably from force of habit. Her silver hair is rolled severely back from her reproving glance, her pursed lips, and the artificial graciousness of her smile. Her manners at dinner are impeccable, but she often reads other people's mail during their absence.

MRS. MERTY *

Mrs. Merty trusted no human being alive and watched the dead out of the corner of her hard eyes. She had a figure that strangely resembled a pear. Her slightly grey hair fought continually for freedom and inevitably won. Her face was a complete sag from the circles under her eyes to her several chins below. She smiled every Christmas.

HUCK *

Huck was a man to be depended upon. His barrel-like body was as hard as the steel in the truck he drove. Two of his front teeth were missing. He had not gone far in school, but he was a master of human nature. His truck was a continual haven for children who wanted to see the country. He knew and spoke to every person in town and was always greeted with a smile.

SCARLETT O'HARA [5]

Margaret Mitchell

Seated with Stuart and Brent Tarleton in the cool shade of the porch of Tara, her father's plantation, that bright April afternoon of 1861, she made a pretty picture. Her new green flowered-muslin dress spread its twelve yards of billowing material over her hoops and exactly matched the flat-heeled green morocco slippers her father had recently brought her from Atlanta. The dress set off to perfection the seventeen-inch waist, the smallest in three counties, and the tightly fitting basque showed breasts well

[5] Margaret Mitchell, *Gone with the Wind*, The Macmillan Company, 1936.

matured for her sixteen years. But for all the modesty of her spreading skirts, the demureness of hair netted smoothly into a chignon and the quietness of small white hands folded in her lap, her true self was poorly concealed. The green eyes in the carefully sweet face were turbulent, willful, lusty with life, distinctly at variance with her decorous demeanor. Her manners had been imposed upon her by her mother's gentle admonitions and the sterner discipline of her mammy; her eyes were her own.

LIGHT IN THE WILDERNESS [6]

Milford E. Wence

Mary Roland lay in her great bed with the high carved back and the thick feather ticks, her brown thin face, with the sharp nose and iron-gray hair, deep in the heavy bolster. Only a faint ridge in the red and white quilt showed where her bony frame stretched beneath. She did not move; her eyelids, half-closed, scarcely flickered; her breath came faintly and inaudibly.

With a slight turn of her head she could have seen into the other room where Ed and Joe and Alice sat whispering together. Mary knew they were there; she had known all afternoon that they sat there, believing her unconscious. Smiling to herself, she thought: "Let 'em sit. It'll do 'em good. While they're sittin' they can't pester me."

Happily she looked through the window toward a wide stretch of flat land that once had been fallow prairie. Her land! Suddenly she wanted to walk across it once more, to feel the brittle crispness of autumn grass beneath her feet, and the cool air on her cheeks. The fields were peopled with a thousand memories, John breaking the sod on that far-off spring morning, and still later the children playing there, bruising their bare feet on wheat stubble.

She remembered the night when the horse thieves came; how John had been fast asleep, and how she had slipped from her bed to search for the guns. . . . The moon had made a bright light in

[6] Wilbur L. Schramm (ed.), *American Medley*, Prairie Press, 1937. The story is reprinted by the courtesy of the author, Professor Milford E. Wence, University of Maine.

the yard. Cautiously she had opened the door and raised the musket. . . . Grinning, she recalled how she had staggered from the kick. . . . One fired, his bullet tearing through the sleeve of her gown. . . . Mechanically she felt for the scar now. Another had fallen across the well platform. She had not hesitated. At a half-run she had reached the well before he could rise to his feet. . . . Taking no chances, she aimed in the direction of his head. . . . Served him right. . . . Nothing but a low-down horse thief. . . . She'd do it again. . . .

Outside the October wind blew cold against the house; and she was thankful for the heavy covers which protected her from the strong drafts. The elm's branches, already bare, rasped against the shingles. She opened her eyes a little wider to look at her Seth Thomas clock, high on its shelf against the opposite wall. Its numbers seemed blurred among the handpainted roses. "The light's too poor; I can't see the hands," she thought, listening to the ticking. The clock labored over each stroke, then rested a moment, wearily, preparing for another. It might be climbing up a hill, for all the effort. Probably needed cleaning, if she could get somebody who wouldn't ruin it.

She smiled to herself, proudly, defiantly. "Those works will never wear out," she thought. "They're made of wood." Intently she listened to it again. . . . There's the funny catching sound. It's going to strike! . . . Guess it's four o'clock. . . . She made a silent wager with herself that it would strike four—an old game that she had invented years ago, when she started to sleep less at nights, and she could lie deep in her soft bed and count the hours, the half-hours, the quarter-hours, and the tick-tocks as they slid off into the darkness. "Bong". . . . Two, she counted. . . . Someone was stirring in the next room. . . . Then three more strokes. . . . Funny she had missed hearing it strike four. . . . Maybe it was off again. . . . Must have dozed, she admitted grudgingly to herself.

Across the room a door opened. Ed was coming in; probably wanted to see if the clock would wake her up. She kept her eyes closed. Now his breathing sounded loudly over her face and she pretended to be awakening. One dark brown eye opened and regarded him with studied vacancy. He looked more like he used to as a young boy—if she didn't look at him too closely. His eyes were bleary. Large saggy folds of skin hung under them. Wrinkled, brown, and gray . . . an old man. He isn't so terribly old. . . . Why, he's younger than Joe. Joe never drank so much. . . .

Ed watched her intently. "How do you feel, Mom?" His large calloused hand that always trembled now, fumbled at her cheek.

She waited until she uncurled her toes before answering. The other eye opened. "Pretty good. Are they out there?"

He nodded. "Better get some supper. Fry that ham from the last hog you killed: it's hanging in the smoke-house. . . . Don't let Alice make a pig of herself—Pork gives her gas." She chuckled.

Ed shifted his weight. Cautiously: "They want to see you—that is, if you feel like it."

"Well, bring 'em in."

Her other son and his wife tiptoed into the room. Joe smiled but there was no change in her expression.

They pulled chairs near the bed and sat down. "Listen, Mom," Joe began: "The *Journal* wants to run a special article about you next week. Dave Hanson says that since you're one of the few old-timers left—well, he thinks it would be great stuff to have something about your experiences when you and father first moved out here. Now, Alice has written something I think is pretty good, but I thought perhaps you'd like to hear it first." Joe smiled his broadest.

The old lady signaled Ed for an extra pillow under her head. This done, she pulled her gnarled brown claws from beneath the covers. Something else was wrong. Oh, yes, her teeth. How did they expect her to talk her best without her false teeth? "Get me my teeth"—she had to open her mouth quite wide to be commanding. Ed brought the glass of salt water in which they were kept. Opening her mouth as far as possible, she popped them in, enjoying the way Alice turned her head in disgust. That was better! She clicked them once to see if they fitted. "Get on with it."

Alice carefully opened a purse, took from it several sheets of neatly folded paper, and began to read in her precise, best lodge-manner voice: "Mary Ann Roland was born in Winchester, Virginia, November 25, 1842 . . ." She got no further.

"What's the matter, Alice—got a cold?"

"Why, no, Mother Roland, I just . . ."

"You sound like a rusty hinge. Better gargle some salt-water tonight."

Alice squirmed.

"Well, get on with it," the old lady said. "Don't sit there like a bump on a log."

"Oh, for God's sake," Ed mumbled. "Hurry up and read it."

Alice wet her lips, and rustled through the pages. She tried another passage: "Noble heroism marked her life. In the War of the Great Rebellion she risked her life nursing at the front. She was of the stuff of which great heroines are made: a trail-blazer in a new country, one who helped to carry the torch of civilization farther into the untamed land of the frontier, a light in the wilderness. A symbol of the pioneer woman throughout all ages, and yet, withal, the embodiment of feminine purity, of righteousness, a good mother and a devoted wife."

As Alice paused, silence filled the room. Between ticks of the clock, the children looked from each other to the fragile old lady. Calmly she flicked a speck from the comfort, then looked up at Alice.

"That's a hell of an obituary," she said.

"But that's not what—"

"It's enough to make a body rise up out of a coffin," she continued. "You'd better not read tripe like that unless you want me to get up and walk out on you. The trouble with you, Alice, is you haven't any horse sense. . . . You print one word of that, and I'll snatch you bald-headed as sure as the day you were born."

Ed pushed his mother back into her pillow and straightened the ruffled quilt. "Be quiet, Mom. Doc says you aren't to excite yourself. There, be a good girl. Alice meant all right. . . ."

"She always means all right." Mrs. Roland glowered. "That's what ails her."

As Alice methodically put the papers back into her bag, Joe straightened his tie, and walked over to the bedside. "That's all right, Mom. Now you just lie still. I'll explain to Dave about the article." Joe paused, looked at his mother, then looked out the window. "How would you like to have that new minister see you? He'd want to, I'm sure. . . ."

The old woman grinned. "What are you trying to do—make an ass of me? You know I haven't been inside a church for ten years. And I don't like that mealy-mouthed fool's picture. . . . Probably chases half the women in town, from his looks. Keep him out o' here."

Joe shrugged. "But Mom, if something should happen . . ."

"If something should happen you can have 'em bury me beside your father. No frills, mind you. Just dig the hole deep enough so I won't stink."

Alice ran out of the room.

"Mom, you know how Alice is. What'd you say that for?"

"She hasn't any more spunk than you can shake a stick at. Too puny, and skinnier than a rail. I always told you it was a mistake to marry a woman that thought more of diets than babies." Joe rose to leave, but his mother stopped him. "Send Judge Herrick in to see me tomorrow, Joe."

The brothers exchanged glances. "Mom, if you want to make a change . . ." Joe began.

"Who said anything about making a change." Mrs. Roland fussed with the blanket that kept scratching her neck. "I might want him to write my obituary." She got the edge of the blanket tucked between the sheet and comfort. Then she looked up at her son. Her eyes blinked once or twice as a smile moved her lips. "You're getting fat, Joe. If you don't watch out Alice'll overfeed you. Then you'll have a stroke and she'll marry somebody else on the insurance money."

Joe turned and went out the door.

She looked toward her other son. "Do you think I'll get well, Ed?"

"You're too tough to die, Mom, and too damn bull-headed." Ed straightened the covers and looked down at her once more. "Anything you'd like to eat?"

"You know I can't eat anything. Go way and let me sleep."

Alone again, she lay and watched the shadows gathering in the corners. A neighbor had tuned in WLS. She could hear the "Barn Dance." . . . That was good. She wished Ed would turn on the radio. But he wouldn't. . . . The doctor said she must lie quiet.

. . . Damn the doctor, anyhow. . . . The old fool didn't know enough to come in out of the rain. . . . Tomorrow she'd get up whether they liked it or not. . . . She'd show 'em! Her legs needed stretching. . . . This time the rheumatic one gave a sharp twinge. She muttered a soft "Damn it!" From a long way off came the faint smell of frying ham. . . . Her lips moistened exasperatingly. She'd get up now! She'd let 'em know they couldn't order her around. As she folded the covers back, angrily, the chill of the room struck her breast.

Better wait till tomorrow, she reflected. Lots warmer then. . . . She sighed as she pulled the covers back around her throat.

Her gaunt old body sank farther and farther into the softness of the bed. An old saw came to her: "The man who made the bed was a good man." The feather mattress bulged around her, and she yawned softly, luxuriously, stopping suddenly to remove her false teeth. There now, she thought, it's more comfortable this way. With the tip of her tongue she moistened her dry lips, then closed her eyes, relaxing slowly until she felt her body slipping away, and there were only her thoughts in the room, her thoughts, the ticking of the clock, and the slow thrum of blood in her ears. Then gradually the ticking became dimmer and dimmer, until she couldn't hear it any longer. The wind which had been blowing outside began to die slowly. The billowing curtain gradually collapsed and hung limp and breathless in the darkening room.

QUESTIONS

In the one paragraph on Scarlett O'Hara, in which the author is introducing a major character at the beginning of a long novel, how much information is suggested about the time, the place, and the environment? What conflict is implied in the character, or what basic trait contrasts with an outer shell of behavior? Do the details about her dress and physical size seem appropriate? Is this an effective introduction for a main character in a novel? Would it be more or less effective for a short story? For a brief character sketch?

Has the author of "Light in the Wilderness" chosen a good situation to bring out the character of Mary Roland? Why? As a reader do you feel a unity of impression? Do you find it difficult or easy to name her basic quality? If difficult, is the cause really a lack of unity or is it the writer's skill in implying one trait, in her memories of the horse thief, her attitude to her sons, to Alice, to the minister, the article about her, and her burial? What is implied in the closing sentences? Has there been sufficient but not too much preparation for this ending? Does the author blend successfully the specific details of setting, the talk, the action, and the physical appearance of characters? For what characters does he use good details of physical description? In what passages? Do these details help characterize the people?

ADDITIONAL HELPS

1. As you walk along behind people, pick out individuals who interest you, studying each one carefully before you go on to the next. How would you describe the walk of each, as you view him from the rear? The general physical shape? What is your tentative impression about a basic trait? Your tentative emotional attitude?

2. Try the same observations on several strangers who approach you. How would you describe the face of each, in a word, in a phrase, in a sentence? How would you describe the walk, the physical shape? What is your tentative impression about a basic trait? Your emotional attitude?

3. As you sit in a college grill or some other place where many people talk in groups, close your eyes and listen. Judging from sound only, what is happening? Hear and describe the whole sound, some individual speech rhythms, the character of one or two people, your attitude to one or two people.

4. Choose some person to whom you are strongly attached—father, mother, sweetheart, intimate friend. (a) Express your attitude to him by a general but exact statement. (b) Describe him so as to give a clear objective picture—to help a stranger meet him at a station or pick him out in a crowd. (c) Describe him so as to give a clear objective picture and at the same time suggest your personal feeling.

5. Study some person whom you think you know well until you have changed your mind completely or have discovered something entirely new which you would like to communicate.

6. Select two or three of your favorite pieces of fiction. Notice how the author first introduces his chief character and how he presents him at two or three other main points in the story. Does he let you see the character? If not, would he succeed better in his purpose if he did let you see his character?

7. Read the opening chapter of some serial story in a daily paper—

a story that you consider cheap or superficial. How does the writer present his chief character?

8. Study a writer's introduction of his character in each of these types of magazine story: sentimental, feminine fiction; stories of action for men; ultrasophisticated stories; sincere stories which you consider excellent.

9

Character:

TALK BLENDED WITH NARRATIVE

In almost any descriptive or narrative writing you need the ability to use good dialogue. Through dialogue, or through talk of some kind, you can reveal basic character, emphasize attitudes and relationships between characters, develop action, and even turn your essential information into human drama. Talk is merely one important kind of specific detail which leads you from exposition to drama; it helps you to stop *telling* us about your characters and to begin *showing* them to us.

QUALITIES OF GOOD TALK

What is *good talk*, for you as a writer? It is talk so individual that it reveals the character who uses it; it is also shaped to a listener, to an occasion with its circumstances, to a time and place, to a specific mood or attitude. Hence the diction of your good talk often tends to be informal, contracted, colloquial, ungrammatical. Sometimes it is tangy, firm, shaped by people who use their hands and their muscles. Sometimes it is sprinkled with expletives, by-words, "swear words," and words or phrases that have become mannerisms. Also, the structure of your good talk is often quite informal: sentences are broken off or finished with additions and afterthoughts; phrases or simple words to express strong feeling or to say *yes* and *no* take the place of sentences. As good talk is like the person who speaks, here is its ultimate test: *without any narrative tags or explanations, would you know by its individuality which character is speaking?*

You cannot learn what good talk is, in the writer's sense, by reading general statements about it; you must hear it, detect it with your eyes on the printed page, respond with your muscles to its rhythm. Listening to people is probably your only means of learning, in the real sense, what it is. Listen, then, to speakers, on formal or informal occasions, to one person talking to one other person and then to several others. Listen to waves of talk ebbing and flowing in a restaurant or at a tea. Close your eyes and listen. Hear speech rhythms, revealing the mental, emotional, and physical characteristics of the speaker.

Compare the following three passages. Decide which one represents best the talk of the average citizen arrested for speeding, and whether the others are poor talk or whether they represent other types of people:

"But Officer, you are unaware of the reason for my haste. Let me explain that my wife is dangerously ill. Her physician asked me to use all possible haste in reaching her bedside."

"But Officer, my wife is sick. I am rushing home to see her. The doctor told me to hurry."

"Say, Officer—well—uh—my wife's sick. Doc said make it snappy; so I stepped on the gas—and—uh—well—you see how it is."

Estimate what you can about the speaker or speakers in each of these passages:

Well, yes, she's pretty enough, or the men settin' around the post office watch her as if she is, but pretty *is* as pretty *does*.—No, and I reckon she wouldn't tell *me* if she done anything bad, but I wouldn't trust her any further 'n my man Jake kin sling a bull by the tail.

No, son. I'm sorry, but last time you used the car you broke your promise. The accident wasn't your fault, I know, but you tried to conceal it from me, until Judge Evans phoned me about it.

No! No! You can't have the car, I tell you. Not till you learn to keep out of accidents. I didn't have a car when I was your age. Always getting in some kind of trouble.

But Kathleen, not that dress, not to the Pan-Hellenic formal—with Ken Ebersole! Ten years ago it might have done—for your mother. Here, try my white one.—Oh, I've worn it twice—that's my limit.

Mrs. Evans, I've known Mary Jane since she was knee-high to a grasshopper, and she's a good girl. She likes a good time, and she's thoughtless at times like all youngsters, but *you* can't tell *me* she's bad.

But my dear Johnson, we don't listen to "Façades" for the *meaning*. It is art in its purest form. We listen to the sound.

> O, she doth teach the torches to burn bright!
> It seems she hangs upon the cheek of night
> Like a rich jewel in an Ethiop's ear . . .[1]

> Worcester, get thee gone; for I do see
> Danger and disobedience in thine eye.
> O sir, your presence is too bold and peremptory,
> And majesty might never yet endure
> The moody frontier of a servant brow.[2]

PREPARATION FOR USING TALK

As your aim here is to use talk to characterize the person who talks, you will need to plan many details of your sketch before you write any conversation.

First, find a character who stimulates your interest and one whom you can partly characterize by his talk. Try to know him with your mind and to select his basic trait, then realize your attitude to him, and observe him with your senses until you can see and hear him. If you can do so, blend observing and creating, according to the discussion in Chapter 8.

Second, choose a minor character with whom your main character may talk. This minor one may be yourself; thus you may simplify your planning. If he is not yourself, you will still need to know something about him, perhaps his basic trait, and the attitudes which he and your main character have to each other. You need to know because he will talk a little himself but also because your main character will shape his talk to him. Of course this

---

[1] Shakespeare, *Romeo and Juliet*, i, 5.
[2] Shakespeare, *Henry IV, Part I*, i, 3.

minor character should be carefully chosen to help your main character reveal himself.

Third, choose a definite time and place for your two characters to talk to each other. At seven-fifty-five in the morning surrounded by a cold, November fog, people shape their talk in patterns that differ from those of a leisurely sunny afternoon in April.

Fourth, give your characters a subject to talk about, not a world-shaking event but perhaps some trifle which will give you a framework and at the same time will help you bring out a basic trait. Suppose that your main character is merely being asked whether his cough is better. In a minute or two he can suggest by his answers whether he is self-centered, interested in other people, inclined to grumble, cheerfully optimistic, or ready to laugh at himself. Or suppose you ask a girl, "Wasn't Anne stunning last night at the dance?" As she answers she will soon reveal her malice, fairness, or generosity.

Fifth, if your subject permits, find in it an active situation or a simple conflict. Perhaps one character wishes the other to lend him ten dollars or another cigarette or to double-date with him. Then, in an elementary way, you have a conflict which ends when the active character succeeds, fails, or gives up his aim. Thus you will be able to foresee a definite ending and to shape it more firmly for your purpose. But with your individual subject you may find it advisable to bring out one character's tendency to agree with everything the other says—not any conflict at all.

Sixth, you will probably find that unity of focus is useful again, unless you have unusual skill in using objective techniques or being an "omniscient eye." You can secure this unity by "getting inside the skin" of your main character, using not only his talk and action but his thoughts and feelings; thus you will gain subjective resources but lose some objective resources of physical appearance. You can instead use a minor character for unity of focus; you can use him freely to bring out the talk, action, and physical appearance of your main character, and you will also have all the resources of his thoughts and feelings about the main character. Unless you have a strong preference for another method, try using yourself, either in the first person or in the third person with an assumed name, for unity of focus.

Seventh, you will need at some time, consciously or unconsciously, to create a unit of imagined experience, shaped by your
senses and infused with your attitudes.

Eighth, you will probably be more successful with your character
when you use repetition with variety to emphasize his main trait.
If his basic trait is laziness, for example, do not merely *tell* us that
he is lazy; *show* us by his dress, his facial expressions, his action, his talk, and keep on showing us. Let him be lazy through
the whole unit, as if we were seeing him in life. You will try in this
assignment, as in others, to give initial and terminal emphasis to
important details, not only in sentences and paragraphs but in the
whole unit; to give more space to important things unless you can
point them up by inverse proportion; and to emphasize important
details by putting them in talk and action. You will need to emphasize by planning a whole unit which progresses to a firm ending
instead of dwindling away like a clock running down. It is "natural" for you to visualize and to write better at the beginning of a
composition, but education and thinking may be used to overcome
nature. If your conflict, when it is resolved, does not bring you to
a firm close, try to choose early some remark or gesture which has
finality, or double your care in visualizing at the end, or keep your
main character active because you know what he is going to do
next and you let us see him moving toward that action.

Of course you need also to emphasize one character, making your
attitude to him and his basic trait stand out as your aim. When
you are a seasoned professional you may be able to stress two characters equally, but in short narratives even professionals are likely
to emphasize one character or at least to create sympathy for one.
You can throw the spotlight on one of your two by your selection
of a title, by the space you give to the main character, by concentration on his actions, talk, or thoughts, and by stress upon him
at the beginning and the end.

USING TALK WELL

You already know that talk should be natural, that it should
sometimes be individual enough to tell your reader which person
is speaking, and that you need to do some planning of your whole

unit before you are ready to write the kind of talk that char-acterizes.

Other special methods of using talk well are these: First, put on paper a smaller amount of total talk than your characters would use in real life. Second, break the talk into small bits, instead of letting any character make long speeches. Third, try to avoid the "he-said" and "she-said" method of tagging your speeches. Fourth, learn to blend the talk of your people with action, specific think-ing, and all the other elements of good narrative.

The total amount of talk we use in real life would often be amus-ing if we could detach ourselves and listen. We say three times what we need to say only once. Why? We are embarrassed, we are poor in ideas, or, as in saying good-by, we just don't know how to stop talking. But in writing, unless your basic aim is to show that your character talks too much, restrain talk. Someone has said that a beginner should write his narrative and then prune his talk until he has half of it left. Thus he will achieve his aim better. The comment has some validity for the average writer.

Talk broken into small bits is probably better nine times out of ten than the same talk would be if the characters were permitted to make long speeches. Professional writers sometimes succeed with long speeches, just as the Mississippi River sweeps away logs that would stop a small creek, and they sometimes use well in novels the long speeches that would be ineffective in short narratives. But sometimes professionals would improve their work if they shortened their speeches. It is true also that long speeches on a printed page tend to seem longer than the same ones would seem in life, for in life you can use your mind and senses on other things as you listen. Long speeches in reading create the effect of a vacuum. Short speeches with frequent give-and-take are more active, even though a listener does nothing but ask a brief question or say *yes* or *no*. They help create suspense when they are well used, or they give narration the quality of drama. They reveal the tension between people which is essential to most literature that is significant. One writer on drama made a comment that is equally true of good narrative:

So far as I am concerned, action is only something that follows the inside of a human being. You can have guns booming, people running in and out, punching each other in the nose until everybody goes crazy, and your audience will yawn its head off. But have two people quietly talking, with tension growing between them, and you can hear a pin drop.[3]

Of course you prefer to escape the "he-said" "she-said" monotony in dialogue. But how? You may try to achieve a dialogue so individual that it stands alone without narrative tags; then you may trim out the "he-saids" and their equivalents. If you have even one individual character in a scene with a conventional person, or if you have two people who differ sharply in their views as they talk, your speeches may not need tags. These two contrasted characters, for instance, need little detail to identify them:

. . . Philip was impatient. He went into the other waiting-rooms and looked at the people sitting in them. Suddenly his heart gave a great thud.

"There you are. I thought you were never coming."

"I like that after keeping me waiting all this time. I had half a mind to go back home again."

"But you said you'd come to the second-class waiting-room."

"I didn't say any such thing. It isn't exactly likely I'd sit in the second-class room when I could sit in the first, is it?"

Though Philip was sure he had not made a mistake, he said nothing, and they got into a cab.

"Where are we dining?" she asked.

"I thought of the Adelphi Restaurant. Will that suit you?"

"I don't mind where we dine."

She spoke ungraciously. She was put out by being kept waiting and answered Philip's attempt at conversation with monosyllables.[4]

In this passage, too, the boy and the constable do not need to be identified when they speak:

. . . The constable watched him, watched the way he drank the milk, watched him when he winced away from questions.

"What made you run away? Playing truant, eh?"

"I don't know."

[3] Samson Raphaelson, *The Human Nature of Playwriting*, The Macmillan Company, 1949.

[4] W. Somerset Maugham, *Of Human Bondage*, copyright 1915, 1936, by Doubleday & Co.

"You oughtn't to do it, young fellow. Think how anxious your father and mother will be."

"They are away."

"Well, your nurse."

"I haven't got one."

"Who looks after you, then?" That question went home. Philip saw Mrs. Baines coming up the stairs at him, the heap of black cotton in the hall. He began to cry.[5]

But when a number of characters with similar attitudes are speaking, narrative tags may be necessary:

Art ran his hand slowly over the wrinkles in his waistcoat. He felt Jen's eyes burn into him. She was sitting rigid.

"Well—of course we want to do what's best for the old people," he began, in his ministerial tone, for which he hated himself.

"Oh, of course, certainly," Sam agreed hastily.

"Yes, but just what is best for Mother and Father Shafer? That's what we all want to know," Lou put in sweetly.

Jen gave a jerk. "I'm sure that Arthur and I are willing to do anything," she cried touchily, with her air of putting them all in the wrong. "I'm sure that no one has been a better son than Arthur, whether anyone realizes it or not."

Lou smiled inscrutably. They all knew that Sam was Mother Shafer's favorite child.

Art flushed. "It's a delicate thing to decide," he murmured.

"Yes, of course," said Sam soothingly. "We're all willing to do whatever is—of course."

Now that the thing was started, he felt at ease.[6]

You may try the escape of using synonyms for *said*, trying each time to use a more exact word, such as *shouted, reiterated, exclaimed, shrilled*; but these synonyms quickly become strained. You may find the remedy worse than the disease.

Perhaps your best method of avoiding the "he-saids" is to give up the narrative tags which are put into the same sentence with part of the quoted material and to use detached details that explain what a speaker is doing or how he is reacting as he talks. Compare the two passages below, passages with the same material, as an

[5] Graham Greene, *19 Stories*, copyright 1947 by Graham Greene, Viking Press.

[6] Ruth Suckow, *Iowa Interiors*, Alfred A. Knopf, Inc., 1926.

illustration of using a small total amount of talk, breaking it into small bits, and avoiding the monotony of "he-saids" by using detached comments:

"Now, Johnny," said his mother as he entered the living room after her return from shopping, "I told you not to go to the swimming pool while I was away. But I have reason to suspect that you disobeyed me. You were not here when I returned, and I heard you come in at the back gate just now. I don't know where else you could have been." She waited for Johnny to answer.

"Johnny?" His mother's voice came from the living room. So she was back from shopping. Moving toward the low rocker where she was sitting, he did not raise his eyes.

"Johnny, did I hear you come in at the back gate just now?"

"Er—why—I mean, yes." He watched her deftly bite off a thread before she looked up from mending the shirt he had torn climbing over the back fence that morning.

"Where have you been?"

"Er—well—you see—Ed just happened along—and I talked to him —and—" Johnny's bare toe began tracing one of the yellow triangles in the green rug.

"And then?"

"Well—ah—we just eased along down to the corner by the drug store—"

"And then what?"

Her voice was as calm, Johnny thought, as if she were asking about the weather. But he stirred uneasily, and a dull flush spread over his face and down his neck.

"Why—ah—Ed wanted me to see his airplane model, and—"

For good illustrations of narratives that blend talk well with action, thoughts, settings, and all the other elements, you need to study long units instead of brief extracts. For this purpose, turn to the readings at the close of the chapter.

In this chapter you are considering talk as one way of characterizing people. But you have already been using it in earlier compositions for other purposes; and in future assignments, whether you develop a mood, an idea, a situation, a setting, or whether you use it to characterize people in short stories, you will still need the specific methods discussed here: using a small amount of talk; breaking talk into small bits, instead of letting a character make long speeches; eliminating the "he-saids" and trying detached comments; and blending talk with all the other elements in a narrative.

WRITING YOUR COMPOSITION

Write a brief narrative which emphasizes a specific character, bringing out his basic trait and your attitude to him. Use the talk of this person as an important means of characterizing him, but do not limit yourself to talk alone. Use his actions, details of his physical appearance, his specific thoughts, or the specific thoughts of another character about him, or any other means as you need them.

Plan your unit first, according to the suggestions which have been given above. Use not only a person who stimulates you to creative activity but also one who does reveal himself by his talk; choose time, place, situation, perhaps a simple conflict, and a minor character who will induce your main character to say what you wish him to say.

When your conscious planning rests easily in your mind, write your whole unit, preferably at one sitting. It should be just long enough to accomplish your own artistic aim without any wasted words.

TESTING AND REVISING

1. Have you achieved your aim, so that your reader will realize a basic trait and an attitude in your main character?

2. Does your character's talk really bring out his main trait, or does he just talk?

3. Have you used a small amount of total talk (unless your individual subject requires more), used it in small bits rather than long speeches, and used detached comments rather than many "he-saids"?

4. Have you blended talk with all the other elements in your narrative?

5. Have you achieved an effect of tension between characters if it is essential to your subject?

READING

NAME OF JOHN *

Bernice A. Fox

The line of civilians waiting to be interviewed by WAVE petty officers stretched the full length of the long central corridor of the NAS Administration Building. By eleven o'clock the heat of the day was beginning to press down on the island, and there was still an hour to go before I could secure the office and go to chow.

I slammed another card atop the "done" pile and went to yank open the door and call "Next." This time the door slammed, and quick staccato footsteps followed me so closely I barely reached my place behind the desk before the applicant was there. I remained standing, staring. He was taller than most Hawaiians—taller and tensely erect.

"I am waiting three hours already," he sputtered.

Our eyes clashed. In his, I saw discs of impatience.

"The Navy," I said, "can't put people to work on a military base before they have been thoroughly . . ." He wasn't listening. His lips were flattened into hard lines of indignation. How like a proud young chieftain he looked, come here to discuss peace terms —his narrow hips accentuated in tight-fitting dungarees, his faded work shirt unbuttoned, showing the tough tan of his chest, his shirt sleeves wadded high on his strong brown arms!

"Your screening slip?" I indicated the temporary identification slips that had been issued at the Labor Office, pointing to the stack of them I'd collected from the others before him.

The man remained motionless, staring. It wasn't a rude stare, only disturbing with its unwavering, almost innocent intensity.

"These things," I repeated, sharply. "You can't be interviewed if you don't . . ."

He drew out a worn billfold, unfolded it, and reached inside. Oblivious to my outstretched hand, he scrutinized the slip for a long moment before handing it over.

"Okay," I said, snatching it and smoothing it out beside my typewriter. "Sit down."

Still he remained standing. I scowled. Maybe he didn't want to understand.

"Look." I reached over and picked up a finished personnel card to show him. "This is going to take a while. So *will you sit down* . . ." The authority faded from my voice as my eyes swung up to meet his head-on, and to recoil from the calm pride in them. I was shaken to hear myself adding, meekly, ". . . please?"

There was a faint flicker of triumph in the black depths of his eyes. At once he dropped his lean body easily into the chair and waited.

"Your name," I said, looking over to his identification slip, and spelling it aloud as I typed it in the blank, "J-o-h-n." Then I stopped to puzzle over the scribbled last name on the slip. "John— what's the last name?"

He seemed not to hear.

"Your name—the last name." I was waiting with the shift key down. "What is it?"

His eyes flicked down to the scribbling on the slip, then met mine blankly. I frowned. Maybe he didn't understand.

"What *is* your name?"

His shoulders hunched. "J-o-h-n," he mimicked, then was contrite, but offered nothing more.

"Yes. I know it's John. But John what? I can't make out what's here . . ."

He craned his neck to inspect the writing on the slip. "That? Is not *my* name I have told the man, is not *my* name. Is my grandfather, *his* name there. But the man say I can use it. So . . ." he shrugged.

He returned my long gaze with an equally long look of indifference.

"Okay." This was turning into a scene from Gilbert and Sullivan. "So this isn't *your* name. It's your grandfather's. But *what is his name?*"

"Is John Rodrigues. Is right there—the man, he wrote it. He tells me, is all right that I use—"

I broke in with a flurry of typing, making a wild stab at spelling Rodrigues. Anything to move beyond the impasse.

"How old are you?" I asked, moving down to the next blank.

He understood at once, I knew, but his attention had settled on my hands and he'd been watching, rapt, as I'd fingered the keys of the typewriter.

"Soon now I am seventeen," he announced, calling up a calm pride in the fact. I stole a skeptical glance. He appeared to be at least twenty-two or twenty-three.

"Okay." I typed that in. "Where were you born?"

Again, he hesitated, waiting for me to prod him with a stern glare. He had suddenly found himself the central figure in an unrehearsed drama and he would not hurry his lines. He drew a pack of cigarettes from a breast pocket and glanced around. I nodded permission for him to light up. He twirled the match in his slim, brown fingers a long moment before applying it to his cigarette, watching me unblinkingly over the flame.

"Where were you born?" I asked again.

"In Honolulu—I guess." He exhaled the answer along with his first long puff.

"You guess?" The tiny pin pricks of annoyance were spreading now. This was just another smart-alec island kid trying to bother me. "Don't you even know that?"

He was startled at my tone, but there was still a relaxed, playful attitude which infuriated me. There was a blind moment when I felt that—to him—all my questions were irrelevant and he was the one who was exercising patience.

"Look," I appealed to him afresh, "I've *got* to know these things. Personally, I don't care—but see these cards? They *have* to be filled out *completely* and the Security Office has to investigate every single one before anybody is hired. If you don't want to answer these questions—"

"I am answering."

I sighed. "But you can't 'guess' you were born in Honolulu."

"I cannot say—if I do not know."

I blinked and leaned back to frown at him. "But you *must* know your name and where you were born!"

His answer was a flick of cigarette ash and the careful shift of his gaze from my face to the open window behind me.

I typed in "Honolulu" in the proper blank and went on.

"Your address? Where do you live now?"

"In Wiawa."

"Where in Wiawa? What street?"

"Is no street names in Wiawa," he explained with a faint smile. "All the same. I live with my grandfather there."

"Well. What is *his* name?"

"Is *John!*" His tone rang with surprise that my memory was so feeble.

"Oh, yes." I moved on to the next blank.

"Your father's name?"

Slowly his eyes lifted from the cigarette butt he was studying. There were shadows of reproach in them, but he shook his head tolerantly. "That," he said, as if explaining something to an imbecile, "is what I am not knowing."

"Oh."

I turned the roller to the next line and suddenly my irritation was gone.

"And your mother?" I asked meekly. "Do you know who she was?"

His eyes flared. "Yes! I know."

I waited. Then, at last, "Who?"

"Antoni Rodrigues."

"And where does *she* live?"

"She? Is not living—since I am only a baby."

"Oh."

I slipped a quick side-long glance, meaning to add, "I'm sorry," but he gazed off into space dreamily, undisturbed by my stupidity.

"Your nationality?"

His chin lifted quickly. "American."

"No—I mean . . . *nationality* . . ."

A curious, fanatical gleam burned in his eyes. "I *am* American," he insisted feverishly, "I am just like you—American . . ."

I nodded quick agreement. "But see," I explained, "I am also part French and part German. That is *my* nationality because that is what my parents were. That is my blood—and yours?"

He toyed stubbornly with a packet of matches and would not look up. "This is a territory of the United States," he said firmly, "so! I am born here and I am American . . ."

I leaned back and groped for my own package of cigarettes.

Instantly he was on his feet, holding a lighted match for me. I nodded my thanks, took a long puff, then went back to considering the blanks still unfilled on the personnel card in my machine.

"Now then," I began, putting my cigarette aside. "Your mother. You know who she was. Was she French? Dutch? English? Japanese? What?"

"My mother," he spoke hastily, "*she* was Portuguese. But I . . ."

"And your father," I broke in, "what was he . . ."

Too late, I realized. I looked over at young John, wanting to apologize, but he was not looking at me. His eyes had narrowed pensively and were focused far out in the bay where a PBM squadron was coming in for landings. I saw the sharp clearness of his profile, the clean olive of his skin, the silky softness of his black hair. I looked back at the unfinished card. What difference did it make who his father had been? I moved to shift the carriage over to the next blank and as I moved, John stirred.

"My father—he was a sailor." His tone of intimacy unnerved me. "That much I know. He could have been killed—maybe. That *could* be why he did not come back. He was American I think. Don't you think? Don't you think he could have been?" His eyes burned into mine with pleading. I looked away quickly and busied myself grinding out my cigarette.

"Sure. He probably was an American sailor," I said.

John sighed profoundly as if my opinion had settled his last doubt. I realized he'd been expecting me to laugh, and when I hadn't he'd been confused. There was a sheen of moisture in his eyes which he blinked back furiously.

"How—how far have you gone in school, John?" It was best to leave his nationality unsolved.

"Just a week ago I am graduated—from high school in Wiawa." There was a broad note of pride in his voice. I smiled and typed in "H.S. Grad. June, 1945."

I flipped the card out of the machine and reached for a pen to insert his Civil Service rating. He rose reluctantly.

"You realize," I explained, "this is only a temporary job. When the war is over, the job will be over . . ."

He nodded. "But," he confided impulsively, "I am hoping the war is not over for one more year yet."

I lifted a sharp look of suspicion. "Why?"

"Because then," he flashed a wide boyish smile and really looked seventeen, "I am old enough to enlist in the Navy and my grandfather he cannot stop me!"

I frowned at him. "What has the war got to do with your joining the Navy?"

"They will not take us from here," he explained, "when it is peacetime. They will not take me without my grandfather's—his consent." He shrugged. "*He* does not like the Navy."

I handed him the slips he must take to the Photo Lab for his identification picture. He started toward the door, but paused as if waiting for some further comment from me.

"No." His eyes flared. "But they would send me to the Mainland for boot camp. I could always—you know . . ." one eyebrow lifted significantly, " 'go over the hill.' "

I was puzzled. "If that's how you feel, then why are you so anxious to . . ."

He had turned the door knob and was about to leave, but now he carefully turned back to face me. "How *else* could I ever get to the United States?" he asked simply. As I started, his face broke into a warm smile and with a jaunty wave he jerked open the door and was gone.

I rose to go and call "Next," but my eyes dropped to John's card with the nationality blank only half filled-in. I slipped it back in the machine and added "American."

THE BALLET MEISTER *

Margaret Mattison

"What a ball," called Luigi in his best New Jersey slang. He put another tablespoon of Mexican sauce on his hamburger and repeated the phrase for anyone who might be listening. "What an absolute ball." He was describing the party after the opening of the ballet. As composer of the ballet, he had a right to celebrate. It was the best ballet that Scott Theater of the Arts had ever produced.

"But where is Mr. Johnnie Beggs? No party is complete until

the choreographer comes," he said as he looked over the crowd around the fire.

"I haven't seen John since before the curtain calls," said little Don Fibenger. "I can't figure out why he wasn't there to get his applause."

"Last time I saw him, he was wandering around back stage." Bill Allison was at his usual station—beside the coffee pot.

The long and narrow Nancy reached for another slice of onion. "You know, troupe, I just can't figure that out. Remember when John danced the part of the Hairy Beast of the Enchanted Cave? He was supposed to carry Greta into the forest." She popped the onion into her mouth and said the rest through the onion ring. "He leaped right by her as if she were just another tree." Nancy demonstrated with a young aspen. She pranced around the tree like a young giraffe. "Greta had to dance around in front of him so he could lunge again."

"I can't figure out why he forgot to leap. After all he composed the dance. He seemed to be looking through Greta instead of at her." Don's mouth twitched as he spoke. His mouth always twitched when he thought he had said something nasty.

"Listen, kids, we all make mistakes. Imagine the strain he was under tonight." That was Ann. Always on the team that needed another player. You could tell by her eyes that she was on your side.

Frank sat in the wicker rocker with a pickle in one hand and a piece of devil's food cake in the other. "Anyway, John is one great guy. How many professionals do you know who would give up their summer to come out here and teach a bunch of amateurs?"

"Shh!" Ann looked toward the gate in the back yard. "I think I hear John now."

We listened. We heard a few curses, a cry of "Bring a man a light so he can see where he's going," and then John stepped into the lantern light.

"For heaven's sake, John." Luigi called from the cake table. "What took you so long? The party's almost over."

"I've been scrubbing that damn grease paint off my face. I look like a white man again."

John was wrong. He didn't look like a white man. In fact, the orange paint was almost as thick as it had been in front of the stage lights. He stood in front of the lantern a minute, soaking up the party spirit. John Beggs, ballet meister. Narrow hips, large thighs, muscular arms, that had been trained a lifetime to lift from the shoulder. His face was almost handsome, in spite of the orange paint. Perhaps a few too many worry lines for thirty-eight, but still handsome. He lived behind thick horned-rimmed glasses. Even in class when he showed us turns, he snapped them off, whirled around, and slipped them on again as if it were all part of the technique.

John walked toward the banquet table. Somehow he missed the first step onto the porch and there lay our ballet meister sprawled out in the currant bushes.

Nancy thought it was a good joke. "For a ballet instructor you sure don't go in for this graceful stuff. You stumble around more than any two people I know. Myself included." Nancy turned to her audience. "Remember the time we were walking home from town and John walked smack into the sign in front of . . ."

"Are you hurt, John?" Ann asked as she ran over to him.

"I'll be all right if I can just find my glasses," he said as he felt around on the ground under the nearest bush.

"You have them on."

He stared at Ann as if he had never seen a face before.

"I'll get your hamburger," and she backed away from his stare. She brought the plate and ushered John to a seat near the fire. She certainly was taking him under her wing. That seemed funny. He must have been at least fifteen years older than she.

Then the party really started to roll. Tall tales of Greenwich Village. Past shows. Inside information on big names in the theater. And John always had the tallest tale and the biggest laugh. He started telling stories of his past accomplishments. That surprised me. It didn't sound like John. When he started another, Ann began a story about one of her students in New York.

"Damn it, Ann. Quit interrupting. This is my night." He stood up to get the absolute attention. "I'm going to shine tonight. Shine while I can still enjoy the glitter."

He stood before us in fifth position. We all knew what was coming. His take-off on Swan Lake. Grand battements that looked like a stretching crane. Relevés that looked like a kid at a candy counter. This was his favorite stunt. It had been my favorite, too. But tonight it seemed too much like the Dance in the Currant Bushes.

"Someone stole my cocoa," Frank called as he crawled around the lawn looking for his paper cup.

"Here it is, Frank, right next to your plate." Don pushed the cup under Frank's nose.

"You must be going blind, too," John said in a loud voice. He laughed hard. I felt as if I were the only person who heard him.

"You must be going blind, too."

"He leaped right by her as if she were another tree."

"Bring a man a light so he can see where he's going."

John was going blind. John Beggs was going blind. Bring a man a light so he can see where he's going. Where he's going.

Tell me, John, where does a blind ballet dancer go?

THE FRILL [7]

Pearl S. Buck

"My dear, the only way to manage these native tailors is to be firm!" Mrs. Lowe, the postmaster's wife, settled herself with some difficulty into the wicker rocking-chair upon the wide veranda of her house. She was a large woman, red-faced from more food than necessary and little exercise over the ten-odd years she had spent in a port town on the China coast. Now as she looked at her caller and thus spoke, her square hard-fleshed face grew a little redder. Beside her stood a Chinese manservant who had just announced in a mild voice:

"Tailor have come, missy."

Little Mrs. Newman looked at her hostess with vague admiration.

"I'm sure I wish I had your way with them, Adeline," she murmured fanning herself slowly with a palm-leaf fan. She went on in a plaintive complaining way: "Sometimes I think it is

[7] Pearl S. Buck, "The Frill," *The First Wife and Other Stories*, The John Day Company, 1933. This introduction to the story is used by permission of the author.

scarcely worth while to bother with new clothes although they are so cheap here, especially if you buy the native silks. But it is so much trouble to have them made, and these tailors say—my dear, my tailor promises me faithfully he will make a dress in three days and then he doesn't come for a week or two!" Her weak voice dwindled and ended in a sigh and she fanned herself a trifle more quickly.

"Watch me, now," said Mrs. Lowe commandingly. She had a deep firm voice and round hard gray eyes set a little near together beneath closely waved dead brown hair. She turned these eyes upon the Chinese manservant as he stood looking decorously down to the floor, his head drooping slightly, and said, "Boy, talkee tailor come this side!"

"Yes, missy," murmured the servant and disappeared.

Almost instantly there was the sound of soft steady footsteps through the open doors, and from the back of the house through the hall following the manservant there came the tailor. He was a tall man, taller than the servant, middle-aged, his face quiet with a sort of closed tranquillity. He wore a long robe of faded blue grasscloth, patched neatly at the elbows and very clean. Under his arm he carried a bundle wrapped in a white cloth. He bowed to the two white women and then squatting down put his bundle upon the floor of the veranda and untied its knots. Inside was a worn and frayed fashion book from some American company and a half-finished dress of a spotted blue and white silk. This dress he shook out carefully and held up for Mrs. Lowe to see. From its generous proportions it could be seen that it was made for her. She surveyed it coldly and with hostility, searching its details.

Suddenly she spoke in a loud voice: "No wantchee that collar, tailor! I have talkee you wantchee frill—see, so fashion!" She turned the pages of the book rapidly to a section devoted to garments for ample women. "See, all same fashion this lady. What for you makee flat collar? No wantchee—no wantchee—take it away!"

Upon the tailor's calm patient face a perspiration broke forth. "Yes, missy," he said faintly. And then he pressed his lips together slightly and took a breath and began: "Missy, you first talkee frill.

then you say no frill. Other day you say wantchee flat collar, frill too fat."

He looked imploringly at the white woman. But Mrs. Lowe waved him away with a fat ringed hand.

"No, you talkee lie, tailor," she cried sternly. "I know how I talkee. I never say I wantchee flat collar—never! No lady have flat collar now. What for you talkee so fashion?"

"Yes, missy," said the tailor. Then brightening somewhat he suggested, "Have more cloth, missy. Suppose I makee frill, never mind."

But Mrs. Lowe was not to be thus easily appeased. "Yes, never mind you, but you have spoil so much my cloth. What you think, I buy this cloth no money? Plenty money you make me lose." She turned to her guest. "I have been counting on that dress, Minnie, and now look at it! I wanted to wear it to the garden party at the consulate day after to-morrow. I told him a frill—just look at that silly collar!"

"Yes, I know. It's just what I was saying," said Mrs. Newman in her tired, peevish voice. "What I want to know is how will you manage it?"

"Oh, I'll manage it," replied Mrs. Lowe grimly.

She ignored the tailor for a while and stared out over her trim garden. In the hot sunshine a blue-coated coolie squatted over a border of zinnias, glittering in the September noon. A narrow sanded path ran about a square of green lawn. She said nothing, and the tailor stood acutely uncomfortable, the dress still held delicately by the shoulders. A small trickle of perspiration ran down each side of his face. He wet his lips and began in a trembling voice:

"Missy wantchee try?"

"No, I do not," snapped Mrs. Lowe. "What for wantchee try? All wrong—collar all wrong—what for try?" She continued to stare out into the shining garden.

"Can makee all same frill," said the tailor eagerly, persuasively. "Yes, yes, missy, I makee all same you say. What time you want?"

"I want it to-morrow," replied the white woman. "You bring to-morrow twelve o'clock. Suppose you no bring, then I no pay—

savee? All time you talkee what time you bring and you never bring."

"Can do, missy," said the tailor quietly. He squatted gracefully, folded the dress into the cloth again and tied it tenderly, careful to crush nothing. Then he rose and stood waiting, upon his face some agony of supplication. His whole soul rose in this silent supplication, so that it was written upon his quiet high-cheeked face, upon his close-set lips. Sweat broke out upon him afresh. Even Mrs. Lowe could feel dimly that imploring soul. She paused in her rocking and looked up.

"What is it?" she asked sharply. "What more thing?"

The tailor wet his lips again and spoke in a faint voice. "Missy, can you give me litty money—one dollar, two dollar—" Before her outraged look his voice dropped yet lower. "My brother's son he die to-day, I think—he have three piecee baby, one woman—no money buy coffin—no nothing—he very ill to-day——"

Mrs. Lowe looked at her caller. "Well, of all the nerve!" she breathed, genuinely aghast. Mrs. Newman answered her look.

"It's just what I said," she replied. "They are more trouble than they are worth—and the way they *cut*—and then they think about nothing but money!"

Mrs. Lowe turned her rolling gray eyes upon the tailor. He did not look up but he wiped his lip furtively with his sleeve. She stared at him an instant and then her voice came forth filled with righteous anger.

"No," she said. "No. You finish dress all proper with frill, I pay you. No finish dress, no pay. Never. You savee, tailor?"

"Yes, missy," sighed the tailor. All vestige of hope had now disappeared from his face. The atmosphere of supplication died away. A look of cold despair came over his face like a curtain. "I finish to-morrow twelve o'clock, missy," he said and turned away.

"See that you do," shouted Mrs. Lowe triumphantly after him and she watched his figure with contempt as it disappeared into the hall. Then she turned to her caller. "If I say to-morrow," she explained, "perhaps it will be ready by the day after." She thought of something and reaching forward in her chair pressed a bell firmly. The servant appeared.

"Boy," she said, "look see tailor—see he no takee something."

Her loud voice penetrated into the house, and the tailor's body, still visible at the end of the hall, straightened itself somewhat and then passed out of sight.

"You never can tell," said Mrs. Lowe. "You can't tell whether they are making up these stories or not. If they need money—but they always do need money. I never saw such people. They must make a lot, though, sewing for all these foreigners here in the port. But this tailor is worse than most. He is forever wanting money before his work is done. Three separate times he has come and said a child was dying or something. I don't believe a word of it. Probably smokes opium or gambles. They all gamble—you can't believe a word they say!"

"Oh, I know—" sighed Mrs. Newman, rising to depart. Mrs. Lowe rose also.

"After all, one simply has to be firm," she said again.

QUESTIONS

How is the young man characterized in "Name of John"? By his actions, physical details, the subjective reactions of the Wave petty officer, and his talk? How important is his talk and how individual is it? What is his basic trait? If several traits seem important, how closely are they related to each other? Is the talk used in small bits, not long speeches? Is it blended well with other elements? How important is the attitude of the other person in bringing out John's character? Are time, place, and situation well chosen? Are they indicated clearly enough at the beginning? Is the whole unit effective?

In "The Ballet Meister," how is John's entrance prepared for by the talk of others before he comes? Is this talk adapted to the writer's whole artistic aim? Is John skillfully introduced, by his talk, his physical appearance, his missing the step, his failure to realize that he has his glasses on? Why is he telling stories of his past accomplishments? Where is his own realization that he is going blind made clear to us? How is author comment used in the beginning, through the unit, at the end? Is this comment effective?

In "The Frill," who is made the dominant character? Why? What attitude do Mrs. Lowe and Mrs. Newman have in common? How do they differ in their ability to express this attitude? How are they contrasted in physical appearance, in their talk? Is the native tailor skillfully introduced? Do his actions and appearance, before he speaks, create an attitude in the reader? What details? Why? When the tailor and Mrs. Lowe disagree on the details of their previous talk about the collar, which one do you believe? Why? What final insult does Mrs. Lowe offer the tailor? How does he react? Where is the writer's sympathy throughout, with the tailor or with the two women? Do you as a reader develop the same sympathy? Why? How does the writer use details of talk, action, and physical appearance for each of the three characters to establish this sympathy? If this were the complete unit instead of the first scene of a story, would Mrs. Lowe's last comment be an effective conclusion? Why?

ADDITIONAL HELPS

1. Watch yourself through one day, or only one hour if you have many conversations on specific subjects or for definite reasons. In each talk what is your attitude to the situation or your inner reaction to the other person—friendliness, antagonism, superiority, humility, fear, awe, amusement, an emotional distaste unsupported by logic? What is the attitude of the other person to you?

2. Listen to three or four conversations between two people, preferably ones in which you have no part. In one conversation at least, close your eyes or turn your back and listen. In others, watch and listen. Would you use selection and arrangement if you were writing about this talk, or would you transfer it to paper without change? Can you find some center of interest in each talk?

3. Characterize briefly *one* person by writing a *dialogue* between him and one other person. Use talk only, without setting, action, or any explanations. Realize the attitude of each character and make the talk of each one individual, but emphasize one character. Use a specific aim in the talk: one person wishes to give or to get information, to ask a favor, to offer a favor, etc.

4. Rewrite the preceding scene, expanding background, action, thoughts. Keep one character as the dominant one, bringing out by suggestion his basic trait and your attitude to him.

5. Write another scene in which you emphasize a basic trait of a character and suggest your attitude to him through a scene in which he is talking with another person. Visualize the scene fully, including time, place, action, the reason and subject for the talk, etc. Start, perhaps, by letting one character ask another a simple question: "How's your cold today?" "Did you get question number four in today's assignment?" "What did you think of the quiz program on TV last night?" "Did you have a good time at the dance last night?"

6. Choose one of your favorite short stories, preferably one with much conversation. At what points in the story is talk used most?

Where is it most effective? Is it individual? Is it used in great blocks or in small bits? Is it used alone or blended with setting and action? Is it well selected and well arranged? Does it really help in characterizing people? If so, select two or three of the best examples of character suggestion through talk. Does it advance action? Does it suggest attitudes? Does it do several of these things at once?

7. Analyze the talk in some novel that you consider an excellent one—or at least in two or three scenes of that novel. Where is it most effective? Why? Where is it least effective? Why?

10

Character:

MONOLOGUE AND SOLILOQUY

The terms *monologue* and *soliloquy* may be applied to short units which emphasize character, to short units with other aims, and to short stories. The monologue is often used as a device for telling a complex short story, and the soliloquy is occasionally used in the same way. In this chapter the discussion will be concerned entirely with their use in short units for character. Later, if you wish and if your material is appropriate, it will be possible for you to use either one in telling a well-developed story.

Considering both of them, then, as units emphasizing character, a monologue is a composition in which a speaker (at a certain time and place, in a specific situation, and with one or more listeners) reveals himself by his own talk. Sometimes the writer adds a few brief explanations, like the stage directions in drama; sometimes the listener as well as the speaker is characterized. But the chief aim usually is to emphasize the speaker, and the chief means is entirely or almost entirely the talk of the speaker. When you read a monologue you are like a person listening to a skillfully guided telephone conversation. You hear one person in a two-sided talk; you realize by implication some comments of the other person, perhaps his character, his attitudes, and the situation. The main elements of the usual monologue are *speaker*, *listener*, the *situation* or *circumstances*, the *time*, and the *place*. Though the implications of a monologue are often or even usually subjective, the talk is an objective technique.

A soliloquy, as distinguished from a monologue and as discussed in this chapter, differs in having no listener. Though the main character in a monologue is a speaker, the main character in a soliloquy is an emotional thinker, not a thinker in the philosophical or scientific sense, but one who lives an experience within himself. Hence the technique is subjective.

PLANNING YOUR MONOLOGUE

If you wish to write a monologue you will choose a *speaker* or main character who reveals himself well by his talk, not one whom you could show better by his physical appearance, clothing, gestures, movements, or moody silences. You will need to understand this character fully, as if you had him under a giant microscope powerful enough to lay bare not only his physique, but also his emotions and his thoughts. You will become conscious of your attitude, which will give flavor to your unit. You will choose a basic trait to guide your planning. If your character is complex, you need not make him lifeless by eliminating all other traits; instead, make the basic trait serve you like a dominant color in a design or a main motif in a symphony.

You will choose a *listener* to help your character reveal himself. If your aim is to show how your main character browbeats inferiors, you will provide him with an inferior. If you wish to emphasize his obsequiousness to superiors, you will put him with a superior. If your speaker is to reveal his unsuspected depths, his listener must be one who would move him to self-revelation.

You will choose a *situation*, with circumstances which will bring out the speaker—a crisis, perhaps, when he is surprised, caught off guard, tempted strongly, irritated, pleased, or frightened beyond his usual self-control. This crisis may be an intangible one which you make tangible by talk. If your character is forced to a decision which seems small yet determines his whole future, if he must act to save his pride or his reputation, you have a sufficient situation. Again, trifles may serve to bring out traits which are anything but trifles. You need not develop the situation into a complex plot now;

you may perhaps show character better by leaving the problem unsolved.

You will choose carefully a *time* when your character can reveal himself best. Though a certain time of year or day or night may seem unimportant, you give flavor to your writing by such specific choices. As your character talks, the change of time from dawn to daylight, sunset to darkness, calm to storm, may help direct his talk, giving it an authentic background. Or weather may be useful because it heightens the mood of your character by likeness or contrast. Your character may talk at a time of national calamity, at a family crisis, at a personal crisis. The amount of time in your monologue is only the number of minutes required for your character to speak the words you give him, but as he talks, of course he may hope and remember.

You will choose a *place*. It will perhaps follow naturally from your decisions about the other elements in your monologue. It may be the habitual surroundings of your character, the place where you like to watch him, the place where he is most himself, the place where he tends to free himself from inhibitions, or a strange place to which he cannot adjust. In any choice, you will relate your place to your artistic aim, and you will also correlate carefully your *speaker*, *listener*, *time*, *place*, and *situation*.

DIFFICULTIES OF THE MONOLOGUE

You will probably discover that writing a good monologue is difficult. Why? First, you must know many things well: speaker, listener, time, place, situation. Second, you must have the important details completely fused, so that they will pervade the whole unit, becoming a natural part of the talk. In any good writing you need to plan and then to create an emotionalized unit, unless you already have the power to combine the two processes quite spontaneously; but in a monologue especially you will need the help of careful planning. Of course your scene will not remain rigid as you write. You will add, enrich, select, because your material is growing, but you will not shift from mere restlessness or from a lack of something to say. Third, you have a more highly specialized job of selection in the monologue. After you have fused your chosen details, you must select from the talk of only one person the details which will suggest the essentials. Hence you must blend and arrange your details with great skill. But though it is not easy to write monologue, it is not too difficult if you really wish to develop skill in writing.

You may overcome some of the difficulties by using a foundation of reading to stimulate your *creation*, not your *imitation*. Besides the selections in this chapter, look up other Browning monologues, such as "Fra Lippo Lippi," "Andrea del Sarto," "The Bishop Orders His Tomb," or read modern monologues, such as "Haircut," by Ring Lardner, "The First Short Dress," by Huguette Garnier,[1] and "All Around the Town," by Stephen Vincent Benét. When you read a monologue, discover the writer's artistic aim and his reasons for his choice of listener, time, place, and situation. In your writing you may begin with rather simple situations, as long as you find something individual to say, to bring out their full significance. In Additional Helps at the close of this chapter you will find some suggestions about subjects.

PLANNING YOUR SOLILOQUY

Since the soliloquy is like a monologue without any listener, you are ready to apply to it most of the suggestions from the preceding discussion and to consider other suggestions. A soliloquy should not be harder for you to write than a monologue, but the soliloquies written by college students are often ineffective. Two reasons stand out. First, soliloquies bog down in the subjective, turning into mental abstractions; second, the talk seems unnatural.

The cure for floundering in the subjective is a clear perception of the objective—a creation which uses many kinds of specific details. First, you can *know* your character—his physical appearance, his mind, his emotions—and you can use this knowledge as a foundation for specific details. You can know the *time*, the *place*, the *situation*, with the attendant circumstances, the complete surroundings, even the weather, with all its changes as the soliloquy proceeds, the little noises which please or annoy the chief character, the comforts or discomforts he feels, the movements of other

---

[1] Alys Eyre Macklin, *Twenty-Nine Tales from the French*, Harcourt, Brace & Company, 1922.

people about him—all these things you can know with authentic accuracy. After all, you are either observing or creating these details. You can use your character's physical movements. You can give him a pattern of action, combining the subjective with the objective. You can use some of his thoughts about his past and his future. You can realize sharply the difference between his opinion of himself and the opinion which you convey to your readers. You can change his conflicts from vague debates about right and wrong to specific struggles; for example, shall I conceal that five-dollar bill I found, when I feel sure it is Joe's; shall I copy that chemistry problem instead of working it myself? If he is trying to decide or to accomplish something, you can give him a deadline; for example, it may be a half-hour till dinner, when his friend will ask him what he has decided.

The cure for unnatural talk may not be so simple. Perhaps any soliloquy seems a little strained to you; your friends do not go around talking aloud, and you might be startled if you caught yourself forming the habit. This unnatural quality of the talk may disappear as your words become specific. But if you wish to write a soliloquy and the talk refuses to become natural, write it in the *third person*. W. W. Gibson's poem, "The Shaft," has an effective use of the third person:

> He must have lost his way somehow. 'Twould seem
> He'd taken the wrong turning back a bit
> After his lamp . . . or was it all a dream
> That he'd nigh reached the cage—his new lamp lit
> And swinging in his hand, and whistling, glad
> To think the shift was over . . .[2]

To change this poem to the first person apparently weakens it:

> I must have lost my way somehow. 'Twould seem
> I took the wrong turning back a bit
> After my lamp . . . or was it all a dream
> That I'd nigh reached the cage—my new lamp lit
> And swinging in my hand, and whistling, glad
> To think the shift was over . . .

[2] W. W. Gibson, *Collected Poems*, The Macmillan Company, 1925. Used by permission of the publishers.

Whether you write a monologue or a soliloquy, you are concerned with a character, a situation, a time, and a place; if you try a monologue you are concerned also with a listener. In either you will blend these elements into a scene, an experience fused by your mind, senses, and emotions. You have a challenge to a difficult job but a chance to achieve dramatic power.

WRITING YOUR COMPOSITION

Choose one of these assignments, the one best adapted to the material you wish to use:

A. Plan and write a monologue to emphasize the character of the speaker, including his basic trait and your attitude to him. Analyze the character of your listener also and adapt the talk to his attitudes and reactions. Choose carefully your time, place, and situation. Know well the whole drama implied in your material and the tension between your characters, if there is tension. Write with selection, using the fewest and the most powerful details for good communication of your artistic aim.

B. Plan and write a soliloquy in either the first or the third person, whichever will serve best your material and your artistic aim. Choose your time, place, and situation carefully, so as to give some tangible quality to the talk; if possible, let your character be doing something or watching action in which he is vitally concerned, so that his thinking will be specific, not abstract. Emphasize the character of your soliloquizer, and use his mood or his reactions to a personal problem if these details will help to characterize him.

C. Plan and write another monologue in which the speaker emphasizes the listener by the way he talks to him, instead of emphasizing himself.

TESTING AND REVISING

When your composition has been written and put aside for a time, test it by any appropriate suggestions given you for earlier assignments, and by these questions:

1. Have you emphasized one character, his basic trait, and your attitude to him?

2. Have you succeeded in making your prospective reader admire, dislike, sympathize with, feel sorry for, or laugh at this character?

3. Have you used talk effectively, so that it sounds like your character?

4. Is the talk adapted to time, place, situation, and listener?

5. Is the whole unit concise and powerful?

READING

KIVER *

Esther S. Warner

No more feelin' out of them old legs than ef they belonged to some one else, 'cepting when he sat too long, and pinpricks chased through the skin like pieces of sharp sand blown into him. He'd have to heave himself up and shake that stinging sand out of his flesh or the old posts wouldn't hold him a'tall.

Gettin' hard to get up, too. All sixty years layin' heavy on him like layers of soggy leaf-mould, weightin' down the red undersoil heavier every fall.

Knee j'int crackin'? No, musta been the splints squeakin' in the rocker seat. Glad to be shed of the weight o'him, was it?

Wild air gusted through the cracks in the cabin wall, and chased blue-bitter smoke out of the back log to make him cough. Savannah'd always chinked the gaps tight before leaf-fallin'—till this time. Now she was sleepin', down under the yellow maple leaves— he'd wager she fancied the way the wind rustled and stirred them over her. Mayhap the sap tumblin' down with fright of the cold w'd tell her how empty he felt, startin' t'winter without her.

Reckon she'd grieve big if he sold the Kiver for medicine-money? Couldn't wait till green-up time for the maple buds to give him her say. 'Tw'd be too late come sap-risin'!

If he just had the bitter stuff in the brown bottles, it might keep his old ticker spurtin' blood through him till spring. Leastways, 'twould take the edge off the pains that came rantin' fury-hot through his chest and eased out again through the ribs under his shoulder blades after they'd got him weak and tremblin'; and his forehead covered with dew beads from the hurt of it.

The Kiver—he'd spread it out on the bed so he could see it all. Whig Rose, it was. He'd never forgit the look of it ef he never saw it again. He could even remember how it looked stretched in the loom years ago, with Savannah bent over it, hummin', and watchin' it grow as she worked. She'd just laughed about her fingernails bein' blue-rimmed all winter from the indigo vat where she'd dyed the wool. Trim, she was, and shy like the wood things—just a mite of a bride, and him proud as ever of her.—He'd lie down a while under the Kiver and think of Her.

Before the last medicine'd given out—that he'd bought with money from sellin' their old cherry table—he'd been able to sleep more, and he'd dreamed he and Savannah were lyin' snug and happy down there under the maple's heart, wrapped together close and warm with the Kiver. What would She think if he came down to rest beside her, without it? 'Twould be tradin' part of Her for a little ease.

Better for him to let the medicine go. He could get some one to bring him in some spice bush twigs to chew. 'Twould take his mind off'n the pain, when it set him quiverin', to bite hard, and taste the cinnamoned juice flowing out on his tongue from the crushed bark.

He'd given her spice bush twigs to mash with her teeth that night long since when the wind had howled so, and the Least One was born. Her pain was too great, and she'd bit her knuckles till the blood spurted out, sickening him, and at last, he'd thought of the spice twigs. When it was all over, he'd covered the two of them with the Kiver. Funny how the feel of it against his face took him back to those long-ago things.

Seemed like the light was dim in the cabin. Funny! He'd thought it only past noon-time—the shadow of the window frame was dark, but it did lay just where the worn corner of the cherry table used to be. He'd get up and brew some sassafras bark d'rectly, but first he'd rest a bit. He was tired, so heavy-tired.

'Twas good to waller down in the corn-shuck mattress—the husks rattled like dry maple leaves—and feel the wool of the Kiver. Chill was in the room, and 'twas getting 'most as duskfilled as the barn-shed loft.

And the indigo wheels—blue agin the lamb-white of the Kiver—why, they'd come to be nought but dark patches, treebark color, restin' on gray.

And them sheets of light in the fer corner, slidin' through where the logs gap after fallen chinking,—not golden with dust specks jiggin' in them like they was—just gray streaks in a room getting cave-dark.

'Twas gathering thick, and moss-soft, this noon-day blackness, like the deep night that filled the hollow, ridge-high. 'Twas good to let it close over him.

HYMN OF HATE *

John Fogelson

Fifth round, fill-in bout, Rainbow Gardens. David Aaron versus Casmir Dublinsky.

Brring, goes the bell.

"Davey, you got him," said the trainer. "Finish it this round."

Up on your feet, then across the ring—you Polack louse, I got you. Bounce a little, look like you've just started and are good for another eight rounds. He comes out of his corner. Jab a straight left, another, more. Now retreat to the center of the ring, make him follow; get under the big, hot lights right in the center of the ring. Maybe someone *big* wants a good boy to manage. Who's better than you—no one. Left, feint with the right, a left hook. Now work on his guts. Feint left, throw a straight right, bend from the knees so it goes between the elbows. Under the heart, good place; grunt, you Polish pig. I'll kill you if you last the whole fight; I hope you do. I could have finished it last round; your right was down and your shoulder sagged. I'm close for some body work, a left under the ribs and toward the side, a right under the heart. A right that starts from the fist, goes up the back, and makes you feel the jar in your wrist and shoulder. Back off; it's only the first minute and his eyes are staring. Stand and fight, you drek—try a fold and I'll catch and foul you. A little more body work, you persecuting blond pig. Some in your kischkiss? You'll love 'em, no ribs to get in the way. Grunt, you blood-sausage, pork-eating pig; we've almost two minutes left. Let go—let me up, will you, you son of filth. Ouch, your forehead in my eye—try my shoulder under your chin. Wait till the referee parts us and you're done. Now, Polack, we'll go on the ropes, heh? Two straight lefts, a right cross. We're there, my Casmir; I can hold you till I'm done—you dirty, jew-baiting, **blond swine. Push my brother's nose in the spokes of a moving** bicycle wheel; take this right, slime. Chase us, yelling, run, sheeny, run? Another one or two; one low, one high. Stand up, pig, lean on those ropes—If I can keep hitting you fast enough you won't fall. On the side of the head and straight to the mouth. I won't want your head or gums tomorrow, Casmir. Take some more—you blond, white, pudding-faced pig. Wait for my brother after school, feel up my sister on the el train? Look at me out of your glazed, blue eyes, pig. You're not seeing anything, are you? Throw snow balls at my old man and holler kike; through your teeth will come hissing, you Polish slime. Stand, lovely Casmir, only a little to go. Too bad we're so soon before the main bout; maybe boos for me and cheers for you from a larger crowd would have made a man of you. You've fallen, swine. Shall I stand here so they can't start counting, and hope you get up? No, I've a date later on, and there are always other pigs to schlag. Remember me, Casmir, 'cause I'll never forget you.

MY LAST DUCHESS

Robert Browning

That's my last Duchess painted on the wall,
Looking as if she were alive. I call
That piece a wonder, now: Frà Pandolf's hands
Worked busily a day, and there she stands.
Will't please you sit and look at her? I said
"Frà Pandolf" by design, for never read
Strangers like you that pictured countenance,
The depth and passion of its earnest glance,
But to myself they turned (since none puts by
The curtain I have drawn for you, but I)
And seemed as they would ask me, if they durst,
How such a glance came there; so, not the first
Are you to turn and ask thus. Sir, 't was not
Her husband's presence only, called that spot
Of joy into the Duchess' cheek: perhaps
Frà Pandolf chanced to say "Her mantle laps
Over my lady's wrist too much," or "Paint
Must never hope to reproduce the faint

Half-flush that dies along her throat": such stuff
Was courtesy, she thought, and cause enough
For calling up that spot of joy. She had
A heart—how shall I say?—too soon made glad,
Too easily impressed; she liked whate'er
She looked on, and her looks went everywhere.
Sir, 't was all one! My favour at her breast,
The dropping of the daylight in the West,
The bough of cherries some officious fool
Broke in the orchard for her, the white mule
She rode with round the terrace—all and each
Would draw from her alike the approving speech,
Or blush, at least. She thanked men,—good! but thanked
Somehow—I know not how—as if she ranked
My gift of a nine-hundred-years-old name
With anybody's gift. Who'd stoop to blame
This sort of trifling? Even had you skill
In speech—(which I have not)—to make your will
Quite clear to such an one, and say, "Just this
Or that in you disgusts me; here you miss,
Or there exceed the mark"—and if she let
Herself be lessoned so, nor plainly set
Her wits to yours, forsooth, and made excuse,
—E'en then would be some stooping; and I choose
Never to stoop. Oh sir, she smiled, no doubt,
Whene'er I passed her; but who passed without
Much the same smile? This grew; I gave commands;
Then all smiles stopped together. There she stands
As if alive. Will 't please you rise? We'll meet
The company below, then. I repeat,
The Count your master's known munificence
Is ample warrant that no just pretence
Of mine for dowry will be disallowed;
Though his fair daughter's self, as I avowed
At starting, is my object. Nay, we'll go
Together down, sir. Notice Neptune, though,
Taming a sea-horse, thought a rarity,
Which Claus of Innsbruck cast in bronze for me!

QUESTIONS

Is "Kiver" a third-person soliloquy? Would the first person be more or less effective here? What specific decision is the main character making? How does he decide? Why? What memories of his past are used? What trait or attitude causes him to make his decision? What is implied in the conclusion by the dim light and the darkness? Is the conclusion effective?

Is "Hymn of Hate" a monologue? A soliloquy? Who is the main character? What do you learn about his past, his motives, his attitude to his opponent? Does the writer blend successfully the subjective feelings and the immediate, objective events?

In "My Last Duchess," who is the listener? Who is the speaker and what is the real motive? Do you think that the speaker succeeds in his aim? Why does he say to his listener at the close, "Nay, we'll go together down, sir"? Is it a gesture of friendliness, or a desire to keep the man from talking to the Count privately first? How is the Duke characterized by his attitude to the art he owns? By the difference in his attitude to the picture of his Duchess and the Duchess in real life? Why does he resent her enjoyment of the sunset, of flowers, of the mule she rode? What does he reveal about himself when he says that she seemed to thank people as if she ranked any gift with his own gift to her of "a nine-hundred-years-old name"? Do you accept his attitude to his Duchess or do you form your own conclusion? What possible meanings could he have when he says that he gave commands, "Then all smiles stopped together"? Does he intend this as a mere fact or an insinuation about the conduct he expects from his new wife-to-be, the Count's daughter? What basic trait does the Duke reveal about his own character? Even though you do not expect to write in blank verse, does the Browning monologue stimulate your thinking about possibilities with the prose monologue?

ADDITIONAL HELPS

Analyze rather fully the details in one monologue, perhaps "My Last Duchess." Try to determine why the writer has made his choices of listener, situation, time, and place, or at least what effect he would get by changing any of these in certain specific ways. What is the writer's attitude to his main character? Is the talk in the monologue diffuse or concise, and how does your own method of writing dialogue compare with it?

If you feel uncertain about subjects, try some of these as practice work, or change these general situations into specific details from your experience:

1. A person who tries to hide a real opinion or a feeling.
    a. One who succeeds.
    b. One who fails.
    c. One who thinks he succeeds but doesn't.
    d. One whose motive is selfish.
    e. One whose motive is unselfish.
2. A person who feels inferior to another.
    a. For a good reason.
    b. For no good reason.
    c. For a reason but without realizing himself that his uneasy feeling is a sense of inferiority.
    d. One who struggles to overcome the uneasy feeling and succeeds.
    e. One who struggles to overcome it and fails.
3. A person meeting the disapproval of another person.
    a. An outspoken disapproval.
    b. An unspoken disapproval.
    c. A person who yields fully to the disapproval.
    d. A person who defies fully the disapproval.
    e. A person who yields within but continues to act defiant.
4. A person defending himself against some accusation.
    a. A spoken accusation from another person.
    b. An unspoken accusation from another person.
    c. An inner accusation.
5. A person who is triumphing over another.
    a. One who rejoices but conceals his rejoicing.
    b. One who flaunts his victory.
    c. One who is generous and modest.
6. A person who tries to persuade another to do something contrary to his convenience, to his disposition, or to his principles.
7. A person who tries to persuade himself to do something against his real interests or against his principles.
8. A person reporting his interview for a position—one who is
    a. Reticent because he realizes his own deficiencies.
    b. Unhappy because he is competent to fill the position but realizes that his appearance or some other factor which he cannot control will prevent his appointment.

    c. Boastful when he has little to boast about.
    d. Boastful when he really did make a good impression.
    e. Modest.
9. A person who feels superior to another
    a. For no good reason.
    b. For a good reason but one which he is modest about.
10. A girl who is questioned about whether she had a good time at the party.
    a. She is modest but had a very happy time.
    b. She is boastful.
    c. She is jealous of another girl for some specific reason, and this jealousy colors all her remarks.
    d. She is conscious for the first time of her deficiencies.

11

Organic Plot:
CHARACTER STORY

Perhaps you are one of those students who say, "I couldn't write a good story, I'm afraid; I'm no good at making up plots." If you make such a remark, you are probably thinking of plot as a complex structure to be evolved from thin air, completed, and then given to a group of characters. Such a plot would hinder or even defeat your effort to express your experience.

WHAT PLOT IS

A good plot is called organic because it evolves from your material and thus it lives and grows. It is usually simple. You start with a character who has your interest and understanding. You put him in a situation which stimulates him to act in accordance with his basic trait. You give him obstacles to overcome, so that he has time to think and feel, while the reader has time to taste the significance of his actions. You cannot make a good story out of reflex action or out of an accident that gives your character no time to struggle. But when you have a character and a situation, your plot develops naturally from your character's efforts to handle his situation.

In any plot, your character struggles against some obstacle or opposing force. Life furnishes many possible obstacles. A man may struggle against inanimate or animate nature, like fire or flood, or tigers or bears. If a man meets a bear who is not hungry and if he does not irritate the bear, he may escape without a struggle; or if he has no desire to save himself from being eaten, there is no struggle. A man may struggle against other men or women. He may struggle against people organized in the social, political, or economic groups which we call society. He may struggle against an environment. He may struggle because there are conflicting desires in himself. As presented by some writers, he may struggle against larger forces personified as Satan and God, or described as moral law.

Whatever a character opposes in his struggle, your interest as a thoughtful reader is captured by character or meaning, not by objective events alone. You are saying, perhaps half-consciously, "How will the character work out this problem? How will he take that defeat? Um! This is serious. I hope he succeeds." But though you are interested in character, your hopes and fears are doubled because a character is acting, trying to do something significant.

If your narrative is worth while, plot is the least important of the four main elements: plot, setting, theme, and characters. Any narrative must have setting—a time and place where people act, with a mood, perhaps, and a social background. It must have actors, usually people. Any good narrative has theme: meaning significance, artistic purpose. Sometimes the theme is a basic trait of a character, sometimes a fully emotionalized idea, sometimes a mood; but always the theme dominates other things. A story with meaning exists for its theme. The plot is merely its skeleton, attractive when clothed with flesh and blood. Plot is merely the servant of the theme, but a very useful servant.

WHY USE PLOT?

If plot is the least important of the four elements in narrative (except in the detective story or the story of pure adventure), why should you use it? It is true that much excellent contemporary writing is plotless; its aim is to present vividly a moment or moments of experience for their own sake. It is certainly true that authentic experience without plot is better than lifeless material carefully plotted.

Why, then, should you use plot? First, activity is more interesting than inactivity; even a man who starts digging a hole attracts a crowd. Second, plot gives you a tangible framework for your intangible material and, in the end, makes your writing easier. Third, plot will probably help you to write with more power—if you have the courage *to shape action from your material.* Fourth, your mastery of plot is a technique which will help you in future writing. Of course if you can already write powerful units without it, go ahead; you have earned your freedom. But if you need help, plots may guide you to a new stage of confidence.

WHERE YOU WILL USE PLOT

Your composition problem at present is a brief story in which you use plot to bring out character. Later you will develop plot to emphasize mood, and then to communicate a fully emotionalized idea. Each of these compositions may be brief; each will probably be one scene, with no change of time or place. But for each you will use in miniature the skills of the short story; each is an "infant" short story.

After you have completed these three assignments you will plan and write a short story. You will emphasize in it either character, mood, or idea, according to your material and your own preference.

HOW TO BEGIN USING PLOT

As the basis of this assignment you have two assumptions: first, *good plot evolves from the reaction of a character to a situation;* second, *good plot will help you to write with ease and power.*

You will start with one kind of plot, called the accomplishment plot.[1] Probably it is not the *one* way to build a story; perhaps there are a hundred ways. But it is a practical method for a beginner, and it is useful for subjective as well as objective material. You begin with a *character* who confronts a *situation.* He resolves to change his situation, to accomplish some definite thing. His *resolution* is the initial action, starting the movement. He makes a series of efforts to carry out his resolution; these efforts form the body of the story. Finally he comes to a moment when he succeeds or gives up all effort; this is the *climax.* It may serve as the conclusion also,

[1] John Gallishaw, *The Only Two Ways to Write a Story,* G. P. Putnam's Sons, 1928.

or it may be followed by a *formal conclusion* which emphasizes the effect of the climax.

As your character struggles he may make a series of successes. He may make a series of failures, leading to a climax of giving up all effort. He may make efforts which are a mixture of success and failure leading to either kind of climax. Or he may resist stubbornly, step by step, someone else's attempts to stir him into action; and at the climax he may realize that he will never take action about the situation.

You will begin your character story with a person who interests you; you will become conscious of his basic trait. Then you can easily choose a simple situation in which he will act in accordance with that trait. What definite thing will he try to accomplish? The answer to that question is the *resolution* he will make. Will he succeed or fail? The answer will probably be clear at once; it is the climax.

Then you are ready to plan the events between the initial action and the climax—to develop the body of your story. A story which jumps at once from the initial action to the climax is like a human being with legs and arms but no torso. A good story, as you remember, is not a sudden reflex action but a struggle in which your character and your reader have time to savor the experience.

After planning the body of your story, you can begin to determine its emphasis and proportion, to ask yourself, "What are the important moments in my story? Am I giving these moments space, making them active and vivid, perhaps developing them by talk?"

EXAMPLE OF AN ACCOMPLISHMENT PLOT

Suppose that you are interested in a charming young man's lack of responsibility, and you wish to write a little story about him. You make your young man a chairman of ticket sales. To secure unity of time and place, you choose a meeting at which all committee chairmen report to the general chairman. Suppose the young man, Johnny, is called upon to report and says at once: "Mr. Chairman, we planned 250 sales. I am sorry, but we have the cash for only 61." Such a story has no body, no development which allows us to realize its flavor; and Johnny has not acted like a charming, irresponsible person: he has been too direct.

Perhaps you might develop your situation more like this, with Johnny trying to postpone the moment when he must admit the facts:

1. The general chairman, Don Adams, after letting Johnny postpone his report at the beginning of the meeting, comes back to him for a statement on ticket sales.
2. Johnny hedges; he still doesn't have his total, he says.
3. Don asks him how many subchairmen he had.
4. He admits that he had three.
5. Pressed further, he names them.
6. Asked about Bill Jones, he says that Bill sold twenty-five.
7. Asked about the cash, he admits that Bill gave him cash for only twenty.
8. Asked about Ed Wilson, he says that he turned in the cash for twenty—no, eighteen.
9. Asked about John Everett, he says that John reported fifteen sales.
10. He admits that John gave him the cash for only ten.
11. Asked about his own sales, he thinks he will have twenty-five— if a few uncertain fellows decide to go.
12. Questioned again, he admits that he has cash for thirteen from his own sales.
13. He admits that he did agree to have the cash for two hundred today.
14. He admits that he did agree to sell two hundred fifty or more.
15. Finally he says that he has the cash for sixty-one tickets.

Such a list of events furnishes plenty of material for the body of a story; and all the events grow out of Johnny's basic trait, an evasion of responsibility. As the events result from character, you can visualize at the same time details of the character and the actions which make the plot. When you write, you will not need to follow precisely the list of steps in this formal planning; these steps are the mere skeleton of a story. But when the skeleton is articulated, you can give your entire attention to creating *an experience*; you can cover the skeleton with flesh and blood.

You have been thinking of the ticket salesman's story as an outgrowth of Johnny's lack of responsibility. So it is. But it is founded in part upon another trait of character: the firmness of the chairman in bringing out the facts. You will often need to choose your minor character so that he may make an important contribution to your plot.

SUSPENSE

Good suspense in a story is like the tenseness of a football game—a well-blended mixture of hope and fear, until the final whistle blows. If your home team scores three touchdowns in the first quarter and the enemy never threatens your goal, suspense is gone: *you have no fear.* If your enemy scores two or three touchdowns in the first quarter and your team never threatens his goal, suspense is gone: *you have no hope.* But if each team persists in threatening the other's goal and if the score is 7–7 and then 13–13, suspense is good: *hope and fear are balanced.*

In a good game, too, your suspense is increased by knowledge. You know exactly *what* your team is trying to do; you know something about its strength and the strength of your opponents—what games each team has won or lost, whether any important players are out of the game. Your suspense may be increased by prejudices from past knowledge if you are playing a chief rival; or you may know that the result will settle a conference championship. Thus you hope and fear as you know about the game.

Suspense in a good story, as in a good game, is based upon some knowledge. You will increase suspense if you let your reader know at once *what* your character is trying to do, instead of keeping him guessing because you are unconscious of this need or because you cannot make up your own mind. You will increase your suspense if you show a reader almost at once the basic trait of your main character, his handicaps if he has any, and the nature of the opposition. You will greatly increase suspense if you show your reader *why* the outcome of the struggle is important. To conceal such basic information is like keeping a spectator in doubt about whether a team will play football, baseball, or croquet, and not giving him the facts about the opposing teams.

If good suspense is based upon knowledge, it is also based upon an emotional interest. Probably you as a writer need to care about your character. Certainly you need to make your reader care, make him experience your story with his mind, emotion, and senses. The best kind of suspense does not exist until you capture your reader; then it is *born in his mind*.

Good suspense, based upon knowledge and emotional concern, is different from *surprise* and from *curiosity*. Complete surprise results from inadequate information or deceit; it makes a reader feel that he has been cheated or kept outside the writer's confidence. Curiosity is a detached, nonemotional feeling. Though it may be a chief concern in detective stories, it is not sufficient in stories of character.

When your suspense flows throughout your story, your work is active; you have *forward movement*. If you let your reader know what your character is trying to do and persuade him to care about what is going to happen, you have started a forward movement. Your reader will begin to realize, half-consciously perhaps, reactions like these: "So that's what the character wants! Well, he has courage. But he's up against a tough opponent. Well, let's see." As your reader goes on, he realizes each effort of the character as a part of the same movement forward, thinking half-consciously, "Well, he succeeded this time! I believe he'll come through." At the close of the final effort, the reader thinks, "Oh, he's succeeded. That's good. It's what I hoped—but I was never sure." (Of course a reader's reactions are reversed if a character moves steadily to failure.) If your forward movement is good, your reader never forgets your central aim; your minor character contributes to this flow of events; your setting is not obtrusive but appears bit by bit as part of your character's experience; you do not have diversions or huge blocks of explanation, like hunks of undigested food. Instead, your characters explain as they talk and act, and your story is more than a static scene or a series of static scenes. It is one flowing movement.

Forward movement is like a spiral which enlarges as it moves upward. It is like a snowball rolling along the ground, gathering more snow, grass seed, or small sticks and stones. It is like a smooth-flowing river, with no logs or boulders to divert the stream, but only branches and pebbles which the current carries along.

Another way to describe the suspense which is a steady movement through your story is to say that the story has a *single tension* throughout. Your character is trying to do *one* thing, not several things. If your material seems to include several, you will, until you are more skillful, choose the one which is most significant. For example, you are concerned with a self-centered girl who is determined to go to a picnic: she wins her mother's consent to her going, after a struggle; she finally gets some attention from a popular young man at the picnic; afterward, she scores a triumph over another girl who had been interested in the young man. Would you put this material into *one* story or *three* stories? An experienced writer might weave these three struggles into one story. If you are less experienced you may do better to choose the one which is most significant to you and develop it from start to finish with a single tension.

WRITING YOUR COMPOSITION

Plan and write a simple, rather brief story in which you use a conflict developed in a plot, to *emphasize your character.*

First, know your character fully, with your mind, emotion, and senses; know your attitude to him; know his basic trait, as you understand his character; bring him to life for yourself by a complete visualizing, according to the suggestions made in earlier assignments.

Second, choose also a minor character who will help your main character do whatever you have chosen for him.

Third, choose, as usual, a time, a place, weather, all surroundings and circumstances, and a situation which will help you bring out the basic trait of your character.

Fourth, plan a complete but simple little plot which evolves from your character's reaction to his situation. Decide on your character's specific resolution, the forces which oppose him, whether they are inner or outer forces. Decide your climax by finding out which force will win. Plan events in the body, so that hope and fear will interplay; find ways, if it is necessary, to make an inner struggle tangible.

Fifth, when your plot has become a part of your thinking, so that it rests easily in your consciousness, create a unit of imagined experience. Use *all* your senses sharply, even your perception of odors, just as you did in earlier assignments. Return to this created unit at intervals, allowing it to grow each time because your senses set free your emotion and your mind joins in creation. Make this unit vivid and interesting to you, until you enjoy it as if you were living it.

Sixth, write your story, selecting from your emotionalized details and moving concisely to your objective. Stop to visualize again any parts which do not come to life. If the closing sentences give you trouble, visualize them with special care, letting your character act, and knowing what he is going to do next after he vanishes from sight.

TESTING AND REVISING

Test your work, preferably after you have put it aside for a few hours, by asking yourself these questions:

1. Have you used the skills for characterizing which were suggested in earlier chapters? The appearance of the person? His talk? Essential details about the minor character?

2. Have you secured unity through the basic trait of the character and your own attitude to him?

3. Does the main character come to life? Is he an individual as well as a type?

4. Does the action, however simple, flow with a single tension through the whole story?

5. Does your plot really aid your artistic aim, instead of hindering it? Are you using it as if it had evolved naturally from your situation and the basic trait of your character?

READING

SEND ME ORCHIDS * 2
Miriam Clure

The Sugar Bowl was unusually quiet. Most of the stragglers were sitting in the back in little groups of twos and threes, their heads bent over books.

Patsy stood in the front door surveying the scene. "No one here," she thought. She marched up to the counter and perched on one of the stools.

2 This story was written at the University of Iowa in a class conducted by Eric Knight. Then the writer transferred to Iowa State College and offered it for publication in the literary magazine.

"Bottle Coke with lots of ice, Pinky," she called.

She glanced at her reflection in the mirror behind the counter. She wasn't awfully bad looking. Her hair was pretty and thick and her eyes a nice brown. After that—well, her mouth wasn't bad either—when it was closed.

"Did you hear the one about the little boy in church?" she asked Pinky.

"Yah, ages ago," he said.

"How about the one about Little Audrey and the mountain lion?"

Pinky shook his head and set Patsy's Coke in front of her.

"Well, it's the cutest story I've heard for simply ages. In fact it's my prize."

She broke into a gust of too-loud laughter at the prospect of telling it.

The groups in the booth looked up quickly. Two boys sauntered up from the back and leaned against the counter. "Two chocolate sundaes with."

Patsy turned to them grandly.

"Hello, Jim! Hi, Bob! I didn't see you kids back there."

"We've been sort of quiet—studying for a test," Bob explained, ducking his head slightly.

"I was just telling Pinky my prize."

Patsy laughed loudly, and plunged again into the story, punctuating it with anticipatory giggles. Pinky went to wait on the customers in the back booths. Bob and Jim fidgeted uneasily and laughed politely. Patsy was encouraged. She pursued her tale to the bitter end.

"But what could little Audrey do?" she almost screamed, reaching the climax. "After all, he was a great big mountain lion, and she was just a teeny, weeny girl."

Pinky came back. "You make more noise than the cash customers," he said.

Patsy pulled out a wooden cigarette case, and, after toying with it, offered its contents to the boys. They shook their heads. Bob mumbled something about a big test. They hurried to their booth.

Patsy subsided, but brightened again immediately as four girls came in and seated themselves in a row around the counter. Patsy welcomed them warmly.

"Ellen, are you going to the Old Maid's Party Friday?" she asked. She liked conversation to flow.

"Of course! I asked Joe last week. He was thrilled to death. He's going to send me orchids."

"Is he!" Patsy marvelled. "I was talking to him last week and he said he had a date."

Two of the girls glanced at each other and quickly exchanged lights for their cigarettes.

In the long silence that followed Patsy tried to blow smoke rings. Ellen looked up.

"Who are you going to take then, Patsy?"

"Oh, I don't know. Maybe I'll ask Bill Railey or Paul Mallory, or maybe Pete Fields."

"I'm taking Pete," Lucile said quietly. "I've asked him already."

Patsy dropped her eyes. Then she looked up, undaunted. "I got the most wonderful letter from Father today," she said. "He writes the nicest letters I receive. You know he has such a wonderful job now. We're all so proud of him. He says he's making such wonderful plans for us for next year. I think he and Mother should take a trip to Bermuda this winter. He really needs a rest. I wish Father would go into politics. He'd be such a success in it. Father says—"

The four girls were paying their checks now and didn't hear what Father said. But it was all right. Patsy had spotted someone more to her liking.

Elinor Beach and Tom Andrews were coming, hand-in-hand, through the door. Patsy waited until they were seated in a booth. She picked up her Coco-Cola glass and hurried back to them.

Elinor had placed her books beside her in the seat.

"Oh, goody," cried Patsy delightedly. "Now I get to sit by Tom."

Tom moved over in the corner to make more room, but Patsy snuggled up to him. He hoped she wouldn't talk baby-talk as she often did. He remembered that when she did it, she showed her gold fillings. But she was Elinor's friend—

"Are you going to the Old Maid's Party?" Elinor asked Patsy.

"I don't know, yet. I've asked two or three, but they have dates.

The way some girls just rush out and snap up the men! Elinor, why don't you ask someone else so I can take Tom?" Patsy looked up coyly. "Or else maybe both of us can take him. He's so big."

Elinor giggled a little and Tom shifted his weight in embarrassment.

"I'm afraid not. Tom's already ordered me roses."

"I want orchids," Patsy said slowly.

There was a silence in which Elinor and Tom seemed to lapse into their own little world, leaving Patsy an alienated onlooker.

"Jamie Pine, the fellow I'm in love with, is so far away I really don't care whether I go or not." Patsy stole a quick glance upward to see if she were impressing Tom properly.

"He's in Annapolis, you know."

They nodded. They did know.

"This is his second year," Patsy went on. "I think so much about him I haven't time to spend looking around this campus for good dates. And, anyhow, there aren't any—besides you, Tommy. He writes to me all the time. I just live for his letters, they're so wonderful."

"Whom do you think you'll take, then?" Elinor asked.

"I thought maybe I'd ask Paul Mallory or Ray Pamperien. Ray has a swell big car."

"Patsy Burge is taking Ray. And Jeannie Busch—I suppose she and Paul will patch it up and go together."

"Oh, did they have a fight?"

"I don't know—just a spat—so they say."

Elinor looked at Tom, and then back at Patsy.

"Look," she said. "Why don't you ask Harvey Lynch? You know him well—and he isn't dated."

"Oh, he's from home and he can't dance! I want someone exciting."

The crowd was increasing. Three o'clock classes were out. The Sugar Bowl was jammed and everyone was talking at once. Pinky yelled something about less noise, please, and more money.

A crowd of boys were at the counter. Patsy stood up. She saw Paul Mallory.

"Excuse me, I see somebody I want—"

The boys saw her coming toward them. They knew what she

wanted, for they had seen Lucile and Ellen a few minutes before.
Paul Mallory watched her coming. What if Jeannie didn't want
to make up again? Then he really ought to be at that dance just
to show her he didn't care.

But then he saw Patsy coming through the crowd purposefully.

He got up suddenly and pushed to the door. He slacked his pace
as soon as he reached the street. He heard Patsy after him—yet a
fellow couldn't run through the streets. And if he did—Patsy was
the kind that would as soon race after a fellow as not. He heard
her voice.

"Hi—Paul!"

"Why, Pricella!"

He waited.

"How's about draggin' me to the brawl this Friday, Big Boy?"
she asked.

He cleared his throat and then nodded.

"O.K.," he said.

For a second Patsy stood in the sunshine without speaking. She
swallowed twice, and her eyes almost shut in a grimace.

She blew her nose, and when she was through she looked up at
him. Her face wore its usual impervious grin.

"O.K.," she said. "Send me orchids."

BLACK WATER BLUES [3]

Montgomery Culver

His name was Rohrs. They called him the Lion, of course; they
could not be expected to do much else. The name was out there
with the others, on the big poster by the box office: Bump Roxy
and his Famous Blue Band. Featuring Adelia Roxy, Step-Up Tate,
"The Lion" Rohrs.

He sat in front of the dimly lighted hall and chorded lightly
with long knobby fingers on eighty-eight keys. The hall was be-

[3] Copyright, 1950, Ada P. McCormick, Tucson, Arizona. This story won a
first prize in the *Atlantic Monthly* contests for college students, 1948–1949,
when the author was a college senior, and a "First" award in the *Atlantic
Monthly*, 1950. It was selected for *Prize Stories of 1951: The O. Henry
Awards*, and was published in both Swedish and Danish anthologies, 1953.

ginning to fill. Couples straggled through the door, circling timidly around the vastness of the bare dance floor, staring at the young white man who sat on the piano stool. A few were young: tall buck Negroes in high-hitched pants and bulging shoulder pads; girls in gay dresses, giggling up at their grinning escorts. But most of the early comers were the older folks, who came to listen only and not to dance. They came before eight o'clock to get the choice seats underneath or at the ends of the footlights. Often they sat without moving for the whole five or six hours, tapping their shoes along with the big bass, flashing grins that gleamed weirdly in their black and brown faces.

The Lion Rohrs sat alone on the big stage, playing gently, quietly, to the early comers. He had learned that it took the Negroes a little time to get used to the idea of a white man playing in a colored man's band. He usually managed to get up on the stage while the others were unpacking the paraphernalia.

He looked up from the keyboard and into the eyes of a staring young couple across the lights. He grinned at them—a savage grin, a grin of joy born of the chords that chortled under the long hands. And the couple grinned back.

He pressed the loud pedal and did a sudden trick in the bass, watching an older couple sitting near the stage. As they jerked their heads up, he winked at them, into their startled faces, and heard their laughter, clear and relieved.

Tonight a few white men were out there to listen. That would be a nuisance. Bump Roxy hated to play to white men. But there was no sense worrying about it now.

Bump strode from the wings, nodding curtly to Rohrs. Stage-hands followed him on and began setting up the traps on the platform in center stage.

"Here sits the Lion, warmin' up the audience," said Sam Lester. The others straggled in: Hadley the number one horn man, LeRoy Bunner with his guitar, Clarence Jackson, the incomparable Step-Up Tate. Tate and Willis Shepherd stopped beside the Lion. He cocked an eyebrow at them and rolled the treble playfully.

"M-m, mm," Willie sighed. "That Lion, you just never know what he's gonna do next."

"Lion, he don't know what he'll do his damn self." Step-Up chuckled and touched Rohrs lightly on the arm before moving away.

It was funny, the Lion thought, funny how easy it was to get along—with everybody but Bump, at least. All you had to do was smile most of the time and play music all the time. The music was the thing, of course; it sometimes thawed even Bump Roxy's scowling distrust. He had sold himself to Bump by sitting on a piano stool and touching the keys as he talked.

"Man, it wouldn't work," Bump had said. "It wouldn't work at all. I ain't taking on no white man. . . . Man, play some more. Play that damn thing some more."

Rohrs looked up at Bump, sitting up on the high chair behind the traps, the sticks in his hands. Oh, Lord! thought the Lion, for Bump was glaring across the lights at the little knot of white men in the near corner of the floor. Most of them were all right—kids, college kids maybe, who paid their way into a colored dance hall to hear the music they wore out on records. But a couple of them, big smirking men in sport coats, looked mean.

The lights distorted their faces, but Rohrs could see the coats and the sport shirts with the tight-buttoned, long-pointed collars— the uniform of the toughs.

It was bad enough when there were just decent white men out there for Bump to glare at. A couple of mean ones might spoil the whole show. They might make cracks at Adelia, and that would really be something. Bump usually tolerated a white audience, but it was different when his wife came into it. He had raised a lot of sand in St. Louis when a white man had just whistled at his wife. And he had snapped at the Lion for a week afterward.

The Lion watched Bump grip the sticks. Bump Roxy was a great drummer and a great musician. He told them when they overdid it or underdid it; he mapped the order of the solos. He held the band together.

It was worth holding together, the Blue Band. They were one of the few low-down outfits left in the country, perhaps the only great one.

To Rohrs they were a way of life. He had left home to play piano against his family's wishes. When he joined the Blue Band, a year ago, he had written of it to his father. There had been no reply. It hurt him, but there were things a man had to do.

He watched Bump drop his eyes to the drums, touch the sticks to the snare. The muttering roll grew slowly, rising, fading, then higher still. Rohrs, although he had heard the theme a thousand times, held his breath until he heard the alto wail, the shuddering note of Step-Up's break.

It was a loafer for the Lion, nothing but rhythm and a couple of quick breaks. He glared from Adelia's empty chair to the wings, wondering where she was, what the hell she was doing. Bump always got sore when she was late getting on, and Bump would be sore tonight as it was, with those two nasty-looking white fellows out there. Besides, she had to do It Ain't Necessarily So in the first set.

Then, while he worried, Adelia came. She glided out of the shadows of the wings in her bold red gown, dazzling band and audience with her smile. The dance hall sighed.

And she spoiled Bump's big drum break. She walked on and grabbed at the eyes and minds of the audience just when they should have been fixed on the wooden blur over the tom-toms. The Lion thought, I wonder if she did that on purpose.

As she sat down, someone in the white corner whistled. Bump jerked his head up and stared deadpan over the lights. Rohrs heard Clarence Jackson's fingers stumble on the big fiddle.

They played a couple of pops for the dancers, and it was time for It Ain't Necessarily So—the bawl of Hadley's muted trumpet, Lester's slim clear notes on the clarinet. And Adelia with her head bent a little to one side, Adelia calling to the lovers in her husky voice.

When she finished, and the band started another dance tune, she came and stood by the piano. As the saxes played, she leaned down and gave the Lion that brilliant smile.

"How was I?" she asked. "Better than usual?"

"There's nothing better than your usual," he replied, and she laughed and touched his shoulder. Even as she did it, as the brown hand rested there for a second, he saw her eyes flicker over his head, up to Bump on the high chair, looking for a reaction.

Damn it, Rohrs thought, I wish she'd cut that out. He gets sore at me often enough as it is.

Aloud he said, "Why don't you put that thing away?"

"What thing?"

"That needle you're stickin' in him all the time," Rohrs said. She giggled, and he grinned at her. He went on, "No kidding, you better lay off him. There's a couple guys out front he don't seem to like the looks of."

"He just frets about them on account of me," she said. "If he ain't got sense enough to know better, let him worry."

She walked away and sat down in her chair; it stood at the end nearest the white corner, the Lion noticed. He shook his head, worrying.

He had been warned about that situation when he first joined the band. On the night of his first trip with them, he had ridden alone in the coupé with Sam Lester. He had asked questions by the dozen, anything about the band that came into his head. And naturally he asked about Adelia.

"Bump and Adelia married?"

Lester looked sidewise at him. "Yeah, they're married. That's a good thing for you to remember."

"Jesus! Do I look like forgetting it?"

"Lots of white men do," Lester grunted. "Lots of white men come to hear the band try to make her forget it. Lots of colored men, too. We had a horn player once, tried to fool around with Adelia. Bump damn near kill that man. Hard to tell what he'd do to a white man. Damn if I ever want to see."

Rohrs had remembered that. He was friendly when he talked to Adelia, but he only did it when he had to, and he was always careful to avoid giving any impression of talking confidentially to her. Even then, Bump sometimes resented it.

Clarence Jackson once told the Lion that Bump had a sister who ran off with a white man. That would explain a lot. And if Adelia knew that, she ought to have more sense than to dog him all the time.

Another time Step-Up Tate had said, "That man crazy about that woman. He ought to tell her so more often."

The Lion was still thinking about that as they wound up the

fox trot. Bump Roxy shoved a handkerchief across his scowling face. He sat staring at the drums.

Rohrs was suddenly concerned. Bump always wanted to play loud when he was mad; he liked to hit the drums as he would hit the heads of the whistling white men; he liked to hear the horns open up and blast, maybe blow the leering faces off the floor.

That was all right, but they weren't in shape to blast. It was nine o'clock and they had nothing but a few dance numbers behind them. They would blow their brains out on anything like High Low Jack or Shattered Slumber. . . .

Bump lifted his head and called it. "Shattered Slumber."

The Lion said, "Hold it now." He slid off the stool, grinning, seeing the startled faces of the band staring up at Bump. When he stood by the drums, he said, "Man, you know better than that."

"Goddamn it, Lion. . . ."

"Man, it ain't ready, it ain't ripe," the Lion went on. "We ain't ready and the audience ain't ready. You got to build up to a thing like that. You know that." It was true; the boys would kill themselves and the audience wouldn't give a damn.

"That's right, Bump," Sam Lester said. "You know that."

"I figured it was Lion's time," Bump said lamely. There was a long piano solo in Shattered Slumber. "I figured it was Lion's time for a big one. Everybody else had one."

"Crosstown, then," said the Lion. "Crosstown, if it's my time. It's too early for the other."

Bump's face was sullen. Rohrs grinned at him and said confidentially, "Man, we can't all warm up as quick as you do."

He walked away, chuckling at the relief in the faces of Hadley and Step-Up, winking at Willie Shepherd. He wondered how mad Bump would be.

They played the Crosstown Blues. Nobody would ruin himself on melancholy Crosstown, but it was something, just the same.

The horns started: Hadley, Step-Up, and Lester, in turn, wailing the mournful one-bar phrase, then together. They held one, cut it off.

The Lion broke, with tingling chords.

He talked to Step-Up for a while, piano and sax alternating and then mixing in dialogue. There were little appreciative chortles from the faces that crowded each other and peered over the edge of the stage.

The horns swept it up again and carried a chorus, fading, dying into silence. Bump took a rimshot. The Lion rolled one, high on the keyboard, held it, did tricks with it. He broke it, walked his hand down the board. With the left he reached deep down for the boogie bass.

A Negro bellowed throatily. The bass thundered in the great hall, striding up and down the scale, pacing the keys fitfully. The treble clashed.

They said that the Lion had it; everyone who knew, who had ever heard him, said so. He had the touch, they said: the touch of the great ones that had gone before; the touch that twitched the muscles and boiled the blood. There is music that can grow only of the love of music, and its greatest and supreme thrill is in its playing. This the Lion knew.

He gave it back to the horns, and the yells at the solo's end drowned even the trumpet.

He wiped sweat from the corners of his eyes and swiveled on the stool to watch the boys finish it up.

As his head swung, he saw the ugly smiles on the faces of the two white men who stared up at Adelia.

It was midnight, fourth intermission time. The Lion, alone, leaned against the wall outside the stage door and watched the rain drizzling into the alley. It pattered in the puddles and dribbled from the roof's edge over his head. He knew that the puddles were dirty, black with the soot and grime of the mill town, and he grinned, singing his song to himself.

> I wake up in the morning
> Black water drippin from the eaves
> I wake up in the mornin
> Black water drippin from the eaves
> It's runnin in the gutters
> Soakin down the grass and leaves

Bump Roxy said, "Move youh goddamn chair!"
The Lion jerked away from the wall. The voice was so close

that he was sure it spoke to him, but when he looked around the edge of the door he saw Bump and Adelia in the tiny vestibule.

"What you talking about?" said Adelia.

"You hear what I say. I say move that goddamn chair!"

"Why should I?"

"You know why. You know I don't like them men lookin' at you," Bump said. His fingers clenched.

"What harm that do you?"

"That's all right. I don't like the way you look at them, either!"

"How can you tell how I look when you sittin' up there behind me?" Adelia was angry now, Rohrs realized. "You talk like you crazy. In the first place, I move my chair, those men move right with me if they want to. In the second place, I can't move my chair anywhere without sittin' right in front of somebody. You must be out youh head."

She stalked back toward the stage. Bump, following, yelled, "And stay away from that goddamn Lion, too!"

Rohrs shook his head. He thought of Step-Up saying, "Crazy about her. Ought to tell her so more often." He shrugged and walked back to the stage, flopping his hands loosely from the wrists, wriggling and drooping the fingers, trying to relax them. The last set was coming up.

The last set was the big one. It was mostly their own stuff, and it was all what they loved to play. The fox-trotters had heard their last ballad, and they knew it; they moved from the edges of the hall and crowded toward the stage.

The last set had Shattered Slumber—the shouting horns, the thunder of the drums, the hilarious vocal dialogue between Jackson and Shepherd. The last set had Basement Stuff, and High Low Jack, and Adelia singing the haunting Ride On. The crowd gulped it and howled for more. They groped over the edge of the stage with their hands, trying to pull more music from the grinning, sweating players.

Bump did a specialty, Rohrs turned and watched admiringly. That man is great, he thought, great enough that this white-audience business is going to hurt him some day. . . .

It was time for Adelia's last song. Hadley stood up and scatted it, and the bawl of the trumpet filled the hall, made the Lion shiver. And Adelia sang.

> Some day he'll come along,
> The man I love . . .
> And he'll be big and strong,
> The man I love . . .

The guitar carried the accompaniment alone, and the Lion had turned to look. Oh, Jesus! he thought. . . .

She was singing it at the toughs, at the two leering white men who stood directly below her. She swayed her body, and smiled and flicked her eyes at the two men.

This is going to be bad, the Lion thought as he had to swing back to the piano. This is going to be hell.

And when, at the end of the number, he fearfully turned again, what he saw was so unexpected that he literally rubbed his eyes and looked again.

The two men were gone.

He didn't have much time to wonder about it. Bump called them into a huddle. He was wet all over; he wiped his eyes and cheeks as he talked. "Now Black Water," he said hoarsely. "Black Water, and then we got to slack it off. We got to tone it down or they'll never let us out of here."

Black Water Blues was the Lion's favorite specialty. He had written it himself, and it was a little poetry, and a lot of sadness, and all the old-time blues scheme and rhythm. It was the only thing he ever sang. He was no Cab Calloway, but he carried a tune well enough, and he could put the mourning in his voice.

> Black water is somethin
> Lord that I sure do hate
> Black water is somethin
> That I sure do hate
> Fortune teller told me
> Black water gonna be my fate

He stroked the keyboard and listened to the soft play of the band. The thing was his and theirs at the same time. They had taken it in; they played it happily, lovingly. And the audience strained forward over the lights.

> I wake up in the mornin
> Black water in my bed
> I go to eat my breakfast
> Black water in my bread
> Well I believe
> Believe I better go my way
> Black water gonna haunt me
> Until my dying day
>
> I had myself a woman
> She liked to dress in red
> I found her in black water
> Found her lyin dead
> Well I believe
> Believe I'll go far far away
> Black water gonna dog me
> Until that judgment day

The crowd yelled and clapped. The boys were grinning. Jackson leaned over and hit him on the back. Rohrs gave LeRoy the flat-hand sign of approval for the guitar solo.

It was all good: the joy of playing it and the sadness of hearing it; the way the crowd clapped and the boys grinned.

A stagehand stood in the wings, trying to get Adelia's attention. She heard his whisper and walked to him. He said something, pointing offstage, and she nodded and went off, out of sight.

The Lion watched her go out, wondering.

They played three more, quietly and sweetly, tapering-off tunes to calm the audience so that they could quit. Then it was closing time, theme time, and Adelia had not returned. Bump was scowling again. The Lion shook his head in disgust. She was going too far, not being on stage at theme time.

The drums rolled again, and Step-Up broke. He had finished and Hadley was standing, when the terrified face of the stagehand appeared over the piano.

"Man! Man, there's trouble!" He was almost crying.

"What's wrong?"

"End it! End it, man, quick!"

"Start the curtain down," said the Lion, and called out, in the singsong, syncopated voice that they used for communicating during numbers, "Knock it off, right now! There's trouble brewin'!"

They stared at him, but Hadley cut the solo, and they blew the final blare as the curtain fell.

Then everything happened fast. The stagehand cried out, "I didn't mean nothin'! I didn't know nothin' was wrong!" and the manager, calmer, said, "Mistuh Roxy, I'm afraid youh wife hurt bad."

Then they all charged off and were in time to see two stage-hands carrying Adelia through the hall backstage—Adelia with her red gown torn mostly off, and what was left smeared and dripping with the dirty water from the alley; Adelia crying in little gasps of amazement and horror. . . .

Bump Roxy roared and the stagehand gibbered and the manager soothed; a doctor followed the bearers into a dressing room, and Bump plunged after them.

"Two white men," the guilty stagehand babbled to the frozen band. "Two white men told me ask Mrs. Roxy come out 'n' autograph . . ."

"You know you hadn't ought to do nothin' like that!"

"I didn't know nothin' was wrong! They gimme five dollahs, Jesus I didn't know nothin' was wrong!"

The manager guided him gently away.

There was an old piano in the end of the tiny hallway, near the dressing room door. The Lion sat heavily on the stool. A stack of folding chairs was heaped against the wall; the band opened them and sat down, lined along the hall, waiting for the door to open.

Rohrs was staring at the keyboard when someone touched his arm.

LeRoy Bunner's face was grave. "You better get out of here, man."

The Lion shook his head.

"Lion, you crazy. Don't you know what them men done to Adelia? It ain't gonna be safe out here for no white man."

"You might be right," said the Lion. He touched the keys softly, hit a B-flat chord.

"I tell you that man like to kill somebody," LeRoy said. He looked around for support.

"Let him be," Step-Up said. "The Lion, maybe he know what he's doin!"

"Bump gonna go for the first white man he sees!"

"That's all right," the Lion said. "This way he won't have to go out in the street and chase one." Old Step-Up, he thought, he sees it, he sees it like I do.

He started to play quietly. He took a simple, four-note walking bass figure and worked over it gently, playing sadness. LeRoy looked around, licked his lips, and then sat down.

The Lion played, waiting.

It was for Bump so he wouldn't go raging the streets and get arrested. But it was for more than that; Rohrs knew it and Step-Up had seen it. It was for the great Bump Roxy, who might never be able to face another white audience if this wasn't handled right. It was for the music; for Crosstown and Shattered Slumber, and the Black Water Blues that might never be played again; for the grins and flat-hand signs when they finished one. It was for Adelia, and for himself. It was for Bump Roxy and his Blue Band.

He did not look up when the door opened and the footsteps came out slowly and then stopped. He heard Bump move toward him, felt him standing directly behind. He made himself stay loose when the huge hand touched his shoulders and the back of his neck.

The hand did not move; it lay there gently. He did not let himself sigh; he sat and played the blues. He did not look up even when the hand began to tremble and he heard the ugly, harsh sobs.

The chords rippled the stillness of the room.

QUESTIONS

What is the basic trait of Patsy in "Send Me Orchids"? What specific thing is she trying to accomplish in this story? Is Patsy's behavior here unusual for her, or is it merely one specific instance of a usual pattern? Does the slow beginning justify itself? Why? In spite of unity of focus, how is Patsy's appearance brought in? What two-edged implication appears in her thought, "Her mouth wasn't bad either—when it was closed"? Just what has been accomplished before the four girls enter? What specific efforts of Patsy make up the whole plot? What does she find out in her talk with the four girls? With Tom and Elinor? What does she accomplish in her talk with Paul Mallory? What single statement in the talk with Paul Mallory is the climax both of that scene and of the whole story? Is there some suspense in the story? Is it based on knowledge and foresight of the reader, or is the ending a complete surprise? Why does the writer use Patsy's stories about Father and Jamie Pine? What is the effect of the conclusion on you as a reader?

Who is the main character in "Black Water Blues"? Is he used for unity of focus, or a modified unity of focus, or is some other method used in telling the story? How are important past events brought in? Important relationships—Rohrs and the other members of the band, Bump Roxy and Adelia? How and when is the fact that there are two white toughs in the audience on this particular evening brought in? Is the fact made to seem important or not? Why does the author develop the scene when Rohrs applied for membership in the band? The scene during the story when Rohrs argues with Bump Roxy about calling "Shattered Slumber" and wins the argument? What effect do they have on the suspense? On the outcome of the story? What effect does the quarrel scene between Bump Roxy and Adelia, when he asks her to move her chair, have in creating the final situation? Is the main plot organic—does it grow from Rohrs' efforts to adjust and to save the situation? Just what is he trying to do or to save, at the final climax? Does he succeed or fail? Exactly where, in what sentences, do you know the outcome or the climax? Is there a conclusion? Is the whole story effective? What reasons do you have for your answer?

ADDITIONAL HELPS

1. Choose your own character and use him as the basis for planning a simple plot growing from each of these situations:
- a. A person who looks at an article of clothing or a piece of jewelry with the thought of buying it.
- b. A person who discovers that a meal isn't ready for him at the time he expected it.
- c. A person who is trying to find something which should be in its place to help him in his usual work.
- d. A person who explains why something he had promised or had been expected to have ready is not ready.
- e. A person who tries to find out why he had a misunderstanding or a quarrel with a friend.

2. In each of the preceding situations test the amount of variation you introduce by changing the basic trait of your character—by making your shopper decisive and well informed, decisive usually but not

well informed for this purchase, fond of driving a good bargain, ill at ease about bargaining, hesitant because he is always so, enjoying for once a purchase where he has funds enough to do as he likes, self-centered, anxious to please another person with his purchase, hesitating between two loyalties.

3. In each of the preceding situations test the amount of variation you introduce by changing the sex, age, social situation, education, race, the immediate circumstances and motives which lead him to his purchase.

4. Plan a simple plot resulting from your own choice of a character with his basic trait and your attitude to him, your situation and circumstances, etc. Plan definitely your situation, the initial resolve or problem of your character, the steps in the body, the climax. Try deciding on your climax first and then filling in the steps for the body.

12

Organic Plot:

MOOD STORY

The term *organic plot* again implies that you will find a conflict in your living material and then develop your plot from this material. It does not mean that you will think up a lifeless chain of events and impose them on your material. But your conflict may be both simple and intangible.

You may need to recall now, as well as later in this chapter, that, when we talk of a character story, a mood story, or a story about an idea, we are talking of relative values, not absolutes. Nearly all stories have all four elements: plot, setting, theme, and characters. Mood may grow from theme, and characters may be emphasized by setting and be developed by plot. When you have chosen certain material you may realize that the material itself puts a stronger emphasis on a character, a mood, or an idea; or you may discover that the three are well balanced and that you may make a conscious choice of the one you wish to emphasize.

When you read an excellent story by a professional writer you may be uncertain which he is emphasizing most, because all the elements are there and because they are so perfectly blended. But it is still true that you, as a comparative amateur, will probably do better to aim at one of these elements. To aim at a bull's-eye is better than to aim at space.

What is mood? It is an inner feeling, a strong, emotional reac-

209

tion; it is the personal attitude which infuses all your creative writing; but when you permit the attitude to dominate everything else in a story—plot, characters, physical setting, even the style—you have a mood story. By derivation, the term *mood* means "mind," "thought," "spirit"; by use it implies a strong emotional feeling. Hence it may be considered an attitude which is deeply rooted in mind and emotion.

Even when a mood is significant, it is likely to be less fundamental and less constant than a basic trait. A mood is more often the result of circumstances, changing when they change; but a basic trait remains constant, unless you have the will power to dig it up by the roots. For example, if your basic trait is stinginess, you are not likely to lose it by a mere change of circumstances. But if a drought has caused you to feel despair and a sense of insecurity, you will probably change your mood as you meet rainy seasons with prosperity, even if you never forget your experience with the drought. A mood and a basic trait differ in another important way: you tend to be conscious of your own mood; but you may remain unconscious of a basic trait, even though your friends agree that you possess such a trait. A mood and a basic trait may, however, have a close relationship, even one of cause and effect. For example, you feel a sense of frustration because you are living in unpleasant surroundings; but your desire to avoid unpleasant surroundings may be the basic trait which causes the mood. Or your attachment to your native soil may be a basic trait, ready to lead you to an action or a decision; but your feeling of homesick longing in a strange land is the mood resulting from your basic trait. Or if you suffer because you have lost a friend, your feeling is a mood; but back of the mood is a sensitivity to loss which is a trait of character. But the emphasis, the emotional shading, is quite different when you write a character story of sensitivity and when you write a story emphasizing a mood of sorrow.

Only significant moods are worth your best efforts in writing— not the whims and fancies of a moment, not the light feelings which vanish as soon as you examine them under the searchlight of your mind. But after all, you are the judge of what is important for you; you can make us care about any mood which you feel keenly, even a mood which you do not quite understand—if you convey your bewilderment honestly. Experiences which you tend to share with most other human beings—life, death, birth, love, hate—may be significant because they are universal; but your honest experiences which are strangely different may be just as illuminating and interesting. Significant and insignificant moods may be associated with the same subject. For example, you feel the physical discomfort from a few hours of hot weather; if that is a mood, it is unimportant. On the other hand, in a prolonged drought, you feel the same physical discomfort plus a mental and emotional tension because your future life is threatened; that mood is important. Thus you may often judge the importance of moods by their causes and effects and by their basis of mental and emotional experience.

But the term mood, as it is used here, does not imply mere somberness or brooding. Contentment, carefree laughter, mischief, satirical amusement, ironic contemplation, optimism, satisfaction in living—any of these moods may be the controlling spirit in a life. Again, do not forget to look at both sides of your human coins.

Why are your moods important as subjects for your writing? First, they are usually inner experience, which you are likely to bury under activity and the other essentials of a practical life; they need to be examined. Second, you will develop skill as you probe beneath the superficial, clarify, select, and find your form for an inner experience. Third, you will gain in understanding yourself. Fourth, if you write with complete honesty, you will help other people to understand themselves and to enlarge their knowledge of human emotion.

USING PLOT

Your starting point in a mood story is naturally an inner feeling or a mood. Of course you use a character who feels the mood, either yourself or someone else whose inner life you understand; you may even be concerned with a basic trait of this character, to express better your mood. Your setting will serve you well because you need objective details—time, place, weather, surroundings— to express the inner feeling by likeness or contrast. Your plot in a mood story has no value for its own sake, but merely as it helps you express a mood. Here are your working hypotheses: first, *you may evolve all the plot you need from a character's expression of his mood*; second, *as moods are often intangible, your plot will tend to give you a tangible framework, helping you write with ease and power.*

In Chapter 11 you used the accomplishment plot in building a story of character. You will find this plot useful for some mood stories. For example, you wish to present an old woman's loneliness. Suppose you choose the day when her grandson, her only near relative, is coming home between jobs after a long absence; you begin with her resolution to establish a friendly intimacy with him. She cleans the house, prepares his room, decorates with wild flowers, cooks his favorite foods, and plans to draw him into satisfying talk. But each effort breaks against his indifference, and the whole story ends in her recognition of failure. Such an accomplishment plot might serve well to emphasize her mood of loneliness.

But mood stories often grow from the need to make a decision. A character finds himself in a situation. The initial act is his realization that he should make a decision. The body of the story results from his weighing two, or possibly three, choices. The climax is his decision. The conclusion emphasizes the result of his decision or his reaction to that result. These are the main steps in a decision story. But the body of such a story is likely to be shorter; the introduction and the conclusion are both likely to be much longer than they are in a story with an accomplishment plot.[1]

You may find that the decision story is hard to handle, though, just as moods are hard to express. Both tend to be subjective, and the inner experience turns into mental generalizations. There are several ways to overcome this tendency. First, though you use material which seems to imply a decision, handle it from a different angle and shape it into an accomplishment plot. For example, John is debating whether to quit college; Ed tries to get him to stay—and you have the beginning of an accomplishment plot. Of course your choice between the two types of plot need not be arbitrary; you will be guided by your material and your

[1] John Gallishaw, *The Only Two Ways to Write a Story*, G. P. Putnam's Sons, 1928. The discussions are very good; the stories used as illustrations are sometimes less good.

desire to handle it well. Second, you may use a decision plot but give your character a confidant or use some other way of telling the story through conversation. Third, you may find a set of outer happenings so closely associated with the decision that it clarifies or hastens it. As an example, see "Rhodes Scholar" later in this chapter.

PLANNING A MOOD STORY

Your plot, for almost any story, develops as you turn your central meaning into specific details—action, talk, circumstances, at one time and place. Sometimes your material gives you plot almost ready to use; but sometimes you need to make plot where none is apparent. First, find the beginning of plot by asking yourself what forces in your material are conflicting, whether they are subjective or objective, or both. *Who* is trying to accomplish or to decide something? *What* does he wish to do? *Who* or *what* opposes him? *What result* will come from the struggle? Second, find the active moments in your material—the moments of change, growth, discovery. These moments are probably significant; and they may help start the simple plot. Third, find the initial action (the moment when conflict begins), and then the climax (the moment at which the character succeeds or gives up his effort). Both of them should grow directly from your character's mood and his situation. Fourth, plan the body of your plot, prolonging important moments and giving a reader time to taste the flavor of your experience. Fifth, choose a specific time, place, and set of circumstances for your action. Sixth, continue turning your generalities into specific actions.

All these steps will of course need to be adjusted to your subject, so that your techniques help the expression of your living material.

Suppose we take as an example two young men who become interested in the same girl! Any one of the three characters, with his own mood, might become the center of a story. If the young men are friends and roommates, their relationship promises more tenseness. If the girl is self-centered, she may feel only triumph that she could break up a friendship; if she is social-minded, she may feel regret at her helplessness in the situation. Suppose that one young man, John, is beginning to date Bob's girl, Esther—not a very special girl but one whom people expect to see with Bob. Suppose that Bob is to be the center of the story and that he is more hurt because John has deceived him than because Esther has deserted him.

You see that we have already made many choices in this triangular situation. In such choices you are sometimes guided by a flash of intuition; sometimes you make a conscious decision—it does not matter so long as you are interested and your imagination is working. The choices we have just made, so far as they are conscious, result from a desire to present the feeling of man for man, not man for girl.

What behavior could best show Bob's hurt feelings? When? Where? Under what circumstances? How could unity of time and place be managed?

In real life many little happenings with intervals of time are likely to reveal a crisis. In art one decisive happening is easier to manage, though memories of other events, used as flashbacks, may be a great help.

In life, then, events for Bob and John might be like this:

1. Bob notices one Thursday night that John, his roommate, is carefully concealing his plans for the week end, though they usually plan together.
2. John remains evasive Friday and Saturday.
3. Sunday afternoon (when Bob's girl, Esther, had told him that she could not go out with him this week) John disappears.
4. Eight days later, after Bob has been home for the week end, another fellow teases him about seeing Esther with a big blonde. (The phrase describes John.)
5. Wednesday evening at six, Bob happens to see John and Esther coming out from the informal afternoon dance. He is quite sure, from their attitude, that they are not together by chance or for the first time.
6. Bob talks to John that evening.
   a. Bob makes clear that the loss of Esther is not the grievance.
   b. He resents John's deceiving him.
   c. He cannot bring himself to trust him again.
   d. As he believes that friendship is based on trust and fair play, they are no longer friends.

You can bring out this story of Bob's regret, it seems, in one scene, the last of the six points. But you will need to know all the previous events; and you cannot get the two boys to talk about them naturally unless you realize them as specific events.

What is Bob, the chief character, trying to do? He is trying to make clear to John his attitude—that John's deception has destroyed their friendship. Of course John tries to defend himself and even to recapture Bob's friendship. The body becomes an informal debate between the two. Bob's final declaration that they are no longer friends is the climax.

Most plots which are not ready at hand in the material probably evolve from a series of specific choices like these. As you plan, you make each step more and more definite—until your material becomes talk, action, specific thoughts, blended into an authentic unit with forward movement.

Using this method, you make a plan, create until your plan becomes an experience, and keep on creating as you write. You need to feel a mood, understand characters, and then visualize, if you are to succeed in creating an authentic scene.

SUBJECTS FOR MOOD STORIES

Your experience in everyday life or in greater crises will furnish the beginnings of mood stories—if you explore your material until you understand it fully. Do not overlook your best subjects because you think, "Nobody else would be interested in that." The important questions are these: Are *you* interested in that? *Why?* How can you communicate your interest to others? Begin with your interest; if you communicate it with sincere power you will gain the interest of your readers.

You may find subjects in experiences which appear at first to be physical struggle: crises in wrestling, in football, baseball, and other organized sports; efforts to catch a fish, shoot a deer, fly a plane, to do some complicated work in a factory or a foundry. These subjects may not be significant without the loyalty, rivalry, pride, desire to prove manhood, or other feelings which make inner drama, but they are easy to manage because the pattern of outer action helps to carry the mood. But your best subjects may lack a pattern of outer events; they need objective, active development. These subjects are as varied as human sorrows and joys —loss, death, growth in maturity, a discovery that another person understands. Such subjects may ·seem passive at first, but try new approaches to them.

If you have been keeping a diary which records your growth, you may draw upon this bank account for mood stories. Perhaps you have details like these:

> Moonlight at the cabin on lake.
> Scene from Lookout Point last summer.
> Letter from Norma: she's changed.
> Autumn bonfires.
> Discovery that Nell, my roommate, is jealous. Too bad—it spoils everything unless I can get her to snap out of it.

If the scene at Lookout Point led you to discover the smallness of the individual, or the moonlight evening started you realizing love as a force in an individual life, you may use either as a basis for a mood story. The letter from Norma may be a possibility, if you rejoice at the change or dislike it; but a conflict is not yet apparent. The autumn bonfires need to be united with some inner activity. The item about Nell seems promising but, like much living material, it might be turned in either of several directions. If Nell as an individual interests you, plan a story of character; if you learn a fully emotionalized general truth—that people do develop unexpected qualities after you think you know them—write a story of theme. But if your regret or sorrow is uppermost, develop a mood story. Of course your character story will have a theme and probably a mood; your theme story will have characters and probably a mood; and your mood story will have a theme and also characters. Every good story tends to have all these elements. The difference is in the emphasis. A *mood story* is one in which the mood dominates, stands out as more important than characters or theme. The material about Nell suggests two possible mood stories because it has two different phases of activity: first you *discover* that Nell is jealous; second, you *try* to turn her away from jealousy but you fail. Either one has possibilities of specific action and of a well-developed mood.

Most subjects have potential action of some kind. For example, here is one which seemed passive at first: *a beautiful but deserted old house, which had a strange attraction for a young man.* As the young man tried to analyze the subject, he said that the house would not have interested him if people had not lived in it and that he often visited the old house with the girl he came to love. Then he realized that his consciousness of a past life led him to recognize himself as a future link in the chain of life. At last he planned a love story, to be told through a visit when he and the girl admitted their love for each other. When you can plan significant stories centering around such apparently passive material as a deserted house, you can develop a plot from almost any material which is significant.

TECHNIQUES

You may find useful in the mood story almost any technique which has been discussed: specific details, suggestion, tone color, pictures of the past and the future. You are not likely to need new techniques, but you may find former ones useful in new ways. For example, you have used surroundings to suggest emotion; in a mood story you may find a color or a lack of color in surroundings effective as a symbol of a feeling. You have used detail of a character's memories or hopes; in a mood story complete scenes, glorifying the future or replacing past scenes which left the ego unsatisfied, may become plot. In "The Little Wife" William March builds his plot from the fabrications of a character who will not face reality. Or you may express a character's mood by a series of contrasts between outer words or actions and inner thoughts. You will find such a contrast in "The Broken Boot," by Galsworthy, or an extreme experimental use of the contrast in O'Neill's *Strange Interlude.* Used in moderation, this technique may be helpful as you develop your story of mood.

WRITING YOUR COMPOSITION

Find a subject that stimulates your imagination, one that permits you to emphasize a mood. Explore the subject, letting your senses live the details that come into your consciousness. Find the moments of discovery, change, or growth. Ask yourself who is trying to accomplish or to decide something; what opposition, either external or internal, he meets; whether he will succeed or fail or what decision he will make. When he wins or gives up or makes a decision, you have the climax of your story. Your conflict will usually involve a minor character (though the opposing force may be an animal or a mechanism); if a person, be sure that you understand him well enough to let him talk and act.

Remember that your conflict and its resulting struggle may be simple—so simple that you will fail to see it as plot. For instance, a student, making a final effort to overcome his loneliness and win another student as a friend, offers to lend his car for a big dance; his offer is refused, he fails. A girl accused of misconduct tries to establish her innocence in the eyes of a friend, her mother, or the president of her sorority; she succeeds or fails. A man makes a personal application for a job; he doesn't get the job but he learns his own strength and weakness. If you feel the significance of some situation as simple as this, you have the material for enough conflict. Examine again the ideas which were discussed in the main part of the chapter if you need to do so.

Try to use talk, action, objective details, objects, and a framework of outer events so far as your material permits.

When you have created an experience, forget techniques so far as your conscious mind is concerned. Write the first draft of your story at one sitting, if possible.

TESTING AND REVISING

Try to forget about your story for a few hours or a day. Then read it aloud to yourself or to a wise listener, criticize it, and revise it as usual. Test your work by these questions:

1. Have you expressed a mood, so that other people will see that it is your artistic aim?

2. Have you communicated it with power, so that your readers will care?

3. Have you emphasized the important parts of your story?

4. Have you achieved a single tension from the beginning to the close?

5. Are the elements of your story well blended—talk, action, setting, mood?

6. Is your whole unit individual—because you have found ex-

perience which is significant, shaped it by individual creation of specific details, and expressed it in fresh, individual words?

7. Have you used all the other skills that you might demand of yourself at this stage of your writing?

READING

FOURTEEN *

Jean Austin

Breathing in short, quick jerks to keep out the smell of medicine, Sarah backed slowly toward the door, her eyes fixed intently on Mom's yellow face. When the hinges squeaked, the taller of the two doctors looked around as if to say, "Aren't you gone yet, Fourteen?" Then Sarah turned and fled blindly to the kitchen.

The dishes had dried too much during the hour since breakfast, but Sarah was glad to dig fiercely at sticky egg and at sugary cups. Why couldn't she be in there with Dad and Les and Esther, listening to the unintelligible mumble of the doctors as they examined Mom? But she remembered how her knees felt, feeble and bending, whenever she heard Mom's low moan. Something, maybe the hot dishwater, made her skin tight and hot. They probably knew it, too. They knew how she might act if—if anything happened.

The goosegrass next to the walk looked dull and quiet in the sultry June sunshine. Sarah wondered again if the vague apprehension she always felt when there was sunshine like that really meant that rain was coming. It usually happened, though, that Mom had noticed the east wind the day before, and Sarah never had a chance to test her own prediction. They always said she had heard Mom's sure-fire prophecy.

She would now, though. Mom hadn't known which way the wind was blowing for four days, ever since she came home from the hospital. The operation was successful, they said, but a strange fever in her legs— This morning two doctors came. Oh, why couldn't they do something? She sprinkled cold water on her forehead to cool the ache, and dried dishes without seeing them.

After the dishes and the sink, there were the floors to do. She usually liked sweeping, since she was tall enough to do it well, but now her strokes were ragged and desperate.

It had been this way before, about the way her feelings behaved. She was seven when Les pushed her away because she wanted to listen with the rest to the first station he was able to get on his homemade radio set. She wasn't too big to cry. But they didn't notice. A sense of unworthiness, of being too young to participate in the family pleasure, shook over her. She had gone out the pasture lane to the old gravel pit. There the smooth, mysterious shapes of new stones for her collection comforted her. They were cool to her hot hands. They were firm to her trembling lips. She was lost there until distant "Yoo-hoo's" called her to supper.

One summer she was given a pup. He was rather an unfortunate color, too many colors, in fact. But he was friendly, furnished bouncing companionship, and learned to speak very promptly. Sarah anxiously taught him where not to dig. When she had to feed him a highly peppered egg, she suffered patiently. But he *would* chase the cows back into the pasture at milking time, and when he snapped at the horses' heads he was properly blamed for the runaway. Nothing much was said. They all knew the rule of the farm. Sarah set her teeth, and after the distant shot she was very brave until that worn-out phrase, "Never mind, you shall have another," broke her composure. Then she had run out to the orchard, to climb her favorite apple tree. The bark was musty, rough, and real. It was something she could understand, and better to think about than this weak incompetence she felt. Lying flat on a long, high limb, with spattery sunshine playing on her long legs, she could feel the calm of the stalwart tree. It had been there, practically the same size and shape, as long as she could remember—not much good for apples, but the best in all the orchard for climbing. A strong west wind flickered the tapering leaves, but the branch scarcely quivered. The wind was always there—high and tempestuous in March, low and sweet in June, heavy with fruit odor in September, and fierce with a blizzard in December. The tree and the wind were different, yet each was a part in her slow peace.

When Sarah was twelve she was in a county spelling contest. No, she wouldn't have said she wanted to win, and she was never found studying. When she was third from the end she left an "l" out of "occasionally." Nobody thought she cared. A few remarks about "letting the family down" were aimed at her silent face. That night Sarah carried a blanket to the lawn and lay there watching the stars. Altair was marching grandly across, supported by his two companions; Vega seemed distant, cold, and beautiful; Sarah stared at the sisters of Pleiades, hunting for the elusive seventh star. Gradually her mortification faded away, leaving a sort of awe that these simple moments should bring her comfort.

But that was long ago, when she was seven, ten, and twelve. Childish pain, and easy consolation. Bigger things would happen. If the doctors—Sarah thought how the rest of the family would react. Esther would find relief in her music, playing her heart out with Bach. Les would seclude himself for hours with some special transformer problem. Dad would go into Farm Bureau work with great zeal. Sarah—would she disgrace herself and them by losing control of herself?

It had been an hour since the doctor came, and ten minutes since they left, with a professional gravity that told nothing of their thoughts. Sarah righteously set herself at peeling potatoes. The sun was hazy on the faded moonflowers, and half-way to the road a raincrow complained moodily.

Les, his face gray and set, came out of the bedroom. From the side of the kitchen table Sarah could see plainly that he went to Mom's desk, and back into the bedroom with papers from the little inside drawer. He looked so stern; and well—he probably wouldn't have heard if she had asked.

She wondered: The little inside drawer. What was in it? Hadn't she seen papers in there, sometime? What did Les get? A faded memory of talk about some debt—Uncle Ben, who never did have enough money—Mom and Dad talking in worried tones— those fat envelopes. . . . Then Mom must have asked for them. . . . Sarah knew what it must mean.

Something in her throat throbbed, and the paring knife slipped against her thumb. Before she knew where she was going, she was out on the shady walk. The slight breeze stung her eyes while she stood heavy and awkward, clenching her fists. Frantic loneliness gripped her throat until she could hardly breathe. On the oak branch hanging near the clothes line she saw an absurd small leaf, fluttering as if it couldn't endure the wind.

At last something rubbed her bare legs. She stooped and lifted the little black kitten, her latest pet. With the ease of an old melody returning, a familiar tranquillity entered her hands and flowed through her whole body. Touching the kitten brought that mood, or touching stones, or trees. Yet how could a humble kitten soothe her fear for Mom? It seemed to be the warmth of the body and the symmetry of shape. Thinking back, she recalled digging in soft garden soil in the spring, when she was so small that she couldn't plant peas without a little stick that Mom made to measure the distance apart. That was related to this mood, too. A starry sky and whitecapped waves came back with the same emotion.

For the first time, she tried to analyze this strange, welcome feeling, which grew as she thought. Did other people know it? Mom, in there on the bed, used to fondle apples when she was selecting them for the Fair, and forget her weariness. Father often stayed out late after doing the chores on Sunday morning, looking at the cattle.

This special awareness was simple, yet a little mysterious. Power to enjoy and endure—it was a part of wisdom.

Sarah felt taller. She brushed her cheek with the soft, warm fur, then put the kitten down. Her fingers found the handle of the screen door. Stepping into the porch, she saw her father standing near the kitchen doorway. He was smiling.

JOURNEY AWAY *

Ervin Krause

In the crevices that were the narrow bluff road, Jethroe Stevens could still see the double row of tracks he had made four days before. They were nearly covered with dust now, but he could still make them out. One pear-shaped set of tracks coming and another set going. He did not stop to consider them, but walked steadily on in the afternoon heat. His head slumped, like his shoulders that held the two suspenders of faded and dirty overalls. A string from a Bull Durham sack hung from a bib pocket. The buttons at his waist were open, letting a part of his shirttail spill out. The yellow, powdery dust that rose with each step settled lightly in the little creases the shirt made. He did not look back. Now and then he turned his wrinkled, olding face upwards to watch the clouds go scudding overhead.

Ten paces behind Jethroe walked his son, Garvin. He was bigger by half a head than his father, and heavier. But where his father had a hard stringy leanness, Garvin was soft and plump. He shuf- fled through the dust with a lop-sided unstable gait, kicking the fine dirt up and across his unlaced shoes and over his bare feet. His sweat and dirt-stained blue shirt and overalls were too small for him and suggested they had been his father's. His thick, fine-haired wrists and neck were exposed by the smallness of his shirt and were beginning to turn red in the sun's heat.

The two moved up the road, silent, and the sun and the earth were silent around them. The hot south wind slid delicately be- tween the yellow banks and curled the dust before it, mixing it with the heavy heat belts that shimmered up. The wind licked up into their faces and into their clothes, making them sweat, and then dried the sweat too quickly.

Garvin's eyes squinted beneath the mottled and torn straw hat. His father walked ahead, steadily, his shirt growing darker as the sweat soaked, leaving dusty imprints. Whenever his father looked up at the clouds, Garvin would look up quickly too. Garvin shook his white, fine-veined hands and hitched up his overalls, easing the tightness. He stopped beside a mass of plum trees that sided and overlapped the road.

"Pa, can I get a plum?" he asked, peering down the road at his father's back.

Jethroe stopped and turned slightly. "If you want one," he said.

Garvin leaned in among the thorny branches and then stopped, looking at his father with a twisted, unsure expression on his round face. He began to whimper suddenly.

"Go on, pick one, ferchrissakes," Jethroe said.

Garvin leaned in to the brush again. He picked two purple-black plums, both big and overly ripe. He squeezed them between his thumb and forefinger. The plums split softly open, and the juice dripped darkly down the warm skins.

"I seed some plums with worms in onct," he said softly, as he closely inspected the plums. Satisfied, he carefully hid one of the plums in his overall pocket, and then moved back onto the road.

Jethroe Stevens had walked some distance farther and had reached the top of the rise to where the bluffs leveled off for a piece. Garvin began to shuffle quickly down the road, his shoulders hunching each time he took a quick step. He sucked on the soft plum, smacking his thick lips and talking to himself.

"Pa," he said. "Pa." He peered up the road.

"I got two plums," he said softly. He giggled suddenly as he felt for the hidden plum in his pocket.

Jethroe turned to look back at him. "What took you so long?" he asked. "Jees Christ, do I gotta carry you to Newton?" He turned his back and walked up the road again.

Garvin hung his head uncertainly, and shuffled after. "What we goin' to Newton for, Pa?" he asked. His father didn't answer. "I only been to Newton onct," he said, loudly. They were silent again.

A whirlwind broke with a rushing sound out of a twisted swirl of grass and onto the road, rolling the heavy dust up into a delicately balanced liquid cone. It slid gracefully down the road and into the grass again, losing the dust as it went. Garvin watched it till it had bent the last blufftop grass before it slid down into the valley.

"Ma always said that was the finger of the devil stirring in the dust," he said. "It looks like that to me too. It looks like the finger of the devil."

He lifted his thin voice to his father. "Pa, did you jist see the finger of the devil?"

There was no answer. "I jist seen the finger of the devil," Garvin said, softly and wisely.

The two plodded steadily on, heads bent down, shielding the faces from the glaring white sun. Jethroe looked up at the light-blue sky, and then he stopped and turned to look back down the bluff and at the bottom, faint in a blue haze. The brown Missouri dozed down there as a snake dozes, sluggish and deadly and silent and knowing. As far as he could see in either direction the great

Missouri coiled. Behind him he heard his son speak. His shoulders sagged suddenly and he turned from the river and back to the road.

"Is it gonna rain, Pa?" Garvin asked. Jethroe said nothing.

"I wonder if it's gonna rain," Garvin said to himself. "Do you like lightning much?" he asked. "I don't like lightning. It always scared Ma too." He recalled the stark white light as it played along the wall of the cabin, and the thunder, and his mother trembling as she talked to him just before the first heavy drops of rain thudded down. "Lightning used to scare me and Ma," he said.

He paused suddenly, his forehead tightened, thinking. "Pa, where's Ma? Pa, what happened to Ma?" He shuffled on, his round face puzzled.

"Oh, she must be in Newton." He giggled, suddenly, happy at the simple explanation. "Pa, is Ma in Newton?" he questioned, hardly able to suppress another giggle at the secret he had discovered. They were going to Newton to see Ma. He wished Ma had been home to be with him and talk to him the last few weeks.

Garvin squinted at his father's back, and then wiped his large white hand across his forehead where the sweat had begun to trickle down. The two walked silently down the winding road, on the back side of the bluff, ten paces apart as before.

They shuffled across a little wooden bridge that pursed itself across a dry gully bed. Yellow butterflies clustered on the edge of a small waterhole that had been left from a rain of a few days before. The butterflies tumbled in a whirling, wing-beating mass as the two passed over the rotting timbers. Garvin stopped and leaned over the gray weather-beaten rail.

"Did you see the butterflies, Pa?" he asked. "I bet I could catch a butterfly. Can I catch a butterfly, Pa?" He peered intently, smiling at the vibrating yellow cluster.

Jethroe turned to look back. "Come along, boy," he said. He waited for Garvin to move from the bridge, but he stood as before, excitedly watching the butterflies, his mouth hanging open, sucking the air quickly in and out with a parting noise. "Come along, boy," Jethroe repeated, more loudly. He took a weary step back. "I allus got to drag you along," he said. "No better's a baby." He took Garvin's arm and pulled him sidewise across the bridge. Garvin hung back, still looking towards the butterflies that were beginning to settle on the cool wetness again.

"They sure are purty butterflies," he said.

"Allus lookin' at purty things. You can't do nothin' but you can always look at purty things. I gotta work like a fool and haul you around like a baby, and you look at purty things."

"I ken do lotsa things."

"What! You, you can't do nothin'. Can't even wipe your hinder, but I gotta do it for you. No wonder Ma died. You could kill a dozen people, the burden you are."

Garvin scraped his heavy shoes in circles in the dirt and looked at the ground. His full lips trembled as he started to whimper. "I didn't kill nobody," he said.

"No?" Jethroe said. "Well, your Ma's in the grave, and I'm halfway there, and the reason is you're crazy, boy." He turned away. "Why did it gotta happen to me, that I gotta send my only boy away?"

"I ain't either crazy, Pa," Garvin said, shaking his head. "Ma said I ain't crazy."

Jethroe made a short movement as though to begin walking down the road again, but he stopped short and looked intently at his son a long moment. Garvin pulled away from his stare.

"All right, boy, let's go down to Newton," Jethroe said. He took Garvin's arm and pulled him gently. The large loose body slowly, unwillingly yielded. "Everything's all right, boy," Jethroe said softly.

They walked slowly up the last slope and cleared it, leaning lightly against each other, both tired in the sapping liquid heat of the afternoon. Beneath them the dusty yellow road wound down the long hills, curving this way and that from farm to farm, and at last marked a straight white path into Newton. The town was hidden by trees, the town and the trees clustered thickly along the banks of a creek. Only the white Baptist church steeple showed, and the red brick schoolhouse hung on the lip of a hill overlooking the town.

The father and son sat down in the brown, dust-soft Indian tobacco and sunflowers that grew thickly along the road. Garvin sat, his head hanging and his large pink hands loosely across his legs. Jethroe slapped him on the knee.

"That's all right . . . son," he said. He paused, shielding his eyes and peering down into the valley. "They put in a new road through Newton," he said gruffly, coughing behind his hand. There was a long moment of silence. Somewhere far off a meadowlark piped his six-throated warble.

"I guess it's gonna rain," Jethroe finally said. "We better get along."

They stood up, shaking the sweat-clammy shirts loose from their backs, and moved down the road, their eyes squinting in the hazy sunlight. They were silent as they walked, now side by side. Off to the west a bank of heavy clouds crawled up into the sky to meet the sagging sun.

When the two reached the hundred yards of gravel road that bridged the distance between the dirt bluff-road and Newton, the sun was hidden. Streaming from the forward edge of the cloud were long, somber, dust-colored shafts of light.

Garvin turned to look up at the heavy banks of clouds. "Is it gonna rain, Pa?" he asked, lurching against his father.

"I think it will," Jethroe said.

"I don't like rain and lightning much. Do you, Pa?"

"Oh, the rain's all right. It washes everything clean, the rain does."

"I like the rain too." He turned to smile up at the clouds. He was glad he and his father both liked the rain.

"We should get home before it rains," Garvin said, "or else we'll get wet."

"We can't. There's nothin' else I can do now."

Garvin turned to look at his father, a puzzled expression on his face. The two were silent again. They shuffled into the town and down the gravelled main street. A sudden coolness had come over the town, and the men and women in the stores came out onto the sidewalks into the cool to watch the tremendous black thunderheads roll overhead.

Jethroe and Garvin moved the length of the street and at last stopped before a car parked in front of a square brick box of a building. In one window of the building, "U.S. Post Office" was printed in gold, shadowed letters. A heavy-set man, dressed in a gray suit, who looked as though he had been waiting for them, came out of the building.

"Hello, Jim," Jethroe said.

"Hello, Jethroe. Hello, Garvin," the man called Jim said. Garvin could not remember having seen him before. There was a lull as if they were listening for something, perhaps the thunder.

"It's gonna rain," Garvin said suddenly.

"I think it will, yes, I believe it will," Jim said. "Have you told him where he's going?" he asked Jethroe quietly. Jethroe shook his head.

Jim turned to Garvin. "We're going down to the city," he said. "They'll take care of you there. They'll have people your own age, and doctors. You'd like that, wouldn't you?" he asked, with the exaggerated care and simplicity one uses with foreigners, children, or fools.

Garvin stared silently at him, his brow furrowed in thought.

"Here, get in the car," Jim said gently. He opened the door and nudged Garvin in. "How's that?" he asked.

Garvin peered out the open window at Jethroe, his eyes terrified and dumb. Jim moved around the car and got in the other side. "Well . . ." he began.

"Ain't you goin', Pa?" Garvin asked, his high-pitched voice squeaking in fear. He fumbled for the door handle, searching for a way out. When he couldn't find it, he leaned his head against the door and began to bleat hopelessly.

"No, I ain't goin', but it's all right, it's all right," Jethroe said, holding the door shut. "You're gonna have friends there, and people who can take care of you, and . . . and Ma's gonna be there, too. I'll be down, too. . . ." his voice trailed off.

Garvin relaxed suddenly, his soft, sun-burned face creasing into a grin. "I'm gonna see Ma?" he said, half wondering, half questioning.

"Yea, you're going to see your Ma," Jim said, soothingly. He leaned forward and started the engine. He looked over at Jethroe. "It's for the best," he said quietly. "It's only an hour or so drive down to Columbia. They'll take good care of him." He leaned over behind Garvin and locked the door. He backed the car out onto the street. "I'll drop by and see you in a day or two," he called to Jethroe. The car purred down the street and away.

Jethroe turned and shuffled tiredly down the street. When he reached the dirt road, where the heavy cold drops of rain were already cratering the thick dust, he looked up at the sky. The blackness of the clouds was over all the sky, turbulent and overpowering. "I had to do it," he said. "I had to do it, Ma. I'll go down and see him . . ." He paused, his head and eyes finding the ground again. With the high rattle like that of nails pouring into a barrel, the thunder knifed across the sky on the heels of the lightning, and the rain whipped down in wavering gray sheets, hiding the man and the heavy tracks he made as he walked up the road.

RHODES SCHOLAR [3]

Allen Walker Read

Over one of the college halls at Oxford University hung an expectant silence. The fifty freshmen who were gathered on the hard benches for the induction ceremony realized that the Principal was about to arise. They sat stiff and self-conscious, timidly glancing about at the gilt-framed portraits on the walls or looking straight ahead toward the dais at the front. On this platform, a few steps above the main floor, sat a row of gowned men behind the heavy oak table. These—actually in the flesh—were the dons that the freshmen had heard about; and in the center, below the intricate coat-of-arms, was the most venerable of the group, the Principal, whose scholarly bearing befitted this somber medieval hall.

One of the new students—he seemed slightly detached—had a more mature cast of eye than the eighteen-year-olds about him. The rims of his glasses were heavier and darker and his clothes had a broad, un-English cut. He glanced about furtively, and the trace of a smile gathered at the corners of his mouth. He was contrasting this solemn scene with that at an American college. There you waited your turn in the hubbub of your adviser's office and

[3] Allen Walker Read, "Rhodes Scholar," *The American Oxonian*, XVII (July, 1930), 121–125; reprinted in Edward J. O'Brien, *The Best Short Stories of 1931*, Dodd, Mead & Company, Inc., 1931. Used by courtesy of the author.

later filed hurriedly past a registrar's clerk-girl who whisked papers about in a wicker wire booth.

This student recalled his first American college, where he had got his B.A.—a denominational institution in a little Iowa town. It was a small school, but he had some true friends on the faculty. Then at the age of twenty-one he had gone up to the State University for a year and got a master's degree in history. He had enjoyed the work and his adviser had liked his thesis. He had proved that the early Iowa settlers were largely Southerners, and that ten years before the Civil War, Iowa would have sided with the Southern cause. His biggest ordeal of the year had been trying out for the Rhodes scholarship to come to Oxford University and he had trembled before the examining committee. But after a long discussion they had called in the candidates and announced their decision: "Mr. Ross." Now Mr. Ross, a freshman again, was starting out at Oxford, waiting for the induction ceremony.

He sniffed at the faint sour smell of beer that hung over the room. He would learn later of sconces and convivial "bump suppers."

His eyes and those of all others in the room converged upon the Principal as that aged man put his hands on the carved arms of the chair and lifted himself up. The long, swinging sleeves of his black academic gown gave dignity to his figure. He smiled in a grandfatherly way and squinted as if the dim light hurt his eyes.

His informal words of greeting had a smoothness that made them seem perfunctory. For many years, probably, they had welcomed each new freshman group. "You will first read this Latin oath, placing your hand on the Bible," he intoned, "and then sign your name in the Buttery Book." He nodded toward the Vice-Principal, who sat at the end of the table with a double-sized ledger in front of him. "You will then be full members of this ancient and honorable college. Now I shall call the roll of candidates for admission to membership."

From the paper in his hand he began reading the names alphabetically: "Mr. Adcock."

The word "Present" came shakily from a freshman off at the side, and everyone turned to look at him.

"Mr. Alford."

The answer was a guttural syllable probably meant to be "Here."
"Mr. Arnold."

This was a man with self-assurance. He might become president
of the debating society before he left college. With a softly-
turned modulation he enunciated, "Heah." His answer seemed to
give courage to those who followed.

"Mr. Bartlett." "Heah."

"Mr. Broadhead." "Heah."

The Iowa Rhodes scholar noticed that they used the kind of
"r" that he called "Eastun." He had affected it jocularly when he
had put a note-book ring to his eye for a monocle and pretended
to have "cultuah." But it seemed to come natural to them. Probably it did come natural. His own "r," he reflected, was actually
pronounced in a word.

There was a long list of "c's," about a dozen, and the answer
came with regularity. "Heah." "Heah." "Heah." "Heah."

With a squirm of the tongue he formed the word as he pronounced it: "He-er." How outlandish it would sound in this group,
he realized.

"Mr. Dallam." "Heah."

"Mr. Dunsworth." "Heah."

The Rhodes scholar edged forward on the hard bench and a
sort of panic came over him. Why, he couldn't flout this whole
group of people, this whole university. He'd have to give in to
their pronunciation, of course. He could force himself to say
"Heah" if he wanted to.

But he was an American.

"Mr. Edmons." "Heah."

And a Middle-Westerner at that.

"Mr. Farrell." "Heah."

As the steady march continued, the muscles in his shoulders
tensed. The "r's" would come along now in a matter of minutes,
and he would have to decide one way or the other. He loved the
Middle West. People seldom talked about it, but he knew that he
did. He remembered his flare of wrath upon reading an article in a
big magazine by a man from the Rockies who said that the prairie
was monotonous and no one could love it. Why, the prairie was
something you could bathe yourself in!

He remembered a certain afternoon during his high school years when the feeling had taken hold of him possessively. He had driven out with his mother from their town home to the farm she had inherited. As she talked about the place with the renter, the son had climbed to the rear door of the haymow that overlooked the fields beyond. The summer's heat held the corn rows in a gelatinous silence and pressed so heavily on the crumbly loam that a soil-whiff rolled up and sent a twinge deep in his throat. These fruity undulations of prairie made a home-land. In cultivating these fields here—

"Mr. Hassall." "Heah."

—his grandfather had spent his life. The boy had thought of his grandfather's stories of early days, stories of hardships and failures and victories, stories that gave this soil a history and a background. This was the boy's region by inheritance.

"Mr. Huddleston." "Heah."

But there are circumstances,— he began to himself with a feverish compression of his lips.

"Mr. Janson-Smith." "Heah."

The Rhodes scholar recalled the thesis he had written for his master's degree at his State University. He had fairly immersed himself in the early history of his state. What fun it had been, sitting in the State Historical Library, slowly working through the several panels of county histories. These bulky, old-fashioned volumes, padded with Civil War rosters and records of early business machinations, had chapters that effervesced with pioneers' lives—their dreams, their brawlings, their courage in breaking sod that was matted with roots of prairie grass.

"Mr. Knox." "Heah."

The scholar gripped the bench. Were they already at the "n's"? No, a Knox was a "k." At that only a few more moments remained until the fatal words "Mr. Ross."

"Mr. Lansdowne." "Heah."

Perhaps he could say "Present" and avoid the difficulty. No, no one had said it since the very first man, and that would be side-stepping the issue anyway. He would have to bend his action one way or the other all during his Oxford time.

"Mr. Lawrence." "Heah."

He darted his eyes feverishly among the English boys. They were still and intent with "first-day" stiffness. They all had on the little commoner's gown, like his own. Each person in front of him was an item of black uniformity. Could he stand out against them all with his own kind of a "here"?

"Mr. Martin." "Heah."

Isn't it the better part of discretion to "fit in"? Didn't his grandparent pioneers adapt themselves to the prairie? Everyone had told him not to remain an outsider in Oxford.

"Mr. Murray." "Heah."

He didn't want to be an outsider.

"Mr. Niblett." "Heah."

He was becoming part of an "ancient and honorable" college, with centuries behind it. Shouldn't he submit to its ways? He was sent here to fit in, to get what Oxford was supposed to give. Everybody said "Heah." That was the way. It doesn't pay to make a fool of yourself.

"Mr. Otley." "Heah."

He could change his pronunciation. People had done it before. But it was nasty business, he realized. His teacher in freshman composition had been brought up in Iowa and had got her master's degree at the State University, and then after one summer session at Columbia in New York City she had come back with a full-fledged Eastern accent. How people had razzed her behind her back and recounted incidents where she had forgotten for the moment!

"Mr. Padwick." "Heah."

God, the "p's"!

And there was that fat returned Rhodes scholar at his American college whom everybody had disliked. He had kept his handkerchief in his sleeve and had lifted his hat even when he met another man. He was the kind who said "Heah."

The scholar formed the syllables on his lips, experimentally— "He-ah." How—a—perverted it sounded. He gulped laboriously and swayed forward with his head bent.

"Don't be an outsider," he snarled at himself. "Don't make a show of yourself here at the beginning!"

"Mr. Partridge." "Heah."

"But I'd be a traitor!" he gasped. "I'm an American, and I know I love my Middle West, my prairie."

"Mr. Pennington." "Heah."

"Don't be a fool!"

"Mr. Radford." "Heah."

"Mr. Ross."

He felt the attention of the room riveted upon him, and before making his answer he rumbled his throat in a preliminary way.

QUESTIONS

In "Fourteen," is the question whether Sarah's mother will recover used as the main narrative question? Or is Sarah's subjective struggle made more important in the telling of this story? What is Sarah trying to do? What bearing does her memory of incidents when she was seven, ten, and twelve have on her struggle now? In each of these incidents what caused her problem, and what special thing or activity helped her solve the problem? What helps her in this crisis? What idea does she form from her own experiences and the actions of her parents? Does this idea emphasize the fact that a mood story can have ideas and characters also? Does Sarah succeed in her subjective struggle, and does she find out that her mother will recover? What bearing does the last paragraph have on the preceding question?

Who is the main character, that is, the one who acts and decides, in "Journey Away"? Whose fate is being decided? How? From the details which are eventually given about Garvin's mother, why, probably, had this decision not been made sooner, and why is it being made now? Is the introduction of Jethroe, in the first paragraph, effective when viewed in relation to the whole story? Is the introduction of Garvin in the second paragraph effective? Does it suggest in any way his abnormality? What effect does the talk about plums, the finger of the devil, and the butterflies have? Where does the reader first realize that Garvin is abnormal? Where does the reader first learn the purpose of the trip to Newton? Does he learn it by a single direct statement, or does he realize it by degrees? Is the characterization of Garvin convincing? Give reasons for your answer. Do the nature details seem authentic? Why did the writer choose a hot, dusty day with a threat of rain? Is there an objective suspense based on a doubt about which decision will be made or what will be accomplished, or is there a subjective suspense that is many-sided? How is suspense built from such things as our gradual discovery of the boy's condition, the father's purpose in taking him to Newton, and our wonder how Garvin will react? Is the suspense satisfying for this material? Whose mood unifies the story? Jethroe's? Garvin's? Or is a larger mood, which is a semiomniscient blend of their feelings with the heat, the landscape, and the author's pity, more important than either? What is the specific moment when you know that Garvin will be taken to the institution? Is the conclusion effective? What is emphasized in it? Why does the writer play up Jethroe in the opening paragraph and in the last paragraph?

Why, in your opinion, does the author of "Rhodes Scholar" begin with a comparatively objective paragraph? Is unity of focus used in the rest of the story? Does the material lend itself to unity of focus? Give reasons for your answer. What is Mr. Ross's problem, when the story gets under way? When does he first realize his need to make some decision? What three possible and different decisions does he think of? Which does he eliminate at once? Why? Which ones does he debate to the end of the story? What desires or attitudes of his are involved in these two? What are the effects of his using an actual roll call for his story, or what dangers of the decision story does he avoid by doing so? Does the story have an idea as well as a character and a mood? Is the ending satisfactory to you as a reader? What decision do you think he made? Why do you think so?

ADDITIONAL HELPS

Follow for a day or a half-day all of your own attitudes that you can capture. Try to find the cause of each attitude. Explore your happy, carefree moods, as well as boredom, hate of monotony, disappointment. Do these moods center around situations? Could you evolve a plot from each situation, so that you could succeed better in communicating the mood?

Evolve a simple, specific plot, related to a mood and a character, from one of these situations:

1. An attempt to make another person understand an attitude or a mood.
2. The suffering of a sensitive person wounded by another who is quite unconscious of wounding him.
3. The suffering of a sensitive person wounded by another who is quite conscious of wounding him.
4. The stubbornness of a person who harms himself by his stubbornness.
5. A person meeting another person who once had authority over

him and struggling against his psychological return to his former attitude.

Select a favorite novel or a book of short stories. Find four or five passages, each of which is dominated in content and style by the mood of a character. Is each passage effective? If so, what techniques or methods make it effective?

13

Organic Plot:
EMOTIONALIZED IDEA

Your composition assignment at the end of this chapter assumes that you will choose whether to develop an emotionalized idea as an animal fable, an allegory, or some other kind of fantasy, or to use realism. Do not try the animal fable unless you have a strong urge to do so and a specific idea which needs that treatment. Most amateur attempts at animal fables are comparative failures. But you may enlarge your vision of what it means to develop an idea in creative fiction by reading Dunsany's fable. And if you try to write an animal fable, even though your success is imperfect, you may stimulate your imagination for later more effective work with realistic creation.

An organic plot, again, means a simple conflict developed from your living material. In this story, too, you will need to plan setting and characters, and to use all the means to give your story flesh, blood, and clothing. Again, your question is one of emphasizing an idea, not of excluding the other elements which make good narrative. An attempt to work without any setting or to repress your character would only lead you to write a dull, wooden story.

A *fully emotionalized idea* is a conclusion or a belief which you have drawn from your own experience. The term *experience* as used here means something more than intelligent reading, intelligent reading checked by detached observation, or participation in a hot debate about ideas. Experience means being involved in a life situation which keeps you in suspense about a reward or a penalty and which calls out your physical, mental, and emotional response. When you find an idea by this kind of experience, you are sensitized to it; when you meet it again, your nerves and muscles respond.

For example, you may be familiar with the term *possessive instinct* as an intellectual idea. Then one day in a hot quarrel your best friend says to you, "The trouble with you, John, is that you can't have a friend without thinking you own him, body and soul." The term, from that time, is emotionalized for you; when you hear it again you relive the hurt feeling of the quarrel. Later, when you read of Soames' possessive feeling, in *The Forsyte Saga*, you react with sharp, first-hand knowledge. You have a fully emotionalized idea, a personal truth.

Personal truth is quite different from scientific truth. When— and if—Newton saw an apple falling from a tree, he watched a *specific objective happening.* When he found out why, he had a *general objective truth:* the principles he formulated would always hold true under the same conditions; he could persuade other scientists to accept them. As he was a human being, perhaps he had an inner attitude, or a series of attitudes, about his discovery— a hope, an exultation when he finished formulating and testing sound principles, a glow of satisfaction when other scientists accepted his principles. Each time he experienced one of these attitudes, he had a *specific subjective experience.* Perhaps he drew a general conclusion, something like this: to discover scientific truth is, for me, the greatest possible happiness. Such a conclusion is a *general subjective truth,* a fully emotionalized idea, a personal truth. Most of our human wisdom is enriched because people have taken the trouble to communicate personal truths.

PLANNING A STORY BASED ON AN IDEA

Writers who are shaping their experience often tend to begin with noticing *specific events*; then they draw *general conclusions*; next they find or create *specific details* to express the general conclusions. In previous assignments you usually began with specific events which you interpreted. In this assignment you are beginning with material in the second stage, a general conclusion or idea. You may need to go on to a third stage—to find or create the specific details for expressing your idea. As you plan your story, you need to find or create a situation, a plot, one or more characters, and a setting; all these must evolve from your idea or be planned to illustrate it.

You may find this process difficult or easy. If it is easy, so that your idea brings a flash of perception about your method, so much the better. If it is hard, it is no harder in writing than it is in daily living. Unless you are conscious of ideas back of your actions and sensory perceptions, unless you perform actions which express your ideas, your life remains unintegrated.

Here are some general suggestions to help you in handling any story based on an idea. First, find your idea. You have a wealth of material in educational, social, political, and economic experiences; apply some of these to family or personal relationships or consider them in the imitative actions of children. Second, limit and clarify your idea; use its smallest possible fraction. Third, find out whether it is emotionalized enough to stimulate your creative activity; if it is not, throw it away. Fourth, become conscious of your emotional slanting—whether the idea, for you, is tragic, pathetic, humorous, satirical. Fifth, choose your method of telling your story—a *realistic incident,* an *animal fable,* an *allegory,* or some other form of *fantasy.* (Consult the readings later in the chapter when you need them to guide your choice.) Sixth, choose the characters for your story. If you use people they may be types rather than individuals; but you will need to know their minds and emotions, and you may gain in vividness if you realize differences in the physical appearance, voices, actions of your conflicting characters. When you are in doubt, make your characters more, rather than less, individual. At least, let your readers feel that through your characters they are meeting a living idea. Seventh, choose a definite setting. As authentic details have been a source of power in other assignments, it is possible that a definite choice of *one time, one place, one kind of weather, one situation,* and *one individual set of circumstances* may further your creative power in this story.

THE REALISTIC STORY

The realistic story emphasizing an idea is probably the easiest kind for you to handle—though it may not be your best choice at this stage. It is easy because you can plan it just as you planned your previous stories of mood or character, beginning with some person whose basic trait interests you, or even with some mood; then when you write you can merely shift your emphasis a little to make us think less of the specific event and more of the underlying idea. It is easy, too, because you can probably draw your characters, setting, and situation from real life.

If you have an idea but no situation, and if no characters present themselves from real life, find types of people who would have opposing attitudes and choose a time and place where they would cross swords in an emotional debate. Of course you will need to create many specific details for their debate.

Such a realistic story was developed by a student who wished to dramatize the difference between an interest in people and an interest in making money. He developed a dialogue between two stock owners who had met at the bank. One reports the sudden death of a neighboring stock owner; he is concerned because the man, who is still in debt, has left a wife and four small children. His listener can't remember the dead man at all, shows no concern about his wife and children, and wakes to interest only when he places the dead man as the owner of some fine Hereford cattle he wishes to buy.

THE FABLE

The modern fable is perhaps harder, but it may be both a challenge and a satisfaction in achievement. You have a chance to use animals, birds, or insects, as long as you use them to illustrate the behavior of people. But your story will differ greatly from the Aesop fable. Here are a number of suggestions. First, choose animals or other characters with whom you are thoroughly familiar, so that you can make their appearance and their actions vivid. Second, let your animate characters talk and think but in other ways let them act like the creatures they really are. Dogs who wear silk dresses and bears who sit in rocking chairs and wipe tears from their eyes are merely grotesque; they tend to hinder the development of an idea. Third, find a situation with a conflict which is natural for your chosen characters and is also fitted to illuminate your idea. Then develop the conflict into a plot, with a climax and a conclusion. Fourth, infuse your whole story with a subtle suggestion of your chosen idea, instead of adding a moral tag at the close. Fifth, give your unit enough sensory development so that it will stir you and your readers to use imagination, you in creation and your readers in perception.

THE ALLEGORY

The allegory will probably be difficult, but it may be a stimulating kind of story for you to use in clarifying an idea. An allegory is an extended metaphor—so extended, for this purpose, that it becomes the basis of a whole story. A metaphor has been explained as a comparison between two objects of entirely different classes; the comparison, if effective, intensifies a quality of one object more because of the great differences.[1] A good metaphor helps your communication because it surpasses a literal statement in clarity and power; and an allegory, if it is effective, will surpass a realistic story in clarity and power.

One student wrote an effective allegory based on the idea that some philanthropists impoverish other people to get the money for their gifts. She developed her idea by a comparison with trees and called her story "Old Millionleaf." One tree, the chief character in her story, choked out other trees by taking their space and nourishment; but when this tree was old and large and covered with golden leaves in the autumn, people praised it for dropping leaves to fertilize the soil.

Galsworthy's story called "The Novelist's Allegory" has an effective use of the extended metaphor. The business of a thoughtful novelist, Galsworthy implied, is to show his readers life as he finds it, including the unpleasant and dangerous. The novelist is represented by Cethru, the lantern bearer, who obeys Prince Felicitas and holds up his lantern that people may see the Vita Publica. But many people accuse him of causing the situations which he is merely revealing.

[1] See Chap. 2, on comparisons and figures of speech

OTHER METHODS

A personification or some form of symbolism may help you turn an idea into a specific story. For example, the term *rugged individualism* leads you to think of industry as a man who has grown into a giant. The individual worker was once more of a match for him. The contest is like a prize fight with a giant and a dwarf in the ring. (Compare this idea with newspaper cartoons, in the discussion which follows a little later.)

When you use symbolism you select a concrete object, a person, or an action and use it to suggest a whole class of objects, people, or actions. Often your concrete object represents an intangible idea. Symbolism, then, is one form of substitution—the use of the concrete and tangible for the general and intangible. Hawthorne's story, "The Birthmark," uses a scientific experimenter who tries to remove the one blemish from his wife's cheek as a symbol of humanity seeking absolutes.

You may be stimulated to imaginative ways of expressing ideas by studying newspaper cartoons. The best ones often follow lines of thinking that might produce a story—for example, a cartoon which presented the tendency to postpone laws to prevent strikes. A little man labeled *The People* is coming out of a house with a bad roof to empty a bucket and a washbowl full of water from the leaks. A burly giant labeled *The Politicians* has put up a ladder and seized a hammer from his box of tools. But a full sun, *The end of the strike*, is rising over the roof of the house. While the little man gazes at him in open-mouthed dismay, the giant says, "Look! Sun's out. Mebbe the roof don't need fixin', huh?" [2]

In such a cartoon, the designer seizes ideas and changes them to tangible form, as one might do with words.

Which type of story will you choose? Try the realistic form if you lack confidence and courage, or if you do not care for fantasy. Choose one of the imaginative forms if you are ready for it. It may give you the pleasure of freedom, challenge and release your creative power, or help you to communicate your emotional ex-

[2] A cartoon like the one described here appeared in the Des Moines *Register*, December, 1946.

perience with more power than you can achieve with realism and to give your reader a lasting memory of your idea.

SUGGESTIONS ABOUT SUBJECTS

Of course you must find your own subjects; you are the only authority about the ideas which are emotionalized for you. If you lack ideas, examine again your personal code of conduct, consider the disagreements between you and friends or members of your family about your behavior, or list the new ideas you have recently acquired or the old ones you have discarded. One idea may lead to many different kinds of stories. For example, these situations are all suggested by one idea, the *search for perfection*:

1. A college student who is failing because he never covers half an assignment—though he does everything perfectly.
2. A boy who struggles for perfection in feeding a prize calf.
3. A student in dairy industry courses who yearns to make perfect butter but has never questioned why butter should be perfect.
4. A person whose attempts to reach individual perfection make him an inhuman bore.
5. A girl whose standards at home emphasized perfection and who reacts violently against these standards when she has a taste of freedom.
6. The tendency for standards of perfection to change as one approaches them.
7. The American desire for a sort of exact perfection or complete success, which leads us to emphasize mechanical problems and to avoid human and social problems.
8. The arts as expressions of the struggle for perfection.
9. A woman whose attempt at perfection in her housekeeping makes her family miserable.

From the last example alone, you might make many stories, according to your choice of character, your mood, and the exact shading of your idea. You might tell the woman's story: she discovers the cause of unhappiness in the family and changes or refuses to change her ways, or she accepts the unhappiness as a situation she cannot solve. You might tell the husband's story: he accepts or revolts. You might tell the story of a son or daughter, driven to desperate ways of finding relief from perfection. When you see that one idea or theme relates to many phases of life and may be developed in many directions, you have increased your control over living, as well as writing.

WRITING YOUR COMPOSITION

When you have found a fully emotionalized idea which you wish to write about and have reduced it to its smallest usable form, think about it as specifically as you can, in terms of your experience. What has emotionalized it for you—one happening or many? How far can you trace it back in your life? As you use all your senses freely, dwell especially on your most vivid memories. Does any memory furnish you a situation, a conflict, a character, a setting, to start you on your creative work? Be receptive to anything, in either your past or your present. Then try the future, as your hopes shape it into tangible or half-tangible form.

If nothing stimulating comes from your experience, look for comparisons, perhaps similes or metaphors. Think of animals or birds which are familiar to you—pigeons in New York City, horses, pet dogs, wild deer, monkeys in the zoo. If you find something tangible, continue to use your senses on it as you have done before, and change it to something more tangible.

If you do not find another approach, create a scene in which two characters debate your idea. What types of people would naturally disagree about the idea? When? Where? In what situation or circumstances? Is the disagreement fundamental, so that neither character will change? Are the characters equals in type, or do circumstances impel one to submit to the other, at least outwardly? Can the idea be illuminated best by presenting an extended discussion or by revealing the view of one character to another in a dramatic surprise?

When you have your method as well as your idea, plan your complete plot, specific setting, characters, and means to unity of focus. Create sensory details to stimulate your own feeling, making everything a little more specific than you think necessary for this kind of story. Be sure that your plot, setting, and characters have all grown from your idea and that they are integrated to help you express it.

Visualize, as usual, until you have *an experience* which you enjoy. Your visualization may be harder here if your details are unlike actual life, or it may be easier because a departure from reality stimulates your powers.

Write your composition. Forget to worry about your formal planning—and write.

TESTING AND REVISING

Later, after an interval of time, test your writing by these questions:

1. Have you expressed your idea with clarity but by implication rather than direct statement?

2. Have you achieved emotional power, so that your experience will be communicated to a reader and secure a response from him?

3. Have you developed your unit with emphasis, proportion, and forward movement?

4. Have you successfully blended dialogue, characterization, and setting with the action?

5. What pruning will improve your work? What other changes or substitutions?

6. If your unit lacks life, do you need to revisualize and rewrite the whole composition?

READING

A GOOD AMERICAN *

Martin Hoffman

The neon sign fizzled in the rain, sounding like an overdose of Bromo Seltzer when you are drunk. "Hamburgers," said the sign, and underneath it, just to make sure people knew that we serve hamburgers, Bud put up a sign, "Hamburgers, fifteen cents."

The February rain gave no hint of letting up, a bus swished past the deep puddles on the avenue . . . I felt like having a cup of hot coffee. I poured two cups and took the other one back to Bud in the kitchen.

"Front's empty," I said.

"Yeh, it's the rain, relax." Bud was cutting up buns and squeezing meat into tiny little hamburger patties.

"Going to lose money." I felt like heckling the rebel. But he was a good Joe, came from Alabama, had a picturesque drawl and promised me a nickel wage-hike if I made good. He scowled, and I looked out at the rain and drank my coffee.

The door to my right opened with a jerk. A big figure in a blue overcoat came in. He looked up, and then a smile covered his chocolate-colored face.

"Hi there, Geof. You a working man?"

"Yep, Don, got to eat." I had known Don for quite a while. His desk was next to mine in engineering drawing. Don took off his coat and sat by the counter.

"What'll you have?" I took out a green guest-check.

"Coffee and a hamburger."

"O.K." I walked over to the little kitchen window and shouted, "One."

"One to go," came the answer.

"No, just 'ONE,'" I shouted, thinking that Bud had not heard well.

Bud came closer to the window, looked hard at me and said, "We don't feed niggers in here. He's taking it out."

I said nothing. There was no suitable reply. If he wrapped it up, I'd unwrap it and put it on the counter for Don. Damn Bud. I found a cup without left-over lip-stick on it and poured coffee.

"Cream?"

"Please."

Don took a drink. I wondered whether he had heard Bud. I hoped not. Then Don looked up and asked, "Do you have a rest-room here, Geof?"

"Why, sure. Through the kitchen and then turn to your left." I washed a couple of plates. If I were a bacterium I'd like to bathe in lukewarm water. Bacteria have it good, I thought, better than lots of folks . . . especially people like Don . . . Better put a bit more soap into the sink.

I heard Bud's voice from the kitchen. It was loud and irritated. "Employees only . . ." Wasn't he going to let Don use the rest-room? Why, the damned rebel. "Health department rules . . ."

I realized suddenly. "Where I come from," Bud had said one

day, "the niggers are all right; they know their place. But these Northern sons-of-bitches don't know where they belong."

Don came through the doorway. He looked at me. The creases in his face, when he smiled, were replaced with deep wrinkles. "Apparently," he frowned, "you don't have a rest-room for . . ." and then he stopped short and shook his head . . . "customers."

I looked down at the floor. The floor looked very dirty. I felt like being sick into the Soilax-green rinse water in the sink. "Yeh." That's all I said.

"About that hamburger . . ." Don's voice wasn't cross or irritated . . . "better put it into a paper bag when it's ready. I . . . I . . . want to take it out."

I nodded. I looked everywhere but at Don. I looked through the little window to the kitchen. Bud said, "Come 'ere!"

"You no-good God-damned Englishman." His eyes said more than his words. He need not have spoken at all. Then, as if he had not made his position quite clear, he asked, "You a nigger-lover?"

I didn't say a word. I looked him straight in the face and went back to cut pie. I had to do something to keep me from thinking . . . to keep me busy. The pie was near Don. I miscut three pieces, then I stopped.

"I . . . I . . . He's from the South." I was going to say that I was sorry, but it was easier to talk about Bud, to project the blame.

"That's O.K., Geof. It happens every day." Don smiled again, and his smile was disarming, sincere.

"One to GO!" Bud slammed a bag on the window-ledge. I took it over to the cash register, where Don was waiting and said, "Twenty-one."

Don handed me a quarter. "How long are you going to work here?"

"If he doesn't fire me, I'll work till after Easter. Got to help pay spring quarter's tuition.'

Don looked at me hard. He would have liked to see me quit. I would have liked to quit.

"Need the money, huh?" he asked.

"Yeah." I handed him four pennies. "Don't get too wet."

The door slammed. Then Bud was standing beside me, his hands deep in his pockets. He scowled and shook his head. I saw a little bead of sweat on his forehead. I clenched my fist. I should have insisted that Don eat his hamburger in here. It was easy saying that now, now that Don had gone.

If Bud was going to say something I wish he'd get it said. He just looked at me. Then he started speaking slowly. Thank God he had his temper under control.

"Geof," he drawled, "have you ever tried to get half a jar of mustard off of a hamburger? That nigger-bastard won't ever come back in here." He laughed and slapped his knees. Then he got serious. "In Birmingham, they lynch people like you—nigger-lovers. But you're O.K., Limey, you'll learn. You'll be a good American yet."

SOME CATOIDOID BREED *

George Cowgill

Jess Garvey made out that he thought lightly of me, calling me no more than a cosmic crap shooter, a blind gambler in the infinite casino of space, a feather blown by the lips of those old, old sisters, the fates. He mocked me now as I stood in my control room, before my digamma lever, saying that I was for all the worlds like an idiot before a dekakred slot machine, and that I had traveled a long way for the simple sake of putting my hand to a lever and taking a chance. Himself, he maintained, being in charge of the *Dosfando*'s nuclear jets, and being concerned with such things as the setting and following of courses, leaving nothing to chance and depending altogether on his cleverness, was to be compared to a chess player, the very antithesis of the gambler.

Jess Garvey was right, and he was not right. For in those flashing instants when I pulled down my digamma lever the *Dosfando* changed position, but she followed no course. She simply dropped out of the continuum that we call space-time and re-entered with absolutely equal probability at any point where the gravity field was the same as what we had left. Ninety-nine times out of a hundred we found ourselves circling a sun barren of habitable planets, as we were doing now, and had no choice but to repeat the process, for Garvey's puny jets, limited as they were to speeds below that of light, were only good for maneuvering within the narrow bounds of the solar system.

Yet it was not without labor and precision on the part of myself and my crew that these instants of effortless imprecision were ever reached. In the entrails of what Garvey called my slot machine were roughly three tons of transistors; were superconducting bus bars the thickness of a man's body; were the four tuned horuntodes that we cleaned after each use in bosun's chairs suspended from a gantry, speaking in whispers to escape the mournful booming of our echoes; were the banks of two farad condensers (a man shorted one once and was vaporized—I suppose we are still breathing his atoms in our air); were ten or twenty acres of fragile printed circuits; were more branched feedback servo-tubulators than in West Nome and New Zimbabwe together.

That this was all so, Garvey well knew, and his taunting of me was but the token of our long togetherness. All those who had left earth with us twelve years before had had but two things in common, the knowing that wherever in space they would ever be, they would never be home again, and the idea that that was how they wanted it. There had been those like ourselves who went for the sheer call of the differentness and the loneliness that was less lonely than the crowds of our home, a few who bought trade goods, hoping for a planet where they could be sold for ten or a hundred or a thousand times their cost, and by far the most offered no reason for their need to leave, nor were ever asked. Some had grown tired of our changeless change, some had found planets to their liking, many had been killed over money, or over creatures that were almost women, or other matters; finally myself and Jess Garvey were all from earth that were still on the *Dosfando* when she left Uyalamba, our last planetfall.

Most of our crew were Uyalambans, decently humoid and musical of speech and no worse people than any of our other crews, but they did not know, as only Garvey and I did, what it was to see through branches of leafless trees the moon among clouds, or to sit in the sun with three hundred thousand others and watch motopolo in the great arena of Passhogan, or to spend a night surrounded by philosophy and damp circles on table-tops in some bohemian little bar on Knapp Street in the decaying old center of Greater Ames. Equally they had their own memories, their own reasons for lying awake and thinking or singing softly, but they were not our reasons, and served more to drive Garvey and myself to one another.

Musing on this, I had been with my eyes and a part of my mind routinely checking my meters, when I was stopped by that which was not routine. "The Devil has got into the Kandaki triggers, Garvey," I said.

"The Devil my foot," he made answer, "this is your own fault, Ennis. I told you three years ago that the thurg shields that you bought of the Groombians would never hold up."

Garvey behind me, I climbed the ladder on one wall of my control room and passed through the hatch and out onto the catwalk that led through my machinery. "It is indeed a Devil," I said after a moment of search. "She has taken the form of one of the dear mousoid creatures of the Uyalambans, but I see through her. There is no hiding her black heart with that little spotted orange skin. Why else would she have chosen Kandaki triggers, out of all my machinery, if not out of Devilish cunning?"

"Blast the mousoids and their pseudo-rodent ways! Will she wreck the triggers, do you think?"

"Garvey, must I forever and forever struggle with the errors of your pig-headed mind? The plural of mousoid is most clearly miceoid. No, she is not big enough to do the triggers lasting hurt, but the capacitance of her little body is enough to put them out of kilter. My machines will not work until we can get her out of there." And I began to wonder how this was to be achieved.

I suppose you could say I was fortunate in a manner of speaking in that I did not long puzzle over the problem. For Garvey tugged at my sleeve and silently pointed. The mousoid itself I forgot, for there was Gustave, one of the half-grown kittenoids which had also come aboard with the Uyalambans, and paid some small part in their keep through the destruction of miceoid. There was no mistaking that Gustave, stock still but for the twitching of his middle tail, was stalking our little mousoid. Gustave weighed at least a kilo. One leap and the triggers would be gone forever, for Kandaki triggers are not to be repaired with chewing gum and thumbtacks. There would be only the creeping along on Garvey's nuclear jets and the starvation in six months or so, or a little longer if we ate one another.

"Here kittyoid, here kittyoid," I called while Garvey withdrew into the control room, and Gustave took no notice save only to switch his tails with more impatience.

I made haste to the galley, returned with a bowl of the warm milkoid which Gustave and his brothers and sisters downed with such relish. Gustave now would have none of it, he was not to be turned aside from his prey, and his meat-hungry eyes sneered at me and the warm green fluid high above him on the catwalk.

Was there then no way to stave off this leap, to save this creature and the rest of us from himself? I thought of roping him or of a net perhaps, but there was no way in all the worlds that I could see of getting such a thing through the spiderwebs of glass and wire between myself and Gustave.

Then I thought myself of Sarmdugu the Uyalamban and his little blowpipe. I did not know what Sarmdugu put on the darts that he used in it but I had seen him use them, and I knew that whatever they hit did not move again.

I wanted to stand there and watch Gustave. Painful as it was, it was less so than being out of his sight, not knowing his progress, not knowing the instant of his leap that would mean an end of leaping for the Ship *Dosfando*. But I drove myself back slowly along the catwalk, keeping Gustave in sight, then, reaching the hatch, leapt down the ladder and ran for Sarmdugu's quarters.

His room was foul with the odor of the schi root, and he and the other Uyalambans there were far gone in the chewing of the cursed plant. That was the way of these folk. They helped me well enough in preparing my machinery for operation, but they had no love for machines for their own sake, and so soon as their duty was over they were back to their quarters and into the vices of their people, the schi root and the endless game of atsanac. Now on the floor in one corner five or six of them were squatting, arguing in fuzzy fashion about the score and speaking of cheating and making threats, but too befuddled to be of any danger. One of these was Sarmdugu. Only with trouble and shaking did I make him aware of me.

"Sarm," I cried, "where is your little blowpipe, where are your darts?"

"None . . . a' yer . . . darn business, Ennish," he answered thickly and between chews.

"Hear me, Sarm! Do you want to die out here in this void of voids? There is a beast in the Kandaki triggers. One false move and they are done forever!"

Sarmdugu was a little aroused by this, and seemed to perceive what I meant. He arose, and tottering followed me to the control room and out onto the catwalk. Most of the others followed behind, hardly knowing what was afoot. "An' I still say it was seven cloober, four bobsnik I had on that last round, you farn," someone muttered. I tried to shush them, but it seemed not necessary, for Gustave still ignored us. He had scarcely moved, and the little mousoid seemed rooted with fright where she crouched.

I pointed out Gustave, and saw Sarmdugu stiffen and turn pale.

"Give me the blowpipe, Sarm."

"I cannot, Ennis."

You sweet murdering dopefiend, I thought to myself, did you really then leave the blowpipe back in the room, to cost us minutes that mean forever? But aloud I said, "Then we must go back and get it."

"It is here, Ennis."

"Then if you are so steeped in the schi root that you cannot even give it to me (and God knows I did not expect you to be able to hit any target with it yourself), tell me where you are wearing it."

"You do not understand, Ennis. The creature is sacred. It is a sin to harm him."

"Sin? Oh merciful God, Sarm, this is no time for good or evil. You have bragged to us enough in the past. Did you think of sin when you burned the orphanage for the sake of one child rumored to wear an aluminum ear charm? Or did you think of sin when you sank ships in shallow seas so that you could skin dive to loot the corpses and save the bother of prisoners?"

"You still do not understand, Ennis. This is different. This is death to the soul. I cannot kill Gustave." There was no more thickness in his voice, and I could see that the blasphemy of my proposals had shaken them all loose from the spell of the schi root.

"Will one of you others kill the beast then?"

But they were of the same mind as Sarmdugu. As bloody a batch as any in space they had been a moment before, but on this they held fast, that they would not see their darling catoid killed; sooner would they starve here where the nearest inhabited worlds invisibly circled suns that were pinpoints of light.

And so we sat and kept vigil over Gustave and his quarry. With all my heart I looked death at Gustave, but he did not quiver. Time swept onward, but some bitter syrup, distilled of my dread and despair, arose and entered the works of my watch, gumming them so that they lied and called the hours that passed mere minutes. My mind struggled and shuddered in this same morass, and could focus itself on no plan of salvation, on nothing but the bitterness of ending.

It was then with relief that this sudden silence was broken by the yowl of a catoid and the cursing of Garvey in the control room. At least the doubly distilled idiot would bring a quick death on himself, I thought. The Uyalambans turned to meet him as he appeared on the catwalk. At arm's length he carried by the tails the infuriatedly scratching Theodosia, the tabbyoid mother of Gustave. For the second time I saw the Uyalambans stars in fixity and pale silence. Then they began to relax, and some of them broke into nervous laughter while others began to weep, and Sarmdugu produced his blowpipe, put it to his lips for an instant, then grinned like a spoiled child who has gotten its way. Gustave seemed to stretch, quivered ever so slightly, and lay down in absolute stillness. The mousoid perceived her chance, moved tentatively at first, then was off in a blur of orange.

As I trailed the others back into the control room it was as though it was myself that had been chewing of schi root.

Seeing me too numb for questions, and unable to contain his cleverness, Jess Garvey waited only until the last of the Uyalambans, headed back for their atsanac game, was out of earshot, "Ennis, my boy, did you not know that those catoids were most sacred? I'd never left you alone if I had dreamed that you knew no more than to try to kill Gustave outright."

There was silence from me.

"Since I know that in your stubbornness you will never ask me about my taking Theodosia by the tails," he went on, "I will tell you that all Uyalambans know well that no catoid can be picked up by the tails. They have known from their cradles that carrying a catoid in this fashion is starkly impossible. They are so sure of this fact that they have never wasted time in vain attempts to pick one of the beasts up in that fashion. And so when they saw me carrying Theodosia by the tails they could not at first believe their eyes, then began to look for an explanation. And, from their premises they proceeded with perfect logic. Since I was doing with Theodosia what could be done with no catoid, then Theodosia was no catoid at all, and neither was her child Gustave. They were mere impostors, some catoidoid breed picked up from some odd corner of space, and no more sacred than you or I."

THE TRUE HISTORY OF THE HARE AND THE TORTOISE [3]

Lord Dunsany

For a long time there was doubt with acrimony among the beasts as to whether the Hare or the Tortoise could run the swifter. Some said the Hare was the swifter of the two because he had such long ears, and others said that the Tortoise was the swifter because anyone whose shell was so hard as that should be able to run hard too. And lo, the forces of estrangement and disorder perpetually postponed a decisive contest.

But when there was nearly war among the beasts, at last an arrangement was come to and it was decided that the Hare and the Tortoise should run a race of five hundred yards so that all should see who was right.

"Ridiculous nonsense!" said the Hare, and it was all his backers could do to get him to run.

"The contest is most welcome to me," said the Tortoise. "I shall not shirk it."

O, how his backers cheered.

Feeling ran high on the day of the race; the goose rushed at the fox and nearly pecked him. Both sides spoke loudly of the approaching victory up to the very moment of the race.

"I am absolutely confident of success," said the Tortoise. But the Hare said nothing, he looked bored and cross. Some of his

[3] Lord Dunsany, *Fifty-One Tales*, Little, Brown & Company, 1915. Reprinted by permission of the author.

supporters deserted him then and went to the other side, who were loudly cheering the Tortoise's inspiriting words. But many remained with the Hare. "We shall not be disappointed in him," they said. "A beast with such long ears is bound to win."

"Run hard," said the supporters of the Tortoise.

And "run hard" became a kind of catch-phrase which everybody repeated to another. "Hard shell and hard living. That's what the country wants. Run hard," they said. And these words were never uttered but multitudes cheered from their hearts.

Then they were off, and suddenly there was a hush.

The Hare dashed off for about a hundred yards; then he looked round to see where his rival was.

"It is rather absurd," he said, "to race with a Tortoise." And he sat down and scratched himself. "Run hard! Run hard!" shouted some.

"Let him rest," shouted others. And "let him rest" became a catch-phrase too.

And after a while his rival drew near to him.

"There comes that damned Tortoise," said the Hare, and he got up and ran as hard as he could so that he should not let the Tortoise beat him.

"Those ears will win," said his friends. "Those ears will win; and establish upon an incontestable footing the truth of what we have said." And some of them turned to the backers of the Tortoise and said: "What about your beast now?"

"Run hard," they replied. "Run hard."

The Hare ran on for nearly three hundred yards, nearly in fact as far as the winning-post, when it suddenly struck him what a fool he looked running races with a Tortoise who was nowhere in sight, and he sat down again and scratched.

"Run hard. Run hard," said the crowd, and "Let him rest."

"Whatever is the use of it?" said the Hare, and this time he stopped for good. Some say he slept.

There was desperate excitement for an hour or two, and then the Tortoise won.

"Run hard. Run hard," shouted his backers. "Hard shell and hard living: that's what has done it." And then they asked the Tortoise what his achievement signified and he went and asked the

Turtle. And the Turtle said: "It is a glorious victory for the forces of swiftness." And then the Tortoise repeated it to his friends. And all the beasts said nothing else for years. And even to this day "a glorious victory for the forces of swiftness" is a catch-phrase in the house of the snail.

And the reason that this version of the race is not widely known is that very few of those that witnessed it survived the great forest-fire that happened shortly after. It came up over the weald by night with a great wind. The Hare and the Tortoise and a very few of the beasts saw it far off from a high bare hill that was at the edge of the trees, and they hurriedly called a meeting to decide what messenger they should send to warn the beasts in the forest.

They sent the Tortoise.

QUESTIONS

In "A Good American" what idea is the writer's artistic aim? How much does the writer's emotional attitude contribute to the expression of this idea? Does he emphasize it by serious or satirical details or both? How important is subjective feeling in the whole unit? Is the situation well chosen for the aim? Are the three characters well selected? What differences exist between them? What are the motives of each? Is the conversation natural? Does it create suspense and advance the writer's aim? Is the ending skillfully managed? Does the whole unit have power, or is it lifeless?

How much time passes in the story "Some Catoidoid Breed"? (Base your estimate on the assumption that the five opening paragraphs are the musings of the main character ". . . Now, as I stood in my control room . . . routinely checking my meters . . ."). What do these opening paragraphs tell us about the space ship, the *Dosfando*? Her control? Her mechanism? Her position in space? The number of years that Garvey and the speaker have been together? What information is given about the Uyalambans? Where in the opening paragraphs does the writer best give us the "feel" of the interplanetary space? Is the author consistent in his use of mousoid, kittyoid, catoid, and other fantastic details? Is the presenting of the Uyalambans consistent? Do you suspect the writer of a satirical intent when he talks of their vices as if he is contrasting them with the dwellers on earth? Why did Sarmdugu refuse at first to let the blowpipe be used? Why did he consent a little later? What result came from its use? Does the author of this fantasy seem more interested in space travel or in satirizing views of good and evil and tendencies to reason so as to make new facts fit conventional premises? Is the method used in the whole story more effective than a realistic method would be?

How does "The True History of the Hare and the Tortoise" differ from an Aesop fable in its tendency to state an idea or to make subtle implications about it, in its use of talk, and in the amount of narrative detail? Exactly what is Dunsany satirizing? How is his opening paragraph related to the preceding question? How are sentences like these related to his aim: "Hard shell and hard living. That's what the country wants" and "It is a glorious victory for the forces of swiftness"? What connection do the last two paragraphs about the forest fire have with the whole artistic aim of the writer?

ADDITIONAL HELPS

What specific and fully emotionalized idea, if any, do you find in connection with each of these themes:

1. Stubbornness.
2. Leadership.
3. Telling the whole truth.
4. The pursuit of happiness.
5. Differences between your generation and the older generation.

Choose one of your specific ideas from the preceding question—perhaps your best one—plan a situation, characters, and a plot by which you might develop the idea.

What ideas have become so emotionalized for you in the last year or two that you have added them to your personal philosophy? Are there any ideas which you have subtracted from your philosophy in the same period?

What ideas in the last year or two have led to clashes between you and your family, you and your new friends, you and your former friends?

What ideas in the last year or two have you sharply questioned—in your own reading, in college classes? Were any of these ideas political, social, or economic?

Select a favorite novel, one that is told rather specifically. Does any idea, implied or stated, seem to be the purpose of the whole novel? If the purpose seems to lie in individual character, instead of an idea, how could the attitude to the chief character be stated as an idea?

14

Writing a Short Story

You do not need to develop any new skills for your short story. You have already expressed your attitude to an activity or an environment, to a place, a scene, or an object. You have brought to life a character by his physical appearance, talk, action, specific thoughts. You have used plot, with forward movement and suspense, to emphasize a character, a mood, a fully emotionalized idea. In all your writing you have used specific details with suggestion, communicated your attitudes, and created an experience, with your mind, emotion, and senses.

But although you do not need new skills, you may find it necessary to use some of your former skills in new ways. Perhaps your short story will be more complex than your earlier compositions; you may need to unite several scenes by a single tension of suspense or to use one scene with complex implications about previous events. Perhaps your story will be longer than your earlier compositions, though you will not be judged by mere length. Certainly it should be the best and the most significant piece of work that you can do. You have complete freedom to choose any material from which you can make a good story and to emphasize a character, a mood, or a fully emotionalized idea. You have also freedom to choose a method of fantasy or realism— or to make any other choice, as long as you write a short story which is a genuine creation.

What does the term *short story* mean as it is used in this chapter? It is not a mere incident or a sketch. First, it has *plot*—a significant struggle, prolonged enough for mental and emotional flavor, carried to a conclusion of victory or defeat, and developed by suspense and forward movement. Second, it has *singleness of impression*, a unity which is emotional and intellectual and which results from a close integration of all the narrative elements. In previous discussions you have met the admission that much good writing is plotless; and you have also considered reasons for using plot. Even for this assignment, if you can write beautiful units without plot, as a newly hatched cygnet swims without lessons, go ahead. But if you need help, try plot as a means to that happy state where your stories evolve as organic growth. And do not forget that the best plots are sometimes subjective.

FINDING MATERIAL FOR STORIES

Your best stories will probably develop from small beginnings, like tiny seeds—vital seeds, but so small that you do not at first see their value. You may start with a character if he stimulates your imagination and if you can create a situation for him:

1. A sensitive person. What would be likely to hurt him most? Would the experience help him or harm him? Would he run away or face facts?
2. A greedy person. What would he be most greedy about? Why? With what results?
3. A slow person. What causes his slowness? What effect does it have? What situation might bring him to complete defeat? What situation might bring him success?
4. A stubborn girl. Why is she stubborn? With what result? Why? Could she be placed in any situation which would stir our sympathy?
5. An inarticulate person. Why? In what situation is he most inarticulate? Why and when will he suffer most? Will he overcome the trait? Will the trait be an advantage to him in any situation?
6. A mechanical, uncreative person. Why, if there is a reason to be found? Where will he succeed or fail? In what situations will he be happy or unhappy?

7. A creative person. Is he creative in handling machines, in aesthetic activities, in working with people, or in all of these things? Where will he succeed or fail? What will happen to him if he tries to work in some field because his relatives think it the thing for him?

You may start with the desire of a character: the desire of two dogs to crunch the same bone; the desire of two sisters for a trip or a new dress when only one can have it; the desire to win a prize, to live a different sort of life, to escape an environment; a man's desire to go fishing against the desire of his wife and daughter for a city vacation. Sometimes a desire is the specific result of a basic trait; at least, when a character with a desire meets opposition, the outcome usually depends on the character of the person involved.

You may start with a problem or a situation: the wish of parents to cut a son or a daughter by their pattern; a daughter's need for the experience of a summer job or an informal vacation, against a mother's preference for having her companionship at home. The result in these examples will be decided by character or by several characters. Sometimes a student begins a story by finding an honest answer to this question: *What is my own greatest problem at present or in the immediate future?* One student met the question by saying, "Oh, that's easy to answer. I've led such a carefully planned life with such normal people. What's going to happen when I get into a tough job with all sorts of people?" At the time he stated the problem it had already become more specific: "Shall I stay in my groove, with a fellowship for graduate study next year, or shall I take that tough job bossing a construction gang out west?"

You may begin with a fully emotionalized idea: the effectiveness of self-discipline, the need of leading people rather than driving them, the attainment of happiness, the right of a person sometimes to conceal the truth, the helplessness of city workers in a depression, the problem of being oneself instead of imitating other people, the desire to escape monotony in something creative. Your idea, too, sends you back to character and situation. By choosing different characters—a middle-aged bookkeeper, an intelligent young factory worker, a lazy young man with an itching foot, a young woman who dislikes housework—you might make a dozen different stories from the desire to escape monotony. You might also make several more stories from each of these characters, according to your attitude and the character's basic trait.

You may begin with moods or psychological attitudes: loneliness, a love of forests, a love of the city, a hate of the city, a fear of death or illness, a sense of inadequacy, an adjustment to change as the norm of life, a desire for security. But a mood also sends you back to the questions: Who feels this mood? In what situation? Why?

You may begin a story with environment: a farm, a city, a store, a creamery, a lumber yard, a doctor's office, a mining town, an oil town, an army camp, the office of the Air Corps Ferry Command. (New industries and occupations, if you know them well, make good settings for stories.) Raising questions about effects will further your planning. How could this background warp or develop a character? What conflicts have I seen in this environment? How has it made people unhappy or happy? Or you may ask of your own environment: how has it helped or harmed me, formed my tastes, or developed my future? Again your questions lead you to some person who is influenced by the environment.

You may begin a story with almost any genuine interest. A zoology major, with experience in government wildlife projects, began with a desire to write about beavers.

DEVELOPING YOUR MATERIAL

Building a good plot, as you recall from Chapter 11, is mainly a process of turning generalities into specific details and then turning each detail into details that are still more specific. When the details evolve from your attitude and from the significance of your material, your activity is creative. Though it should continue while you plan, write, and revise, it need not occur in any rigid order or result from any one kind of detail. If one detail does not further creation, try another. Consider these suggestions, then, as if they are possible "toe holds" in climbing a cliff.

Again, look for the active moments in your material—the moments when someone changes, discovers, decides, or gives up. You may remember actual moments or invent natural moments of activity. *Who* experiences these active moments? Is the experience *inner, outer,* or both inner and outer? *Why* does the experience begin?

What does the main character wish to do at these active moments? *Why?* Does opposition appear? Is this opposition inside the character? For example, does a character's ignorance of a mature feeling change to full realization—to the conviction, "So *this* is what one feels"? Does a character who wishes to do something struggle against a conventional attitude, a fear of new behavior, or a sense of wrongdoing? (These tenuous conflicts inside your character are likely to be significant; do not overlook them in your haste toward outer action.) Does opposition come from another character? Is it concealed or open? Which force will win? What initial act will start the conflicting forces?

When does this conflict take place? *Where?* In what *situation* or *circumstances?* Can you change any of these details, to make your feeling more effective than it was in your actual experience?

What behavior does your main character use at his moments of activity? Does he talk, act, have specific thoughts, recall sensory impressions, betray his feeling in little physical signs, mostly unconscious? Does he experience an inner emotion quite different from his outer behavior? Does he talk about his inner feeling, or does he repress it by talk and action? If he represses the inner feeling, is he trying to mislead himself or an onlooker?

What behavior does a minor character use in the same scene? Is he approving or trying to thwart a main character?

What is the most important element in your material to you, the writer? What is *the source of your power, your ability to care?* Is it, first, a *character,* with a basic trait; second, a *mood* of a character; third, a *fully emotionalized idea?* You will find your artistic aim (your main purpose, or theme) in the answer to this question. But your story of character may have a mood and an idea; your mood story will need a character and perhaps an idea; your story of an idea will need a character and may have a mood. In choosing your artistic aim, then, you are selecting only a dominant quality, like the main motif in music; you are not suppressing other elements, producing a thin, barren story; you are using the other elements as helpers for your main purpose.

No matter what your main purpose is, you need a main character. What do you know about him? Is he like you? If he is, can you handle him best by complete identification with you, or by giving him another name and a different physical appearance? If you are using another actual person, are you both observing him and analyzing your past knowledge? If you are creating a character, can you give him a past as well as a present and a future?

If you are writing a *character story*, do you know your character with your *mind, emotion,* and *senses*—even his foibles, small interests, vanities, and secret sins, great or small? Though you emphasize one trait, you know many traits; people are seldom single-minded; they merely have their single-minded moments. If you are ready for creation you may gain much from it—the joy of freedom and the power of a living unit.

But whatever the source of your character, can you bring him to life according to the needs of your material?

Your framework, which these questions may help you find, should be individual. No one can give you a pat foolproof formula. But *find* your framework. You will need it—if you still need any book on writing. Consider a plot as a pair of crutches if you wish; some day you hope to throw them away; meantime they may help you to rise and to gain strength.

Probably your usual planning will proceed something like this —though your order is not important so long as you are making progress:

1. Choosing the germ of your story.
2. Finding your artistic aim.
3. Planning a main character.
4. Finding a situation for the character.
5. Finding the climax.
6. Building the *body* of the plot.
7. Planning for economy of plot, scenes, time, place, characters.
8. Getting the emotional "feel" of the story started.
9. Creating *an experience.*

KINDS OF PLOTS

You met the accomplishment plot and the decision plot in preceding chapters, but a brief restatement of them may help you.

The accomplishment plot has these steps:

1. A situation exists.

2. A character resolves to do something about that situation. (The initial action.)

3. He makes an effort or several efforts, each ending in success or failure. (The body.)

4. A last effort leads him to *succeed* or *to give up efforts.* (Climax.)

5. A conclusion, if there is one, emphasizes his reaction to his success or failure.

The decision story has these parts:

1. A situation exists.

2. A character realizes that he must make a decision about it. (The initial action.)

3. He weighs his alternatives, or possibly three choices, realizing the effect each will have. (The body.)

4. He makes a decision. (The climax.)

5. He reacts to his decision; perhaps he experiences its effects. (The conclusion.)

You may find useful another analysis of the way to plan a short story.[1] According to this plan, you begin with a character; you are conscious of his basic trait. Then you find for him a human problem which he will solve because of his basic trait. The body consists of his efforts to solve his problem; the climax is his realization of success. (The climax might be his failure, also; but the writer who analyzes this plan prefers his characters to succeed.) The chief character is the means for unity of focus, or the x-ray method; readers experience nothing except through him; his suspense is their suspense.

This plan differs from the accomplishment plot in its initial emphasis on character.

Which of these plans is best adapted to the material you have chosen for your story?

SUSPENSE IN YOUR STORY

At this point you may wish to review the discussion of suspense in Chapter 11. Notice especially the remarks on the need of

[1] Stewart Beach, *Short-Story Technique,* Houghton Mifflin Company, 1929.

blending hope and fear, the basis of *knowledge* for suspense, the basis of *emotional concern* about a character or about the significance of action, the nature of *forward movement,* and the power of a single tension. Again, weigh carefully the statement that good suspense is *born in the mind of your reader.* Plan your material carefully so that you may call up in your reader's mind emotional, perhaps half-conscious responses. Make your situation clear at the start; impel your reader to say: "So that's what the character is up against! Hm! What can he do?" A few seconds later, cause the reader to say to himself, "Oh, that's what he means to try! Can he do it? He has pluck all right, but he's up against real opposition. Well—I hope he succeeds." At the end of each effort of the character to accomplish his purpose, let your reader think: "Well, he won this time. What next?" Or "He failed this time, but he's learning. Maybe he could win at the close." At the climax, have your reader thinking, "Ah, he's won. Good for him!" If there is a formal conclusion, let it impel your reader to think, "He's happy about it, isn't he?" or "He's unhappy about it!"

Your reader's thoughts, of course, will be reversed if he does not sympathize with a character or if the character fails, and they will be much more specific as he reads your particular story. But if your reader makes inner responses like these, you are succeeding; you have suspense, forward movement, a single tension based on meaning or character.

No matter which method of plotting you use, *your readers will be interested when your characters play for high stakes.* The desire to win a spelling match or an athletic contest, the desire of a child for a toy—these things seem to be lower stakes than the desire to save human life, to win domestic happiness, honor, love, friendship, inner peace. But a second principle which seems almost the reverse of the one about playing for high stakes is just as important: an objective trifle may become a high stake when we know why it is important to a character. For example, if a child with an ambition to rise above a shiftless environment finds confidence from winning a spelling match, that match becomes a high stake. You may handle double or triple stakes; but do not substitute them for vital feeling and do not trust to mere complexity. You will perhaps find double stakes most effective when you use an objective aim to emphasize a subjective aim. You may sometimes handle double or triple obstacles well. For example, a man who tries to establish his title to land by filing a claim at a federal office works against time, a rival claimant, and a flooded stream.

Suspense may be furthered by whetting a reader's curiosity about small details. An example occurs in Maupassant's story, "Vendetta." The reader has heard the old woman's vow of vengeance for her son's death. But when she ties up her dog and starves it, he says to himself, "Now what is she up to? I know she thinks this will further her plan, but *how*?" But until you have more experience, be wary about the use of curiosity unless some example of it grows spontaneously from your material.

ECONOMY IN PLANNING

Here are some suggestions which may save you difficulties and increase the power of your story.

First, use *economy* of plot. Let the effort of *one* main character to accomplish *one* thing dominate your planning. Even if your hero is going to get the job and win the finest girl in the world, use *one* as your main plot and subordinate the other. Unless you can handle a love story well, subordinate it and play up the getting of the job. But suggest early the subordinate action also, so that it may increase the suspense. Make your main plot a source of your tension, from the first words to the last sentence of your story.

Second, use *economy of scenes.* List the essential events of your story in time order. You may have many of them. Find the smallest number of scenes which will enable you to tell your story; reduce the number to two or three or to one. Do not use a scene in which nothing essential happens. If your characters can do two things in one scene do not give them two scenes; you will only waste effort. (It is like making two trips to a grocery store on a hot day—one for a pound of sugar, another for two lemons.) Often you can let your characters refer to previous events in their talk, or you can let a character tell us the past through his memories used as "flashbacks." Of course you will need to know previous events as well—perhaps better—if you are going to weave them into an effective scene. The best way to begin a story is to "pick it up as you would pick up a puppy—a little in front of the middle."

Third, use *economy* in the number of characters. If you plan to use three or four people but you can manage with two, kill off the extras. Your judicious murders will be rewarded later in ease and power. Emphasize and subordinate in dealing with the two who remain; plan to keep your main character dominant from beginning to end. If your main character's aim is opposed by his whole family, select one member of the family, if possible, to lead the opposition; subordinate the others. Of course there are exceptions to all suggestions on writing; in a certain story you might find it effective to bring in one by one all the members of a large family. But scrutinize your material to see whether you can gain by simplicity.

Fourth, use *economy of time*. If you plan for years, try months; if for months, try weeks or days; if for days, try hours. If your material really permits, tell your story in a half-hour or an hour. Prove your power before you take on needless handicaps. But if time gaps serve your purpose, use them.

Fifth, *use economy of place*, unless your material demands a change. Don't let theories of variety delude you. Every new setting which you must develop or leave vague is a liability.

Sixth, use *economy of mood*. If you are interested in the disillusion of a young man who has been jilted, do not develop his happiness, his growing suspicion, his doubt, his development of doubt into certainty, and his disillusion. Begin at a moment when doubt is changing to certainty, and emphasize the disillusion. Of course you will need to know the facts about the former happiness and to use the emotional impact upon his memories. But if you limit the time and secure unity of mood, you can enrich your story.

MISCELLANEOUS PLANNING

You may find the point of view for your story by answering these questions: Whose story is this? What is the best way to tell it—from whose point of view? Sometimes you can answer these questions easily because of your material; sometimes you might do well with any one of several slants and may as well take your personal preference. For example, if an aunt offers to take one of two nieces on a trip but refuses to decide which one, you may write the story of the aunt, of either niece, of their mother, of their father.

You also have many possible methods of telling a story. You may choose one of the special, occasional devices, such as monologue, soliloquy, dialogue, letters, a diary, or a story-within-a-story. Even if you stick to the usual methods you have many choices. You may use the first person, with your chief character as a narrator. This method is simple and easy to keep in focus, but your character must be interesting if he is to hold a reader's attention; his presence, normal and alive, may reduce the suspense, and he is likely to be limited or to seem biased and boastful. You may use the first person with a minor character as a narrator. This method often works well when your story has a double edge—one meaning which is obvious to the narrator and another which he reveals to us unwittingly.

The third-person omniscient point of view, either limited or complete, is a common method. An author uses complete omniscience when he assumes full knowledge of the minds of all his characters at all times. This method was frequently used in nineteenth-century novels. An author may limit his knowledge to one person; but if he is truly omniscient he steps in to explain to us things about that character which the character does not understand. On the surface, these omniscient forms look easy, just as all objective writing looks easy to a beginner, but it is difficult to infuse them with power.

Using the mind of one character for unity of focus has been assumed as the best method in the preceding chapters. It is probably the best for your short story. It requires penetration, the ability to "bring to life a character." It permits the first or the third person. It is effective if your main character is *you*, apparent or hidden. It is effective if your main character is someone else whom you understand. It may be used with a double edge of understanding, too, as it is used for the minds of children in "A Trip to Czardis," by Edwin Granberry, and "Innocence," by Rose Wilder Lane. Even if it is hard at first, you can probably secure more power with it than with any other method until you are sure of your techniques.

How will you begin your story? If it is well planned, with a character who knows what he wants, with an artistic aim, with the complete plot which makes one tension, it will *almost* begin itself. An obvious beginning is to introduce your chief character in a situation and to make that situation clear to your readers. You may do this either by talk or by the specific thoughts and acts of your character. Until your situation is clear your reader cannot develop a sound interest. To keep your reader uneasy about the situation is like keeping him guessing about what mathematics problem or conundrum you are going to give him—instead of letting him get started on the solution. When you have made the situation clear you are ready at once to show us the main character's attitude and intention about it.

The use of dialogue has been discussed in earlier chapters. (See Chapter 9 especially.) As we have seen, talk reveals character in a natural way, conveys information, and advances action. It is excellent for conveying information by specific bits instead of formal exposition. It is especially desirable for developing those parts of a story which need emphasis because they are significant. It is most useful when you are able to blend it well with description, setting, action, and specific thoughts of a character. It is much used in the best contemporary writing. It is almost indispensable in a short story.

UNITY IN YOUR STORY

We have already discussed the unity of a theme or an artistic aim in your story. If the story is well planned you will actually have many kinds of unity. You may have unity of time and unity of place. You may have unity of plot, with a single tension, unity of an emotional slant on your material, and the additional unities of one main character, one basic trait, and one attitude of yours to that character. You may also have subordinate unities, growing out of your attitudes to minor characters. You may have the unity of one mood or of one fully emotionalized idea as the center of your story. If these unities grow naturally from your material, use them, but do not distort your subject by unnatural unities.

HOW STUDENTS PLANNED STORIES

Occasionally a story comes so directly from experience that the planning is simple. Such a story was "Brown Boards." It was evident almost at once that the college girl was the chief character and that her false pride was the artistic aim. The steps of the conflict, written down in time order, were these:

1. Ellen's parents write her that they have put up rough brown boards across an open side porch to keep the kitchen warmer.
2. She feels ashamed because the boards look bad.
3. A young man in her group, Bill, tells her that he will be in her home town spring vacation, to visit mutual friends; and she says casually that he must drop in to see her.
4. She writes her father asking him to take down the brown boards.
5. Her father refuses.
6. She answers that she will not invite Bill to their house unless the boards are down.
7. As her father brings her home for spring vacation, she sees that the boards are still up.
8. She remonstrates with her mother.
9. She goes through the familiar pattern of home life that evening, noticing her mother's shabby dress and hose and little economies that she had forgotten. She also feels the additional warmth from the brown boards.
10. Later in the evening her father asks her about inviting Bill and the other friends.
11. When she refuses, he explains further about their finances.
12. He makes her admit that she is ashamed, though the boards have made her mother more comfortable.
13. Finally she conquers her pride and steps to the telephone to invite her friends to Saturday evening supper.

The main problem in this story was where to begin the narrative. The planner decided to start with the seventh point, bringing out previous events through the talk of the girl with her father and mother and through her specific thoughts. This plan secured unity of time, place, and mood.

The story which began with an interest in beavers was not so simple. It developed something like this:

1. A plan to use beavers in relation to people.
2. Main trait of the beavers: persistence.
3. A human character who rediscovers his own persistence.
4. Main character: a college student, discouraged from overwork and lack of money.
5. Situation: his temptation to quit college or his decision to return.
6. Type of plot: a decision story.
7. A plan to center the story about the problem of his going back.
8. Place of the decision: a logging camp in the north woods—a place familiar to the writer, natural for beavers, and near enough for him to reach by hitchhiking when he ran away from college.
9. Time of year: April or May.
10. Perception of two halves in the story; a period of discouragement at college with a hasty decision to run away; a period of readjustment at the lumber camp, ending in the decision to go back in the fall.
11. A plan to use the lumber camp, with flashbacks.
12. The young man's rescue of the beavers as a tangible framework for his decision.
13. Characters
    a. Main character: a young man like the writer.
    b. Minor character: the manager of the lumber camp, intelligent, sympathetic.
    c. Other minor character: a boss who orders the beaver dam blown up.
    d. Another minor character: a girl who is an indirect influence but never appears.
14. Plot plan

    Situation: a young man who has run away from college is given a job at a lumber camp.

    Initial act: he realizes that he must make a decision about his future—his running away is merely a postponement.

    Efforts to make a decision:

    a. He watches the lumbermen blow up a beaver dam. He realizes that his attitude to his own work has already changed, with mental rest and exercise. He thinks of Jane and his profession.
    b. He goes back alone next day (Sunday) to find the beavers rebuilding.

He does more thinking about a future without Jane and his profession.

c. He takes the manager to the dam with him and shows him just how they can carry on the work of the camp but still save the beavers.

Climax: He wins the manager to his plan about the beavers. He refuses the offer of a more permanent job, telling the manager that he will go back to college in the fall.

The story needed several scenes with time intervals, but after the plot was planned, the story was not difficult to write.

A group of students offered these beginnings of stories in a single set of conferences:

1. A pacifist changes his mind because he himself knocks out a bully to protect a weakling.
2. A girl discovers her growth to maturity as she changes her mind about marriage.
3. A daughter has a chance to be with her father after his retirement and finds that he is really an interesting person.
4. A girl prefers creative work for its own sake.
5. A character has a conflict between his own sense of integrity and his desire to be a good fellow in the crowd; the conflict is deepened because he is fond of a girl in the crowd.
6. A college student whose parents shelter him wishes a chance to grow and to be independent.
7. A girl feels hostile to men; she finds the origin of her hostility in the depression, when her father lacked initiative about finding another job, and her mother took over the responsibility.
8. An educated Anglo-Saxon owner of a Texas ranch discovers that his uneducated Mexican employee has better practical judgment about the ranch.

Each of these students had significant material which for him was emotionalized knowledge. Each idea or germ needed to be changed to specific details—situation, plot, time, and place—by finding moments of change or by making plots to resolve feelings which spread over long periods of time.

The story of the girl who preferred creative work was furthered by asking these questions: *When* would the girl show this preference? *Where*? *What* would she *do*? *What alternative* would be offered her? *Who* would offer the alternative? The answers led the writer to use an October afternoon at home-coming on a college campus, a sculpture studio, and an offer of marriage from a wealthy young man. The young man, who was coming for the week end, arrived early and caught the girl still at work in the studio. He resented her soiled, informal clothing; and though he was willing to buy "good" art for her, he did not care to have her messing about with sculpturing in the elegant home he wished to give her. The climax is implied in the theme: she refused to marry him. The writer had two chief tasks in developing her story: to know a set of previous events which were essential as memories, and to bring out the issues naturally in an emotional debate. Each was a problem of turning ideas into sensory details.

From such a beginning you too can evolve a story; you can find emotionalized knowledge and turn it into specific details—time, place, mood, conflict, climax, complete plot, talk, action. Where experience does not serve, you can use full creation.

PLANNING YOUR STORY

Find your richest, most significant material for a short story; or rather, develop a significant story from some vital bit of your experience. Plan the story carefully; know these things:

1. Your main artistic aim—a trait of character, an idea, a mood.

2. Your main character: his chief trait, your attitude to him, his ideas and emotions, his physical traits, even his past and his present. Know him as you know yourself, either by creating or by using your own background.

3. Your essential minor character or characters. Know more about them than you think it necessary to know.

4. Your plot, if it is an accomplishment plot:
   Situation, with the conflicting forces.
   Initial act, or resolution of your character.
   The efforts he will make to carry out his resolution and the success or failure of each one.
   Climax: his success or his final failure.
   Conclusion: effect of the struggle on him.

5. Your plot, if it is a decision plot:
   Situation.
   Realization of a need to decide—why.

One possible decision—its results.

Another possible decision—its results.

Climax: what the final decision is.

Conclusion: satisfaction or lack of satisfaction in the outcome.

6. Your setting: reasons for your choice.

7. Your economy in planning: one plot which will make a single tension from start to finish; no unessential characters, no extra scenes, no changes in time and place unless your story cannot be told without them; a single emotional effect.

After you have planned and visualized your story so that it is imagined experience for you, test your planning by these questions:

1. Does the material of my story mean enough to me so that I have a chance to make other people care?

2. Is my story significant for the chief character? What does he want? Will he get it? Will his getting or not getting it change him, give him a new attitude to life, or a different life? (*Your* uncertainty is not a good way to create suspense.) What opposition will he have?

3. What emotional effect do I plan for my story? Can I convey this effect to my reader?

4. Have I found the most individual way of telling my story?

5. What is my artistic aim—to emphasize a certain trait of a certain character, a mood, or a fully emotionalized idea? Am I ready to state this aim specifically in a sentence?

6. Am I ready to bring to life my main character? Do I know him with my mind, my emotions, and my senses? Do I know his past and his future, his basic trait, other traits, prejudices, desires, and little foibles? Am I ready to give him physical reality and physical activity in my story?

7. Do I understand minor characters enough to let them act and talk?

8. Is my plot an organic growth from my artistic purpose, my situation, and my character? Will it help and not hinder me in bringing out the living quality of my story?

9. Is my action tangible enough, especially if my material is subtle and subjective, to keep me from floundering in generalities?

10. Do I know the essential things which have happened *before*

my story begins? Am I prepared to make these clear through specific thoughts or talk?

11. Am I ready to make the fundamental situation clear to my reader at the very start—to base my suspense *not* on uncertainty about what the main character wants but on the problem of his getting what he wants? How soon will I make my reader say, "Oh, that's what he wants"?

12. Will my character start some kind of activity at once—or will he refuse to act, if he is that kind of character?

13. Have I planned unity of focus—unless I have a good reason for not using it?

14. Do I visualize my climax and my conclusion with special vividness?

15. Is my setting clear to me, whether I plan to use much or little? Is it integrated with my visualizing throughout the story, so that it will be natural and continuous, instead of coming out in lumps of exposition? Does my setting include weather, or do my people move in a vacuum?

16. Do I hear talk in my imagination as blended with other elements in a give-and-take fashion, not long orations blocking off other experiences? Will my talk further action and reveal character? Am I using it for the most important parts of the story?

If your story has several scenes, visualize each by itself at first; then merge them into one, with tension and forward movement for a story, not a series of static pictures.

WRITING YOUR STORY

When you have finished your other planning and you feel the tension of your plot, forget your conscious planning and write. While you are writing, feel free to make any changes which further your artistic aim, especially to use any emotionalized details you had not thought of earlier. If your material is alive, your senses will be creating as you write, and you will be selecting out of the riches they offer, instead of putting on paper every detail that comes into your consciousness.

Write the first draft of your story at a single sitting if possible. If your story is long and there are several scenes, write at least an entire scene at a sitting.

TESTING AND REVISING

After you have put away your story for several hours or days and have forgotten it as completely as you can, read it critically yourself, aloud if possible; also hear it read aloud by another person, preferably with other listeners. Notice these things:

1. Would the listeners have cared if the reader had stopped in the middle of the story?

2. What comments made by the listeners, after the reading, were valuable because they were both perceptive and free of personal prejudice? What comments were not valuable?

3. If you were misunderstood at any point, why did this happen? Was it your fault or the listener's fault? If it was your fault, what can you do to prevent misunderstanding?

4. Was your artistic aim clear to your readers, and did it seem significant?

5. Did your main character come to life (especially if you have written a character story) and did your listeners see and hear him, understand him, and care what happens to him?

6. Is your whole story now, in your opinion, as individual as you can make it, in both the plan and the details? Does it seem authentic?

7. Is there forward movement, so far as you can judge, or do you have only a static scene or a collection of static scenes?

If you and your readers are not completely satisfied, rewrite the whole story or at least the weaker sections. Unless you are semiprofessional you will be doing very well to get a good story in two or even three or four writings. But if you are doing much revision, revisualize and let the story grow from within you as you rewrite it. Avoid a mere detached tinkering.

READING

PENNY SALE *

Irving Spaulding

"Well, have things started?" Molly asked dryly.

Pete nodded his answer to his cousin's wife as he slammed the door.

"Who's the auctioneer?"

"Weston. Two clerks with him today. Another family affair between him and Burns. That banker can't get anyone but his brother-in-law to cry these foreclosure sales for him." Pete's corduroy cap hurtled into a straight-backed chair, and his blanket-lined jacket slid from his shoulders.

"We've got some dinner saved for you."

"Don't want much. They started at twelve o'clock; it'll be half an hour before they get that row of old corn plows sold. Gotta be there, then. How are you, Rob?" He tousled the hair of the ten-year-old lad who came toward him.

Sighing, he sat down at the kitchen table. Molly quickly set some warmed-over coffee, a few slices of corn bread, and a dab of boiled potatoes before him.

"I'll have a couple of eggs fried in a jiffy."

Pete waited silently. He was tired. Three hours' sleep showed him up. Not so young any more.

"Where's Luke?"

"Down at the barn showin' 'em which teams and cows to bring out first. Your husband's a plucky fellow. He's looking up."

"Any place else to look?"

"Nowhere."

Pete clasped his hands, his elbows resting on the table. Before him, from the kitchen window, stretched eight miles of half-snow-covered fall plowing, fields of corn stalks, and unplowed stubble, dotted with box-like groves from which windmills protruded.

"Mamma! Can I go out in the barn where Daddy is?"

"No, Rob. You stay in here today. Here are your eggs, Pete. Now, don't whine," she added as the boy showed signs of fretting.

"Better stay in here a while, Bub," Pete admonished. "Wait until the crowd's gone, and we'll go out and have a look around."

He began gulping food.

This was different from his sale back in 1930, he thought. Every fellow who came then brought at least one kid, or so it seemed, and they'd played around, getting in and out of the way, until their dads had corralled them when the sale broke up. This afternoon there wasn't a kid on the place. At least, not one who couldn't handle a gun.

Yep. They'd sold him out in '30. Three years had passed. Three years of hard living for him and his wife. They'd bought a team and a couple of cows with what was left from the sale. By working out they were able to exist on the acreage they'd rented near town. It had been hard, at first, to work as a hired hand for fellows with whom he had traded work when he was farming for himself.

But now—it'd be different with Luke. There wasn't work to be had. There wouldn't be anything left from the sale. He would go on relief, unless he could get some machinery and some livestock. Then he could move on to his mother-in-law's eighty.

If things went right this afternoon, Luke'd have his machinery and livestock. There were at least two hundred men in the yard. Neighbors—good neighbors! With guns in their cars. They wouldn't use guns less they had to. Blanchard's sale last week had been bad—two men killed and half a dozen in the hospital. But—if they had to use 'em—rifles and blank shotgun shells first —in the air. A fellow could always lower his sights! They wouldn't have to, though, if they could bid things in for less than a dollar this afternoon! Then they'd give 'em back to Luke!

A sudden pounding on the door brought Molly from the front room where she'd been watching the crowd of "neighbors— good neighbors! With guns in their cars." Wrenching the door open, she paused.

"Hello, Loren."

"Pete here?"

"Yeah. Come on in." She turned to Pete, "It's Loren Schmitzer," and returned to the front room with Rob, who had followed her to the kitchen.

"How near the end of that row of corn plows are they, Loren?"

"Close. Ya better get out there pretty quick. Pete, this is my nephew, Roger Layden, from Lone River."

"How are you?" Their hands clasped.

"They're foreclosin' on him. Sale's a week from Thursday."

"Burns?"

"Yeah—and the local bank at Lone River." He shook his greyed head, and his stooped shoulders jumped in a little shrug. "Well, he's wonderin'—if this scheme of yours works—if you'd come over and run his sale."

"I don't know. We aren't sure we can put it over. You can rent a place if you have equipment?"

The nephew nodded. "There'll be some cash or beef for you, if you come."

"Pete!"

A boy of sixteen burst into the house. "One corn plow left, Pete! Luke's ready to have 'em start!"

"See me when this is over, Loren," Pete said, glancing at his nearly finished dinner and reaching for his cap and jacket. "If we're able," he added. "Where are you stationed, Larry?"

"I'm with the guns in the four cars at the end of the chicken house."

"Well—take care of yourself." Pete strode from the house, Loren and the nephew at his heels.

As he reached the gas barrels by the machine shed, Pete stopped. Yes—the roans were being brought out! Luke's favorites—tall, broad, husky—their harness jangling—walking—trotting—now standing in the large space between the orchard and the corn crib. The crowd shifted its position, circling the team. By the crib— Pete glanced—yes!—a half dozen fellows apparently not interested in horses, their hands filled with long, tapered ears of corn which they were examining carefully. Swinging up to a position on the barrel racks, Pete scanned the yard.

Weston, flanked by his two clerks, stood near the team inside the circle of men. Crisply his lingo ran across the space to the gas barrels.

"Now, men—here's a pair of eight-year-old roans. Both of 'em sound—except the left one. She was caught in a fence once and has a scar on her left shoulder! The injury doesn't bother her, and she's a good worker! The other one's as sound as a dollar! Now, we're gonna sell 'em as they are—in the harness! A right smart good team! Who'll start 'em off?"

There was a long pause.

"Anybody? Who'll start 'em? Ya've seen 'em in action, boys! They're a good team! Wha' da' I hear?"

Another long pause.

"Fifty cents." The drawled bid came from the edge of the crowd.

Pete smiled. Harley could be relied on. Trust him to start things off.

"Fifty! Fifty—a— What did you say?" he asked the bidder.

"Fifty cents." Again the slow drawl.

Weston grinned.

"O. K. Fifty cents! Anybody give fifty dollars? Fifty dollars?"

"Fifty dollars."

Pete gazed at the bidder—a well-dressed young fellow—near the edge of the crowd. Quailing under the farmers' glances, the smooth-shaven chap drew the collar of his trim, grey overcoat high and pulled his grey hat over his face. Quietly an ear of corn spun low across the crowd and shattered with a bang on the steel snout of the corn picker. The roans jumped—three men grabbed their bits.

Pete waited, watching the crowd draw closely about the team; good fellows, these neighbors—they knew what they were here for! Weston's call rolled out:

"Got fifty! Who'll give sixty? Sixty, sixty, sixty,—"

"Fifty-one cents!" It was not the drawl this time.

"Fifty-one cents, the gentleman says! Who'll give sixty dollars?"

"Sixty dollars!" Again from the grey overcoat.

Anxiously, Pete glanced toward the men at the corn crib. Again corn spun over the crowd. Half ears this time. A heavy butt struck the grey coat squarely in the right shoulder. With snakelike rapidity the chap turned, striking with his left hand, only to find himself in the embrace of a wiry, denim-clad pair of arms.

"Look out! The team!"

"Get out of the road!"

"Quit throwin' corn!"

Pete flinched as the roans reared, excited by the mob and the crash as a couple of pieces of corn hit the picker again. Farmers scattered. Snorting, the team plowed their way to the edge of the ring of men, where they broke into a dead run, then cavorted aimlessly about the yard.

"Must 'a' been hit with some corn!" "Let 'em run!" "They'll be all right as long as they run together!" "Better catch 'em 'fore they run into some machinery!"

"HEY! Whose car is that?"

A blue sedan was crawling onto the graveled road at the end of the rutty driveway. It paused as though to set itself for the five-mile sprint to town.

Pete dropped from the barrel rack. "Who's in it?"

"One of Weston's clerks and the guy with the grey overcoat." "Who is that guy?" "A cousin of Weston's, I guess." "Oh!" "Well, they're gone."

"Let's get the team!" Pete called, and a dozen fellows headed for the far side of the orchard where the roans now stood nervously in the fence corner.

The team being caught, Pete watched the road from the corner of the wellhouse. The blue car had disappeared. A tough break! What now? A posse, perhaps. And the men—the men, in little groups of five or six, were dropping away from the crowd to return a few minutes later with shotguns and rifles slung under their arms. Neighbors—anxious to help! By pairs, a score of them strode through the orchard to the road. A dozen clustered at the end of the driveway. Two pairs stationed themselves in the far corners of the barnyard. Above Pete, dangling his feet over the edge of the small platform at the top of the windmill tower, a red-scarfed little Irishman sat where he could watch the road and fields. "No posse's gonna slip up on us!" he'd muttered.

Calls of "Get the sale goin', Weston!" "Bring out another team!" "Bring out some cows!" "Come on! Get goin'!" rolled through the air.

Pete motioned for a team to be brought from the barn, as he stalked toward the crowd of men. Moving close to the auctioneer, he picked up an ear of corn. Slowly, he shelled a few kernels, watching them slide from their long even rows as a team of bays trotted up. Pete raised his head; his eyes met those of the auctioneer. "All right, Weston! Let's start!"

Reluctantly, Weston started. The bays sold quickly at 90 cents; the roans were sold next at 99 cents. Luke could use four horses. The five best cows—Luke would need them; the year-old corn planter, the two-row corn plow, the gang plow, the four-section drag, the harrow—Luke would need them, too. Weston sold rapidly —with apparent disregard for the word "cents" which followed every bid. An ear-splitting whistle from the windmill tower brought activities to a halt.

"Keep selling," Pete said quietly to Weston.

Three rifle bolts clicked.

As Weston took up his call, Pete hustled to the foot of the windmill. He exchanged shouts with the Irishman. Two cars, eh? Blue? Grey? Turning, he sprinted toward the road, as the fugitive clerk and Weston's cousin stopped the blue sedan in the "Y" of the driveway. Burns' long Packard followed. Guns in their hands, the cluster of men blocked the drive.

Sliding through the group of men, Pete halted as Burns rolled down the window of his Packard.

"What's goin' on here?" The words were wrapped in cigar smoke.

"We're havin' a sale. Want to go up and look around? Or'd you rather watch from here?" Empty-handed, Pete stepped near the open window of the Packard.

"What's this about bidding in cents?"

"We're buying things at a price we can afford—with corn at ten cents a bushel."

"What's the idea?"

"Just savin' enough stuff for Luke so he can go over and work his mother-in-law's place."

Pete watched a curl of smoke twist thoughtfully from Burns' lips. In the silence Weston's voice—Burns' brother-in-law's voice— hummed from the yard, "Got twen'y-three! Anybody give twen'y-four? Twen'y-four? Twen'y-four, twen'y-four—" hummed from the center of a ring of determined men, men with guns! Guns which had been used with accuracy on rabbits, squirrels, and pheasants; guns which could be used on deputies, auctioneers, and bankers!

Behind him—facing Burns—stood a dozen half-amused men— grimly amused. Seven of them had been at Blanchard's sale last week. Two fellows killed. The auctioneer's shoulder filled with shot. Five others in the hospital. Grimly amused men.

Weston's cousin could be glad that only an ear of corn clipped his right shoulder! Burns knew that!

Slowly Burns let a cloud of smoke stream from the Packard's window. Steadily, he gazed at Pete. "Well," he began. Pete's fists tensed in his jacket pockets. "Settle up with the clerk as soon as you can," the banker stated crisply.

There was the sudden closing of the Packard's window—the throb of two racing motors—two cars backing jerkily into the road, heading toward town—Pete's clenched hands relaxed in his jacket pockets; he turned, slowly, to face a row of smiling men.

An hour and a half later, Pete learned against the side of the wellhouse and pushed the corduroy cap back on his head. Slowly he glanced across the vacant yard; then at the fellows with him. "Well, Loren—the sale's a week from Thursday, eh?" he said to Schmitzer.

"That's right. Six miles east of Lone River."

"It's Burns and the local bank there," Pete told the men. "Anybody not interested in going over?"

There was no answer.

Schmitzer looked at his long shadow. "Gettin' close to chore time," he remarked. "Want a ride toward town, Pete?"

"Sure. Riding's better than walking."

"Anybody seen Luke during the last half hour?"

"He's probably out in the barn with the team of roans."

"Well—he's with the roans, but they're down at the tank."

Pete stepped around the corner of the wellhouse. By the low cement stock tank stood Luke, the halter ropes of the drinking team across his arm; at his side—Rob. Stooping quickly, he caught the boy under the arms and flipped him to the back of the nearest mare.

Pete smiled. Turning to Schmitzer, he half-chuckled, "Luke'll make a good farmer out of that boy in the next ten years!"

NEITHER HERE NOR THERE [2]

Ruth Portugal

The soldier was tall, so that to sling his kit bag and his cap and tunic into the upper berth was no more than a gesture of wrists. There were the blue eyes and the fresh yellow hair of northern farms. Somewhere close by might be the place he had always lived in.

[2] *Harper's Bazaar*, September, 1943. Reprinted by permission of the author.

From her berth across the aisle Caroline watched him for a moment, saw him settling himself with pretended ease, as though he were accustomed to this sort of thing. In the canteens in New York, in their aimless wandering through the streets of the city, she had seen them—like this one, the strong colors of sun and wind in their skins—painfully casual, to cover up the startled uprooting that the war had brought to their lives. She felt a helpless pity for the bewilderment and shock there must be behind that deliberately hardened face. Chicago, she thought, as she fastened the curtains of her berth, was a long way from where he was going.

In his privacy now, behind the curtains of the shelf he lay on, the uniform and the sudden manhood put aside, he would be staring at whatever fears and denials congregated in the dark, knowing he had to fight, and not knowing at all how or why it had happened to him.

All the following long day they saw Nebraska. The land looked sick, the old cornstalks rotting, and everything the one brown-yellow color.

Across the aisle the soldier dozed. Without lifting his head from the hand it rested on, he would glance out only long enough to see that nothing had changed in fifty miles, and then he would close his eyes again. There were other soldiers in the car; down front were four privates and a corporal. Perhaps only yesterday they were unknown to one another, disparate and alien. Now, by an alchemy of uniform and orders, their faces were indivisible from other soldier faces. And hiding behind the new looks of unconcern might be the private wonder at what had happened to them, finding no answer in the futile landscape. These wastes could not be the fruited plains they were expected to fight and die for.

After lunch Caroline fell asleep, drugged by the perpetual sounds of the wheels and the sunless day and the deadness that was all you could see. When she awoke the soldier across the aisle had disappeared. She decided to go forward to the club car for a drink while the crowds in the diner thinned. She was unprepared to see him there. He was looking through one of the magazines in the railroad's bindings, quite at ease in the urbanity of the car, drinking beer. The only vacant chair was near him. Now that she was so close to the soldier she did not look at him at all.

And then he was in the chair just vacated beside her. "Care for a beer?" he said. At first Caroline was not sure it was to her he spoke; he did not turn his head toward her.

She managed a pleasant, even smile. "Why—yes. Thank you."

He waved two fingers at the barman in a gesture as definite as a salute. When the beer was brought, he poured it easily into the two glasses, tilting the glasses' rims to the bottles and controlling the foam, and then, after handing a glass to her, he settled the bottles with a sure extension of arms on the unsteady metal table in front of them.

He was silent as they drank the beer, not looking at her.

"It's too bad you're not traveling in a group like the others," Caroline began. "You're alone, aren't you? I didn't know they did that to you."

He shrugged slightly. "In the Army it don't happen two times the same way." He said it as though it were an ordinary fact anyone might know.

She started again. "Have you been in long?"

"Yeah, kind of."

"My brother"—my brother who knows why he is doing it—"is leaving college next month to enlist. He could stay on and finish his course, but he doesn't want to. He wants to be in it right away." She felt the pride rise in her for what her young brother was doing; she wanted to let this soldier know that the war touched upon her. The soldier was steadily drinking beer. "I don't know what branch of the Army he'll be in. He's very good at languages. He had always hoped when he finished college to go over to the Sorbonne—that's a university in Paris," she explained. "He did say once that he wanted to be with the infantry because that's the real army."

The soldier made no comment.

"You're in the infantry?"

"Yeah," he said.

At Service men's dances she had often found herself with shy soldiers; it was an effort to talk to them, to get them to talk.

"How far're you goin'?" he asked.

Caroline was pleased by the first direct thing he had said to her. "All the way." Then she saw one corner of his mouth lift a little in a smile; she realized suddenly the innuendo his smile had given to her words. "San Francisco," she added hurriedly.

The soldier's glass was emptied and he looked at hers. "Drink it down." He waved his two-fingered salute again.

"Not another, thank you." She hadn't really wanted beer.

"Sure, why not?" he said blandly, and that was that.

It was the unhesitating way in which the soldier did it—flipping the coins on the steward's tray and again pouring the beer with practiced eye and hand, and his calm existence beside her that had by this time set awry the image of him she had formed the night before. She wondered where he had gone, that other one, lonely and confused. Watching the smooth rhythm of the soldier's drinking, the strong free throat receiving the large drafts, she floundered among the questions she might have asked that other self she had thought him to be, of the home somewhere and the homesickness, of the time ahead, of what he had dreamed of being before the dreams had been torn from him.

"How about somethin' to eat?" he said after his final swallow of beer, and he pointed to her half-full glass, so she quickly drank it down.

The simple earnestness of his eating brought back again the clear farm look to his face. Caroline felt more at ease. Nebraska, he said when she asked him where his home was. Barrow, "coupla miles outside of Omaha." At ten-thirty that morning they had stopped at Omaha. She had seen no one come to be with him during the long wait at the station.

"But you boarded the train at Chicago," she said.

"That's where they stuck me. Bin goin' to school again. Uncle Sam's spent a cool ten thousand, adding in everything, just sendin' me back to school like a kid. Jeez, some Army," and he shook his head. But Caroline detected at the same time a pride expanding in him that he was worth that much money.

"Where are you going now?"

"I gotta play teacher to some of those new punks they got up at Sacramento. What a goddam job. They'll be callin' me Joe Palooka 'stead of Joe Purvis."

Like her brother, he was impatient, too. "But you have to get your training here before they can send you overseas."

"Hey . . ." He looked up from his plate and stared at her. "You got me mixed up with a coupla million other guys. I bin out there."

She sat there looking at him readjusting her picture, seeing him against the name places of the war. Bataan, Corregidor, Guadalcanal, New Guinea. . . . "Where have you been?" she asked.

"Put in ten months in Hawaii before I landed back in Frisco last summer."

"Pearl Harbor—you were there?"

"Didn't get over much. They stuck me the other end of the layout." The way he said it, Pearl Harbor might have been merely another point on a travel-folder island. "Hell," he said, "I bin to all the places." He checked them off on his fingers. "Panama. Porto Rico. Manila. China. Got out on the last troop boat from Shanghai when those monkeys walked in. Shipped to Hawaii." He leaned back in his chair and placed his hands behind his head. "I'd kinda like to get the hell out and go back there." His voice sounded withdrawn from her and from the table and reaching beyond the window. "I wonder who's taken over. If it's one of those new punks I'll twist her goddam neck."

"You've left your girl there? In Hawaii?" Caroline asked uncertainly.

Joe looked at her abruptly, as though her speaking recalled her presence. "Left her? That's where I found her. On the beach along with the seaweed." He was looking at Caroline with his mouth pulled back in the odd smile. "Those half-breeds sure know what to do. She was part Chink." He looked at her directly, seeming to measure her side by side with that girl. "Took one in Panama—she was part nigger," he said.

"How long," Caroline asked quietly, "have you been in the Army?"

"Seven years," he said.

Caroline looked at his shirt sleeves, bare of any stripes that might explain the seven years. His eyes were the same simple blue that might have last looked over the farm lands. But behind those eyes now were the women of strange bloods he had taken, and the ports of call he had wandered in, and the scattered garrisons he had had for home in the years of peace when the Army was in eclipse, its existence remote and forgotten, its men never seen.

"You must have been just a boy when you went," she said, partly to herself.

"Sixteen, fooled 'em on my age." He sat back to survey her. "Makes me twenty-three. Older than you, huh?"

Caroline was twenty-four. "No," she said. "I'm a little older." And the year's difference seemed a vantage point that she needed.

"Guess I got a coupla kids I don't know about," he said, grinning slightly and making her conscious of the sheltering walls that had always been up around her, and opening the door a little wider into the secret world he had chosen.

"But what made you go into the Army?" she asked, to fathom the sixteen-year-old mind of seven years ago.

There was a chunk of meat on his fork and he lowered his mouth to it and she saw the jaws grinding it thoroughly. "Well," he said; he took his time with the words, "that's neither here nor there." His words were not spoken as something to hide behind, but as though that were the closest he could penetrate to whatever had sent him into the Army. Perhaps he had become another person in the seven years and had forgotten why it had happened. Here I am—who cares how I got here?—was what his face seemed to say.

"Never much to do," he said when Caroline asked him what Barrow was like. "Nothin' to do at night but listen to those goddam train whistles."

To Caroline these words lifted some of the mystery from him. They brought back her sympathy for him. She could see him, his boy's face raised to the night sky and his ears echoing long hours afterward, the train's call to him across the prairies, until he had to run off to the world beyond the landlocked birthplace. He had joined the Army because that was a way to do it. Even that flash of homesickness which she had first seen written on his face fitted into the picture: the homesickness of the wandering soldier returned after the long odyssey and finding he loved the old places, and being torn from them to an Army more sober than the one to which the night wails of the train had first called him.

"You've been home," Caroline said softly. Tell me about it, she wanted to say, because no one again might ever care.

"Got over to see my sister once."

"I'm glad," Caroline said.

"Yap, yap, yap," he said, and his face grew slack with boredom, "about why didn't she hear from me when Pa died. Maybe she expected me to sprout wings or somethin' and fly in from Shanghai."

The waiter came just then with their dinner checks. Caroline started to reach for hers.

"Hey," Joe said, "what the hell!" And he drew off some bills from a thick layer in his wallet.

"But I don't want you to," she protested. "I'd have to have my dinner anyway."

"Got paid off before I boarded." He handed the money carelessly to the waiter. "And I got an expense account, you might call it, on the train."

She felt awkward. "But—a private's pay—"

"Oh, I'll be gettin' a boost soon as I report in. They're pinnin' the stripes back on me again." He grinned in his twisted way.

"What do you mean?" she said, puzzled.

"They broke me." He said it without bitterness, philosophically in acceptance of the rules of a game. He did not say more about it, so that Caroline did not know what he might have done to lose his rank: A.W.O.L. or drunkenness or a brawl or women. . . .

The train was slowing down. "Cheyenne," he said. "We got fifteen minutes."

There was a clarity to the mountain air, it was air to drink. Caroline walked along the platform with him, absorbed in the exercise and the muscular pull as she stretched to his long stride, until they passed two soldiers coming out of the station building.

"*Wuh-whoo*," she heard them whistle after her. It was like a code. She could feel the answering grin on Joe's face. It made her just one in a million, a grass-skirted native girl he had found—or some tart he had picked up in one of a thousand cities in the world.

"I'm going back," she said, standing a little apart from him already. "Good night." And without looking at him again she walked away.

She knew his eyes—and the other two soldiers'—were focused on her back, inspecting the carriage of her body, following its lines and halting frankly, as she had caught men's eyes traveling over other women passing along a street.

Caroline walked toward her car with a precise dignity. I would never have noticed him anywhere, nor talked nor eaten with him, were it not for the uniform, she told herself.

But in her berth she thought back to the home and the family he had hinted at and was troubled by their neutral meaning to him. The homesickness could not be called that any more and she did not know what to call it; the home was not something to long for nor something to escape from but only a place to grow up in and leave. Perhaps—and her mind swiftly hunted it down—the drained look of his eyes was his sign of grief for some one of those women he really loved, caught up now in the war in some corner of the world to which he would never return.

But even the love and the grief like the homesickness might be only her invention. The emptiness of his eyes might be no more than the projection of something coal-hard and blank at the center of him, impervious to the longings and reasons and hates that were the only gauge she knew to measure him against.

The curtains of his berth were still drawn when Caroline got up the next morning. At breakfast she sat opposite a nondescript woman about whom she need not have any thoughts at all.

Toward noon she looked up from the book she had brought with her to the lounge and there he was.

He wiped the sleep from his eyes. "Guess I'll settle for beer this morning," he said through a yawn. After he had drunk down a glass he spoke again. "Sat up kinda late with a coupla those punks from our car. Got 'em all staggering on their ears." He smiled that one-sided smile that was the closest Caroline had ever seen him come to laughter; sometimes, as now, she was not sure it had anything to do with laughter. It was his signal of pleasure or amusement or some secret attitude, narrowed down to the thin, noncommittal lines of that smile. "Soldiers! They think they know all about it. I gave 'em a lesson. Blackjack. Trimmed 'em."

"Where are they now?" Caroline automatically looked around the car.

"Who, them? Got off back at Ogden this morning." Again he smiled like that. "No sleep and plenty likkered. Guess they won't know what's hit 'em when they get the works today. The corporal too." He said "corporal" with mock respect. "Bin in a coupla months, thinks he's one of us."

She thought of their dismal arrival at some camp, miserable from drinking all night with Joe and losing all their money to him, and the quick destruction of their new soldiers' bravado.

"They're going to camp with nothing, no money at all?"

"Oh, their mommas'll send 'em cookies," he drawled.

"Why shouldn't their mothers worry about them!" She was surprised by the indignation in her voice. "Some of them are just boys." But Joe had been only sixteen when he went off.

"Yeah? They're makin' it a goddam Sunday school." He poured the rest of his beer.

"It's not easy to change from one kind of life to another," Caroline said. "I suppose fitting into Army life when you've had nothing like it is hardest of all." Like some of the men she knew, suddenly transplanted into a new existence with none of their old habits applying. "They've never been in anything like it before," she said, pleading the case of all new soldiers—her brother and the privates and the corporal—to this veteran of twenty-three.

He said nothing. He just grinned and drank his beer.

"They know what they're in to do." Each one of them knows, her mind tolled, that he may be one of those who won't come home again. Perhaps it was harder for them to prepare for death than for Joe Purvis. They knew what they were giving up. They had not been in for seven years, but some of them, on the oceans and in the islands and in Africa and over the sky-pointed guns of Europe, knew more of that death than he did. "They're not asking to be coddled. But you've got to understand what the change means to them."

He did not seem to notice what she was saying. "Joe." She tried again. "You've been in so much longer than any of them. You can do a lot to prepare them," as though to say you, Joe Purvis with your seven years, can afford to do that.

"Sure," he drawled, and smiled again. To Caroline the futility of her plea was clear. The new soldiers were entering Joe Purvis' realm, and in his realm he was master.

Her brother might find himself obeying Joe Purvis.

She felt all the helpless rage and despair of the brother who might be signed over to this Joe Purvis sitting next to her drinking beer, who had never read a sonnet nor traced the design of a fugue nor learned of the golden times in men's history nor recognized the barbarian's shrill voice of destruction screaming down the centuries.

None of these things would matter, and it would not matter that the brother's young eyes saw in this war the barricades against the tyrant at last being thrown up around the world, himself mounting the barricades. This war was no more to Joe Purvis than the job he had been on for seven years. All the brother's ingrained values—the same values she abided by, all his solemn beliefs and hopes would be reduced to a zero when he stood at attention before Joe Purvis.

Joe Purvis knew the craft of war. That was the only thing that mattered.

If I were my brother, she thought, looking at Joe Purvis drinking and unaware, he could do that to me. He could trample down everything I am.

The war had proclaimed his existence. The war could put him and others like him on top; the seven years formed the pyramid of his ascent. Here in the direct, ignorant sureness of Joe Purvis of America was the brutality of the enemy. Facing her was his coarse primary maleness that somehow degraded her as it looked at her.

"Did you ever think of a commission?" she asked on impulse, sensing that in his answer might lie a germ of hope, some ambition she could play upon that would reclaim him.

His eyes spread in surprise. "Who—me? Don't make me laugh. Hell, I make more pay countin' in the time I bin in than the gold-bar wonders." He paused. "Anyway, this way I got more—you know, like a private can eat peas off of his knife." He said it like a child proud of his special prerogative.

There was no way for her to reach him. Watching him cross to the radio, she understood why he was content to stay where he was. On his side of the fence he would be boss.

Without a thought for those who might be listening to the broadcast, he snapped the dials over a series of noisy bands until he found one that satisfied him. Caroline watched the careless and certain movements of his body; his force added a new dimension to him. Even the concentration he gave to settling the elementary problem of one juke-box song over another seemed an act of his power; only what he wanted at the moment counted. It would be the same way if he wanted a woman.

Suddenly, as though in flight, she hurried from the car.

In the evening the train stopped at Reno. Joe walked over to her on the platform. She hesitated over the cigarette he offered, and then took it, and they looked out over the lighted place.

Ahead was another coast, with its constant guardedness.

There was a gaudy brilliance to the city, reeking of silver dollars and a bawdiness removed from war, and an old relaxation.

"It would be fun to stay a while," Caroline said. She was hardly aware that Joe was with her, and she was startled when she heard him say, "Why don't we?"

He looked at her from the corners of his eyes as he spoke; his voice was slightly uncertain.

"You'd land in the guardhouse for overstaying your leave." She tried with a light quick laugh to rub out the meaning of his words.

"Yeah," he said. "That's right." As he turned away to the city's lights he looked like a boy who had tried something beyond him and found he didn't know how to make it work.

There were all the women he had known, the derelicts and the natives and the ripe easy choices. She was unassailable and he knew it. Looking at him now she wondered how she had ever come to feel afraid of him.

In a few hours she would never see him again; he was getting off at Sacramento. So she stayed up with him, drinking beer and playing gin rummy, not thinking of what he had done to the privates and their corporal nor of what he could do to her brother—for he could never really touch him—but seeing him as a soldier who would be gone soon.

It was one o'clock. She started to pick up her bag from the table. "You'll have to be up again in a few hours."

"Come on, have another beer," he said.

There was a hard rain pelting the windows and in a little while he would be walking in it. "All right." She stayed on because he wanted her to and that was little enough to do for any soldier.

Then all the other passengers had left the car and the steward was locking up at the small bar.

She stood up. "We'd better leave now."

They walked silently back through the cars of sleeping people until they came to their Pullman. In the vestibule she paused.

"Well—good-bye," she said, coming to that word at last. She looked up into his eyes, as clear as a farm boy's. "All the luck to you, Joe." And she thought how futile were the last words one spoke to a soldier.

She held out her hand to him and he took it and she touched the stranger's flesh. In the firm-boned hand, in the whole and muscular body that faced her in the uniform was the promise of death. Whoever and whatever he was no longer mattered before the fact of his untimely mutilation.

Who would there be to grieve for him?

They were scheduled to arrive in Oakland at seven-thirty. She was repacking her suitcase, when Joe's head and shoulders appeared through the curtain. He had taken off his blouse and the skin shone high-colored against the white undershirt.

"Have you got an aspirin?" he asked. "I got a headache, kind of."

She was aware of the nightgown and the lingerie spread on the berth, and the open suitcase revealing further details of herself. "Yes—I think so," she said.

He took the tin she handed him and stood there and looked at her. "Can I stay a while?" he said. "Gotta be gettin' off soon anyways." And he sat down on the berth, pushing up the pillow with his elbow, before she could find an answer.

"I don't think you'd better." Caroline did not know quite what to say, how to say it. She smiled. "It's late; everyone's asleep."

He looked up over his head to where the upper berth had been pulled back to give Caroline more space. "It's kinda stuffy where I am."

In all the darkened car her berth was bright. Anyone getting up would witness the preposterous sight of a soldier lying across her bed. "No," she said to him, kindly but firmly, "you'd better go." She held out her hand again.

"Goddam you," he said through his immobile mouth.

Caroline felt her blood like sudden fire. "Will you please leave!"

"What's the matter? Afraid?"

"Of what?"

And then looking at his fingers as they played over the surface of her lingerie, she was afraid, tasted the fear she had known when she was a child and had sensed hands reaching out for her from dark places. She could only stand there, speechless, in the fraction of space between the curtains and her berth.

Joe's eyes moved over her legs and thighs; the breasts suggesting themselves against the buttoned suit jacket; the hips balancing the shoulders' width. His eyes moved up the shaft of her throat, sampled her mouth, met her eyes, marched again over her.

She searched backward with frantic speed to discover when first his ruthlessness had begun to shape itself for her, as though to find the answer would dispel this moment. Just a little while ago they had stood on the platform at Reno and he had turned shy at his first lame attempt toward her; he had stopped short of her. He had recognized the barrier between her and whatever way he had taken women, so that she had been inviolate.

Joe did not take his eyes from her. "You've never met a guy like me," she heard him say.

His hands lay certain of themselves on the blanket, ready to touch her. With those hands he could hold a rifle as he held a woman; they were hands that knew a woman as they knew a rifle. They would be quick and sure. Terrible; splendid.

"Why do you come to me?" she whispered, to break the fascination of those hands.

"Why shouldn't I?" he said. "You're made like all the rest."

Had an hour before we got to Sacramento, took her on her bunk. . . . Took one, she was part nigger. . . . Took one in the seaweed where I found her. . . .

Caroline watched the blond hairs on his arm stir with her breathing, and stood rigid against the magnetism of his flesh. Right now she must get away—but some unexpected will compelled her to wait.

Her skin was taut with the waiting. She was aware of a rising violence in herself, waiting to match the threat of him.

"You're utterly wrong," she said, finding the voice to say it.

His mouth was fixed in the warped smile. "You're just a tease. Make the guys hot for you and then say good-bye, nix on the monkey business, keep it clean. You're no different," he said. "And I ain't your pretty-boy brother. You don't kid me with your smart lingo and all the rest of that craperoo. What the hell didya think I want?"

"I thought you were lonely," Caroline said. "When you came over to speak to me I thought you were lonely." But almost at once he had been something else; she had been repelled by that alien thing in him and had been drawn to it and dreaded its unleashing.

"I don't waste my time."

His eyes changed from their steady blankness. They were luminous; hate seemed to come alive in them. "You think I ain't fancy enough. Maybe I'm a bum, huh? The whole goddam country thinks I'm plenty good these days. I can take any goddam thing I want."

Even me. He has hesitated until now; he's never tested his power this far before.

"I can walk into any goddam place I want," he said.

And his words lit up harshly the years of doors closed to him, backs turned to him, outcast because he had made himself that, his life narrowed down to the company of those like him who had discarded the world. He had exiled himself and now he was back, restored from limbo. He would walk roughshod and bullying over everything. He was the illiterate ready to crumble the world he could never understand.

"You'll be in Sacramento soon," she said desperately, to turn his blunt attention from her. "Back in camp." Inside the barracks that were the only outlines of home he recognized. "You'll be with your friends in a little while," she said to put off the appalling realization of him loose in the world.

"Hell. . . . They won't be around. It ain't the same any more."

The hate and the power seemed to be washed pale in that instant by the look of something lost from him.

Then he stood up. His eyes came back to her. He took her throat in the bruising grip of one hand, and looked full into her thrust-back face that stared at him and refused him. He held her like that. And as suddenly he let her go.

"Save it, lady," he said. The grin was a scar on his face. "Save it."

Then he left, and Caroline leaned her head against the window, weak in the sickness she felt. She was rid of him, herself safe. And she was sad and cold in the wake of his shapeless loneliness. In that brief flash of loss he had shown at last a need. Even he did not want to be alone. Lost member of a lost tribe. All the others like him, the mercenaries cut off from the world, were scattered now, nomads lost among the new millions of men bearing loyalties, who were usurping their garrisons.

Some day there could be a leader—here, too, in America— who could take Joe Purvis and the ones like him and translate their inchoate power into a terrible thing. He would make them an army of occupation in their own land. Joe Purvis would be the enemy among us, the enemy of his people, for he did not belong to them. He belonged to the others like him and now they were gone and he was lost. . . .

She hated her human blind pity for him, the enemy; that was part of the sickness—the tears, even now, for his loneliness and for the hero's death he might die before his power could be turned against them.

This was the dawn hour when armies moved out; a hundred times before he might have slung his bag over his shoulder as he did now, on the path beside the tracks, with the rain dripping off his cap.

As the train started away, Caroline saw him, a darker gray against the gray air, set off alone in the winter mountain rain toward the valley.

BLOODHOUND [3]

James Boyd

The crowd of black felt hats moved from the track.

"Hyer she comes. Hark to her whistle."

"That's good. They tell me with a bloodhound every minute counts."

"That nigger's had four hours' start right now."

"Reckon it was a nigger."

"It's a nigger. All this stealing around town's nigger work. And what white man would take a purple suit with yellow stripes?"

"All I hope, this dog can smell him. They tell me it costs the town fifty dollars to bring it here."

"Heyo, Will, you got a bloodhound aboard?"

"Sure have. Hyer's the man with him."

"Gentlemen, how you all?"

"Howdy."

"Now, gentlemen, stand back and give this dog room. Too many folks is liable to mess him up."

"Look at them great ears. A man could tie them under his chin."

"Now, gentlemen, whereabouts do we start?"

"Right yonder. See that sign 'Bullteel's Clothing Store'? Nigger taken the suit right off the hanger."

"That dog knows what he come for. Don't he walk proud, though?"

"He's a severe dog."

"They tell me, though, a bloodhound's gentle."

"Well, doggone if I'd love to hear one belling on my track."

"They tell me, though, he don't do nothing but smell and holler."

[3] *Scribner's Magazine*, August, 1931. Reprinted by the courtesy of Mrs. Katherine Boyd.

"That's all right, but, as the fellow says, does the dog say it? Yes, sir, I want to hear it from the dog, else I'm gone right now, I—"

"Now, gentlemen, stand back. Don't mess up the sidewalk. You Mr. Bullteel?"

"Yes, sir. Bring in your dog."

"Never mind that. Bring out the hanger the suit was on."

"You reckon he keeps the harness on that dog all the time?"

"I expect so."

"Sure he keeps it on. How could he stay with him else?"

"Yes, sir, without that harness that dog would fly."

"Watch him snuff that hanger."

"Hark to him snuff."

"Now, gentlemen, stand back."

"He's working the ground now. Now he's whimpering."

"Man, he's off."

"Come on, boys."

"Now, gentlemen, keep back."

"Doggone, he's bound to catch that nigger. He's straining in the collar."

"Man, hark to him. I'd love mighty well to hear that tongue on a fox."

"Now he's hushed."

"Hold on, boys, don't push him. This cross street has him bothered."

"Stand still. Let's us see what he will do."

"There he goes. Round the corner and down the hill. Right for Jim Crowtown."

"Didn't I say it was a nigger?"

"Bill, you and some others cut around ahead. Don't let any nigger leave on the other side. You all got guns?"

"We all got guns."

"Now, gentlemen, stay back. All these nigger tracks keeps him studying."

"Look at all the niggers disappear."

"Nothing but dust and doors a-slamming."

"Niggers sure despise a bloodhound."

"They say, though, a bloodhound's gentle."

"That's all right, but does the bloodhound say it? Yes, sir, I want to hear it from the bloodhound."

"Hush, he's hit off his loss. Come on."

"Now, gentlemen, keep back."

"If he branches off yonder they ain't but one house it can be."

"Well, there he goes. It's Sis Highpocket's."

"He's straining on it now."

"It's Sis Highpocket's. Look at him jump at that door."

"Stand back, gentlemen. Nigger, open that door."

"Come out, Sis."

"Sis, open that door."

"Take a run at it, Lon. Pull out your guns, boys, and go right in behind him."

"Hold on, gentlemen, till I get my dog away."

"All right, let's go. Everybody in."

"Oh, my sweet God, gentlemens, oh, my—"

"Hush your fuss, Sis. Who you got with you?"

"God is my judge and witness, gentlemens. They ain't been a man in this house since my man went on the roads."

"What you got under that green wrapper, Sis?"

"Gentlemens, let me tell you the truth, I was just changing my closes to step over to town for my Saturday rations. I was—"

"What man you got here, Sis?"

"Gentlemens, I—"

"Look under the bed, Jeff."

"Oh, my sweet God, gentlemens."

"Yonder he is. I can see his feet. Come out, nigger. Grab his leg."

"Who's got the handcuffs? Nigger, hold out your hands. Anybody know this nigger?"

"Looks like one of them south Georgia niggers that's come in."

"That's what he is. It's them south Georgia niggers been raising all the fuss around here."

"Sis, what ails you? This is as sorry a nigger as ever I saw."

"He's yellow and he's puny."

"Can't you do no better than that, Sis?"

"Gentlemens, God is my judge and witness. I never seen this

person before. He must have crope under my bed when I was sleeping. Black boy, don't you grin at me. I'll slap your head in, ape. Gentlemens, let me tell you the truth. This a mighty big surprise. I declare—"

"Anybody find the suit? Cut open the mattress."

"Done cut it open. Pillows as well."

"Let's get out. Between nigger and feathers I'm about to lose my breath."

"Never mind the suit. We got the nigger."

"So long, Sis."

"Sis, you better tread light. When your Lundy gets off the roads he'll cut your liver."

"Gentlemens, ain't I told you—"

"We ought to tie a rope on this nigger."

"You know what we ought to do? We ought to tie this nigger up and whip him good."

"Road gang don't mean nothing to him. He'll get fat on the roads."

"Nigger, you want to be whipped?"

"No, suh."

"Heyo, here comes Hugh Dave. His face is afire and he's stepping high."

"Look at him raise his knees. That scoundrel sure loves his liquor."

"Howdy, Hugh Dave."

"Hi, boys, howdy. How you all come on? What's the fuss?"

"Nigger yonder been stealing."

"Nigger, you been stealing? Doggone my hide, you ought to be whipped. If they's anything I despise it's a stealing nigger. For two cents I'd lay onto you with a bull whip till you had the gospel in your soul. You hear me? Who caught him?"

"Bloodhound from Twelve Oaks."

"Bloodhound, come here. Rise up, dog. You and me will finish this bottle together. Rise up, dog. Only don't mess up my clothes. They're new."

"Man, keep your liquor away from my dog."

"Whereabouts did you get that suit, Hugh Dave?"

"Taken it out of Bullteel's store. He was gone and I aimed to go on that Birmingham excursion, only I needed a suit and I was drunk."

"You're drunk now, Hugh Dave."

"Then I went to sleep and missed the excursion. And now look at my fix. I've the suit to pay for and I've slept in it already and my liquor is give out and it's a sorry bluegum nigger suit, anyways."

"Doggone if that ain't the suit."

"Sure enough, that's the suit."

"Well, boys, it looks like this is the suit. Nigger, you listen. You can go this time, but mind how you carry on around here."

"Yes, suh."

"Man, what ails your bloodhound that we paid fifty dollars for?"

"You lay off this dog. He's caught twenty-nine niggers and a white man in the last three years. And two of them was hung."

"Looks like they hung the wrong niggers if this fyce dog caught them."

"You call my dog a fyce, you—"

"Now, gentlemen, gentlemen—"

"Well, then, let him lay off my dog."

"Friend, they is no complaint about your dog. Ain't that a fact, boys?"

"Sure is. A dog can't always be right."

"And it's a mighty good thing for this community—to bring in a bloodhound."

"Yes, sir. It will keep the niggers quiet for some little time."

"Why, man, this bloodhound has done a thousand dollars' worth of good."

"What this town needs is a bloodhound."

"Well, gentlemen, times are hard with me. For three hundred dollars—"

"Well, boys, I reckon we better be getting back to town."

QUESTIONS

How has the writer of "Penny Sale" planned the time, place, and situation for his story? Since he had much knowledge from family background about such sales in the Midwest during the depression, would it be difficult or easy for him to limit to one sale? Has he done well to choose a sale after outbreaks of violence and before Pete feels sure of success? Or would a sale with an outbreak of violence make a better story? Give reasons for your answer. What information is brought out by the opening talk between Pete and Molly? By Pete's thinking while he gulps his food? By the talk of Loren Schmitzer and Roger Layden with Pete? What is the significance of Molly's refusal to let Rob go to the barn? What details does the writer use well for suspense through the whole story? What is Pete's character like as it appears in the whole story? Where are the sympathies of the writer, with Pete and Luke or with Weston and Burns? How important are character, setting, theme, and plot in the story? What are the conflicting forces, when larger causes are considered, and when individuals are named? What is the climax of the story? What is the conclusion like—a sharp ending or a continuing effect? Is the kind of conclusion effective or not? What is the writer's artistic aim in the whole story?

What idea is the major aim of "Neither Here Nor There"? Where is this idea given its most complete statement, and by whom or through whose thoughts? What contrasts exist in the education, background, experience, and ideals of Joe Purvis and of Caroline? Is Caroline's comparatively sheltered background essential to the story? Why? What had her first impressions of Joe been? How did those impressions change during her first encounter with him in the dining car? During the stop at Cheyenne? In the lounge car next day when he told her about his gambling with the punks? During the stop at Reno? During the gin rummy games the last night? In the scene at her berth? In which of these scenes does he appear most human? If Caroline had never been influenced at all by Joe's ruthless power, would the author have been able to develop the idea of the story? Does the author apply her main idea to Joe Purvis and Caroline only? How large is her final application of the idea? Is it universal? Give reasons for your answer.

What had happened in "Bloodhound" before the story began? What assumption was made about the identity of the thief? Why? Was this assumption true or false? What were the real facts about the theft? With only one opening sentence of comment, how does the author manage to use well a rather complex set of events? Does the talk characterize the owner of the bloodhound, the men about town, a spokesman for the town, Sis Highpocket, Hugh Dave? Does the story emphasize character, a mood, or an idea which centers on the identity of the thief? If you object to the use of certain words in the story, in most connotations, do you grant the writer's right to use them here for his artistic aim?

PART II
Personalized Exposition

15

The Process:

HOW PEOPLE DO THINGS

From your reading of Part I you perhaps recall the statement that no rigid line separates narration from exposition. Writers of fiction use author comment, analyze characters, and summarize events between specific scenes whenever they need exposition. Writers of exposition also use narration to support, clarify, and make ideas interesting. It may be safely said that neither you nor professional writers start to write merely narration, description, argument, or exposition. You, like the seasoned professionals, probably begin with a specific subject and an urge to inform, interest, convince, persuade, or stimulate; then you blend narration, exposition, and the other forms as you need them. But if you already combine them without much conscious planning, perhaps you can gain skill by using them consciously, as you practice a curve in baseball or a left-handed stroke in tennis.

DEFINING EXPOSITION

When we attempt to define exposition, too, there are few if any absolutes, and thus there is no rigid definition. Exposition, of course, is explanation. The term often implies an explanation of objective facts or principles, causes, effects, analyses of problems, impersonal truths, and the generalizations that satisfy intellectual curiosity. Often exposition has a logical organization. But the term exposition applies also to material that is both subjective and emotional and that has a logical organization. For example, if you wish to analyze and explain your motives for an action, or your tangled feelings at a particular time, you are certainly dealing with subjective and emotional material and you may need a logical organization. When we attempt to define narration so as to separate it from exposition, we say that narration is a series of events that have happened in a time order. We say, too, that narration tends to deal with specific details and emotional attitudes, that good narrative has subjective truth but often uses fiction instead of fact.

Probably no one of the preceding statements is true of *all* exposition or *all* narrative except the statement that narration is a series of events in a time order. But in the *process*, even when we are concerned with scientific or mechanical principles, we use a time order for exposition. Hence it seems impossible to make rigid definitions which are sound.

It is possible, perhaps, to make some clarifying statements about the assignments in Part II. In all the chapters you will be explaining, writing some kind of exposition. In the first four chapters you will tend to use a time order to explain ideas that have importance outside your mind and that are generalizations about effective principles or customary actions. For instance, if you tell how a community manages its apple-blossom festival you are dealing with customary actions; if you tell a reader how to build a receiving set you are of necessity reporting effective principles. In the fifth chapter you will use either space or space and time patterns to explain things which have some objective details. In the other chapters you will tend to use a logical order of ideas; sometimes your aim will be to explain subjective ideas and sometimes to blend objective observation and subjective generalizations. In all these chapters you will be writing *exposition*; but as it is personalized exposition, you will use freely both your own attitudes and also the techniques of description and narration, and you will try to capture your reader's interest.

THE PROCESS

Whenever you try to tell another human being *how* to do something or *how* other people usually do something, you are concerned with a process. (The term might be applied to nonhuman actions;

but, for convenience, in this chapter it will be limited to the actions of people.) You probably follow a time pattern sometimes without conscious planning; that is, you explain the events in the order your reader can follow easily when he tries to understand or apply your directions. Thus your composition is a narrative exposition, a use of narrative to explain *how*. You are not concerned with the feel of experience at one time and no other; instead you are explaining the methods that are usually effective.

You can understand better what the process is if you realize that you have a wide choice of subjects. You may use technical and scientific processes connected with your formal education if you can make them interesting; farm or factory processes, either individual or large-scale ones; methods of work learned by trial and error or by informal education; creative and critical procedures; sports, organized or unorganized; hobbies and all avocational occupations. You may choose a community activity: how a community celebrates Christmas, the Fourth of July, a rodeo, a tulip festival, a clambake, a sugaring-off, a fish-fry, or a grape festival. You may wish to tell us how a family manages its birthday dinners or its annual reunions. If you are interested, you may explain psychological activities: how to apply for a job, set a date under difficult circumstances, sell a gadget, discourage a bore, or get rid of an unwelcome guest. You may select from a large number of miscellaneous activities, such as how to hunt deer, pitch a tent, start a car on a zero morning, criticize a picture or a poem, paint a water-color picture, bake a cake, or do some difficult traveling without undue strain. Additional suggestions to help you find a subject will be made in the latter part of the chapter.

AIMS IN THE PROCESS

In the process which is the work of human beings you may have in mind either of two different aims. First, you may try to give your reader an understanding of the process without assuming that he will undertake it himself. Even with this aim, your process will probably have a solid core of facts which add up to a knowledge of the usual procedures, but your subjects may differ in emotional coloring. For instance, if you wish to explain how a canning factory operates you will aim at clarity and interest; if you wish to explain how a community manages a festival you will still do well to aim at a basic clarity about the events but you may be more concerned with color, action, and human enjoyment. In the festival there are no scientific principles, only customary procedures. Second, though you are still concerned with securing your reader's interest, you may wish to give him directions that he can follow himself. This aim is often the more difficult of the two for reasons which will be explained later. You will write better and more easily if you know which of these aims you have in mind.

PLANNING AND ORGANIZING

If your material is scientific and technical, or even if it is a process you have learned informally, you may need to consider these things: What are the basic principles of the work? What technical or semitechnical terms do you need to define before you can use them freely? How and where can you describe unfamiliar things in familiar terms? Or how can you compare them with familiar things? What things or what parts of the whole are especially difficult to do or to understand? Why? How can you make the difficult details clear?

If your reader is to follow your directions himself, he may need to assemble some equipment before he begins. What tools, materials, and other equipment will be necessary? How can he choose them wisely? Does he need any help about the quality, the cost, or the place to secure his supplies? As you explain the stages of the work, do you need to tell him not only *what* to do but *why* he should do something in a certain way? What difficulties can you foresee? What errors can you prevent? What signs of success will he detect as he proceeds? By way of a conclusion, what will his completed product be like and how will he react to it?

Since you know your subject better than any potential reader knows it, you are the only person who can answer these questions and find other pertinent questions to ask yourself as you plan.

When you use a serious subject in a serious way you will probably need to outline first the stages in your process. If you first state each stage or step in the whole process, using a *concise sentence*, you will clarify your own thinking. These stages will be the main divisions in your composition, and you will probably have three or four or five of them, depending on your subject. Unless your subject is simple, you may need a group of paragraphs for developing each stage when you write your paper; but do not make the mistake of assuming that you must write the same number of paragraphs for each step. Use your plan, but do not let it cramp you.

You may need to plan for unity by asking yourself what quality in the process you wish to emphasize. Is it easy? Is it difficult but rewarding? Is it exacting because it calls for very precise work? Is it fascinating? Is it monotonous at times? What other quality, if any, does it have? Besides analyzing the quality of the process, you may also need to discover your attitude, unless the two are really one, as they seem to be in the implications of some of the preceding questions. From the two, the quality of the process and your attitude, phrase in one concise sentence a central idea. This idea should be large enough so that every main point or stage in your plan will clearly be one part of its support or development. After you have worded your central idea and the steps which will develop it, you may need to plan briefly the ideas which will best introduce your paper to the reader and also draw the most effective conclusion for him. As the introduction and conclusion are like the front and back porches of a house, you can probably plan them better after you understand clearly the body of the paper.

You probably realize that you need also to think about the audience for whom you are writing, since you cannot gain skill in writing by addressing the world. Choose your audience and then plan for that audience. How much does your chosen reader know already? What is the degree of his interest? Perhaps you will do better to assume that he knows little and is not greatly interested. Otherwise, why would he be reading your composition? At least you will develop more skill from these assumptions. And as long as you do not talk down to him or patronize him, you will not go astray. You might, for example, write as if your reader were an intelligent younger brother who has had no experience with your subject; you are trying to make him understand it and to capture his interest.

Whatever your subject is, be sure that you do not undertake too much. Trying to encompass the world in a brief paper is a besetting sin of college students and of other human beings. If you are interested in photography, do not try to tell us in one short paper how to take pictures of all kinds, how to develop the negatives, print them, and enlarge the pictures. Instead limit yourself to only one of these things, or tell us how to take a first-class picture of a child, or of a landscape under certain weather conditions. Then you will have the time and space to make your small unit interesting and vivid.

Whatever your subject, you may gain by stating in concise written form, entirely for its *influence on you*, the effect you wish to have on your reader, the quality of the process itself, and the attitude you have to the process.

STYLE

How will you write a vivid and interesting composition? First, you will use your senses and your emotions on your subject until your details are fused into an imaginative creation. Then you will find fresh, vivid words, not stereotypes, to express your individual experience. (If you are not familiar with Part I of this book, you might read Chapter 2 at this point.)

Since you are writing narrative, use action and movement wherever you can, even though your narrative is used for explanation. Use vivid verbs if they are useful, not only main verbs but gerunds and participles. Avoid heavy expository transitions, like *nevertheless, moreover, notwithstanding*. Use *but, and*, and simple time words and phrases, such as *then, next, the next stage*, and so on.

Personalize your whole composition in some way, but find your own way. Why should you personalize? To keep yourself from falling into passives and abstractions, and to give pleasure to your reader. You may talk directly to your reader, using *you* and *your* if you can be consistent through your whole unit. When you expect him to try the process himself, or even when you wish to give him the feel of the usual experience, you may find this method especially effective. Here is an example of it, from the middle of a chapter on making camp:

The civilized method is to build a fire and then touch a match to the completed structure. If well done and in a grate or stove, this works beautifully. Only in the woods you have no grate. The only sure way is as follows: Hold a piece of birch bark in your hand. Shelter your match all you know how. When the bark has caught, lay it in your fireplace, assist it with more bark, and gradually build up, twig by twig, stick by stick, from the first pin-point of flame, all the fire you are going to need. It will not be much. The little hot blaze rising between the parallel logs directly against the aluminum of your utensils will do the business in very short order. In fifteen minutes at most your meal is ready. And you have been able to attain your hot food thus quickly because you were prepared.[1]

You may succeed with the third-person method, using *he, him, his* to represent any person who tries the work, or you may even use a proper name for this person, giving the effect of one time but not forgetting to bring out the difficulties, errors, and successful principles. A paragraph from an account of pouring the keel for a boat illustrates the use of a name:

Now Pinaud opens the valve and thrusts a brass rod inside. His ungloved hand reaches to the very maw of the dragon. When he withdraws the rod he measures it on the outside of the spout. "Heat it there," he orders, indicating where the lead has cooled inside. The workman with the torch moves it quickly, and the flame describes an orange arc. Again Pinaud thrusts in the rod, and with fearful expectancy we watch him, hoping the lead will not gush forth. He appreciates the danger and procures a longer rod. Now as he prods the slowly melting plug he stands at a safer distance. Chance protects him still further, and he is elsewhere, overseeing something else, when the plug lets go and the lead spurts out, across the spot where he had been standing.[2]

The first person singular or plural, *I* or *we,* may be used, perhaps more appropriately for subjects with a strong personal feeling. In his account of an old-fashioned threshing, for instance, Garland used *we* and *us* for himself and his younger brother; and the reader follows the process through the nostalgia of one who delights in his memories:

In those days the machine was either a "J. I. Case" or a "Buffalo Pitts," and was moved by five pairs of horses attached to a "power" staked to the ground, round which they travelled, pulling at the ends of long levers or sweeps, and to me the force seemed tremendous. "Tumbling rods" with "knuckle joints" carried the motion to the

[1] Stewart Edward White, *The Forest,* Doubleday, Doran & Co., Inc., 1903.
[2] Alfred F. Loomis, "And So the Keel Was Poured," *Atlantic Monthly,* September, 1929.

cylinder, and the driver who stood upon a square platform above the huge, greasy cog-wheels (round which the horses moved) was a grand figure in my eyes.[3]

The style of your process may be humorous or satirical if both you and your subject are adapted to less serious treatment. Satire is usually based on contrast, whether it is used in small bits or in a whole unit; it tends to surprise the reader by the sharp difference between what he expects and what he finds, or by the contrast between what the writer seems to say and what he really means. If you wish to try it in a whole unit use this working hypothesis: Consistently tell your reader to do the exact opposite of the thing that is your serious intention. If you wish to poke fun at bad table manners, advise your reader to cultivate a long reach, help himself to everything first, take big bites, and smack his approval; thus, you tell him, he will gain the approval of the elite. Since you do not wish to seem obvious or to have your readers take you seriously, you will need to adjust your method carefully to your topic and your reader. Sometimes either exaggeration or understatement will be effective. Perhaps the tone of these sentences will guide you away from the overobvious:

Duveen was not snobbish in his selection of pupils; he often lavished his knowledge on the backbenchers, and even on what he regarded as the small fry. Hearst was in the small-fry category; he probably spent at Duveen's no more than five million dollars in all.[4]

SUBJECTS

Here are some subjects that may be suggestive for the process, in addition to those mentioned in explaining the term at the beginning of the chapter. Use them to help you recall your experience instead of assuming that you will write on one of them. For processes in which you plan to tell another person how to do something, consider these: how to clean a rifle, prepare for military inspection, play shortstop in baseball, play any difficult position in football, make camp on a canoe trip, feed a certain kind of dog, train a dog until it is housebroken, teach a dog tricks; how to give first aid for

[3] Hamlin Garland, *A Son of the Middle Border*, The Macmillan Company, 1917.
[4] S. N. Behrman, *Duveen*, Random House, Inc., 1952.

a burn, a broken arm, a sprain, or possible internal injuries resulting from an auto accident; how to buy a dress or a suit; how to make pizza, lasange, or some other special article of food; how to hunt pheasants, deer, foxes; how to catch trout, muskies, or some kind of sea fish. If you are interested in college affairs, perhaps some of these will be suggestive: how to become a fraternity president or to be a successful fraternity president or steward or treasurer, a sorority president, a dormitory counselor; how to become a Big Man on Campus or a Big Woman on Campus; how to get ready for a specific examination, impress a teacher, flunk a course, get an A in a course; how to get a date, treat a girl on a date, treat a young man on a date; how to manage a rushing tea; how to select or how not to select a college. Many of these, of course, may become humorous, satirical, or serious, as you wish.

If you are interested in larger problems, use one similar to these: how a railroad track is cleared after a wreck, how an automobile accident is handled, how a city elects its mayor or disposes of garbage, how a mayor or any other official handles his job, how a grocer or a druggist manages his business, how a clinic operates, how the director of a college housing bureau works, how a research worker handles a specific job. Probably every large university or state college is carrying on a hundred research or technical projects which you might investigate; smaller colleges may also have individual projects; and each community may be doing something that is slightly different. But unless your time is unlimited, beware of those in which you have no background.

If you prefer psychological or creative subjects, try one of those mentioned earlier in the chapter or one of these: how to get rid of an unsuccessful applicant, make a friend, lose a friend, spend a holiday, get the family car for the evening, plan a vacation, look at a specific painting, or listen to a specific piece of music.

If you wish to study unusual examples of the process, in addition to the reading at the end of the chapter, try "Profiles: Mr. President, V: A Weighing of Words," by John Hersey (how one President prepared important speeches);[5] "Preface: How to Write Short Stories," from *How to Write Short Stories*, by Ring W. Lardner; "Traveling in Peace," from *Inside Benchley*, by Robert C.

[5] *The New Yorker*, May 5, 1951, pp. 36–53.

Benchley; or other parts of *Duveen*, by S. N. Behrman, in addition to the excerpt in this chapter.

WRITING YOUR COMPOSITION

A. Write an explanation of some process which you expect your reader to follow successfully. Use either scientific, technical, or informal experience material; but when you have chosen, accept any obligations about information you find when you analyze your subject. Personalize; make your paper not only clear but vivid and interesting.

B. Write an explanation of some community process; or choose some other large process in which you try to give your reader an intelligent understanding, not prepare him to follow your directions himself. Do research on your subject if necessary, the research that consists of observing and asking questions rather than reading. Again personalize; make your account clear, vivid, interesting, and also lively and filled with color and action, or somber, according to your subject.

C. Write a serious explanation of a process which is mainly psychological. Choose one that is familiar to you. Give your reader some basic information. Personalize as usual; make the process vivid and interesting; get a response from your reader.

D. Write about a process which is mainly psychological, but use a satirical tone through the whole unit, or combine humor and satire in any way you can manage successfully.

E. Write a process which explains *how* some person you know usually does something. Emphasize the steps of the process enough to distinguish it from a narration which is a character sketch. Your tone may be serious, satirical, or humorous.

READING

DYNAMITE [6]

Joseph Husband

Isolated and avoided, the high explosive plant lies half hidden in a waste of sloughs and sand dunes. Like the barren country that

[6] Joseph Husband, *America at Work*, Houghton Mifflin Company, 1915. Reprinted by permission of and arrangement with Houghton Mifflin Company, the authorized publishers.

surrounds it, the plant itself seems a part of desolate nature, stunted and storm-beaten as the wind-swept hills. Against the straight line of the horizon rise no massive structures of steel or stone; no sound of man or machine breaks the soft stillness; no smoke clouds stain the blue of the autumn sky. Half buried in the rolling sand a hundred small green buildings scatter in wild disorder along winding paths among the scrub oaks. The voices of undisturbed wild fowl rise from the fens and marsh land.

In the little office at the gate I left my matches and put on a pair of soft wooden-pegged powder shoes. Outside, the faint flavor of last night's frost freshened the morning air, and above the red and yellow of the scrub oaks the autumn sun was shining in a pale-blue sky.

At my side the superintendent was explaining the processes of manufacture I was soon to see, but my mind was curiously unresponsive; in the peace of the morning air an ominous presence seemed to surround me; an invisible force that needed but a spark or the slightest impulse to awaken it, annihilating and devastating in its sudden fury.

Beyond the office, like the letter "S" a high sand dune bent in a general east and west direction, a sweep of marsh land in each sheltering curve. Against the outer bank of its first wide crescent the small power plant and a row of red one-story buildings marked a single street. From the open door of the power house the rhythmic drone of a generator accentuated the stillness. Down a track between the buildings a horse plodded slowly over the worn ties, dragging a small flatcar, the driver leaning lazily against one of the uprights which supported a dingy awning.

The manufacture of dynamite consists of two separate processes, which are conducted individually up to a certain point, when their products meet and by their union the actual dynamite is produced. In the little buildings by the power house the first of these products was in course of manufacture. Here the fine wood dust, mixed with other materials, was prepared, an absorbent to hold the nitroglycerine which was being made a half-mile beyond the nearest sand dune. Packed in paper cartridges the nitroglycerine-soaked "dope," or sawdust, is called by a single name—Dynamite.

In two great open pans slowly revolving paddles were turning over and over a mass of wood pulp, fine and soft as snow. The room was warm from the sunshine on the low roof and the drying fires below the pans; there was a strong, clean smell of sawdust. The building was deserted; unattended the paddles swung noiselessly with the low sound of well-oiled machinery.

Inside the next building a couple of men were weighing great measures of white powder from bins along the wall. The superintendent picked up a printed slip from a desk by the window.

"Nitrate of soda, nitrate of ammonia, wood pulp, marble dust. That's the formula for this batch. Sometimes we put in sulphur, or flour, or magnesium carbonate. It's all according to what kind of explosive is wanted; what it's to be used for."

Far down at the end of the little street the strong, hot smell of paraffine hung heavy in the air. Inside, against the walls of the building, the paper cartridges were drying; racks of waxed yellow tubes half filled the building.

Here the first process of manufacture was completed. Stable and harmless, the fragrant wood dust was being prepared for its union with that strange evanescent spirit which would endow it with powers of lightning strength and rapidity.

With our powder shoes sinking in the sliding sand we climbed the path to the top of the hill which marked the center of the twisted dune. On its summit the frame building of the nitrater notched the sky. Here, in the silence between earth and clouds, a mighty force was seeking birth.

Perched on a high stool, an old man in overalls bent intently over the top of a great tank, his eyes fixed on a thermometer that protruded from its cover. Above, a shaft and slowly turning wheels moved quietly in the shadows of the roof. There was a splashing of churning liquid, and the bite of acid sharpened the air. The old man turned his head for a moment to nod to us. Below his feet a coil of pipes white with a thick frost rime entered the bottom of the tank, a cooling solution to keep the temperature of the churning acid within the limit of safety.

As we stepped inside the doorway, the splashing grew louder; the bitter reek of the acid seemed to scorch my nostrils. Slowly the old man turned a valve beside him and a thick trickle of glycerine flowed heavily into an opening in the top of the tank. Inside the blackened caldron a strange transformation was in progress. Were the glycerine allowed to become completely nitrated by the acid the windows of the distant city would rattle in the blast that would surely follow. Carefully, the nitrating must be brought almost to that danger-point and abruptly arrested; so near, that later in the form of dynamite the nitrating could be instantly completed and the desired explosion obtained by the jarring impulse of an electric spark. Like a child pushing a dish to poise on the table edge the old man was bringing this dynamic mixture to a precarious balance.

The superintendent pointed to a cistern filled with water behind the nitrater.

"Before we had the brine pipes to keep the acid cool, it used to heat up occasionally. It gives up red fumes when it passes the danger-point. You ought to see the quick work Old Charley used to do,—open that faucet in the nitrater to let the acid and glycerine dump into the cistern and drown; blow the alarm whistle, and then everybody beat it!"

The old man looked up from the thermometer. "She's ready."

Deliberately he climbed down from the stool and opened a switch behind him; the splashing of the paddles ceased; the process was completed.

Behind the tank an earthenware faucet opened into a long lead gutter that passed out of the building. Fascinated, I watched him as he slowly turned the handle. From the spout a stream of viscous liquid gushed noisily and flowed off in a sullen current.

"Nitroglycerine,"—the superintendent pointed his finger at the splashing stream; "of course, it's impure now, mixed with acid. We'll see it purified in the separating-houses."

I was disappointed. Vaguely I had expected something would happen; how could this dull, oily liquid be that fearful thing that had been represented.

"There's enough in that trough now to wreck a battleship," he added.

Under the crest of a curving hill a half-mile away, was the mix house. From the nitrater we had followed the nitroglycerine through the dangerous process of its separation from the acid, its perfect neutralization. Here, at last, the explosive fluid would assume its final form. Mixed with the absorbent dope, in a crumby consistency it would become dynamite.

The sunshine filled the little room with yellow light; a blue fly buzzed noisily against the window. Facing the flat marsh land the building rested in a deep cut in the hillside; behind it the solid hill, on either side an artificial embankment or barricade of sand and timber. In the center of the room was a cumbersome machine like an archaic mill for crushing grain. Hung from an axle revolving on a perpendicular central shaft, two great wooden wheels, four feet in diameter, rested in a circular trough; a pair of giant cart wheels with broad, smooth tires of pine.

There was a sound outside the building. Down a board walk that disappeared behind a hill in the direction of the separating-house, came a man pushing a square wagon completely covered with rubber blankets,—three hundred pounds of nitroglycerine.

Swiftly the two workmen filled the circular trough with the prepared wood pulp. The wagon was trundled softly into the room. From a tank in the corner a measure of brown, sweet-smelling, aromatic oil was mixed into the contents of the cart.

Something was going to happen. A sudden impulse to run before it was too late seized me. The cart was pushed beside the trough. From a hose in its base a heavy brown fluid gushed over the powdery dope. Slowly the steady stream became a trickle and ceased.

There was a faint sound and I knew that the current was thrown in; the great axle began to revolve on the shaft. One and then the other, the giant wheels turned heavily. Under the advancing ploughs the brown stain of nitroglycerine faded in the yellow of the dope. Round and round; heavily the smooth wheels pressed the flocculent mass, cleanly the sharp ploughs turned furrows behind them—Dynamite.

I started violently at the voice of the superintendent. It seemed hours instead of minutes since this death-taunting machine had begun; hours in which each second might bring annihilation.

"It's mixed."

The wheels ceased to revolve. With wooden shovels the workmen scooped the dynamite from the troughs and pitched it into fiber cans, as big as barrels.

As though built to withstand the siege guns of an enemy, the dugouts of the packers faced the marsh in a long straggling line against the hillside. Like the mix house, each building sank deep into the sandbank, its sides protected by enveloping barricades.

In each small cell two men were working. There was little talking. Silence hung heavy over the hills and marsh land; a strange blending of peace and terror that made harsh sounds improper and jarring to the senses.

With quick dexterity the empty paper tubes, that I had seen manufactured when I first began this perilous journey, were inserted in the packing-machine. An abrupt movement, and they were packed with dynamite and laid in boxes beside the workers.

I picked up one of the "sticks" from a half-filled box. "Stump Dynamite."

Hour after hour, day after day, the filled boxes were trundled down the board walk to the magazine. "Stump Dynamite." I had always thought of this great industry as a destructive agency, of high explosives as carriers of death and desolation. But where the forests have vanished before the axes of the woodmen, dynamite is clearing fields for the next year's planting. In the black entries of the mine the undercut coal-face falls shattered at the blast of the explosives. Through the walls of mountain ranges it is tearing loose the solid rock, that trains may some day follow the level rails; through blasted tunnels flows water to moisten the lips of a parching city; from ocean to ocean it has opened a giant cut that deep-sea vessels may carry their cargoes by shorter routes; deep under the strata of the earth's crust its sudden shock shakes the oil-well into life; its rending breath tears the red ore of iron from the living rock.

Labors of Hercules! What are the feats of the earthborn son of Jupiter to the mighty wonders accomplished by this tabloid thunderbolt. Death and destruction may come from its sharp detonation, but for every life that goes out in siege or battle a hundred lives are sustained by its quiet labor in field or mine.

The afternoon sun was setting behind a mist of autumn clouds.

In the silence of the dunes and marsh the clear call of a bird sounded sharp and silver-tuned in a run of hurried melody.

A SALE TO JOHN R. THOMPSON [7]

S. N. Behrman

Still another of the small fry, in Duveen's opinion, was John R. Thompson, of Chicago, the owner of the well-known chain of one-arm restaurants. Thompson had begun to nibble at paintings through a Chicago art dealer. As his chain of restaurants increased, so did his appetite for paintings. The dealer, drawing upon the resources available to him in Chicago, gradually built up a small collection for him, but there came a time when the dealer's intuition told him that if he tried to keep Thompson to himself, he would lose a valuable customer. The dealer came to New York and advised Duveen that he had a client who had plenty of money and was ripe for higher things. Duveen agreed to give the restaurant man an audience, and the dealer a commission on any sales. "You mustn't be shocked by my tactics, though," he warned. Thompson, escorted by the Chicago dealer, presently appeared at the Ministry. He was a small man, and was wearing a derby hat. Duveen kept Thompson and the dealer waiting for an hour. Finally, the two men were admitted to the Presence. Duveen was brisk and genial. "I hear you are in the restaurant business," he said. "Anything like Lyons?" He went on to say that he approved of the Lyons tea-shops, and that if Thompson's chain resembled them, he approved of that. He revealed that he often snubbed Claridge's in favor of a Lyons on Oxford Street. The absence of formality there was pleasurable. He grew eloquent on the important social service rendered by those who provided good food at popular prices. He asked about the turnover in the Thompson restaurants, and the problems of refrigeration. The restaurant business, it became clear, was Duveen's liveliest and most intimate concern. "Look here," Thompson broke in desperately when he could stand the strain no longer, "I didn't make this trip to New York to talk to you about the restaurant business. I came to see you because I am interested in

[7] S. N. Behrman, *Duveen*. Reprinted by permission of Random House, Inc. Copyright, 1951, 1952, by S. N. Behrman.

paintings!" Snapped back so rudely to an activity so marginal, Duveen made a quick adjustment. "Oh, paintings!" he said, as if recalling an almost forgotten acquaintance. "Of course, paintings! Oh, well, now, if you're interested in pictures, come upstairs with me and I'll show you some."

Duveen led Thompson, as well as the Chicago dealer, into the elevator, which bore them to sacrosanct upper regions. Duveen strode swiftly through a thickly carpeted, dimly lit room that contained six Old Masters reclining on easels. Thompson, in his wake, was almost out of the room when, like Mrs. Lot, he looked back. He lingered; from the blur of the six pictures he got a quick impression of infinite desirability. He called the hurrying Duveen back. "Here are some pictures," he said. "What about these?"

Duveen took his arm. "My dear Mr. Thompson," he said gently, "there is nothing in this room that would interest you in the least."

"Why not?" argued the new pupil. "Of course they interest me. What would I be doing here if they didn't interest me?"

"These pictures, my dear fellow, I am reserving, as a matter of fact, for a favorite client," Duveen said. "They will interest him far more than they could possibly interest you."

Thompson protested; he would yield to no one in acuteness of interest. "Why do you think they wouldn't interest me?" he asked. "I want you to know, Sir Joseph, that I own some pretty good pictures."

"I am sure you do," Duveen said soothingly. "And if you will just follow me, I am sure that I can add to your collection and, if I may say so, improve it. But not these. You are a busy man, and I don't want to waste your time. Not with these."

"Why not?" repeated Mr. Thompson.

Pushed to the wall, Duveen dropped all pretense of tact. He made it plain that he thought the pictures were over Thompson's head, both aesthetically and economically.

"How much for the six?" Thompson demanded.

"A million dollars, I am afraid," said Duveen, as if pained at having to demonstrate the truth of an unflattering statement.

Thompson was ready with an answer. "I'll take them," he said vindictively.

RED LANTERNS [8]

Aldo Leopold

One way to hunt partridge is to make a plan, based on logic and probabilities, of the terrain to be hunted. This will take you over the ground where the birds ought to be.

Another way is to wander, quite aimlessly, from one red lantern to another. This will likely take you where the birds actually are. The lanterns are blackberry leaves, red in October sun.

Red lanterns have lighted my way on many a pleasant hunt in many a region, but I think that blackberries must first have learned how to glow in the sand counties of central Wisconsin. Along the little boggy streams of these friendly wastes, called poor by those whose own lights barely flicker, the blackberries burn richly red on every sunny day from first frost to the last day of the season. Every woodcock and every partridge has his private solarium under these briars. Most hunters, not knowing this, wear themselves out in the briarless scrub, and, returning home birdless, leave the rest of us in peace.

By "us" I mean the birds, the stream, the dog, and myself. The stream is a lazy one; he winds through the alders as if he would rather stay here than reach the river. So would I. Every one of his hairpin hesitations means that much more streambank where hillside briars adjoin dank beds of frozen ferns and jewelweeds on the boggy bottom. No partridge can long absent himself from such a place, nor can I. Partridge hunting, then, is a creekside stroll, upwind, from one briar patch to another.

The dog, when he approaches the briars, looks around to make sure I am within gunshot. Reassured, he advances with stealthy caution, his wet nose screening a hundred scents for that one scent, the potential presence of which gives life and meaning to the whole landscape. He is the prospector of the air, perpetually searching its strata for olfactory gold. Partridge scent is the gold standard that relates his world to mine.

My dog, by the way, thinks I have much to learn about partridges, and, being a professional naturalist, I agree. He persists in tutoring me, with the calm patience of a professor of logic, in the art of drawing deductions from an educated nose. I delight in seeing him deduce a conclusion, in the form of a point, from data that are obvious to him, but speculative to my unaided eye. Perhaps he hopes his dull pupil will one day learn to smell.

Like other dull pupils, I know when the professor is right, even though I do not know why. I check my gun and walk in. Like any good professor, the dog never laughs when I miss, which is often. He gives me just one look, and proceeds up the stream in quest of another grouse.

Following one of these banks, one walks astride two landscapes, the hillside one hunts from, and the bottom the dog hunts in. There is a special charm in treading soft dry carpets of Lycopodium to flush birds out of the bog, and the first test of a partridge dog is his willingness to do the wet work while you parallel him on the dry bank.

A special problem arises where the belt of alders widens, and the dog disappears from view. Hurry at once to a knoll or point, where you stand stock-still, straining eye and ear to follow the dog. A sudden scattering of whitethroats may reveal his whereabouts. Again you may hear him breaking a twig, or splashing in a wet spot, or plopping into the creek. But when all sound ceases, be ready for instant action, for he is likely on point. Listen now for the premonitory clucks a frightened partridge gives just before flushing. Then follow the hurtling bird, or perhaps two of them, or I have known as many as six, clucking and flushing one by one, each sailing high for his own destination in the uplands. Whether one passes within gunshot is of course a matter of chance, and you can compute the chance if you have time: 360 degrees divided by 30, or whatever segment of the circle your gun covers. Divide again by 3 or 4, which is your chance of missing, and you have the probability of actual feathers in the hunting coat.

The second test of a good partridge dog is whether he reports for orders after such an episode. Sit down and talk it over with him while he pants. Then look for the next red lantern, and proceed with the hunt.

The October breeze brings my dog many scents other than

grouse, each of which may lead to its own peculiar episode. When he points with a certain humorous expression of the ears, I know he has found a bedded rabbit. Once a dead-serious point yielded no bird, but still the dog stood frozen; in a tuft of sedge under his very nose was a fat sleeping coon, getting his share of October sun. At least once on each hunt the dog bays a skunk, usually in some denser-than-ordinary thicket of blackberries. Once the dog pointed in midstream: a whir of wings upriver, followed by three musical cries, told me he had interrupted a wood duck's dinner. Not infrequently he finds jacksnipe in heavily pastured alders, and lastly he may put out a deer, bedded for the day on a high streambank flanked by alder bog. Has the deer a poetical weakness for singing waters, or a practical liking for a bed that cannot be approached without making a noise? Judging by the indignant flick of his great white flag it might be either, or both.

Almost anything may happen between one red lantern and another.

·   ·   ·   ·   ·   ·   ·

At sunset on the last day of the grouse season, every blackberry blows out his light. I do not understand how a mere bush can thus be infallibly informed about the Wisconsin statutes, nor have I ever gone back next day to find out. For the ensuing eleven months the lanterns glow only in recollection. I sometimes think that the other months were constituted mainly as a fitting interlude between Octobers, and I suspect that dogs, and perhaps grouse, share the same view.

QUESTIONS

In "Dynamite" does the writer assume that you will learn to do something yourself? If not, what does he assume that you will learn or feel? What does he do in the first four paragraphs? Are these details clear? Are they vivid? Are they essential? What is the purpose of the fifth paragraph? How many stages of the process are explained, and in how many different places does he tell you that these steps are carried on? What kinds of transitions does the author use? How does he personalize his material? Where and how does he use talk? Is the narrative quality emphasized? How? What kinds of sensory detail are used? Which are most vivid? What kinds are most essential for this topic?

What is done in each of the last three paragraphs? Do these make an effective ending? Why? What is the final impact of the unit?

Does "A Sale to John R. Thompson" seem to you like narrative rather than exposition? Is it fiction or a factual account? Does the unit tell *how* Duveen managed a sale toThompson? Does it also imply *how* he usually managed his sales? (You might compare this unit with the brief quotation from *Duveen* earlier in the chapter.) What methods of salesmanship did he use? Where in the unit is the material more expository? Why? Is there any summary narrative? Any talk? Assuming that this is one of several incidents in the whole chapter, is the end effective? Does the writer use understatement? Contrast? Any other effective qualities of style?

How much factual information does the author of "Red Lanterns" give you? How much does he emphasize his pleasure in hunting partridge? How much does he emphasize the pleasure and the skill of his dog? Is the article personalized? If so, how and where? Is the writer aiming at readers who know nothing about his subject? Those who know something about it? Those who know something and are already interested? Does he add information even for the informed? What qualities, if any, make this different from the usual article on how to do something?

16

The Process:

HOW ANIMATE CREATURES DO THINGS

At the close of this chapter it is suggested that you choose one of these compositions: first, a process, how non-human creatures do things; second, an explanation by narrative patterns of any other interesting things you know about animate nature. A chief difference between the process here and in Chapter 15 is, of course, subject matter. The first reading at the end of this chapter might have been placed there because a man is learning how to tame a hawk; but the reader is probably more interested in the hawk than the man, and the topic requires observation of the hawk. The material in "Biography of a Dancing Ground" (research material made vivid and yet kept scrupulously accurate) is only distantly related to a process, since it explains the effects of careless human action on the sharptails. Hence, the reading and the discussion in this chapter lead to any narrative explanation of animate nature.

Perhaps you should not try to do any composition assignment in this chapter unless you have a strong desire to choose one of them. If you have never observed birds or animals and have never cared for any creature as a pet, if you enjoy nature but tend to large generalities about its beauty and have no definite information to explain, you should not try any of these assignments. Instead, you might try another of the compositions suggested in Chapter 15.

SUBJECTS

If you choose to write on animate nature, what are possible subjects? Perhaps you once owned a pet—a dog, cat, horse, or even a snake. You might write a biographical sketch about it, using the chief events of its life in time order but using them for explanation of its habits, its personality, or its changes while you knew it. If you once kept for a period of observation some wild bird or animal—a screech owl, a hawk, a rabbit—you might tell us in time order what you learned about it. Perhaps you have observed how a certain kind of bird usually behaves—how it builds its nest, feeds its young, or trains its young. Or you may wish to depart from the one-narrative pattern and write a series of small incidents illustrating the strange things you have seen birds do.

PLANNING AND ORGANIZING

Whatever your subject, you will analyze your attitude and your assumptions about your reader's knowledge and attitude; you will word your central idea in a concise sentence; and then you will plan the stages of your composition. Perhaps you should check over in your mind the basic facts you wish to imply with your narrative, for you can use well in personalized narrative only the facts that rest easily in your mind; and unless you have some objective material you probably do not have a good subject.

You will personalize in some way, of course, unless you have skill in using an objective method; you will use your senses, your attitude, and your mind; you will create a unit or units of imagined experience; and then you will find vivid words to give your writing freshness and reality.

It is possible to be subjective and at the same time to give objective detail which is accurate. Hemingway wrote like an expert observer when he used a shark in fiction; the same vividness with accuracy is possible in narrative exposition. Perhaps you would like to read *The Old Man and the Sea*, noticing especially Hemingway's active description of the Mako shark.

T. H. White is capable of many moods in commenting on many animals. Talking of snakes, which he used to turn loose in his sitting room, he said at one point:

> The tongue comes out two or three times (its touch on the hand is as delicate as the touch of a butterfly) and flickers on the air. It is a beautiful movement, with more down in it than up. It can be faintly reproduced by waggling the bent forefinger quickly in a vertical plane. Then she goes on with her pour, satisfied, toward her objective in the moss. We sit as still as a mouse.[1]

At times White could be humorous and completely subjective, without confusing the reader about objective fact. For example, in the same article he said:

> I remember particularly two of last year's snakes. One was a baby male (the yellow markings are brighter in the male) only about eight inches long. He was a confiding snake, and I once took him to church in my pocket, to make him a Christian and to comfort me during the sermon. I hope it was not an undue interference with his life: I never carried him about like that again, he seemed to like the warmth of my pocket, and I believe he did not change his creed.[2]

While he was training his goshawk and robbing himself of sleep White understood the feeling of his dog:

> Brownie, who had lived as often my sole and always my chief and most beloved companion for two years, had for days and nights been without notice. Her anxious face, watching this incomprehensible desertion, had become more and more pitiful without receiving pity. Suddenly it was too much for her. She came humbly, heart-brokenly, asking with fear and desolation for any re-assurance. Of this new mad-eyed and absent master she was even afraid . . . So now the man had to pull himself together for a new demand, to comfort the poor creature out of a heart with no energy to spare.[3]

Donald Culross Peattie combined acute observation and love of beauty in this account of hummingbirds, apparently without distorting facts:

[1] T. H. White, *England Have My Bones*, The Macmillan Company, 1936.
[2] *Ibid.*
[3] T. H. White, *The Goshawk*, G. P. Putnam's Sons, 1951.

Here are laid two white eggs, the size of pearls or peas. When they hatch, the chicks are hardly bigger than the nail of your finger, helpless, naked, blind, all gullet and yelp. To see the mother thrust that bill in a lightning flash down the baby's throat, you would think she must surely pin the little things to the very bough. Feeding time is about every minute or two at first; it must be a great relief to the mother when the children have to be fed only every five minutes! [4]

Later in the same article he said:

When I turned the light little stuffed bodies in my fingers, as one would turn a gem, they shot forth an unearthly radiance of color that made me gasp. A tiny throat, at first merely black, glowed suddenly emerald . . . So a hummingbird is a feathered prism, a living rainbow. Darting out of fairyland into your garden, it captures the very sunlight for you and turns it into a jewel on wings.[5]

WRITING YOUR COMPOSITION

A. Write an expository narrative about some animal (bird, beast, fowl, or reptile) which you have observed over a period of time. Have a central idea and some general information to bring out, perhaps a conclusion about the personality, habits, growth, or a change in personality which you observed. Use generalized narrative, a series of incidents, or any combination of explanation and narrative that you need. Personalize. Use your attitude as a means to emotional unity and adapt your wording to the kind of reader you wish to interest.

B. Write an expository narrative which explains *how* some living creature does something that you have observed accurately— how a beaver cuts down a tree, a bird builds a nest, even how a dog manages its master. Give information but use all the pertinent suggestions in the discussion for vividness and reader interest.

C. Write a unit combining narrative and exposition, perhaps in contrast patterns, explaining how living creatures change their habits as men changed their environment for them. (This will probably require extensive information.) As usual, use your attitudes, write vividly, and interest your reader.

[4] Donald Culross Peattie and Noel Peattie, *A Cup of Sky*, Houghton Mifflin Company, 1950.
[5] *Ibid.*

READING

SATURDAY [6]

T. H. White

I got up at six o'clock as usual, and for confused reasons decided to get my own breakfast before the hawk's. I was too sleepy to know very clearly what I was doing (one would make plans as one fell asleep and break them when one woke up) but there was some sort of idea at the back of the mind. There were about five great milestones in hawking: the moment when the hawk first ate, the moment when it gave in to its master after the watch, the moment when it flew to his fist, the moment when it flew to him a distance of a hundred yards, and the moment when it made its kill. I have left out the moment when it could be said to be manned to loud noises, bustle and traffic: it was difficult to determine that moment, so the list may be allowed to stand. As the day broke, then, we were still upon the threshold of the third step: we had been trying for days to make him fly for reward, without success. I knew that half the partridge was still left, of which the bird was madly fond, so that greed and hunger might join battle on my side: and I put off his breakfast until after my own, in order that the hunger might be increased.

At half past seven I went out to the mews, spoke a few words in unlocking the dead keeper's door, confronted the unfathomable raptor. Gos regarded me like the sphinx. I held out the partridge.

It seemed that partridges were not attractive. Rather pathetically trying to cry up my own goods, I turned it this way and that, so that he could get a good view, ruffled the feathers like one of those travelling Indians trying to sell a rug, plucked out a few as if I intended to eat the horrid morsel myself. I could never make up my mind whether I was the master. Gos regarded me with tolerant contempt. He had no doubts about who was the slave, the ridiculous and subservient one who stood and waited. For himself, he had the whole day to fill in.

[6] From *Goshawk* by T. H. White, copyright 1907, 1935, used by courtesy of G. P. Putnam's Sons.

I looked at my watch and stood still for fifteen minutes, saying: "I will give him a quarter of an hour." It meant standing motionless beside the bird, about a yard away from him, leaning forward like a butler and staring out of the door with the butler's distant gaze. Even to look at one's watch, one merely dropped the eyes without raising the wrist. The mangled bird lay in the leather glove, on a plane with the hawk's line of sight, catching the morning sun. The leash was more than a yard long. The hands of the watch went round.

I began to sigh, to straighten myself up, to lower the glove. The time had expired and I began to go away. Began. The reflexes for all these motions were already half way down their nerves, running with the messages of movement to shoulder and knee and back: but before any change had been made, in the moment between the outset and the arrival of the messengers, the great dun-coloured wings had unfurled themselves in half a stroke, the murderous thighs had bent and unleashed themselves for the leap, and Gos was sitting on my shoulder.

An exultation! What a bursting heart of gratitude and triumph (after the first terrified duck) as the ravening monster slowly paced down the arm with gripping steps and pounced upon his breakfast! The rest of the day was a glow of pleasure, a kind of still life in which the sun shone on the flowers with more than natural brilliance, giving them the high lights of porcelain.

THE BIRTH OF A FOAL [7]

T. H. White

I helped Tom Bourne to deliver one of his mares of a foal to-day. It was a grisly business in a way, as you have to actually haul the creature out with a rope; but it makes up for itself. For one thing, you are helping: you did not yourself invent the system of birth, and are making it better for the mare, not worse. Also there is a sense of creation about it. There were more horses in the field when I left it than there were when I went in. It is the kind of visible increase that pleased Cobbett.

It was exciting. She had been due to foal for nearly twenty-four

[7] T. H. White, *England Have My Bones*, The Macmillan Company, 1936.

hours. When we went out after tea Mark was there watching, and he beckoned to us. We went with the rope and an iron bar, in case leverage was needed in emergency, and stood under a hedge at the top of the field, two hundred yards away. She was down, and they said that she wouldn't be long now. We stood and watched, talking involuntarily in low voices. She got up again, looking rocky, but nothing happened. The other mare, Poppet, had foaled two weeks ago. Poppet's foal suddenly came trotting across from her mother and began to suck milk from Blossom, who allowed it without protest. The foal trotted back. We thought it might make him scour. Tom had never seen anything like this happen before. After about twenty minutes Blossom went down again, and rolled on her back. She held her legs unnaturally, as if she were dead or in pain. We began to stir uneasily. It was obviously beginning to happen. She got up again clumsily, and tried to crop some grass, and turned her back to us, and we could see that there was something white coming out. We walked quietly downhill towards her, till she lay down for the third time, and cut the bag, and looped the rope round the soft mushroom-coloured hoofs.

We fell over when he came out, a big foal. He lay there and shivered, all legs and hoofs, but with his head up in a new country, whilst Blossom shuddered. He had come, with his lizard face and unfocused eyes, from another world. He was going to be a black horse, gelded at eighteen months, perhaps a fine specimen. We didn't know. He had the world before him.

The feature of the whole thing was lack of hurry. We let them alone for a minute or two, whilst Tom told me that a foal is born with a kind of false tongue in his mouth. I think he called it "with a crown in his mouth." A filly is not. We found the thing, like a bit of liver, and turned it over with our toes. Mark was reticent and offhanded about the so-called magic properties that it possessed.* Tom suggested letting Blossom see the foal, which was lying behind her, but just then she lifted her neck and looked round. The foal tried to get up, but couldn't, because it didn't know what its legs were for. It had to find out about gravity.

* But when I went to see the foal next day and looked for it, the thing was gone.

Blossom stood up and thought. They had both stopped bleeding. After a bit Tom said we should teach the foal to stand. It seems that if you can teach it to stand and suckle more quickly than it would naturally learn to do so, then its chances of survival are greater. We uncrossed its legs and held it up on them, but when we let it go it would sway, trip up, and subside. However, after we had held it up twice, it knew what it ought to aim at. It began trying to get up by itself. We went round the hedges for half an hour with the gun. When we came back it was standing laboriously on all four hocky pins, and Blossom was snuffing gently at it through her nose.

BIOGRAPHY OF A DANCING GROUND [8]

F. N. and Frances Hamerstrom

The charred stumps of the felled timber had ceased smoldering . . . logging roads wound among the obliterated slashings. The country lay open, devastated and bare, but the first weed growth was pushing up green shoots . . . tiny beginning of immeasurable wealth to come.

The first sharptails appeared in the autumn. No one knew where they came from, but the deep woods around the burn had not proven an insurmountable barrier. From some other open country a flock came in, winging its way over the treetops and alighting on the burn.

The green shoots of smartweeds and ragweed had made good growth on the new ashes. By autumn seeds were abundant and the sharptails stayed.

Just before sunrise on a frosty morning a group of sharptail cocks started gobbling and cooing near an oak stump; and the sounds increased in volume as though each cock, by his gobbling, were urging the others on to gobble too.

Suddenly . . . within the twinkling of an eye . . . one cock spread his wings, blew up his lavender air sacs, and started to dance. For the first time since the white man inhabited Wisconsin

---

[8] Frederick and Frances Hamerstrom and Oswald E. Mattson, *Sharptails into the Shadows?* Game Management Division, Wisconsin Conservation Department, Madison, 1952. This is the beginning of the pamphlet.

a sharptail was dancing on this particular piece of ground. His feathered legs buzzing like a mechanical toy and his feet beating a rapid tattoo, he danced and cooed. So still was the morning that the sound of his cooing resounded far over the open plain. As the sun rose, more cocks took up the dance; and so, in the open plain by the oak stump, a dance ground was born.

No longer did a pileated woodpecker drum on the old oak tree, nor flying squirrels glide in its shade. A new era in the ever-changing pattern of natural successions had begun and the sharp-tailed grouse were among the first to take advantage of it.

It was not till spring that the sharptails returned to dance on the spot by the oak stump. For sharptails spring comes early. In February, weeks before the editor of the local paper was to print his news item about the first robin, the sharptail cocks gathered on the spot by the oak stump and fought their neighbors for possession of a part of it.

So far no hen had appeared; early mornings and evenings the cocks gathered and fought and danced and cooed until each had his own territory.

There was a vehemence to their cooing, not like the gentle-sounding dove. They danced as though possessed, and feathers lay upon the ground—torn out in fights—but still no hen had come.

It was on a morning in April that a new intensity came upon the dance ground. It was still so early that the tails of the dancing cocks gleamed like will-o-the-wisps—white in the half light.

Demurely the first hen walked the dancing ground. If she were aware of the tumultuous dancing cocks around her, she concealed it admirably. She walked slowly, occasionally pausing to peck at a blade of grass or an herb leaf . . . perhaps the avian equivalent of a yawn.

Mornings and sometimes in the evenings the cocks came to dance and as May approached more and more often hens sought the dancing ground, and with each visit the fervor of the dancing cocks increased.

Gradually, one by one, an awareness seemed to come over the hens. They spread or flicked their wings in invitation as they walked amongst the dancing cocks. One and then others, each as she came to the point of readiness, was mounted.

The nests in which they laid their eggs were mostly within a half a mile of the dancing ground. And some of the young cocks hatched from these first nests would try their first dancing steps not four months later.

Year by year the dance ground gained in numbers. Each spring more cocks danced on the spot by the oak stump and more and more dancing grounds became established over the plain.

It got so that people who had settled near the big burn within the last year or two thought there had always been sharptails there and lots of them; for they had never seen it when the woods were deep—they had only heard tell of the big woods. Now pin cherry and birches and aspen were growing up among the stumps and here and there pines were coming in.

Pin cherry, aspen, and birches gave winter budding. The new brushland offered the sharptails all they needed and they throve. Food was abundant: sweet fern, buds, catkins, berries, grasshoppers and other insects for the young birds. Heavy grass near the willows and aspen gave good nesting and rearing cover. Most of the plain was open with bare, grassy spots for loafing and dancing.

Abundance lasted for years and every spring on the dance ground by the oak stump the cocks fought and danced and mated and fought again until the spring was over. Perhaps each spring they kept it up as long as there was the slightest hope that a hen might come.

And then there were fewer sharptails; some dancing grounds disappeared entirely and others that once resounded with the stamping feet of thirty cocks now had but two or three.

A jack pine seedling grew by the old oak stump and cast its shadow over the dance ground in the late afternoons. Shadows are not for sharptails, for they are birds of sunlight and brushland. The shadow was but a forerunner of what was to come.

A blueberry picker dropped a lighted match. He spat casually but missed the small flame flickering in a grass tuft. His friend said,

"Let her go. The berries need a burning."

The picker looked up at the hot sun three hours high, faced the dry south wind and kicked the dry ground with his boot.

"No," he said, stamping the small flame, "she might get a roaring; no telling how far she'd burn."

It was before the days of fire protection; thus with a few half idle words the future of the plain was settled for a generation to come. The plant succession was not to be turned back to open country once more. The forest was to grow and the doom of the dancing ground by the oak stump and of others like it was sealed. Four cocks danced there the next spring . . . one hen demurely trod the dance ground at sunrise two days running. She never came again though the four cocks fought and danced and hooted till the lupine buds showed blue and summer was on its way.

People noticed the difference. One said, "I saw ten deer in my rye field the other night and there's partridge out on the plain."

The plain? It was no longer a plain; it was a young forest. A new and different wealth had come. Young trees and deer and partridges were a part of the new order, and snowshoes where the sprouts were thickest.

"Funny thing the way the sharptails went," said the berry picker. Some thought the foxes got them and some said it was "them white owls." The berry picker said he didn't know and changing the subject to more familiar ground he remarked, "The berries have been scarce for years now . . . seems like they need a burn or something to keep the crops a coming."

Blueberry crops and sharptails were both on their way out.

That spring one cock danced by the oak stump, picking a bare spot of sandy soil among the jackpines. He started early, long before the first robin was to arrive, and the sun lit up his purple air sacs and his feathery tracts left dancing patterns in the snow. He never fought, for there was no sparring partner. Later he kept the grass on the sandy soil stamped bare with his feet, dancing morning and night. No hen was to come, for the last hen was gone from the plain.

He danced till his rump feathers were worn down to their shafts from the movement of his tail as he danced, and then when the lupine buds were full to bursting and showed blue . . . he danced no more.

The music of the dance ground by the oak stump was stilled.

Wisconsin is losing its sharptail range.

The open plains by the old stumps are disappearing. Sharptails are fast losing ground . . . giving way to the inexorable return of the land to forest. The openings and brushlands so necessary to the existence of sharptails are being "crowded out" by the natural process of plant succession and by the man-made processes of plantings and fire protection. The skill of the hunt for this trophy bird is also yielding. The Moquah Barrens in Bayfield county, for example, were once the sharptail hunter's paradise. Few birds are now taken from this area.

What is the status of sharptail habitat now in Wisconsin? A decade has passed since Wallace Grange's work and many changes have occurred. In order to learn what has happened in the meantime, we made a survey of the northern and central counties. We wanted to find out not only the present range of this game bird, but also ways to insure its survival in its struggle with modern land-use. The following pages present the situation as it exists now. We have given special emphasis to the north where the loss of range is proceeding at a faster rate than in the central counties.

The map of the state shows the counties which produced birds for the hunter's bag during the 1951 hunting season. However, this by no means indicates that good stands of sharptails are found throughout the area open to hunting; rather, spots of favorable sharptail habitat are scattered about each of these counties. This is true even in the four counties—Douglas, Sawyer, Rusk and Wood—which are classed as "good" sharptail habitat. In the counties classed as intermediate and poor range, there are fewer such "sharptail spots" and so fewer birds in the county as a whole.

The good range now existing is not a guarantee of the future for sharptails. Even in the best counties there has been an enormous loss of range since Grange's survey during the population "high" of ten years ago. What will be their future ten years hence?

QUESTIONS

How are general exposition and narrative combined in the selection called "Saturday"? Does the writer really explain ideas? What ideas?

Where? What forces are in conflict? Which wins? What statement contains the climax? Does the writer use effective details to make us realize his suspense and his feeling in the suspense? Is the end of this unit effective? Why?

How are exposition and narrative combined in the account of the foal's birth? Is the writer more interested in the specific incident or in the general process of birth? What does the writer mean by the terms *foal* and *filly*? Does he use either with more than one meaning? What is his attitude to his whole subject? What details seem most vivid and individual?

In "Biography of a Dancing Ground" how do the writers combine vivid descriptive-narrative and exposition? Is their combination effective? What ideas do they emphasize? What is their attitude toward the ideas? Is the use of talk effective? Why? About how much time is covered? What transitions are used? As the writers are research specialists, what part do acquired facts, the evaluation of facts, and the vivid emotionalizing of facts have in the whole unit? Where do the writers imply that more expository evidence will follow? Without that evidence, is the relation between their narrative and their expository comment clear to you as a general reader?

17

A Way of Life:

PATTERNS OF LIVING

You are perhaps wondering what "a way of life" means in relation to your writing. As you may interpret it here, it is a rather broad term. You have probably done things yourself which were a temporary way of life—if you have been an office worker, salesman, clerk, house-to-house canvasser, page in a legislature, high-school student, college student, professional ball player, member of a dance band, lookout at a forestry station, construction worker, bellhop, checker, milkman, or had a paper route. You may have belonged to a city gang, the Boy Scouts, a 4-H Club, a fraternity; lived on a farm, in a summer camp, in a small town, in a city; or taken a canoe trip in the Canadian wilderness. Perhaps you have served in the army, the air corps, the navy, or the marines, or have gone on a navy cruise. Each kind of work established a way of life for the hours you spent on the job; each organization tended to give you both a code and a method of living. Perhaps you know a parent's way of life as minister, superintendent of schools, college teacher, traveling salesman, newspaperman, grocer, farmer, real estate agent, bricklayer, member of the diplomatic corps, representative of a business firm in a foreign country, Senator, Congressman, medical or agricultural missionary. Perhaps you have had a chance to learn thoroughly the way of life in a coal mining community, in an industrial center, in an exclusive suburb—either the individual or the community pattern. Perhaps you are familiar with some other way of life that is not mentioned here. The preceding illustrations may serve to explain the term and at the same time remind you of personal experiences you may choose for your composition.

YOUR AIM

You are not concerned with telling us how to follow one of these occupations, nor how other people follow one of them as a process. Instead, you are trying to explain the "feel" of the experience, the satisfactions or lack of satisfactions it brings to the worker or to those intimately associated with him. It is true, of course, that there are no rigid partitions between the topics suggested here and those in Chapter 16. And when you find a personal subject you may be able to decide for yourself whether you wish to give it the *how* treatment or the *feel-of-life-and-satisfaction* treatment.

PLANNING AND ORGANIZING

Again, in writing about a way of life, your problem will be comparatively simple. You will still, with most topics at least, be guided by a time order and be writing generalized narrative. With many subjects your pattern will be narrative without much obvious explaining; with others you may need bits of author comment or longer explanatory passages; with others you will need skill in weaving together narrative-descriptive details and ideas; with still others you may need to mention the stages of the subject each time you take up a new part. With an occasional subject you may need to give technical background or explain technical terms at the beginning or during your composition.

You will need to know and perhaps to express in concise sentences a number of other things before you begin writing. First, what quality or qualities of the life itself do you wish to bring out? Is it easy, difficult, pleasant, monotonous, lonely, or social? Does it have warm human contacts? Or unusual but not intimate contacts? Second, what qualities of the whole pattern do you need to analyze? The occupation itself, its variety, monotony, demand for precision, its hours, its danger or ease, regularity or irregularity, stagnation, stimulus to growth, its chance for advancement? Does the job exhaust a worker physically by the time he is forty or give him richer opportunities as he matures? Is the mental or emotional strain endless and exhausting? What contacts, what recreations and shopping chances are available after hours? What places to establish a home? (Some of these details may, of course, be unimportant for your subject.) Third, what are the other effects on the person who follows the particular pattern of life? What qualities does it require at the start? What qualities does it bring out? What ones does it repress? Does it tend to enlarge the worker's skills and interests? Fourth, what do the people who follow this way of life think about it? Do they like it, dislike it, chafe under its restrictions, find that it gives them good money but little else, that it gives them little money but rich personal satisfactions? If the people who follow this pattern have a certain attitude, what is the attitude of their wives? Of their children? Fifth, whether you are a worker or merely an observer, what is your own attitude to this way of life? Sixth, what audience are you writing for—people who know nothing and feel nothing about your topic, those who are prejudiced against it, or those who view it with unrealistic romanticism? If you are trying to change the attitudes of your readers, you will need to select and arrange as carefully as if you were writing a persuasive paper. Seventh, from what point of view do you wish to write, that of an active participant or of a wife or son or daughter of the participant, or from your own viewpoint as an active observer or a participant? The answers to these questions will have much influence on your arrangement, your selection of details, and the mood or tone of your entire paper. If you try to write all these answers concisely, you will discover whether you are hazy about them; if so, think them through until they are clear.

As part of your planning you may need to consider possible choices in handling your time. It is possible that an hour or so of events, as they usually happen, will serve. For example, if you have been a shoe salesman and wish to show that such a salesman usually leads a hard life, you might explain the demands of three or four customers, and other troubles, in a hypothetical hour or half a day. You might use a typical day for life in a coal mine, a small town, at college, and for a dozen other ways of life. For some jobs requiring night duty (for example, that of a stillman in an oil refinery) a typical night or a dangerous night might serve. For a complete picture of life on a farm in Montana, in Iowa, in Vermont, you might need a typical day in each of the four seasons. Such a plan, with vivid development, will require a long paper; perhaps you would do well to limit it by choosing a season, an occupation, and one day for your composition, and giving the feel of the life within those limits.

STYLE

The discussion so far (as well as the readings at the end of the chapter) is based on the assumption that your tone will be serious. But there is no reason why you may not treat a way of life, like a process, with humor or satire. If you wish to write about a lazy, a shiftless, or an ignorant and intolerant community with your tongue in your cheek, by all means do so.

After you have decided upon a point of view, the personal tone will again make your writing appealing to your reader and easier for you. Personalizing will help you avoid awkward passives and vague generalities. If "we" are going to examine a way of life, then use *we, us* and *our* consistently. Or establish the first person singular and use an *I-my-mine* pattern throughout. With some subjects you might assume the viewpoint of a worker—*he, his,* or *she, her, hers*—and use it from start to finish, and you might use a proper name for a typical worker. Do not be afraid of monotony in any one of these patterns because you are repeating a pronoun; your reader will probably welcome the resulting vividness and clarity.

Again you will wish to avoid stereotyped phrases, and again your best way to do so is the positive way of using all your senses on your material. When you experience details as if they are fresh and original, instead of dried in your memory, and when you have fused the details into an experience, you are ready to write. (Read or reread Chapter 2 if you need its suggestions on vividness.)

If you wish reading, in addition to that at the close of the chapter, try *The Country Kitchen,* by Della T. Lutes, Chapter III, "For All Good Things—", or any chapter you find interesting; an anonymous article, "My Husband Was Elected," [1] written by the

[1] *Atlantic Monthly,* November, 1953.

wife of a reform candidate for mayor; or one of the thirty-five articles in *These Are Our Lives*, the book from which the last article in the chapter is taken.

WRITING YOUR COMPOSITION

A. Write a personalized account of some way of life which you have followed for a time yourself, such as a typical day at college, on vacation, in a branch of the armed services, a typical period in a summer job or a regular job, or a way of life which your family established for you. Limit your time pattern carefully. Use generalized narrative, with talk, action, brief character sketches, vivid but generalized description, and whatever you need for your subject and your attitude. Choose your attitude freely. It may be serious appreciation, dislike, or a humorous or satirical slant. Use it consistently as a contribution to unity in your work.

B. Write an account of some way of life which you have observed or investigated by talking with people who follow it, not one that you have merely read about. Consider the satisfaction or the lack of satisfaction which an individual or a group finds in this way of life. Use any suggestions in the preceding discussion which are helpful for your topic. Personalize in some way. Try to get a response from your reader.

C. Write an account of your own future way of life, as you plan it now. This may involve analyzing your entire philosophy of work, marriage, family life; recreational and social life, with their satisfactions. If you choose this, you may need to use a logical arrangement more than you did in A and B; but use a time pattern if you can. At least illustrate your ideas by description or narration.

READING

LIFE IN LIBERIA: THE FIRESTONE PLANTATION [2]

Esther S. Warner

Perhaps all the isolated pieces of our life will fall into a more sensible pattern if I give the setting first; so I will ask you to come

[2] Esther S. Warner is the author of A *New Song in a Strange Land*, 1948, and *Seven Days to Lomaland*, 1954. Both were published by Houghton Mifflin Company. This material is part of a personal letter and has not been printed elsewhere. It is used with the permission of the writer.

with us in our fiery red pickup Ford, "Chief," from Monrovia, the port, to the research area of this huge plantation. Out of Monrovia we pass through palm groves, past mangrove swamps, through grassy areas with occasional high trees, and between "high bush" which comes down to the road like a green wall on either side, so that one feels the road is excavated out of green moss, rather than that the violent growth is on top of supporting earth. The plantation begins thirty miles from Monrovia; but as there are about 90,000 acres in the plantation, one never feels that he is at home when he enters the rubber trees.

Our house is in the Research Area, which is a lovely location. One leaves the rubber trees and drives along palm-lined roads of brick-red earth and approaches our house by winding up a hill between low-growing oil palms. They are shrubby, and their graceful fronds meet over the lane at a height to brush the top of the car as we drive home. It is like passing through a live green Gothic archway, and it has something stately in it, too, like the arch of crossed sabers at West Point weddings.

Once through the arch of palm fronds, we see our red brick house against a background of low hills, and beyond these, higher hills covered with high bush. The house itself is very big. The red corrugated iron roof looks like red tile, and the eaves are so wide that the house seems to be sulking under a big red hat. The front part is on eight-foot brick stilts. Before we planted vines to bridge the gap between earth and house, I always got the effect of a huge animal resting on his front feet. We built trellises and planted native vines the first week we were here, and they have grown from seed to the top of the trellis in less than fifty days.

After climbing a flight of concrete steps you are ready to enter our living room, which is about the size of the faculty lounge in Memorial Union. Two and a half sides are screened and have French doors which can be shut against rain, although this is seldom necessary because of the protection from the eaves. We are really on the "second story," although there is no first story, nothing but piers beneath us. We feel as if we are in an out-of-door living room, because the palms are so near and the birds sometimes fly against the screens.

Besides the master bedroom and the bath, there is a guest bedroom, *for you*. David, the steward boy, will unpack your bags; and you will probably be a bit uneasy, as I was, at having a strange black boy go through your luggage and hang your dresses in the dry closet where an electric heater is always in operation to discourage mold, and put your jewelry and underthings and hairpins and hosiery, much to your surprise, just where you would have put them yourself.

When you awaken from your afternoon nap, you will be surprised to see that noiseless hands have been at work while you slept. All your shoes have been shined in a way they could never be shined in America. They are sitting in a neat row at the foot of your bed. All your dresses have been taken from the closet while you slept and perfectly pressed, and returned again. Clean underthings have been taken from the dresser and put in the dry closet, so they will be warm and dry when you are ready to put them on.

When you awaken about four, you are surprised that you could sleep in such bright white light, but to shutter out the light is to close out the pleasant breeze, so one learns to sleep with the light.

When you have had your bath and have found that the only way to get dry enough to dress in the humid atmosphere is to stand before a fan, you are ravenously hungry. The fragrance of fresh tea, of fruit freshly sliced, of cinnamon toast, and of freshly roasted and salted ground peas (peanuts) hastens your dressing.

From tea time until dinner is cool and pleasant. We might play tennis or go to the bush to collect exotic plants, or visit a native village or drive to a latex station, but you have had a hard day and we have not seen each other for much too long, so today we will sit quietly and talk of many things. There will be plenty of time later for these other adventures.

Twilight is a beautiful time of bird songs, blue haze, soft breezes, sweet smells from night-blooming flowers, and an insect chorus from the swamp between our house and the mountains. There is an old bull-frog whose pompous bellowings are as dramatic and self-conscious as the vocalizing of a famous baritone. It is the light of the moon, and there will be drums and dancing all night in the near-by labor camp. An occasional booming in intricate pattern gives promise of the throbbing rhythm that will begin later and last until dawn. Christmas is approaching, and that means the Devil is unusually active. The boys will not leave the house except in groups carrying lanterns and armed with cutlasses. Many a boy has disappeared because "the Devil got him." If he is ever seen again it is as a corpse from which the heart has been cut out, but usually no trace is found of him. We will hear the Devil's pipes later. Sometimes they seem to come from the mountain just back of the house and sometimes the sound seems to come from the valley and echo against the mountain. To suggest that the Devil might be men is dangerous. By a great stroke of luck and the help of a civilized native, we were able to obtain a Devil pipe. One night my husband got it out and without thinking, blew an experimental blast. When I went to the kitchen the boys were crouched in the corner, quivering and as pale as it would be possible for colored boys to become. I put them all to work at once, but I am sure they think the Devil passed under our house that night and that they had a miraculous escape.

All food is called "Chop," and chop is at eight at our house, although when we go out to eat, chop is usually at ten or eleven. We will dress for dinner. At first this seems like too much trouble—one is always bathing or sleeping or dressing. Now I have come to see that in a changeless land men must make their own changes through activity and dress and customs. So dressing for dinner is not a foolish vanity; it has a function in a land where women especially are likely to "let down."

My husband sits at one end of a long table and I at the other, and you are between us on the coolest side of the table. It would be quite impossible for us to pass any food to each other, but that is not necessary. David will serve us first because he has been told he must. Why white men prize and honor women is quite beyond him, but at any rate he will manage the serving so that *Massa* gets the choicest portions! In movies, the shot of two people dining alone at opposite ends of a long table and looking at each other over an expanse of white linen, flowers, and candles has always seemed either pathetic or very funny. Here it is just another new experience.

Tonight we are dining "off the land." We start with a shrimp cocktail. A boy named Ga-ga (Kpuesi for "duck") brings live ones every morning in an old rusty bucket covered with banana leaves for shade. No matter what he asks I offer a third less, and he will agree after a time for my price plus a cup of rice "for dash" (gift). We cook them like lobster, dropping them one at a time in rapidly boiling water. They change from a dull olive drab to rosy salmon in a few seconds, after which Sammy Cook shucks them out of their shells. Having the water at a rapid rolling boil was an innovation to Sammy. I went to the kitchen one day and found he was giving them a slow stew in a small kettle, and they were still kicking. I couldn't eat shrimp for several days after that, and Sammy was completely baffled at my anger. The boys are completely unaware of suffering in animals or other people, and very stoic about enduring pain themselves.

We have stuffed water deer (shot by ourselves) for the main course. At first I couldn't eat a bite of deer. They seem to me the most beautiful creatures in the whole animal world. But the scarcity of fresh meat and the poor quality of tinned meat work together to break down one's sentimental ideas.

Then we have baked native sweet potato, fried eggplant, and a platter of browned pineapple slices.

Dessert is papaya pie, which is like pumpkin pie except that it is more subtle in flavor and doesn't need added spices; its own flavors are sufficient. . . . But you have had a big day and I prattle on. The trip into Monrovia in one of the little surf boats which bring you from the ship was hot, the ride out was rough, and the tropical heat makes all newcomers want only to eat and to sleep for several days. So to bed now! Our mosquito net is tucked in under the mattress, David has laid out the night gown he thinks you should wear (always the prettiest one), and your slippers have been set just the right place to step into them. To step even once on the floor bare-footed would invite trouble. A strange animal called a "jigger" lays eggs which hatch out just under the skin. They swell and itch and swell. When they are finally "ready" the egg sack is as large as a pea and must be removed intact or the eggs will hatch more deeply in the tissue. Getting the sack out is not as bad as having the hole poured full of iodine!

When you are under the mosquito net you feel like something on exhibit at an old-fashioned farmers' short-course, before the days of cellophane and show cases. You ring for David to turn out the light; he brings you a "night cap" of mixed fresh fruit juices and disappears with your shoes. It gets to be almost annoying, this business of always having one's shoes whisked away, as though one had a right to them only by keeping them on his feet.

Down in the boys' quarters, the boys and the wives and Jabo, the small girl, are softly crooning Bassau songs, and you fall asleep with the lullaby.

REVERIE [3]

Sherwood Anderson

I sat once all night at a boat landing at Baton Rouge. It was hot and still. Mother Mississippi made a soft whispering little sound as her lips touched the land. The steamer had but one eye—a glowing headlight that shot up along the landing stage to a warehouse on a high bluff.

Soft swaying bodies, dancing, dancing, dancing. In the night the great bugs, that come out of the darkness to the light, also danced about the heads of the negro stevedores.

For a long time all was still. The negroes came out of darkness into the light and the great bugs flew about their heads, striking black faces, but the negroes did not mind. Grain was being unloaded—thousands of sacks.

There was nothing for the white captain and the mate to do. The negroes had fallen into their rhythm. No good swearing now, shouting commands. The night was very hot.

I lay on my back in dusty weeds. Shuffle, shuffle—shuffle along.

Sadness too. The long reach of the silent empty river—the dead river that was once alive.

Ghostly echoes of cries, oaths. Explorers on the river, DeSoto, LaSalle, Tonti of the Iron Hand, keel-boat men, longhorn men, pilots on steamers, Mark Twain, "no bottom, no bottom, no bottom."

Human cries across nights, Mason, Big Harpe, Little Harpe, gamblers, steamboat men.

[3] From Sherwood Anderson's *Notebook*, by permission of Liveright Publishing Corporation.

The Natchez—the Robert E. Lee.

Too late. Too late.

For myself I could have done without many things, Woolworth Buildings, the Henry Fords, the aeroplane, the automobile, modern Chicago, Detroit, the movies, the radio, Los Angeles, Miami.

I lay in the weeds by the big river all night, a thousand miles of empty river, no sound—the soft lap of little waves in soft mud, the shuffle of negro feet.

Hours passed—no song. It was midnight. On the deck of the boat the mate sat under a light reading a newspaper.

Then it began. Generations of load bearers in the bodies of these men, the blacks. Did something whisper to them out of the silent river?

First the soft beginning of laughter—out of the bowels of the ship. The laughter ran up the gangplank.

A cry. Oh, ah, ho, a ho, ah ho. Las' sack now. Soon de las' sack. Oh, ah ha, ah ha.

A dance in the bodies now. Swaying bodies going empty-handed, dancing down a gangplank. (If you ever have to go all night down a steep hill try that step. See how easy it is. See how it rests the body.)

Dance going down-hill, rest that way, dance then coming up with two hundred pounds on your shoulders.

Keep dancing, rest dancing.

De las' sack, de las' sack.

On Sunday go ride in the white man's engine. Rest riding.

But keep the song, black man, don't lose the song.

When you lose that, we've got you, we whites.

We'll get you in the end, of course.

That's what makes the song sweet to hear while it lasts.

Will love of words be lost? Success, standardization, big editions, money rolling in.

When you get money you are respectable.

What has respectability to do with loving words? What words do you love? Who has passed on them? What authority has said they are respectable?

Words for every act of the body, for dark and gay thoughts.

The little singing sound made by a pen on paper. The tale whispered in the night and then forgotten.

Words going the way of the blacks, of song and dance.

Can you imagine sweet words in a factory, sing them, dance them?

In the end they will make factory hands of us writers too.

The whites will get us. They win.

Don't turn your back on the modern world. Sing that too, if you can, while the sweet words last.

ON THE ROAD TO SHERIFF [4]

Nellie Gray Toler and James R. Aswell

"All I ever study about or ever want to do is to be kind to all in every way and do my duty as First Deputy of Brundage County.

"Well, in some ways deputy work jist can't be beat. You git to go so many places. It ain't confining like mill work and they's not any hard hand labor, day in and day out, to wear a man down. You git a better salary than farming and it's stiddy money, too. Dry spells and wet spells and smut and rot will set a farmer back. But a deputy don't have to worry none. His business is always good.

"When you're in deputy work, you have some drawbacks, though. Look at my hours! May git a call any hour, day or night. Never know jist when the county will need me. It seems like it needs me mostly when the weather's the worst. I don't know why, but I git a sight more calls in cold rainy or sleety times than in good weather. And don't let nobody tell you the work ain't dangerous. You risk your life every time you make an arrest, every time you serve a warrant or raid a still. That's what I go through all the time to keep this county peace-abiding.

"Far back as I can remember I always wanted to be on the side of the law. I'm the only one of my family ever went into this business. My father was Horace Squires Marshall and my mother was Betsy Naomi T. Farley Marshall. All of my people has been farmers all the way through and that's the way they started me

[4] *These Are Our Lives*, University of North Carolina Press, Chapel Hill, 1939. The material in this volume was written by members of the Federal Writers' Project of the WPA.

out. My brothers farmed and I guess I'd be messing with farm work right this minute if they hadn't been that little certain something in me that put me on the side of the law.

"I always had a lot of patriotic feeling. So when the war come along I was right ready and was glad to go when they drafted me. The government then trained me to fight and sent me overseas. Well, I sure done my best in that war. I stopped a bullet and got wounded. Stayed in a hospital till she healed and went back at them Germans. So they laid for me and give me a dose of gas and I was out for good that time. Government sent me home and I spent two years in hospitals. That old gas is sure hard to clear out of a man's system. But they finally got me shet of it and I come home to Brundage County.

"Well, I jist knocked around for a couple of years. Didn't feel like fooling with farm work. It was jist one thing I wanted to do—deputy work. But I couldn't git on. Then in nineteen twenty-four I got a place. Served my county and its good people ever since except between nineteen thirty-two and nineteen thirty-six. In that time they had a sheriff that him and me couldn't noways git along. So I jist knocked around until we got a good man in here again and he give me my job back.

"Here's how I make my salary. Well, I don't guess you'd exactly call it salary, either. It's commission work. I mean, I git my money all according to how much arrests and subpoenas and warrants I do. So, you see, it keeps a man hustling on his toes to make a go of it. You've sure got to hit the ball. If business is dull, go out and look some up, I say.

"Now whenever they's a funeral anywheres in this county, like as not you'll find me there, specially if its back off the road somewheres. Most usually they's lot of drinking goes on at country funerals. The family drinks so's to drownd their sadness. Them that comes out of respect for the deceased drinks so's they won't git too low in mind from watching the women folks carry on. And then they's lots of young bloods comes just for the pure fun of it and gits lit up. You can look for a fight before it's all over. If nobody gits to fighting, then you can grab somebody for having liquor on them or in their car or wagon. Any which way it is you carry them before a justice of peace and he fines them and you git your fee. If they can't pay the fee, it's the county road for them and the county pays you your fee. You can't lose on a funeral.

"Next to a funeral is a political speaking and a barbecue. Always drinking then and fights. Almost any gathering where people git together may mean you can pick up a fee. Auction sales where they're selling off a mortgage-due farm is good. The man that's being sold out may git ugly and try to start something and then I can step in and put it on him. Lots of times you can do business at a revival meeting when somebody makes trouble over what they believe. Oh, they's a heap of ways to do if you keep hustling. But I wish they'd give me a regular salary along with my fees.

"I keep right at it, doing my duty. I aim to rise in this work. Right now I'm on the road to Sheriff. If I live and nothing happens you will call Elmore Marshall sheriff before many more years.

"The largest raids or work we usually have now is stills. They's several we've got spotted now to gather in. We'll be going in again in a very few days. Usually we get our tip-off when it's least expected and have to go in all kinds of weather. We almost never find anybody there, but they's always signs of them. The still worm still hot and the mash boiling. But they have time to see us coming and run, no matter how much we try to slip up on them.

"We raided a still a short time ago and found it directly on the Creighton County line, we thought. But we found after we had busted and shot it all up that it was all in Creighton County territory. You jist don't seem to be able to make people quit making liquor. They'll go to jail for it and come out and go right back at it. But still raids is gitting to be pretty tame. The birds is flown usually.

"We haven't had a mob since the time they got the nigger that killed Buck Starwell. The nigger had always worked for Mr. Buck and knew him well. Well, he had a sudden spurt of gitting drunk. They wasn't no living with him, that's all, when he got drunk. Bad nigger then. So he got in a lot of trouble and hid in an old house on Mr. Buck's place. Mr. Buck was then sheriff of the county—you remember when that was. Well, we tried after that nigger. He shot a lot of men when we tried to run him out. Mr. Buck says, 'I'll go git him my own self.' He walked right toward the barn. The nigger shot him before he got to the door in cold blood murder.

"They gathered a mob and went after him. Practically everything in town joined it and shot it out with him. He was holed up in the barn and with plenty of ammunition and it didn't look like we was ever going to get him out till all the ammunition had give way. But some of us got enough of that. We got together and rushed him on all sides at once. He hit a few of us, but none serious, and we got him that time.

"Well, he got such wounds he soon died without living to be hung. The mob came pouring in when we'd disarmed him and jist riddled his body when they got to him before we could stop them. Niggers was in on this hunt as well as whites, for they all loved Mr. Buck, a friend to black and white alike.

"About the hardest shooting scrape we've ever had or the toughest customers is the Garners. Them Garners is into everything happens and always gitting out, too. They was caught cold-handed, almost, in the robbery of the Ten-Acres Postoffice sometime ago. But they got out of it. Some of the Garner girls has served time in prison for stealing and various things. Well, they jist don't seem to be anything much they haven't done, though no proof of murder has ever been put on them.

"One time the boys, Boyd and Skipper, refused arrest and after most of the ammunition in town had been shot, they hid in this log barn with the rest of the family and shot it out. It lasted several days. We'd finally captured them all but Boyd and he jist wouldn't give up. He shot two or three deputies and city officers. Finally, though, his mama seen he would be riddled by bullets if he kept it up. She run in front of our men to the barn begging him to give hisself up for her sake and the girls. So he did, or otherwise we wouldn't never have taken him alive. He already had a bunch of wounds, but he was a crack shooter and fought it out to the bitter end almost.

"We've caught them Garners several times since then. They's always wanted for stealing in other counties. We've found the goods on their land, but they always worm out of it somehow.

"Once I let a man git away in a still raid. I was new on the job and kind of skittish of shooting at a man. Well, this was down near the river. I went down there and was watching. We slipped up on them and they had their backs turned and we didn't see their faces. They all run jist as we yelled at them and we shot over their heads. One run and jumped in the river. He stayed under so long I thought he was drownded and when he swum out right almost at my feet I was so happy that he wasn't drownded I jist stood there and didn't ever recognize who he was or say a word to him. Jist stood with my mouth hanging open, a stone's throw from him, and let him go walking off down through the woods. The other deputies was chasing the others and I let him git clean away. Could have caught him if I'd tried.

"One time Joe Mumpower shot Rae Barfield. He was a high yellow and so was she and she was a cook here in town. They accused him but couldn't find the body. Finally I went to his place and searched and seeing a fresh looking place in his barn, he told me that it was a hog had died with cholera and he'd buried it there. I become suspicious and made him dig there. Well, he uncovered the hog right straight. I told him to keep on digging. And it wasn't long till I soon saw the body of the woman. So I forced his confession there. We put him in jail and he hung hisself with his belt.

"Another branch of the deputy work is this. Lots of cold checks is passed and we have to run them down. We serve subpoenas and warrants and arrest people for failure to pay debt. All in all, it's a pretty hard day's work. It's hard to serve a warrant on or arrest a man who is your personal friend. Have to do it, though, even when it's your own neighbors and friends. We must do our duty by so doing.

"About the only criminal assault case in this county by a Negro on a white was a porter at the hotel. We got him for assault on a white girl here. But it later come out showing she was crazy and only trying to git some money out of the management of the hotel.

"Well, I like my work here among the fine people of Brundage County. They's nothing I'd rather do than serve them as their sheriff and I aim to run in this next coming election. I never was blessed with no children in my married life, but if I had a boy I would tell him, 'Git on the side of the law, work for the good people of this county, and they will gratefully reward you some day like they done your Dad when they made him sheriff of this fine county.' "

QUESTIONS

In "Life in Liberia" how much time is covered? How much space? How much is the material adjusted to an individual reader? Since it was written as a personal letter, just how are pronouns used? For the writer? For the reader? How and where are transitions used? Are they effective? Is the unit vivid? Does it give information about the plantation in general, or merely the writer's routines? Is it "a way of life"?

In "Reverie" Sherwood Anderson comments on the modern mechanized civilization and a creative civilization. What are his attitudes to the two? Which does he prefer? How are the Negro stevedores related to this preference? Why has he chosen the unloading of grain from the boat as the center of his sketch? What time and place are used? Where are impressionistic details used? Are they effective? Does the sketch have tone color?

"On the Road to Sheriff," though written by two other people, gives Deputy Marshall's view of his own life work. What does he like about his work? What disadvantages does he admit? What conclusions, if any, does the reader draw? What is the deputy's attitude to the people of his county? To lawbreakers? How are specific incidents used? Is the article a monologue? Is the method of telling it effective?

18

Autobiographical Sketches

There is one subject, at least, on which you are the main authority: your own life. You know more of its outer events, even though you learned from others what happened in your infancy; you were present more often than anyone else when things happened. You know more of your inner life, or at least you have a chance to know it, because your stream of consciousness makes a never-ending comment to you on your past, present, and future. You know less, perhaps, about your character and personality. You are hampered in learning from others because no one person dares to be completely candid with you and nobody can be completely objective; and to different people and at different times, you seem a dozen or a hundred different people. You cannot be omniscient about yourself—unless you can find a psychic x-ray machine. But you can catch yourself off guard when you do or say something that surprises you; you can ask yourself why you acted or spoke as you did, and what attitude prompted it. You can face all your motives, not merely the noble motives. You can analyze your hopes, fears, and desires. You can watch the reactions of other people to your talk and actions, although you must allow also for their personalities and motives. Thus you can approach but never reach complete knowledge of yourself.

And the results of this self-knowledge? Certainly you need not become morbid from introspection if you are an active person with a sense of balance. You may not like what you find, but in time and with persistence you can change even your emotional patterns. You may develop a sense of humor and an ability to smile at yourself, or a sense of tolerance because you and other people are not perfect.

The results in your writing? Your increased self-knowledge may lend flavor to everything you write, both narrative and exposition. And you may find new material to use now in autobiographical sketches and later in logical patterns.

YOUR AIM

In this chapter it is suggested that you use time patterns in explaining the significance of things in your own life. That is, you will write narrative, either generalized narrative or specific narrative, with explanations. Since you will not be concerned with mere events you will need to find out first what events have been important and why; and thus you may need to know much about your outer and inner life as well as your character and personality. You may start with specific incidents or scenes you remember and ask yourself why you remember them, what consequences resulted, what attitudes you have to them, or any other questions that will help you interpret their meaning. You may start with general questions about your life; for instance, whether it has been happy, sheltered, insecure, lonely, adventurous, and so on. Then you may choose events to help you develop one general idea. You may start with a trait of your own character and trace its relation to events in your life. You may begin with some outstanding event, such as an illness, an accident, or a death in the family, and then trace the results by a time pattern, in the past, the present, or even the future.

Thus you may choose to relate one incident and explain its importance or to use several incidents in time order to explain a quality of your life or character. If some of your ideas do not lend themselves to narrative patterns at all, save them for future assignments in logical patterns. Some suggestions to help you find subjects are given later in this chapter.

PLANNING

To achieve your aim, you will probably need to do what you

have done in earlier assignments: find your material, analyze its meaning, and realize your attitudes to it. You may need to estimate the reader you wish to reach. Certainly you know more about your material than he knows; if you explain your ideas clearly and powerfully he will probably find something universal in them. Or at least he will recognize that your experiences are human. You need, perhaps, to phrase a central idea, a central attitude, or a fusion of the two, in a concise sentence. With certain topics you may need to think of the available incidents for developing, and to select, reject, and arrange them in a tentative order. With other topics, especially with a single incident, you may need to create, to enlarge significant moments, and to make a plan for using explanation at the beginning, the end, or as a running commentary through your narrative. In some instances, especially for contrast, you may use an envelope pattern effectively; that is, you may begin with an incident, interpret it by generalizations, and use an incident, either the same or another one, to end the composition.

STYLE

For autobiographical subjects you may find generalized narrative useful, especially the narrative which suggests customary action at some time in your life ("I would go every morning" or "often I would go . . .") but gives the customary action vividness, with the feel of experience. Or you may use the present tense consistently to carry the suggestion of usual action.

You will need to write frankly and freely if you interest your reader. Of course you will write from a personal point of view. The natural method is probably to use the first person, *I*, *my*, freely and consistently. Sometimes a student, following the method used in *The Education of Henry Adams*, gives himself a name and writes successfully in the third person. Some students free themselves from inhibitions when they use the third person for themselves, but others develop a complete blocking. It is possible that you could use the second person consistently and well—but it is unlikely. Make your own choice about the person to use, but be sure that your choice helps you to write with the greatest possible freedom and power.

FINDING SUBJECTS

Thinking your way through this list of suggestions may help you, not to use one of these, but to find your own subject:

1. An autobiography of your life, to give its feel or pattern. Ask yourself what events have been important, and why. Eliminate, select. Then weave a pattern of narrative and explanation.

2. A general conclusion about the quality of your life. Has it been happy or unhappy, eventful or uneventful, lonely or companionable? Use events or incidents in time order to illustrate the theme.

3. A record of growth toward maturity. Examine your changes in attitude toward love, death, desire for security, desire for freedom to grow, toward giving and getting, and so on. Use incidents with explanations of the changes.

4. One important event. Analyze its past, present, or future consequences. Among events consider a death, an illness, an accident, a discovery of music or reading, and so on.

5. A period of good or bad fortune. The depression has often been discussed; families have often had their own periods of good or bad financial luck. Training in some branch of the service or experience in combat might be discussed for good or bad results.

6. An interest, either vocational, avocational, or professional. Try to analyze the events which caused the development, the consequences, present or future.

7. A trait of character. Start with your best trait, your worst one, or the one which has been the greatest problem. Analyze causes, growth, development, or consequences. Use a narrative pattern with explanation.

8. A fear. Analyze causes, consequences, changes, and events.

9. A desire. Consider a desire to construct things; to find out what makes a thing tick, and why; to seek adventure, freedom from control, larger horizons, or any kind of growth. Look for causes, results, changes, and incidents.

10. Effect of parents, one or both, on your whole development. Find incidents.

11. Effect of your position in the family. If you are the youngest, oldest, or only child, or the in-between child in a large family, analyze the effects; find incidents which illustrate them.

12. An education in the formal sense. Limit to a particular period or make a value judgment about the quality of your education. Select typical events in time order for your whole pattern.

13. An education in the informal sense. If a particular person or a group of people, or a sport, or a way of spending vacations gave you a real education, analyze what it did, and why; then find incidents in time order to develop your ideas.

14. A summer camp. You may analyze yourself as a camper or as a counselor.

15. A conflict with your family. Perhaps you were forced to take music lessons or to do something else you resisted over a period of time. Examine your attitudes, find events that are specific or typical, examine your changes in attitude, and evaluate.

16. Travel. Do not plan a mere record of where you went and what you saw. Be sure that you have definite impressions, evaluate, and then find a narrative pattern.

17. Nature. Beware of this topic unless you have enough events and can evaluate influences.

18. A home. You might use a narrative pattern here to show why a particular place was a home as no other place has been, or to show that no place has been a home.

19. A place in your community, such as an art museum, library, youth center, even a skating rink or a bowling alley, if it was the focal point for some development.

20. The lack of something to do and some place to go in your community during your adolescence. Analyze causes, consequences for you and your friends, and find incidents to illustrate your views.

21. A city. Consider the whole city as a physical object or only such parts of it as affected you, its effects on you and your development, and the effects of people in the city, so far as they were an important part of the influences.

WRITING YOUR COMPOSITION

Plan and write a unified autobiographical sketch which uses some kind of narrative pattern for its explanation of ideas. Use specific, summarizing, or any kind of generalized narrative as you need it to bring out their significance.

READING

COMING HOME *

Gertrude Richards

From that October day when I first saw the campus I had the feeling that at last I was safe. I wanted to fling myself down on

the earth, still warm from the summer sun that refused to believe
the calendar, and try to press my body into it; to leave an impression that would be a permanent reminder of the first time in
my adult life that I had come "Home."

"Home" . . . a funny way to feel about this place when I had
never been further west than Chicago and then only on a flying
visit from New York. Yet I felt I was home . . . as I used to feel
when I was a child and returned from camp after a summer away,
to be welcomed by my mother, who seemed so big, so comforting,
to my childish eyes, which took in every detail of her soft, warm
face and unfashionable figure. "It was good to be home," I had
thought as I nuzzled my moist lips against her neck that was still
flushed from baking my favorite chocolate cookies. . . . I would
snuggle close to her . . . closer and closer, as if unable to believe
I was home, safe from the outside world within the circle of my
mother's arms. . . .

I have run a long way since then . . . always running . . .
always escaping . . . escaping not just from places but from
things . . . things around me . . . things within me . . . night-
mares . . . ghosts . . . ghosts of buildings that stretch their
jagged towers to the sky . . . sway and come together, closing in
on me . . . smothering me . . . trapping me . . . trying to reach
out and drag me back. . . .

But I won't go back . . . I'll never go back . . . they can't make
me . . . nothing can make me go back . . . for now I am on the
path that leads to home and peace and safety . . . and now I feel
the road will be short. It must be short because within me I see
the last bend of the road.

Still in my dreams I am tortured. . . . "The Street" leers at me
. . . leers with a dagger between her teeth . . . Chinatown they
call it—the Chinatown of the Tong War days when Tong fought
Tong with knives, opium, and oriental trickery. . . . But this
wasn't Chinatown.

This was just the name they gave to 38th Street . . . the heart
of the highly civilized Garment District, where they waged a
different type of war . . . Boss cheats Boss . . . Buyer cheats Buyer
. . . Worker cheats Worker, and they all connive to cheat each
other with throat-slitting tactics. . . . This was the street of

golden opportunity for anyone willing to sell his soul for a chance to use the talent and training he had taken years to acquire. . . .

How well I remember that day a few years back when I so naïvely thought that *I* could conquer "The Street" on my precocious ability in art school . . . yes, I was one of the youngest and most promising students in the history of the school. . . . I would be a designer in no time . . . I was so fresh . . . so full of ideas and ideals . . . it shouldn't be difficult for me, I had everything in my favor . . . youth, talent and the clean good looks of a girl who was bursting with enthusiasm for life.

"And all you have to do, little girl," said Mr. X or Mr. Y or Mr. Z, as they let their fat, clammy hands run up my warm forearm, "is to be nice to the right people." What a beginning and end for my childish dreams. . . . Yet I couldn't believe all people were like that . . . I couldn't give up so quickly . . . I had to go on searching . . . finding out for myself.

Of course I managed to get and hold some jobs that were at least stepping stones to my ultimate goal. And then finally that last wonderful offer of a job as a buyer for a chain of stores, and this job apparently had no strings attached.

That first day I optimistically made the rounds of the showrooms. "Sorry, if you haven't an account here we can't give you any merchandise . . . wartime shortage of materials you know, Miss . . . old customers come first . . . but wait a second." His eyes appraised my figure. "Maybe we can go out to lunch and talk this over. . . . No, we're not taking any new customers, but you look like a regular kid. . . . If you play ball with me, maybe I can help you out . . . new around here, ain'tcha?"

Suddenly it dawned on me why I had been given the job . . . the man who had formerly had my job had nothing but cash to offer in exchange for goods . . . but I had a subtler bribe. . . . Run, Sandra, run . . . faster, faster, faster, faster, faster, faster.

Some people might call it war jitters and maybe it was . . . that sick cold feeling I'd have each time I went into the grocery store and saw women, formerly imperious in their demands, kowtowing and fawning over the little man behind the counter, all in the hope of getting a pound of butter or a bit of choice steak to fill their already over-stuffed bellies. . . . Oh, of course they were patriotic . . . weren't they buying War Bonds with the excess profits from their husbands' war jobs and contracts? . . . Didn't Mrs. Stanton wear the attractive Red Cross worker's uniform as she drove around the countryside? . . . And wasn't Mrs. Gardner devoting an evening a week stolen from her busy schedule of card parties and teas, to sell War Bonds in the theater lobby? . . . Of course this did entitle her to see the picture after an hour or two of this strenuous work. . . . And what about Mrs. Reese who was so very active in all the women's war organizations? . . . She had no time to think about her young daughter who gave her time and her youthful body to service men because she thought that was being patriotic.

Run, Sandra, run, faster, faster, faster, faster, faster, faster. . . .

But now the tempo has changed, and my footsteps are paced to the majestic calm of the chimes coming from the Campanile. . . . Eight o'clock classes in winter time . . . and I slowly walk across campus in the darkness. The steady, silent stream of students making their daily pilgrimage to knowledge, reminding me of another pilgrimage so many winters ago when the wise men came to worship at the first great shrine of Knowledge.

And the stars twinkle . . . each one like a captured snowflake reflected on the white robed ground. Each note of the carillon escapes into the stillness of the air, a frozen dewdrop that remains suspended like a halo around my heart. . . . It's eight o'clock in winter time, and slowly the darkness lifts . . . a fine band of light shows through . . . blue and violet and rose and gold . . . real gold . . . the gold I have been unwittingly searching for all these years. . . .

I raise my eyes to the sky and I see no more. . . . A burning tear makes a path over the cold fire of my face. . . . At last I can stop running . . . at last I have come home.

TWO LEGS TO STAND ON [1]

John D. McKee

The weather was near-blizzard proportions that day in December. Early in the evening there was a knock on the door of a small

[1] From *Two Legs to Stand On*, by John D. McKee. Copyright, 1953, 1955, by John D. McKee. Reprinted by permission of the publishers Appleton-Century-Crofts, Inc.

cottage in Emporia, Kansas. A young housewife, heavy with child, answered the knock. A little boy stood on the porch with home-made pine wreaths clutched in blue, gloveless hands.

His face was pinched with cold, and the wind whipped through his worn, thin coat. Would the lady buy a wreath? She would, and she would invite the little waif to warm himself before the fire. *This is a sad way,* she thought, *for a little boy to be spending his time, and so near to Christmas, too.*

The little boy did not tarry long, but his face remained in her memory for many years. Especially would she remember his blue-cold hands, and the clumsily contrived wreaths they held.

My mother always associated the little boy and the Christmas wreaths with my birth, for at 8:30 that evening I made an all too sudden appearance into the world. I arrived about two months ahead of schedule, much to the consternation of my mother and of my father, who at the time was on the other end of his run as a Central Division brakeman on the Santa Fe Railroad.

I weighed at birth a scant two and a quarter pounds. I was christened John DeWitt—John for my mother's older brother, and DeWitt for my father—but anyone could see at a glance that all that name was too much of a load for such a tiny mite, and almost immediately the name was shortened to Jack.

I was born at home and there was no incubator available, so I was bundled into a clothesbasket and surrounded by hot-water bottles and hot bricks wrapped in flannel. Apparently I thrived on this hothouse treatment. When I was only a few days old my father's hand served as a cradle. A short time later, the man who delivered the groceries, on seeing my dangling arms and legs, said, "My, ain't he growed! Why, put him in a piller and you couldn't of found him!"

There didn't seem to be anything the matter with me at this time. At the age of four months I weighed fourteen pounds. When I was fourteen months old I was putting words together into sentences.

But, as the months went on, it became apparent that something was terribly amiss. It was not only that I made no attempt to crawl. I was a year old before I could even sit up by myself.

It was about this time that Mother took me to a clinic. The

doctor gave me a thorough examination and checked each item on the examination card "O.K." until he came to feet and legs. There he put a big X, and under "Remarks" he wrote "Spastic. Suggest stretching exercises."

"All I learned from that examination," Mother says, "was that there was something wrong. I had no idea what spastic meant, and the doctor didn't explain."

Long afterwards, Mother told me that while she was carrying me she had slipped and fallen on an icy sidewalk. Such a fall may have caused my premature birth or injured the motor nerve centers of my brain and sent me into the world with cerebral palsy. The injury which causes cerebral palsy may occur before, during, or following birth. It may be that the birth process having begun early, I suffered cerebral anoxia, a lack of oxygen which is caused by premature cessation of the oxygen supply from the mother to the fetus, and which results in damaged brain tissue.

Whatever the cause, the results are somewhat similar to crossed wires in a telephone exchange. Like ringing Smith's number and getting Jones, if a cerebral-palsied person sends a mental signal to his foot for action, his arm may tighten in sympathetic, or even independent, action. The wires are crossed somewhere.

There must have been some dark days indeed between the time Mother took me to the clinic and the time I was two years old. Most of the progress which has been made in the treatment of cerebral palsy has taken place in my own lifetime, and in those early years, at least among the doctors who saw me, diagnosis of the condition was the only advance made. Treatment was by trial and error if there was any treatment at all. The long struggle to get me on my feet was begun almost entirely by my father and mother.

With a pillow behind me and a pillow propping me up on either side, I could sit up by the time I was a year old. Sometime between my first and second birthdays, I began to sit up alone, and by the time I was two—way behind schedule—I had finally begun to crawl. Although it was a red-letter day when I began to get over the floor under my own power, part of the difficulty I was to have later became apparent then. When I crawled, I thrust my arms ahead of me. Then I drew up my legs, both at the same time, with the action originating from the hip. There was no reciprocal action originating from the hip. There was no reciprocal action between arms and legs, or between the legs themselves. It was to be years before any sort of reciprocation, necessary above all else for walking, was obtained.

But I was crawling. At last I was moving, regardless of how awkwardly. Now, at last, there must be some hope for my walking.

The day I first hunched myself across the floor marked a beginning and an end. Such progress symbolized for my parents the end of a period of black bewilderment and despair when, but for hope and faith, there was no evidence at all that I would ever move from my bed. But the act also marked the beginning of an almost equally frustrating period because for years I did not progress beyond the crawling.

The doctors said I would probably never walk. They considered it something of a miracle that I learned to crawl. Shortly before the age of six, after many false starts and an operation, I learned to walk. After four operations and a great deal of physical therapy I have walked my way through grade school and high school, and am now walking through college; and I have held jobs which required the walking of several miles daily.

I went to Boy Scout camp two summers. One of my favorite ceremonies at the camp was the ritual of the Yellow Ribbon. When a Scout learned to swim, the yellow ribbon which had marked him as a novice was ceremoniously cut from around the initiate's neck with a large butcher knife from the camp kitchen. I was never the star of the Yellow Ribbon ceremony. I wore my badge of aquatic ineptitude throughout my two terms at camp. But in 1947, at the age of twenty-eight, I learned to swim.

Because I fell often and unexpectedly in my early years, I did not so much as walk the downtown streets alone until I was a senior in high school. Yet some of my college years have been spent away from home. I gained confidence as my independence increased, and I roamed the streets of a city much larger than my own with complete unconcern.

Parents have hidden cerebral-palsied children away in their homes because they were bewildered and shamed by what they brought into the world. Cerebral-palsied persons have been committed to homes for the feeble-minded simply because they have been unable to express themselves and demonstrate their intelligence.

Circumstantial evidence is against us in many cases. The average victim of cerebral palsy is often not attractive to look at. His facial muscles may contract uncontrollably, so that he grimaces and grins for no apparent reason. Unable to swallow correctly, he may drool continually. He spills his food and struggles painfully with each word he utters.

I have been spared the facial contortions and the drooling, the garbled speech and the inverted breathing, but I still have to watch myself carefully when I eat in company. Eating out could have been one of the hardest problems for me to face. But in this, as in all things, my parents refused to let me think of myself as any different from my brothers, or from other normal people.

At home with my family, I was perfectly relaxed. If I spilled something at the table, such an act was regarded as an ordinary occurrence, merely as if one of my brothers spilled his milk or dropped his bread butter-side-down on the floor. Once in a while, if I was having a particularly tough time, and was spreading my food around the dining room with a lavish hand, Mother would say "Why don't you sit on the floor, Jack? Anything that falls up, we'll hand down to you." The tension was broken by the laugh that always followed, and I could usually finish my meal with a minimum of spilling.

From my own experience, I am convinced that my parents' attitude is the only one to adopt in regard to the problem of a cerebral-palsied child. My cerebral-palsied friends who have solved their problem indicate a remarkably similar psychological influence.

I met Hubert Shelley when I was going to Kansas Wesleyan University and he was attending McPherson College. Hubert's walking problem was as difficult as mine. His speech was so troublesome as to make recitation a chore. Penmanship, in his athetoid hands, was a scrawl. Yet he was in his junior year in college, and when I met him he was returning from Iowa, where he had hitchhiked to attend a national students' meeting.

We met in the college dining hall, and since our conversation was not nearly finished by the end of the meal, I invited him to my room. Hubert had had trouble getting his food from the plate to his mouth, and the area around the plate showed the effort, but the only reference he made to it came when we were ready to leave. "I'll be ready to go," he said, grinning and reaching for a drink with both shaking hands, "as soon as I spill some more water."

When you have been mentally and chronologically an adolescent but in physical abilities yet a child, and one day for the first time you tie an acceptable bow in your shoelace and, for the first time, the knot stays firm throughout the day, then you may realize something of the magnitude of walking for a period of three weeks without falling. When, after years of having someone tie your necktie for you, you spend an afternoon before a mirror and tie and retie a four-in-hand knot until you finally learn how to do it, you have cut another strand of the web of dependence. When you have done that, then you may realize what a gigantic advance you've made when you can go through the intricate ritual of shifting gears and getting a car under way.

Because of the hypertension of my muscles, and because of the rigid reaction of my muscles to any startling situation—a reaction which continued into adolescence—my parents said it was obvious I would never drive a car. In October of 1949 I passed my tests and got a license to drive.

Suppose for years it has taken you at least an hour to bathe, and you cut the time to half an hour. Suppose only the index finger has escaped the paralytic stiffness of your right hand, and suppose you teach that finger to take its part in typewriting. You would join me then, I think, in agreement with Walt Whitman: "The narrowest hinge of my hand puts to scorn all machinery."

Even if I had not made the physical progress I have, I still would have the compensation of development in other directions. If I had been an active child, I might not have gained my early and still sustained love of reading. If I had been able to participate in organized sports, I might never have learned the intricacies of more than one or two athletic events. I might never have acquired the ability and inclination to write about them.

All of which is at least part of the reason why I do not consider myself handicapped. Handicapped is an unfortunate word. A person is handicapped only when he fails to look on his particular problem as a challenge to be met. Once he accepts the challenge, what could have been a handicap becomes but one more obstacle—of which there certainly are many besides physical ill-being—to the achievements of one's dreams.

If I am handicapped, then everyone is handicapped. Everyone has problems of personality, of capabilities or the lack of them, of desires just out of reach, of visions tantalizingly obscured by clouds of his own making. This individual lacks education, that one initiative. This one is burdened with a crutch, that one with his fears. Indeed, I strongly suspect that the only true handicap travels under the soft and pious name of resignation.

I insist, therefore, that I am not handicapped. I am merely different. And my difference is of no more real importance than the individual differences in temperament, capabilities, and personality which give to each person his own shape and color in the human crazy-quilt.

By no means is that to say that I do not have my doubts and fears. I learned, long before I read the statement, that a cerebral-palsied person is a creature of alternating high-flying elation and profound depression. I have tried to avoid such an emotional see-saw, but I have not always succeeded.

Mine is not, however, a blindman's-buff approach to my physical deficiencies. At times it seems that I have come to the end of my progress. I was in such a mood while I was deciding to write this essay and I discussed the problem with my mother.

"After all," I said, "maybe there are some things I can't do." Mother has seen me defeat all the difficulties I have surmounted so far. She and Dad have driven and goaded and cajoled me into doing things I would not have attempted otherwise.

She looked me in the eye and said, "Name one thing you can't do."

"Well," I said, thinking of certain times of loneliness in my high school and college days, "I can't dance."

"You've never tried," she said, and she left it at that.

BACH [2]

Frank Lloyd Wright

At this time a nervously active intellectual man in clerical dress seated at the organ in the church, playing. Usually he was playing. He was playing Bach now. Behind the organ, a dark chamber. In the dark chamber, huge bellows with projecting wooden lever-handle. A tiny shaded oil lamp shining in the dark on a lead marker that ran up and down to indicate the amount of air pressure necessary to keep the organ playing. A small boy of seven, eyes on the lighted marker, pumping away with all his strength at the lever and crying bitterly as he did so.

Streams of sound went pouring out into the church against the stained-glass windows *fortissimo*. The boy worked away for dear life to keep air in the bellows, knowing only too well what would happen to him should he give out. Then came a long-drawn-out, softer passage. It was easier to pump—the Vox Humana—faraway beauty, tenderness and promise in it stealing over boy-senses. He stopped, tears and all, entranced. Listening—breathless—he forgot, but suddenly remembered just in time to work away again with all his might to keep air enough for the Bach as it broke into the sound-waves of triumphant, march-like progress. The heroic measures brought him back again to strength and for a while he pumped away with fresh energy, hopefully. But as on and on the wondrous music went, more and more the young back and arms ached until again the tears began to flow. Would father never stop? He felt forgotten, and he was. Could he hold out? Pulling all his energies together now, despair gaining on him, eye on that leaden marker. Should it ever drop? But it will . . . it will . . . for he can't . . . No. . . .

Just then the music abruptly ended. The stops knocked back into their sockets. The cover of the keyboard slammed down. His father called him. "Frank! . . . Frank!" There was no answer.

The figure of the father darkened the small doorway, took in the

---

[2] Frank Lloyd Wright, *An Autobiography*, Duell, Sloan & Pearce, Inc., 1943. Copyright, 1943, by Frank Lloyd Wright.

situation at a glance, took the boy by the hand and led him home without a word.

When they got there his mother, seeing the state the boy was in, looked reproachfully at the father.

It was always so. The differences between husband and wife all seemed to arise over that boy. Mother always on the defensive, father taking the offensive.

So the lad grew, afraid of his father.

His father taught him music. His knuckles were rapped by the lead pencil in the impatient hand that would sometimes force the boy's hand into position at practice time on the Steinway Square piano in the sitting room. And yet he felt proud of his father. Everybody listened and seemed happy when father talked. And Sundays when he preached the small son dressed in his homemade Sunday best looked up at him absorbed in something of his own making that would have surprised the father and the mother more if they could have known.

His pupil always remembered father as he was when "composing," ink on his fingers and face. For he always held the pen crosswise in his mouth while he would go to and from the desk to the keyboard trying over the passage he had written. His face would soon become fearful with black smudges. To his observant understudy at those times he was weird.

Was music made in such heat and haste as this, the boy wondered? How did Beethoven make his? And how did Bach make his?

He thought Beethoven must have made most of his when it was raining, or just going to, or when the days were gloomy and the sun was soft with clouds. He was sure Bach made his when the sun shone bright and breezes were blowing as little children were happily playing in the street.

Father sometimes played on the piano far into the night, and much of Beethoven and Bach the boy learned by heart as he lay listening. Living seemed a kind of listening to him— then.

Sometimes it was as though a door would open, and he could get the beautiful meaning clear. Then it would close and the meaning would be dim or far away. But always there was some meaning. Father taught him to see a symphony as an edifice—of sound!

QUESTIONS

Why did the writer of "Coming Home" choose as a beginning a time when she had come to a new place and new work? How does she use the envelope pattern for the whole unit? Is its use effective? What contrasts does she state or suggest between her former life and her present life? What does she mean by "the street," or "Chinatown"? What does she not mean? Are her memories of the past general or specific or both? Where does she use summarizing narrative most effectively? What does she mean to suggest by the words, "Run, Sandra, run, faster . . ."? Are these words used effectively? Does the sketch have any universal significance? Do the examples from the war period detract from the universality or add to it? Are any details ironic? Is the end effective? Does the unit have power?

How does the sketch "Two Legs to Stand On" combine narrative and exposition? Where does the writer use exposition with little or no narrative? Where does he use narrative to summarize events? Where does he use specific narrative without much general explaining? Where does he blend the two most successfully? What fundamental fact is the basis for the whole unit? What does the term *spastic* mean? Is the definition the writer gives both essential and adequate, considering his aim? What general evaluation of his problem does he make? In this evaluation does he recognize differences between himself and others? Does he recognize compensations? What does he say about himself as a handicapped person? How does he treat the question whether there is anything he can't do? What impressions do you form about his character? Why? What impressions do you get of his family? Is his article interesting? Why? Does it have any universality?

In "Bach" what main incident is used? How does the writer use this incident to explain the boy's interest in music? To bring out the conflict between the mother and father? To bring out the relationship between the boy and his father? To lead to other generalizations about the boy's feeling for music? What concept of music did the boy develop? What, if any, is the relationship between that concept and the writer's career as a distinguished architect? Does the whole unit have an effective blending of incident and generalizations? Is the use of the third person effective? Is the writer's artistic aim achieved? What seem to be the unusual qualities of the whole unit?

19

Places, Objects

In this chapter, more than in others, it seems necessary to begin by explaining assignments because you have many choices.

First, you may write about a place, using mainly space patterns. The place may be a house, another building, a room, a camp, a favorite spot by a river or in the mountains. For instance, you might write about a new factory or any other industrial plant, a new gymnasium, or a new kitchen, stressing its beauty or comfort or utility or all of them combined. You might explain the plan of a new house or of the house you hope to have, emphasizing one or more of these qualities. You might write about some object, possibly a chair, an old clock, a building, or a room because it has significant emotional associations. (A student wrote "Benediction" and Marcel Proust wrote "The Steeple of Saint-Hilaire" because of memories connected with the place. Both are reprinted at the end of the chapter.) You might choose to explain modern tendencies in church architecture by writing about the plan of one church, stressing its beauty and modernity. You might explain a small town, a community, or a whole city by showing us the plan of the place and your attitude to its life or its activities. All of these topics assume some objective information; but in the ones that are important for their emotional associations you will probably emphasize subjective explanations. In any one of these subjects you will need space patterns, and in some of them, perhaps time patterns also.

Second, you may explain a mechanism, not to show how it works but what it looks like, perhaps where it is used, and what significance it has for people or society. For example, you might write about a tractor or some other piece of farm machinery, to explain the ways in which a farmer uses it and the changes it has made in his life. Probably you would explain the appearance and size of the tractor, though they might not be essential. You could write in the same way about a cotton picker, a corn picker, or any piece of machinery that has made a radical change in an industrial process. For instance, the student who wrote "The Grinder" knew objective details about the mechanism, but he selected only details to emphasize its power and its danger to a worker who stands in front of it.

Third, you may explain the phenomena of inanimate nature: a typical blizzard, snowstorm, tornado, hailstorm, autumn rain, summer storm, or hurricane. If you choose such a topic here, you will not write a mood sketch or a specific narative only; you will have a basis of accurate observation and some scientific information. You will be concerned with what usually happens, but you may need to explain the locality with which you are dealing and some variations on the usual pattern. In these specific topics time patterns are important, but you will be dealing also with details which you observe in space and which are temporary in that space. Other topics may suggest themselves: the pattern of rainfall in a normal season in your locality, the pattern in a drought year and the effects on the landscape or the crops, and so on; the appearance of dew in a certain kind of weather, from the coming of dusk to bright sunlight next morning. If you choose to write about dew you may concern yourself with its variations in certain kinds of weather, its appearance and disappearance, and the causes of these variations. Since you wish to express yourself with vividness and interest, you may need to follow time patterns in parts of your work and to give us the feel and the look of dew as it exists in space. "Fog" at the end of the chapter is a suggestive piece of reading for this group of topics.

YOUR AIM

Whatever subject you choose from these or similar possibilities, your aim is twofold: first, to let the reader see, in the physical sense, the subject you have chosen and to understand your ideas about it; second, to communicate to him your attitudes about it. (If you choose to write about a mechanism or about inanimate nature, you will also need much objective information.) Thus you will write from your own interest and try to secure your reader's interest. This double task may challenge all your powers.

POINTS OF VIEW

Since you are dealing with problems of space in some subjects connected with this chapter, you will often be concerned with physical points of view. You may need to think of them not as ideas in rhetoric books but as parts of a live subject, and to make a choice for your subject. The first of the three main points of view is the stationary but personal view, as if, for instance, you are explaining the plan of a city from a hilltop. You remain fixed, but you need place transitions to make the scene clear to others: *below, at my right, at my left, at the back, in the foreground,* etc. If the scene changes, from afternoon quiet to rush-hour traffic or from sunset to darkness, you will need time transitions also. Second, there is the moving point of view; that is, the observer moves as he continues to use his personal view. For instance, a writer wishing to take us through the Chinese section of Chicago may say: "But now as you walk . . . Then . . . Through the glass of a dozen store fronts . . ."; and with these transitions he may use details typical of the Chinese section and other details indicating time and place. Of course the writer-observer may deal also with a subject that keeps him stationary while other objects move, as he might if he wished to explain an annual parade; and he would have a similar problem of using time and place transitions. Third, there is the point of view which seems impersonal and omniscient because the writer explains the whole plan of a town or a community when he cannot see the entire unit at any one moment of time or at one point in space. The first example below is an illustration.

EXAMPLES

The following account is factual, autobiographical, infused with the writer's attitudes, and the view tends to be omniscient:

In 1890 the village of St. Mark's in South Carolina was raw; it had more than a touch of wildness and through its life there ran a strain of violence. It consisted of two principal streets, running diagonally to each other, and of half a dozen lesser streets that trailed off into cotton-fields and pine-forests. There was a cotton-seed oil mill, a saw mill and twenty to thirty general merchandise stores. Three or four of these were housed in one-story buildings of red brick. For the rest the village was built of wood and many of the houses were unpainted, showing the browned and weather-beaten boards. There was a Methodist Church and a Baptist Church, each with a grave-yard behind it. North of the village straggled a Negro grave-yard, its graves decorated with colored pebbles, bits of iridescent glass and the broken shards of cheap vases. Here and there, behind houses or in chance lanes were small, black, one-roomed huts inhabited by Negro women. These women were in domestic service in the village and, as I learned later, plied, in addition and quite openly, an equally ancient but less honest trade. Despite eight or ten bar-rooms the streets were quiet except on Saturday. Then the village flared into life. Many hundreds of Negroes came in from the sparsely settled country; they rode in on horses or mules or oxen or drove rough carts and primitive wagons, and were themselves generally clad in garments of which the original homespun had disappeared in a mass of gaudy patches. They traded and drank and, child-like, spent their money on foolish things—perfumes and handsome whips and sweets. Toward dusk they reeled in a hot turmoil and filled the air with that characteristic odor of peanuts and stale whiskey and chewing tobacco.[1]

Another writer explains a mechanical invention, the monotype, in this way:

The machine looks modest, and, to anybody capable of understanding machines, very simple. It stands perhaps 4 feet high, it is 3 feet 8 inches long by 3 feet broad, and it weighs only 900 pounds. It requires very little power to drive it. The buzz of its driving-belt and the click, click of the work it is doing hardly makes itself heard at your ear above the clatter of Leadenhall street. Altogether it is one of the least ostentatious machines that ever made a revolution. But if you look at it closer and realize what it is doing, the machine is one of the greatest marvels of all the marvelous history of machinery, the crown of over five centuries' development in the most vital of all civilizing arts. The machine is casting and setting type all by itself—setting it, too, more regularly,

[1] Ludwig Lewisohn, *Upstream*, Boni & Liveright, 1923.

more clearly, more cheaply, and more untiringly than written words have ever been set before.

Click, click, click; and with each click a fire-new shining letter slides into place in a line print. Click, click, click, till a line is finished; the line slides up into its place in a column, and the machine, before you have finished watching the line fall in, has pushed out nearly half the next. Nobody is touching it—nobody telling it what to say. . . .

Its full name is the Lanston monotype machine; its familiars call it briefly the monotype. It is almost a relief—so much are you hypnotized by the apparent spontaneity of the thing—to learn that it is not saying just what it likes; that it is, after all, like other machines, man's servant.[2]

The author of the preceding explanation has only to expand his first paragraph by using specific supporting details to write a complete composition on the significance of this machine.

Another author had occasion to describe a tractor in action to show its significance in an economic and social revolution:

The tractors came over the road and into the fields, great crawlers moving like insects, having the incredible strength of insects. They crawled over the ground, laying the track and rolling on it and picking it up. Diesel tractors puttering while they stood idle; they thundered when they moved, and then settled down to a droning roar. Snub-nosed monsters, raising the dust and sticking their snouts into it, straight down the country, across the country, through fences, through dooryards, in and out of gullies in straight lines. They did not run on the ground, but on their own roadbeds. They ignored hills and gulches, water courses, fences, houses.

The man sitting in the iron seat did not look like a man; gloved, goggled, rubber dust mask over nose and mouth, he was a part of the monster, a robot in the seat. The thunder of the cylinders sounded through the country, became one with the air and the earth, so that earth and air muttered in sympathetic vibration. . . .

He loved the land no more than the bank loved the land. He could admire the tractor—its machined surfaces, its surge of power, the roar of its detonating cylinders; but it was not his tractor. Behind the tractor rolled the shining disks, cutting the earth with blades—not plowing but surgery, pushing the cut earth to the right where the second row of disks cut it and pushed it to the left; slicing blades shining, polished by

[2] G. W. Steevens, *Things Seen* (memoir by W. E. Henley), The Bowen-Merrill Co., 1900.

the cut earth. And pulled behind the disks, the harrows combing with iron teeth so that the little clods broke up and the earth lay smooth. Behind the harrows, the long seeders—twelve curved iron penes erected in the foundry, orgasms set by gears, raping methodically, raping without passion. The driver sat in his iron seat and he was proud of the straight lines he did not will, proud of the power he could not control. And when that crop grew and was harvested, no man had crumbled a hot clod in his fingers and let the earth sift past his fingertips. No man had touched the seed, or lusted for the growth. Men ate what they had not raised, had no connection with the bread. The land bore under iron, and under iron gradually died; for it was not loved or hated, it had no prayers or curses.[3]

You may disagree with the emotional attitude of the writer in the preceding passage, you may wonder whether the subjective element has led to a kind of falseness; but you will grant, perhaps, that he has a point of view and that he has found powerful figures and other details to express his point of view.

OTHER ORGANIZING PRINCIPLES

You may find it necessary to consider some other principles also. First, you may need a fundamental image or a basic comparison to clarify the broad general outlines of a place or scene. For example, Victor Hugo used an A as a basis for explaining the Battle of Waterloo; and one writer has compared Cape Cod to a human arm, with certain places located at the shoulder, others at the elbow, and still others at the fingertip. In the account of St. Mark's, quoted above, the writer explained the basic plan in literal terms when he said that the town "consisted of two principal streets, running diagonally to each other, and of half a dozen lesser streets that trailed off into cotton-fields and pine-forests"; thus he gave his reader a kind of blueprint of the place. Second, you may have problems of selection and arrangement. You will need to use both principles at once as you emphasize a quality of the place and your attitude to it, and choose a dozen details out of a possible hundred to help a reader see, instead of drowning him in details or giving him no picture.

In developing certain topics you may need to name a center of

[3] John Steinbeck, *The Grapes of Wrath*, Viking Press, 1939.

interest; that is, name some outstanding object and then use it as a point of reference for other details. For instance, in explaining a room, you name the fireplace first and then relate other physical objects to it; if a church spire dominates a town, you mention it first and then use it as a point of reference for other objects. As you struggle with the arrangement of your details, you may proceed from the near at hand to the far away, or from the far away to the near at hand; you may give a general statement, support it with specific details, and then summarize with a repetition of the general statement; or you may use the order of climax, proceeding from the least, to the more, and then to the most important details. Of course you will need to choose from these principles according to your aims and your topic.

If you wish to explain a change in your attitude to a place you may choose one of these plans of arrangement: a series of incidents or scenes in time order; two contrasting incidents or scenes; the same incident or scene used at the beginning and again at the end to envelop a series of flashbacks. With any one of these patterns the aim may be the same. And you will still need to show us the place by space patterns at some point and to interweave scenes or incidents with explanations of the change.

If your topic is a mechanical invention or some other object, you will probably explain it at the place where you have watched it yourself; and its significance will be your own mental problem to solve before you can make any complete plan for patterns in time and space. If your topic is an object but a family heirloom, you may be able to use a specific conversation between an older and a younger member of the family as a device for explaining the appearance of the object, its origin, history, and significance for the family.

SUBJECTS

Perhaps you found enough suggestions at the beginning of this chapter to help you choose a specific subject. Here are a few other possibilities if you need them.

If you are interested in writing about a place and have not yet decided on one, recall places where you have lived, worked, loved, hated, been educated, attended church, visited, felt at home, felt

cramped, spent vacations, played, grown up, or experienced anything else important. Your best subject is probably not the place
that is unusual in itself but the one where you had the most interesting inner experience. The wonderful romantic place you
saw once may be an unsatisfactory topic if you are hazy about the
external details and have no inner details. Perhaps a place you once
thought beautiful, spacious, or awesome seems ordinary now, or a
place where you once went for protection or solace seems different
because you have matured. When you analyze the reasons for
some such change in attitude your subject will probably seem
significant.

If you are interested in an object, try some heirloom: a brooch,
portrait, hand-woven coverlet, silver teapot, or something similar.
You may use an object that is personal property: a violin, a gun, a
medal, a certificate of achievement. Any of these things may
seem significant when the owner asks himself: Why do I have this
object? What failures and successes does it represent? What development has come from my struggle to use or possess it?

If you wish to explain a mechanism, not merely to show how it
works, you probably already know a particular kind that interests
you. Or you may be interested in a larger idea similar to one of
these: What ease and comfort does the owner of the newest model
car have, compared with the owner of a Model-T Ford? Do the
trends in automobile designing tend toward safety or toward eye
appeal?

WRITING YOUR COMPOSITION

Choose one of the assignments which follow. No matter which
one you choose, make the best possible use of space and time
patterns, use your attitude freely as a means to emotional unity,
personalize, interest your reader, and make effective use of descriptive-narrative details. Apply any suggestions in the preceding discussion which are pertinent to your subject.

A. Choose a place that has personal associations for you (a
house, room, summer cabin, lookout, camp, etc.). Explain the
associations; or if your attitude has changed, explain the change
in it.

B. Choose some mechanical invention. If necessary, explain

what it looks like and where it is used; but emphasize mostly its significance to individuals or society.

C. Choose an object that has personal significance, either an heirloom or a piece of property which is associated with your own struggle and development. Make us see the object and understand its significance.

D. Write something about inanimate nature if you have a sufficient basis of observation and some scientific information.

READING

THE GRINDER *

Homer K. Gordon

It looks harmless enough—like all machinery under control. The peaceful purr of its giant motor never betrays the fact that the power of twelve horses is driving that wheel. And certainly just by looking at the wheel one would never realize that its outer edge is traveling nearly two hundred fifty feet a second—it runs that smoothly. It is rather pretty, in fact, to see the brilliant shower of orange sparks mingled with the milk-white cooling solution as the wheel bites into the steel side of a ninety-pound axle, and to hear the br-r-rit, br-r-rit as the axle revolves. It is nice to watch the dull grey bearing transform into a gleaming mirror.

Yes, it is an interesting and beautiful machine to watch—from the side. . . . One doesn't watch from the front, for even the operator is reluctant to stand in front of that madly whirling two-hundred-pound emery wheel. Ninety times a day, four hundred fifty times a week, twenty-three thousand four hundred times a year he walks in front of that wheel, and twenty-three thousand four hundred times a year he casts a wary glance at it.

He remembers too well the time the wheel on Charlie's machine came apart and threw pieces of abrasive four times the size of a man's fist against the wall a hundred feet away with enough force to break three bricks. The company gave Charlie's widow a thousand dollars, but they wouldn't let her see him till the undertaker had made a mask to cover the hole where his face had been.

It is lovely music to hear those six v-belts tapping out amazing rhythms against the steel belt-guard, or the gentle hum of the wheel coasting free, but it is hard for a man to forget how this gentle hum can turn into a sudden maddened roar—a crash—and then silence—silence broken only by the steady drip, drip, drip of his best friend's red blood on the black, oily floor. It's hard to forget how with each step his right shoe clung to the floor and then pulled away with a sound like paper tearing. Who would think that a little blood on his shoe would cause a man to limp peculiarly the rest of his life? It is hard to forget that one clean spot on the floor in this world of grease and dirt. Especially when the repulsive odor of strong disinfectant still seems to cling to the spot, and he can still close his eyes and see that twisted form lying there.

Fifteen years it took him to forget a similar twisted form—another friend killed also by a machine—not a beautiful harmless looking, quietly humming, spark-throwing grinder, but a destructive engine that killed men by design. Fifteen years is a long time to remember how still a man lies when a piece of shrapnel hits him full in the face just below the rim of that comical steel hat. Will it be another fifteen years before he forgets that a man lies just as still when killed while making an axle for one of those engines?

No wonder that twenty-three thousand four hundred times a year he warily watches that beautiful, harmless wheel.

BENEDICTION *

Maurice Kirby

It was a peaceful place, that little prairie town where I first lived. The long summer days were green and pleasant, and free of that hurrying and worrying which we call "progress." Friendly trees shaded the acres of lawn between happy white houses gleaming in the sunlight. The quiet streets were flat and straight, and seemed to run away and away far as the eye could see, until they lost themselves in an eternity of dancing heat or a shimmering ocean of corn. The only sound was the drowsy hum of the fertile summertime, which is more felt than heard. Things happened slowly there, or not at all, and the game of life was not played for keeps.

And the church, resting its quiet bulk at the crossing of two tree-lined avenues, seemed the most tranquil and contented place in all the town. Its mellow bricks grew naturally from the grassy yard, and the fillets of ivy which clung beneath the overhanging eaves gave it a timeless serenity. There, on Sunday mornings, the Gregorian Chant floated gently through the Gothic windows to blend with the warm buzzing of the air, ever outward and away, until it finally became a mere shade of its own echo among the sibilant whispering of the corn.

There, on Sunday mornings, we went to Mass—father and mother and I—and occupied the very front pew on the left-hand side. There were frescoes and murals around the walls, and over our heads was an angel, white and gold. The sunshine entered on tiptoe through the stained glass of the windows, or streamed in boldly where a pane was open here and there for ventilation. The cherubs on the wall smiled in it, and a high little window back of the altar sent a golden bar of it down through the candle-smoke of the sanctuary, like a visible pathway to heaven.

There were services in the evening also, when lights glittered on shining marble or nestled into the warm heart of polished wood, and saints and angels beamed upon the congregation. The rich luxury of incense filled the air; sweet, sad music stirred its listeners with memories which were not their memories, made them relive hopes and fears which they had never known. Always we sat in the very front pew on the left-hand side; it belonged to us then, and we to it.

After ten years I returned to that church, on an evening in September when the waving tassels of the corn reached up toward a huge, red-orange moon. The music was there again, and the lights, and the lazy, drifting perfume of the incense. The people had changed but slightly; some had melted a little farther into the dusk of age; others had reared their heads a little higher into the world of their elders. The same acolytes, it seemed, carried the lighted tapers, and the same candles burned before the altars.

Everything was the same but one. I looked for the place we used to sit—father and mother and I—and the very front pew on the left-hand side was empty.

FOG [4]

Wyman Richardson, M.D.

1

Fog! The terror of all navigators, whether on land, sea, or in the air. Great is its power—for it can slow down and stop all moving wheels, spoil the lawn party at the Casino, cut into the resort proprietor's net, and incite the Browns to wrangling again due to their all-night foghorn sleeplessness. I well remember my Prides Crossing friend's annoyance when I told him that his snoring had kept me awake all night.

"That was Baker's Island foghorn," he explained.

What is fog? The answer is easy. Fog is a cloud. Whenever you are in a cloud, you are in a fog. If you are either above or below fog, it becomes a cloud. What is a cloud? A cloud is a mass of water vapor which has condensed into fine particles of water.

Why is fog? Generalities are easy to mouth. "Fog occurs when warm, moisture-laden air meets cold air." Therefore, heavy fog belts are found where warm and cold ocean currents meet. Also fog occurs when there is a considerable difference between a suddenly lowered air temperature and the temperature of large bodies of water; such as, for instance, the "river damp" which hangs over pond and river during the night and early dawn of a still, cold May or October morning, or the "steam" which arises from the ocean on a below-zero day, and causes such havoc with shipping traffic. But why fog suddenly appears in a certain area, and as suddenly vanishes in the same area, I have never understood.

The waters of outer Cape Cod are in the "heavy fog belt," which I believe means that fog occurs on the average of one out of every three days. Fortunately for us at the Farm House, the fog frequently hangs offshore, where it can sometimes be seen as a

[4] *Atlantic Monthly*, September, 1951. Copyright 1951 by The Atlantic Monthly Company, Boston 16, Massachusetts.

low-lying, rather ominous wall of cloud. Perhaps it will drift in and off the lower end of Nauset Marsh, blotting out for a time the East Orleans headland; occasionally, it will shut down thick across the entire Cape and smother us in a blanket of moisture. The next day, likely as not, a hot "muggy" sou'wester will blow endless strands of fog across and away to the east, the sun gradually lifting them higher and higher into "fog clouds" until finally the sky is clear. Be sure you have your compass, though; for when the sun drops, the wind may drop too. Then that sudden chill east air strikes your cheeks, and you find yourself alone in a strange world, landmarks obliterated, familiar objects distorted. Birds do not like fog; neither do I.

One of my earliest definite recollections of a fog experience was when I was a boy. Mel Marble, our skipper, took me out in my father's 21-foot catboat, the "Kingfisher," to Cleveland's Ledge in order to bottom fish. (Cleveland's Ledge, incidentally, was discovered by my father and Mel Marble when they were trolling for bluefish in the middle of Buzzards Bay with a 2-pound lead tied 150 feet out on a 300-foot line. The wind unexpectedly petered out, and the lead caught in a rocky ledge. A quick jibe saved line and lead, and soon a little sounding demonstrated a large group of rocks. I believe they anchored at once and caught a good mess of rock (sea) bass, and tautog. President Cleveland, who spent his summers at "Gray Gables" at the head of the Bay, and who was a great fisherman, was told of this spot and came so often to fish it that it has been known ever since as "Cleveland's Ledge.")

On the present occasion, a heavy fog shut in and with it came a light northeast air. Does the east wind bring the fog, or the fog bring the east wind?

Anyway, we fished for a spell and then decided to make our way in. Mel got out the box compass and we headed by dead reckoning for Marion Harbor. The jaws of the gaff creaked loudly as the uneasy swell swung the sail inboard and then slatted it back. But through it all came the clear, steady tones of the Bird Island fog bell.

"Gee, this is easy," I said.

Mel said, "Humph!"

We kept the bell to starboard as we slowly made our close-hauled way. The bell suddenly sounded very loud. "We're going ashore on Southeast Ledge, Mel," I said, in some perturbation.

Mel smiled, said nothing, and kept his eye on the compass. Then, just as suddenly, the sound of the bell stopped. I waited awhile, and then got scared.

"Why did they stop it?" I asked Mel.

"Didn't," said he. "Noises hop around in a fog."

Just then the red Centreboard Ledge buoy loomed out. Our craft not drawing very much water, we left the buoy a hundred yards to port, at which point we were dead to leeward of Bird Island, and very close to it. No fog bell. Later on, when we came upon the black Seal Rocks buoy (and left it, also, carefully to port) suddenly the bell became insistently loud. Since then I have often observed that sounds, in a light air, can best be heard across the wind. At the Farm House we hear the whistling buoy, or "grunter," off the Inlet, which is southeast of us, in a southwest air; and sometimes, when the breeze is southeast, we hear the whistler off the Peaked Hill bar to the northeast.

2

Fog can do queer things. Some years ago, a friend and I sat in the grass on Porchy Marsh, at the spot where the then high, sandy Porchy bar made out across the channel toward Teal Hummock. It was a sultry September afternoon; and soon the fog shut in thick. Shooting in thick fog is not much fun; for the fun of shooting lies in being out of doors, in a pleasant spot, with a good view both of the surrounding landscape and of the passing wildlife. In a fog, one's world is limited to a 300-foot radius. Nothing is seen except for an unexpected, ghostlike apparition which turns out to be a herring gull. Occasionally, the clear, pewee-like notes of a black-breasted plover, or the more staccato call of the yellowlegs, bring forth a burst of frantic, and usually ineffective, imitation from our whistles. A flock or two of peep will suddenly swirl over our heads, so close as nearly to remove our hats.

On this occasion, just before dark, we had shot at a bunch of summer (lesser) yellowlegs; and after a vast amount of banging, we managed to bag one—small pickings for two hungry men. As darkness began to fall, we picked up and started to row across the channel toward the just visible Middle Flat. Halfway across the channel, we wondered if we had remembered to put our game inside the boat. We both rummaged around in the cockpit, finally found the bird, and looked up. We still could make out both the Porchy and the Middle Flat shore. We continued on our way home. Fifteen minutes later, when we should have been off Uncle Heeman's Creek, I became uneasy. We came to a wide creek; but even in spite of the tide, it looked too big and did not run off at the correct angle. I took out my compass. We were headed south, out near the Inlet, instead of north, just off the Cedar Bank and nearly home. It gave me a shock I have never forgotten. Of course, what had happened was that when we both were busy looking for our bird, the boat had made a 180-degree turn. When we looked up, the relative positions of the dimly seen shore lines remained the same, and we went south instead of north. I was glad I had taken my compass with me; indeed without it we might have become involved in some real difficulty. Since then, I have never gone out, either in the Nauset Marsh or on the West Shore flats, or in the woods, without a compass.

And fog can do still other queer things. A foggy day on the beach, especially if one is alone, may give one the creeps, although perhaps not to the extent of bringing about a precipitate retreat. My brother was casting off the beach into the fog, one afternoon, and working north along the shore. He came to a man sitting at the top of the rising behind him. "Any luck?" asked Harry, backing up the beach as he reeled in.

There was no answer. Harry turned around and saw to his chagrin that he was addressing a lobster pot which had washed ashore.

My daughter Margaret and I took out the canoe early one black morning. As we left the boathouse at the Salt Pond Creek, a perceptible lightening of the previously black darkness suggested that possibly the almanac was right. We crept along under the Cedar Bank, which by now could easily be made out, and fished up the Cedar Bank Channel. Gradually, the light increased, but we could not see much afield. After quite a long while, the cupola of the Nauset Coast Guard Station suddenly appeared and we found ourselves close to the bluff at the head of Nauset Bay. There was no evidence of bird, or any other, life. However, as we turned back and headed into the Minister's Channel, our friend the musical crow could be heard calling from the vicinity of the Cedar Bank.

A short distance below Minister's Point, which marks the junction of the Minister's Channel with the Beach Run to form the Beach Channel, Marg hooked into a fish and after a few minutes skillfully brought a nice 2-pound bass to the net. This area, between White's shanty and the cut-through below White's, has frequently produced a fish. (One of my friends, however, complains that these directions are insufficient, inasmuch as White's house, some ten years ago, was completely washed away during an exceptional tide and storm; and the "cut" through the dunes, which produced such a convenient sandy point on which to make a duck blind, has for at least five years been blocked by rapidly growing sand dunes.) When at last we paddled out by Caleb's Hummock at the mouth of the Beach Channel, quite happy to have caught a fish, the general brightness indicated that the sun was up. However, except for Caleb's Hummock and the opposite nearby edge of the Middle Flat, we could see nothing. Our world became a peculiarly spherical one, limited to a narrow 200-foot radius. I took my compass out and put it on the canoe bottom before me. For below the mouth of the Beach Channel there is a stretch of wide water at high tide.

"Look," I said, pointing. "There is a man fishing on the Porchy riffles."

I could see him standing up in a skiff and casting.

"Yes," said Marg. "We better not go too near."

"I hear he has caught a lot of fish that way," I remarked, as I headed away to give him plenty of room. Just then he rose from the water and flew off. He had suddenly turned into a young, dark herring gull.

On another occasion, during the war, my daughter Charlotte and I made almost the same circuit in the midst of a thick fog. On our way home, we heard the loud roaring of motors.

"Lost airplane," I said and shuddered a bit. "Thick fog, no radio directions, gas low, hoping for a safe crash landing."

We paddled harder; the engines roared louder; and soon we saw the huge hull of a flying boat coming to rest off the First Hummock, across the channel from the Cedar Bank. We really made time, pushing the canoe so fast as to make her dip with every stroke. And then, suddenly our crippled airplane began more and more to take the shape of a motorboat. When finally we came close, it turned out to be a cabin cruiser, trying to get out on the top of an unusually high tide and well stuck on the flat just across from First Hummock. What in the world, we thought, was a boat of this draught doing inside the Nauset Marsh? We told the disgruntled and somewhat truculent skipper where the channel was (he found it on the evening tide), and ever since have been skeptical as to his occupation.

The suddenness of fog is one of its worst features. Last summer, we went out in the canoe at high water, a couple of hours before sunset. It was a beautiful, warm afternoon, with almost no wind and a clear sky. We again cruised over the Nauset Bay flats, but found no bass. On our way down the Minister's Channel we could see umbrella handles here and there, sticking up out of the marsh grass. Occasionally, one would suddenly straighten out and a great ungainly, yet strangely graceful, loose-jointed hulk of a bird would leisurely take off, trailing long legs behind and eventually curling its neck back over its shoulders. The great blue herons like the Middle Flat and at high water, in September and October, collect in loose groups, each bird striking a different pose. One will stand erect, sharp beak lifted and gleaming yellow eye turned skyward; another hunches up, halving his size, draws in his neck, cocks his head, and eyes the water beneath him. If luckily you have him in the field of your glasses, and if he does not suspect your presence, you may see a sudden motion. So fast is the strike that only the obvious swallowing undulation of the neck, with head uplifted, indicates the destiny of a hapless minnow.

A half hour before sunset finds you out of the Beach Channel below Caleb's Hummock, just as the ebb begins to sweep across the Goose Hummock flats, by every rule the time of times to catch a fish. But the fish do not seem to know the rules and there is no excitement. And then silently and relentlessly small puffets of fog come drifting across the dunes "on little cat feet." A slight chill creeps up your spine; the extra sweater is retrieved from under the bow. Old Sol, a moment ago so strong and invincible, suddenly begins to lose his power. A cold air from the east riffles the water. And then, all at once, your world is blotted out. Abruptly, the roar of the surf seems close aboard.

"Let's get back," you say, somewhat casually, as you fish for the compass in the bottom of the tackle bag.

As darkness rapidly descends, the thought of the Farm House seems good. A fire, so out of place this hot noon, now seems highly desirable. You put a bit more drive to your chunking paddles, follow up the Porchy shore and around Tom Doane's Hummock, and take a bearing just west of north-west from Pull Devil Corner. The gray dimness becomes darker, all landmarks disappear, and you wonder whether the black or the white end of the compass needle points to north. Fortunately, you have scratched the formula on the back of the case: "B = N." Of a sudden, the cricket chorus hits your consciousness. Then a strange headland, with an unusual pattern of cedars, looms out of the fog. Where are you? This is unfamiliar ground. Perhaps you got turned around. This looks like the lower end of Skiff Hill. No! Here is the Salt Pond Creek and there is the boathouse. You are safe in port. Now it seems ridiculous to have been so, yes, scared. The weather is warm, the marsh landlocked except for a narrow inlet; real harm is well-nigh impossible. And yet—and yet, the fog gets you down. You want home. And you are afraid you are not going to get there.

And then, at home at last after the long climb up the hill, standing before a crackling fire with a glass in hand containing just a smitch of bourbon, you forget your fear. Fog is not bad; it is good fishing weather. There is usually little or no wind, and the bright sun, with its dark shadows, is dimmed and does not frighten the fish. You must make an early start tomorrow.

Fog! Terror of all navigators! Yes, even on the Nauset Marsh you cast your spell and bring a chill to the stoutest heart. Birds do not like you; neither do I.

THE STEEPLE OF SAINT-HILAIRE [5]

Marcel Proust

From a long way off one could distinguish and identify the steeple of Saint-Hilaire inscribing its unforgettable form upon a horizon beneath which Combray had not yet appeared; when from the train which brought us down from Paris at Easter-time my father caught sight of it, as it slipped into every fold of the sky in turn, its little iron cock veering continually in all directions, he would say: "Come, get your wraps together, we are there." And on one of the longest walks we ever took from Combray there was a spot where the narrow road emerged suddenly on to an immense plain, closed at the horizon by strips of forest over which rose and stood alone the fine point of Saint-Hilaire's steeple, but so sharpened and so pink that it seemed to be no more than sketched on the sky by the finger-nail of a painter anxious to give to such a landscape, to so pure a piece of "nature," this little sign of art, this single indication of human existence. As one drew near it and could make out the remains of the square tower, half in ruins, which still stood by its side, though without rivalling it in height, one was struck, first of all, by the tone, reddish and sombre, of its stones; and on a misty morning in autumn one would have called it, to see it rising above the violet thunder-cloud of the vineyards, a ruin of purple, almost the colour of the wild vine.

Often in the Square, as we came home, my grandmother would make me stop to look up at it. From the tower windows, placed two and two, one pair above another, with that right and original proportion in their spacing to which not only human faces owe their beauty and dignity, it released, it let fall at regular intervals flights of jackdaws which for a little while would wheel and caw, as though the ancient stones which allowed them to sport thus and never seemed to see them, becoming of a sudden uninhabitable and discharging some infinitely disturbing element, had struck them and driven them forth. Then after patterning everywhere

[5] From *Swann's Way* by Marcel Proust. Reprinted by permission of Random House, Inc.

the violet velvet of the evening air, abruptly soothed, they would return and be absorbed in the tower, deadly no longer but benignant, some perching here and there (not seeming to move, but snapping, perhaps, and swallowing some passing insect) on the points of turrets, as a seagull perches, with an angler's immobility, on the crest of a wave. . . .

It was the steeple of Saint-Hilaire which shaped and crowned and consecrated every occupation, every hour of the day, every point of view in the town. From my bedroom window I could discern no more than its base, which had been freshly covered with slates; but when on Sundays I saw these, in the hot light of a summer morning, blaze like a black sun I would say to myself: "Good heavens! nine o'clock! I must get ready for mass at once if I am to have time to go in and kiss aunt Léonie first," and I would know exactly what was the colour of the sunlight upon the Square, I could feel the heat and dust of the market, the shade behind the blinds of the shop into which Mamma would perhaps go on her way to mass, penetrating its odour of unbleached calico, to purchase a handkerchief or something, of which the draper himself would let her see what he had, bowing from the waist: who, having made everything ready for shutting up, had just gone into the back shop to put on his Sunday coat and to wash his hands, which it was his habit, every few minutes and even on the saddest occasions, to rub one against the other with an air of enterprise, cunning, and success.

And again, after mass, when we looked in to tell Théodore to bring a larger loaf than usual because our cousins had taken advantage of the fine weather to come over from Thiberzy for luncheon, we had in front of us the steeple, which, baked and brown itself like a larger loaf still of "holy bread," with flakes and sticky drops on it of sunlight, pricked its sharp point into the blue sky. And in the evening, as I came in from my walk and thought of the approaching moment when I must say good night to my mother and see her no more, the steeple was by contrast so kindly, there at the close of day, that I would imagine it as being laid, like a brown velvet cushion, against—as being thrust into the pallid sky which had yielded beneath its pressure, had sunk slightly so as to make room for it, and had correspondingly risen on either side; while the cries of the birds wheeling to and fro about it seemed to intensify its silence, to elongate its spire still further, and to invest it with some quality beyond the power of words. . . .

Whether one saw it at five o'clock when going to call for letters at the post-office, some doors away from one, on the left, raising abruptly with its isolated peak the ridge of housetops; or again, when one had to go in and ask for news of Mme. Sazerat, one's eyes followed the line where it ran low again beyond the farther, descending slope, and one knew that it would be the second turning after the steeple; or yet again, if pressing further afield one went to the station, one saw it obliquely, shewing in profile fresh angles and surfaces, like a solid body surprised at some unknown point in its revolution; or, from the banks of the Vivonne, the apse, drawn muscularly together and heightened in perspective, seemed to spring upwards with the effort which the steeple made to hurl its spire-point into the heart of heaven: it was always to the steeple that one must return, always it which dominated everything else, summing up the houses with an unexpected pinnacle, raised before me like the Finger of God, Whose Body might have been concealed below among the crowd of human bodies without fear of my confounding It, for that reason, with them. And so even today in any large provincial town, or in a quarter of Paris which I do not know well, if a passer-by who is "putting me on the right road" shews me from afar, as a point to aim at, some belfry of a hospital, or a convent steeple lifting the peak of its ecclesiastical cap at the corner of the street which I am to take, my memory need only find in it some dim resemblance to that dear and vanished outline, and the passer-by, should he turn round to make sure that I have not gone astray, would see me, to his astonishment, oblivious of the walk that I had planned to take or the place where I was obliged to call, standing still on the spot, before that steeple, for hours on end, motionless, trying to remember, feeling deep within myself a tract of soil reclaimed from the waters of Lethe slowly drying until the buildings rise on it again; and then no doubt, and then more uneasily than when, just now, I asked him for a direction, I will seek my way again, I will turn a corner . . . but . . . the goal is in my heart. . . .

QUESTIONS

What quality of the "grinder" does the writer wish to emphasize? What attitude to it? Does he have any exact information about it? Does his writing seem authentic, as if he knows this mechanism from experience? What positions in space is he concerned with in relation to this object? Is his use of numbers effective? What chief incident does he use? What was its immediate result? Its psychological effect on him? Does his comparison with the friend killed in the war add to or detract from his artistic aim? Is the closing sentence effective?

What is the writer's artistic aim in "Benediction"? Does he describe the place adequately for his aim? What does he stress in his first paragraph? In his second, third, and fourth paragraphs? In his last paragraph? Is the change he records one of circumstances or inner attitudes, or both? Does this unit have tone color? What support can you give for your answer?

Is "Fog" an extended definition as that term is generally used? If it is a definition, how does it differ from a dictionary definition? From a scientific definition or explanation? What answer does the writer give to each of these questions: What is fog? Why is fog? What is a heavy fog belt, and what specific one is he familiar with? What examples does he give of the power of the fog to do queer things? How does he support his statement that fog is sudden? What quality of the fog and what attitude of people to it does the writer stress in the opening paragraph and in the closing paragraphs? Does he suggest the same quality and attitude throughout the article? How much general exposition and how much narration are used? Is the article based on scientific information or accurate observation or both?

In dealing with an outstanding object, "the steeple," from many points of view, how and where does the writer use transitions to secure clarity? Does he use time or space transitions or both? In the last paragraph especially, what transitions does he use? Do these help him complete or summarize his attitude? What comparisons does he use effectively? What details of color? Is the steeple important to him because of its physical qualities or his emotional associations? In how much of his article does he use narrative? Is it specific narrative or generalized narrative? Is it objective or subjective narrative? What comparison does he use to make the last sentences effective?

20

Satirical Comment:

SITUATIONS, EVENTS, PEOPLE

For your composition at the end of this chapter scrutinize your immediate environment. Find situations (rules, attitudes, institutions, customs), either permanent or temporary, which you deplore. Find recent events that will, in your opinion, lead to undesirable consequences. Find instances of people who have just been promoted, demoted, fired, have won some award or other honor or been elected to office; give special attention to those you view with disapproval or those who have been treated in ways you cannot approve. From these situations, events, or people choose a subject which is emotionalized for you because you are a potential victim of its consequences. If you cannot find an interesting local problem, consider national problems that are both simple and universal—high taxes, a comic book, a radio or TV program. When you are ready to write, make a brief satirical comment on your topic; try to get some reaction from your reader, preferably agreement.

PLANNING AND ARRANGING

When you have found your topic, ask yourself what most people already believe about the idea you wish to emphasize. Then ask yourself whether you agree with them. If you do, perhaps you would do better to discard the subject instead of laboring the obvious by expressing a conventional view. If you disagree, put

397

aside fear and conformity and ask yourself this question: What is my honest opinion? The answer to that question is your central idea.

Whatever your subject, you will need to do simple analyzing by asking yourself: Why do I hold this opinion? What consequences do I fear? What results do I desire that will not come from this situation or this person? If you wish, you may anticipate the discussion of analyzing in the next chapter, but it will probably not be necessary. Though this is the first assignment in which your exposition is based on logical order, your topic is limited and your organization is simple. Ask yourself what attitude you have to your central idea. Are you indifferent? Do you feel strongly, so that you cannot analyze the reasons for your attitude? Do you have a cool amusement with a strong intellectual belief in your own opinion? Perhaps the last attitude will help you to work most successfully. What sort of effect do you wish to have on your reader? What sort of reader do you hope to reach and to affect? What order of ideas will win him over? Should you begin by making concessions, by showing him that your idea is acceptable to him in other situations, or by reducing to absurdity some opposing view? Should you recall to your reader a few basic facts about your topic? With the kind of topic you have chosen, you should not have to do much explaining. But even in a familiar situation, there may be facts which most people overlook, and these may be the essential ones. In a familiar situation, too, you will not have to spend your time assembling information; the facts will be at home in your mind so that you can use them.

At this stage you are probably ready to write down three or four statements that will support your central idea and become topic sentences for your paragraphs. Think how you can develop these effectively by supporting material.

STYLE

In a preceding chapter, this working definition of satire was suggested for your writing: you seem to be saying one thing but you suggest the opposite as your real meaning. For example, if you wish to poke fun at the freshman girl who gets herself engaged to every fellow she goes out with, you might advise her to see how many fraternity pins she can manage to wear and then give back; thus she will become well known on the campus, gain experience and the ability to make a shrewd final choice, and develop real wisdom. This method has its dangers. You may be so absurd that your reader loses interest instead of being challenged. You may be taken seriously; against this fate, your best protection is probably subtle exaggeration. Try to walk a successful plank over these failures.

You may use satire in small bits in many kinds of writing, but here it is recommended that you try it for your whole composition. You may use satire, too, with all sorts of intentions—from light-hearted fun to bitter comment, from a desire to stir laughter at the foibles of people to a desire to change social conditions. It is often effective when it has the light touch with serious intentions. If you read the "Talk of the Town" section in several issues of *The New Yorker*, you will probably find varied styles and intentions.

Unless you can use a general approach more effectively than most people do, you will need to personalize. The editorial *we, our* may be used humorously, or even seriously if you can keep it from sounding smug or pompous; *you, your* may be effective. Your title, if carefully planned, can be either a serious statement or a kind of caustic comment. Your tone in the whole unit will not be collo-quial or "folksy" unless you can do something individual or different with it; instead it will tend to be conversational but urbane and finished. If you need slang or new words, have enough confidence in yourself to use them. Of course, try to achieve a high degree of suggestion and power.

WRITING YOUR COMPOSITION

A. Find some situation (a custom, a set of rules, an institutional attitude, a judgment people in your community tend to make) that you wish to see changed. Prefer a local situation; but if you choose a national or international one, be sure that it is simple and well known. Analyze the situation until you know exactly what, in your opinion, is wrong, why you wish changes, and what changes would be desirable. Then select a few essentials. Write a brief but effective satirical comment.

B. Choose another similar subject but in a lighter vein. You are amused, not indignant; you have no burning desire for change; you might even prefer to see this human comedy continue. Choose a time, place, actions, perhaps a person or persons to illustrate the usual elements in this type of behavior. Write a generalized descriptive-narrative unit, using words with a connotation of ridicule.

C. Find a type of person whose actions have a serious effect on you or your community. Analyze his actions, their results, and the changes you desire; then select a few essentials again. Write a brief but effective satirical comment.

D. Choose a type of person whose actions have either a serious or an amusing effect on you. Choose a time, place, and actions to illustrate how he usually behaves. Write a generalized descriptive-narrative unit, using words with a connotation of ridicule.

READING

REQUIRED COURSE *

One of the most fascinating subjects required for Home Economics students is Bacteriology 374. No doubt it should be required. It broadens one's outlook on the world—the world which isn't just trees and buildings and people and violets blooming by the road, but also thousands and thousands of minute bugs and germs floating around. I was amazed to find that 6,304 of these fall on each square foot of a local restaurant each hour. That is by slide rule calculation, of course.

In chatting with one of the founders of 374 the other day, I discovered that the ulterior motive in setting up the course of study was to make us all clean housekeepers, better known as Dutch *hausfrauen*. The scientific way to become an expert dishwasher is to know before you start that little bacteria have a logarithmic growth phase in which they grow faster than they die. A logarithm, as a note to the uninformed, is a power which is turned upside down. This brings us to the important fact that petri dishes must be turned upside down, too, so that the condensed moisture will form right-side up. Both these topsy-turvy details are related to the phenomenon known as upside-down cake, in which the fruit baked on the bottom ends up on the top.

And so it can go on, applications and applications to each scientific principle. And I shall not be ignorant of the fact that in each corner lurks a little *Escherichia coli.*

BROTHERHOOD *

That's the word they used when I officially became a member—brotherhood. And I suppose that's right. When we live together, study together and sleep together, that makes us all brothers under the skin. Yes, that's right, it's much easier to study when the halls are noisy, and I'm sure everyone likes to frequent the Annex usually called Pete's, and we like to sleep in a cold dorm with just two blankets on the bed.

And then, too, we get to understand each other better when we spend two or three hours in the chapter room discussing whether the drapes in the living room should be blue or green. And there is a unifying effect when we all stand outside a sorority house and serenade off-key to sleepy-eyed girls shivering in the cold, winter night. I'm sure the girls don't mind standing on those windy fire-escapes because they know that the forty-odd fellows bellowing below are adding another bond to this brotherhood.

The cook, too, knows that there is a strong bond of brotherhood present. She knows that we think of each other first and of ourselves second. She knows we only want our fair share of the food and nothing more. Sure she does—that's why she locks the kitchen every night.

The most important aspect to me is that the whole system builds character. I'm sure that Chick's character was strongly improved when he was asked to turn in his pledge pin. Chick was a good fellow, but he just didn't fit in, too much of an individual. And that's not good. He'll be given six months now to change and become a conformist. Then he will be acceptable for repledging. Of course, his personal feelings mustn't be taken into consideration. No, it's his character alone that's important. Yes, that word is correct now—brotherhood.

TWO BY TWO *

I sat in the second chair of Andrews' Barber Shop in Campus-town yesterday. I watched the girls walk by. Always two by two. Always in wool tubes and sweaters. Always with short hair, white anklets and loafers. I waited for a girl with braids or green socks, but there weren't any. I waited until I was tired of waiting. Then I looked to the pile of magazines. I wanted to read the "Talk of the Town" or *Harper's* so I could laugh at this world of people. Andy had the remains of a *Glamour, the Magazine for the Working Woman, Men's Magazine* and a *True Confessions*. No *New Yorker*.

"Andy, have you got any *New Yorkers* around?"

The barber surveyed the dip in the butch hair cut he was working on. "*New Yorker*? Who are you trying to impress?"

"Nobody." I picked up the top magazine on the stack. "I like the cartoons. Charles Addams and Arno, you know?"

"Never heard of them."

"Just cartoonists." I pretended to be content with an article on what's wrong with the American woman. I didn't find out her main faults, for Lanky-One in chair one was finished, and it was my turn.

"I just want the duck tail trimmed and the sides a little shorter. Not too much. I have funny ears," I said as Andy pinned the towel around my neck.

He wet the back of my hair. "You girls sure are going for the short hair cuts. How come?"

"They're easy to take care of. Besides, everyone's doing it."

Two by two. No green socks.

"Great game Saturday. You go?"

Typical barber talk. What did he care if I went or not.

"No, Andy, I didn't make it."

"You out of town?" he asked as he cut too much over my left ear.

"Yep."

What a damn liar. Why didn't I tell him that I read Chekhov instead. Is it a crime against the state? Push yourself in that mold, girl. Everyone else is doing it. And you'll step out looking like all the other castings. Laugh at the right jokes. Like the right boys and go to the right parties. Order spudnuts and black coffee and smoke Pall Malls. "I think I am an elephant who's following an elephant who's following an elephant who really isn't there."

In the mirror, I saw Rita come into the shop. Greasy-faced Rita with her red schedule book and white anklets.

"Well, Rita Engler! How are you, kid? I haven't seen you in ages."

There's one girl I can't stand. Be nice to her! She's good to have as a friend. Wonderful name to have as a recommend on a student application blank.

"Say, girl, you having your head shaved this time?"

"Nope, just a little off the back. You know how it goes. When did you take the big step, Rita?"

"Oh, two weeks ago."

"It looks terrific."

Rita, that word doesn't mean a thing. It is last year's word. Your hair is spooky, according to the accepted vocabulary. It makes your face look wider than it is long. Have you ever considered braids?

"How about coming to The Style Shop with me after I get mine cut? I want to get one of those angora collars."

Have mercy. A girl your size will look like the Easter Rabbit himself in all that fuzz.

"Aren't they darling? Gee, I'm sorry I can't go. I'm meeting Donna right after this. We're going to walk home together."

Two by two.

SOCIAL SCREAMING *

I know a lot of people must have lectured to you about the adjustments that have to be made when you move into a sorority house, and I agree wholeheartedly with all of them. In fact, the only trouble is that there are some adjustments that are always overlooked. Screaming is one of them. It's really amazing that people forget about this factor when it's so important to anyone who hopes to be a successful sorority girl. It's an art to be able to apply the correct scream to the right situation, and it takes years of experience before one can really feel sure of herself. Maybe I can help you out, though, by outlining the most important uses of the scream.

One of the first screams you should learn and the one you will probably use most often is the "pinning scream." Naturally it's used when one of the sisters comes in wearing a fraternity pin. If you should be the first to discover the pin, it's especially important that you should know all the details of the pinning scream, for you have to use it to cue all the other sisters. No, you don't have to learn any formula of words for this scream. You can use the girl's name if you want to, but just any sound that will suggest overwhelmed surprise, extreme pleasure and uncontrollable excitement will do. Be sure to yell loudly enough to rouse any of the sisters who might be sleeping or studying. It's very important that no one be left out, and it's your job to see that they are not. Your duties aren't over after you have warned the sisterhood of the event. You have one more duty to perform. It's your job to give the newly pinned girl a feeling of security against the oncoming mob by slipping your arm around her waist and chattering excitedly.

Another scream that you should learn right away is the "five-pound-party scream" which is used at all engagement announcements. You might think that you could cheat a little and substitute the pinning scream here, but that would be a terrible *faux pas*. If you're on the ball at all you'll realize that the five-pound-party scream has got to get across a feeling of sentiment and awe as well as surprise and pleasure. It's rather a touchy situation, so be careful that you don't imply too much surprise or a "Well, you finally hooked him" tone. And never forget that you've got to go from this scream to a sentimental sorority song. That transition is bound to be hard for beginners.

One of the hardest screams is the serenade scream. It's especially difficult because it's yelled in unison by the whole chapter. It's very appropriate in this situation to clap loudly while you scream, and you will also find that the clapping helps considerably to thaw out your hands in the winter time. Your scream in this case can suggest a number of things—that's what makes it so difficult. It should always convey delight, admiration and gratitude. Sometimes it may imply amusement, shocked amusement, or emotional impact. If the song is particularly sentimental you can build up the scream with a "delighted murmur." We'll say more about the delighted murmur later.

We'll just mention this next scream to remind you of it. It's actually the easiest one to learn, mostly because, unlike the others, it is usually given because you feel like giving it and not because it is expected of you. It is the "winning scream" which erupts spontaneously whenever the chapter has won a volleyball game, infiltrated an honorary fraternity, or captured a trophy. You can really let yourself go on this one—even to the point of waving your arms, hugging the sisters, and jumping up and down.

Let's go back to the delighted murmur now. It can be a very handy tool for sorority girls when an out-and-out yell would be frowned upon by the house mother or any other wet blankets. It's very handy at the dinner table and sometimes at serenades. It is a substitute for a scream, or actually a suppressed scream. My only complaint about the delighted murmur is that sorority girls don't use it enough. But then we must understand that it requires great finesse and restraint.

Now, I believe that just about does it. You should be ready to start practice now. Oh, one more thing. When you move into the house, don't forget to bring a family-size bottle of Anacin.

QUESTIONS

In "Required Course," what is the writer's attitude to Bacteriology 374? Is the unit satirical? Does the writer use exaggeration? Are the fantastic details effective? What is the most effective detail, in your opinion? Why? Does the unit have any ineffective details?

What is the real intent of the writer of "Brotherhood"? Does he use slanted words for effect? Satire? Well-chosen examples? Is the personalized example in his last paragraph effective? Does he get a response from his readers, or is he merely expressing personal frustration?

Does the writer of "Two by Two" have a general expository aim? What does the talk about the color of socks, about haircuts, going to football games, reading, collars, and walking home add up to as far as an idea is concerned? What is the writer's method—satirical or serious? How does she emphasize her own attitude as well as the conventional attitude? Could the same effect be secured without talk? Without a one-time, one-place pattern?

What is the author's real aim in "Social Screaming"? Is her method serious or satirical? How does she organize? Is her arrangement effective? Which is her best paragraph, if there is any difference? Is her diction heavy or effective? Does she get a response from you as a reader?

21

Explaining Other People

In this chapter you will be working toward writing a character sketch of some person you know well; and though you may use narration or description to support your ideas, you will need to start by analyzing the person you wish to write about. You will still be writing personalized exposition, of course; but instead of using time or space patterns, which are comparatively easy, you are now working with logical patterns. They are harder because they are based on analysis. To analyze ideas is to break them into their component parts (*ana*, up; *lyein*, to loosen). Ideas are often abstract and intangible. When you try to analyze your own character, that of another person, a personal problem, a social problem, or a philosophy of life, you are struggling with large abstractions. Sometimes you may feel as if you are hunting for missing pieces in the dark.

Analyzing is thinking. The average human animal resists it and will go to great trouble to avoid it, even when his refusal to think keeps him from achieving cherished ambitions. Sometime, perhaps, man may think more easily—if he survives; but his evolution to such a stage may take aeons. You are not exactly the average human animal, though, or you would not be trying to do the kind of thinking and writing you are asked to do here. For you the question is this: How can you do some essential thinking to the best advantage?

407

ANALYSIS: A SPECIFIC PROBLEM

Suppose we consider a sample problem in analysis; and since you are using logical patterns with character, suppose we start with this idea: *My mother is an interesting person.* Such a controlling idea puts on you the obligation to explain what you mean by *interesting,* and to analyze her personality. After you have begun the analysis, you may wish to limit your statement if it proves to be more than you can do well. Try questions like *Who? What? When? Where? Why?* What *causes?* What *results?* Such questions may help you to get a grasp on almost any subject. Expand each question: *Who* finds her interesting? Her children? Her husband? Her other relatives? Her intimate friends? Her neighbors? Her club groups? Her church? Her community in general? Strangers? People with unusual talent or prestige? Write down answers, specific ones, to the preceding questions, and then go on. *What* kind of interest? *Why* is she interesting? What are *causes* of the interest? What are *results?* What *incidents* do you recall? *What* did she say or do? *What* did others say or do? Probably the answers to these questions alone would give you a paper with rich detail.

But suppose you continue. *When* and *where* is she interesting? (The two seem to belong together.) Is she interesting at breakfast on dull mornings? At other meals? At home generally? When other people need her? Only at rare intervals when she feels the need to dramatize herself? With company? With just a few people she cares to interest? Outside her home? In groups of relatives? At community meetings? When she talks about world events? Politics? Work she does outside the home?

Why is she interesting? Does she have a sense of humor? A gift for phrasing everyday things and events? An ability to forget herself in other people? A gift for putting other people at their ease and making them forget themselves? Other qualities?

What *results* come from the fact that she is interesting? Does she make a happier or a more social home? Does she give happiness to other people? Does she put aside trivial domestic affairs instead of boring other people with them? Or, even though she is interesting, does she make people afraid of her because she will stab anybody, absent or present, to seem clever? (Of course your definition of *interesting* has some relation to these questions.)

What traits in her personality make her interesting? Is she kind or unkind, generous or stingy, reticent or communicative, selfish or self-sacrificing, inclined to draw others out or to monopolize the conversation, quick or deliberate in thought and action, restless or composed, tireless or easily exhausted, tense or relaxed, quick-tempered or slow to anger, serene or easily ruffled, hospitable or inhospitable, solemn or blessed with a sense of humor? What skills does she have? The ability to manage a house, to do creative cooking, to teach her children manners, to inspire them with a desire for development? The ability to play, sing, paint, to understand young people or members of minority groups? What interests does she have? An interest in nature, gardens, animals, ceramics, world politics and problems? Is she optimistic, pessimistic, or merely realistic? Does she have faith in herself, in members of her family, in other people, in civilization, in God? These are only a few of the specific questions you might ask yourself. And though your aim remains the analysis of her qualities, you might ask yourself how she is different from you, your brothers and sisters, other relatives, and family friends.

If you were really interested in this topic, you could choose any one of a dozen small points and carry it further by applying the same principles of analysis to it. Suppose, for example, that her optimism is outstanding. *Who* profits or suffers because of it? *Where, when, why,* with what *results* is she optimistic? *What* does she do or say to indicate her optimism? Is her optimism funny, pathetic, tragic, inspiring? Suppose that her faith in her family is outstanding. *Who* has been affected by that faith? *Why? How? When? Where?* What *results* have come from it? What *incidents* or *situations* illustrate that faith? Either of these two traits of her character might furnish you enough material for a well-developed paper. Suppose your character has some fault which might inspire you to write a humorous paper. You could use the same methods of analyzing to find your material.

Suppose you have carried this far some subject that really interests you. Then what? First, you will have material for ten or for twenty papers. (If you start writing a paper and then get stuck because you are not sure what to say about a particular point, stop and analyze that point, no matter how small it is.) Second, you will have material to throw away. And do by all means throw some of it away. Do not act like a miser who hoards every idea that enters his mind. Act like a millionaire. Write out of riches—after you have analyzed your subject and found its resources. It was Hemingway who wisely said that good writing is like an iceberg: only one-eighth projects above the sea, but the other seven-eighths furnish the power.

You may wonder whether you can analyze a subject of your own as this sample has been analyzed. You can if you believe in yourself and your subject, if you persist, and if you really try to think. Do not limit yourself to general thinking either; let your senses and your feelings have free play, and recall everything that bears even remotely on your topic. Jot down on a sheet of paper everything that comes into your mind, or use two sheets, one for ideas and one for specific details. An idea written down, like an insect on flypaper, can't get away. Perhaps ten new ideas will come for each that you clarify by writing it down.

Try to learn well this method of taking a small part of your topic and expanding it from within. Nothing is more important in helping you write well when you handle ideas; and if you are like the average student, there is nothing you more often fail to do. Of course you need not go to the trouble of analyzing if ideas flow for you with no trouble at all and if you can organize them with speed and skill. But most people have some difficulty with abstract ideas.

ORGANIZING

Your next job is organizing your paper. If you can avoid it, do not use the old-fashioned, inefficient method of writing a long paper just to find out what you wish to say. Perhaps you cannot work any other way, because you are entangled in habits; if so, you are unfortunate. On the other hand, do not suppose that many people, even with training and practice, tend to organize with the speed and precision of an efficient machine. Thinking, as we said, is hard work. It is human to try an outline many times before something useful evolves, to rearrange some points when a paper is half-written, and to stop in a paragraph to analyze and assemble more supporting material.

But work as quickly as you can toward a satisfactory organization. Try to phrase a central idea in one concise sentence; it is a large generalization which summarizes your whole paper. Every main point directly supports it but is only a part of it; the sum of the main points is the central idea, since all of them together clarify, explain, and support it. This idea may need to be rephrased from time to time as you work. Try also to discover and to state in words the effect you wish your material to have on your reader. In personalized exposition you do not usually try to get your reader to accept your opinions as his own, but you wish to clarify them for him and to stimulate his reactions or his interest. If he says when he hears your material, "My experience has been entirely different, but I understand how you feel, why you feel that way, and I sympathize with your feeling," you have succeeded.

These small ideas may help you in planning. First, what do you need to define? What do certain key words mean in your discussion? Do you need to explain what you do *not* mean, as well as what you mean? Second, do you need to analyze further some main point, or even some minor point? Third, do you need to name the class to which something belongs, and then show the things that differentiate it from the class? You may need to do this more often in formal exposition; but it might be possible here, for example, to show that your mother belongs to the genus housewife but has many qualities that separate her from the typical housewife. Fourth, have you considered causes, effects, origins, and have you asked yourself what your subject does? Fifth, have you considered repetition in your whole plan, or in important and more difficult paragraphs?

Any of the ideas in the preceding paragraph may help you to find what we call supporting material. But in personalized exposition you need also much descriptive or narrative material. First, you can use incidents, examples, or illustrations. These may be specific or generalized or summarizing narrative; they may have both talk and action. Second, you can use vivid description, rich with many kinds of sensory detail, realistic and incisive, humorous or satirical, according to your subject. When you write about people, you would like us to see them and even experience their background. Third, you can use comparison and contrast: people with other people, settings with other settings, people with themselves at other times, and so on.

You may find certain principles useful in arranging your whole composition. First, try to capture your reader's interest by putting first what will appeal most to him. Second, move from the simple to the more difficult and complex. Third, build on the known, the familiar, the reassuring, and then proceed to the unfamiliar and the unknown. Fourth, put together ideas that are closely related, for your ease in writing and your reader's ease and pleasure in reading. Fifth, when other principles do not interfere, use the order of climax: from the least, to the more, to the most important. Sixth, when your subject impels you, use a time order, not for the whole composition, but for some points and for the arrangement of incidents in your supporting material.

OUTLINING

When you are ready to select and arrange, how much outlining do you need to do? If you can turn out well-organized papers quickly and efficiently without outlining, go ahead. But ninety-eight out of a hundred people cannot do this without struggle, trial and error; the result is a half-organized product. If you have difficulties, try outlining.

Suppose you wish to write about your mother's character and personality (to return to our earlier topic instead of introducing a new one), and you have decided to limit your controlling idea to her ability to put people at their ease. You start asking yourself the usual questions: *Whom* does she put at ease? *When? Where? Why? How?* With what *results?* Your tentative list might look something like this:

> Her liking for people.
> The unhappy Haitian.
> Plumber, with the "innards of the bathroom all over the floor."
> She likes to succeed when she starts anything.
> Her efficiency.
> A harmonious home.
> The timid soul, John Nelson.

In summer.
In winter.
When we children were young.
Now when we come home from college for vacations.
Picture of her as she looks in action.
Anything possible?
Her housecleaning spree.
The stubborn painters.
The client who wanted to shoot Father.

After two or three rewritings, which need not be reproduced here, your version might be like this:

MY MOTHER'S TALENT

Controlling idea: My mother has the ability to put other people at their ease.

INTRODUCTION
I. I will give an active picture of her as she looks in action.
II. I will emphasize how she puts people at their ease.

BODY
I. She can put people at ease in any place, at any time.
    A. In summer she works best on the screened porch; in winter, around the fireplace.
    B. She has proved her ability over years.
        1. She put us children at ease when we were small and when we were conscious of wrongdoing.
        2. She puts us at ease now, when we come home for vacations, no matter what strange ideas, objects, or people we bring home.
II. She can succeed under unusual circumstances.
    A. She won when stubborn painters refused to quit for unexpected guests.
    B. She won when the plumber had the "innards" of the bathroom over the floor and guests arrived.
    C. She won in the middle of her housecleaning when honored guests arrived without notice.
III. She can thaw out the most difficult guests.
    A. She won with John Nelson, the shyest friend I have.
    B. She persuaded my frustrated foreign friend to enjoy himself.
    C. She calmed the hostile client who threatened my father.

IV. She is effective with people for many different reasons.
    A. Her own personality calms people. (Here a further analysis might help.)
    B. She likes to succeed in whatever she undertakes.
    C. She must have harmony in her home, just as she must breathe.
    D. She has a genuine liking for people.
 V. She, along with us, enjoys several results of her success.
    A. Her home is praised and envied by others.
    B. Her home is the center for all our friends.
    C. She knows that we love to come home, often, for as long as we can.

CONCLUSION

  I. Can she succeed under any circumstances?
 II. Here is a vivid picture of the way I think of her in action.

You will notice that the outline uses parallel structure and much repetition, and that it keeps the same viewpoint by using the same subject or pronoun reminder of that subject whenever it is possible. "Isn't that a lot of repeating and sameness?" Of course it is; otherwise it wouldn't be a good outline. An outline is a skeleton; like the skeleton in a medical school it serves its purpose best when the relation of its parts shows up at once. To use variety of style in an outline is like covering up the skeleton in silks and satins.

Do not assume that an outline is ever finished. You may need to shift parts or to add parts. You may use it best by writing in, for your own use only, all sorts of details and incidents to support your points, and then selecting the best from these as you write. A well-built outline is a well-built highway; if you use it well, it helps you decide where you are going, and it gets you there smoothly and quickly. If you let it stop you from using your senses and from creating, because you have a framework, it can hinder you. Do not abuse it; use it, and let it set you free to handle incidents and vivid details with greater effectiveness.

LOGIC, ARGUMENT

You may not often need the principles of logic and argument in personalized exposition, but some of them are essential to clear thinking in any expression of ideas. Here are a few fundamentals; read about them in more highly specialized books if you wish.

First, one instance seldom gives you the right to generalize. In sound *inductive* reasoning you are examining many instances and finally making a general conclusion. Second, in *deductive* reasoning where you begin with a generalization, be sure that your premise or basis is sound and that you use the terms of your syllogism correctly. It is sound to say:

> All men are mortal.
> Ezra Jones is a man.
> Therefore Ezra Jones is mortal.

It is not sound to say:

> All men are mortal.
> Fido is mortal.
> Therefore Fido is a man.

The syllogism which follows depends on a premise which some people will not accept; hence it is not sound:

> All men are corruptible.
> Ezra Jones is a man.
> Therefore he is corruptible.

In cause-and-effect reasoning it is not sound to assume, when two things happen together, that one is necessarily cause and the other effect; or when one thing follows another, that the first is cause and the second its effect. You need to ask whether there is a real connection between the two, whether the first is sufficient to cause the second, whether the first one produces other effects, and whether there are other causes sufficient to produce the same effect.

Argument by analogy is often interesting and appealing, but it may be tricky. It rests upon assuming a likeness between two things, but the two things may have differences which invalidate a conclusion. For example:

> Trees suffer from frequent transplanting.
> Human beings are like trees.
> They suffer from frequent transplanting.

The critical reader asks about the second part: Are human beings like trees? In how many ways? Do all human beings suffer from frequent change, or are some actually stimulated? If a writer wishes to use such an analogy he should choose his wording carefully, give evidence that the human beings he is talking about did suffer, and avoid conclusions about *all* people. But as a means of clarifying, not proving, a debatable point, analogy, like comparisons in general, may be powerful.

Other fallacies that may appear in exposition as well as argument are arguing in a circle, using loaded words before you have offered proof of something that needs proving, and using loaded words in a definition.

Even if you do not use these principles of logic and argument directly, they may help you to think clearly. The first principle which was stated, that one instance seldom gives you the right to draw a general conclusion, may remind you to use plenty of supporting material and to limit your central idea. There is a great difference, for example, between making your reader accept the idea that *all* mothers are interesting, that *the mothers I know* are interesting, and that *my* mother is interesting. Sometimes, even for *my* mother, you need to use more than one instance; sometimes the slanting of your wording will imply the additional material which you need not give. For example, you say: "Of the many instances when my mother put strange people at their ease, perhaps the best is . . ." If you write about this instance with vividness and conviction your reader will probably accept your evidence. But he may also enjoy one or two more examples; and your job is not merely to make him assent but to make him enjoy.

FINDING SUBJECTS

What subjects can you use for character sketches? Your possibilities are as large as your experience. Start with the members of your immediate family, look at your relatives, near or distant (with a humorous, satirical, or serious eye), consider your friends, your teachers past and present, your doctor, lawyer, merchant, grocer, plumber, mayor, representative in the state legislature, Senator, Congressman, radio or TV repair man, cleaning woman, carpenter, landlord or landlady, minister, employer. Consider people in your home community, your college community, the place where you are employed, any organization you belong to, or any other place where you have had a chance to know people.

You might be interested in finding a subject by asking yourself who, among your acquaintances, has recently met a crisis. Who has been elected to office, appointed to a position, arrested for embezzlement? Who has married, died, retired, moved away, broken off an engagement or a friendship? If a recent event startles you into thinking of a person to write about, does this event itself illuminate his whole character? After this approach, you can go on to analyze his whole personality.

Consider also the types of people you like, resent, admire, or think of with satirical amusement. You can find them in your community, on a college campus, or any place else. It could be interesting to study and write about a campus leader, a typical fraternity man, or an apple polisher. Generalized description and narration would be effective for such a subject.

WRITING YOUR COMPOSITION

A. Find an individual whom you admire, one who interests your mind, appeals to your senses and interpretative imagination, and thus stirs you to creative work. Find a tentative aim or central idea, analyze, limit your idea if you need to do so; and in general follow the suggestions given above for analyzing and outlining. As you work, list supporting ideas, become conscious of your attitude as soon as you can, and then jot down incidents and sensory details also. Plan until you feel sure that you are ready to write. Then write your paper, using a logical plan with specific supporting details.

B. Find an individual whom you do not admire; estimate your attitude to him, analyze, word a concise central idea, outline, list supporting ideas and details as above, and so on. Then write your composition, using a logical organization with specific supporting details.

C. Use the same subject you analyzed for B, but instead of logical organization, use generalized description and narration. Either select a time and place where you can do justice to the person by picturing what he usually does, or show him at several different times and places, according to your subject.

D. Find a type of person that interests you because you approve, disapprove, or laugh at him. Using either one time and place or several times and places, use generalized narration and description to make readers understand him and realize or accept your attitude to him.

READING

AUNT BERTHA *

Tom Olsen

My great-aunt Bertha was childish and always a burden. But her worst trait was that she would not die. She was seventy-five when my parents agreed to care for her for the rest of her life, for what she would leave them when she died. She fooled them. When she finally died at ninety-seven, she had used all her own money and was such a burden to my parents that they had to send her to the county hospital.

Sending her away killed her. I think she could have cleared a hundred easily if we had been able to keep her well fed and provide her with lives to torment. It was a kind of mutually agreed murder, that business of sending her away.

My mother's health was failing, mostly because she had spent more than twenty years catering to the whims of this old woman. My father had employment dropped on him by the government, and we were eating more than we ever had before in my memory. My sister was in high school and wanted to go to college, and I myself thought that I must have a new baseball glove. It was a culmination of these things that sent my great-aunt to her death.

She wasn't sick. She had never had a sick day in all those ninety-seven years. She had put her husband away (pneumonia) and all of her brothers and sisters had been dead of old age for a long time. That's not a bad record considering that she was the oldest in the family. She liked to think about dying, or at least gave the impression that she did. Whenever people brought up the subject of getting old she would tell them about the plot where she would lie, alongside Andrew, her husband. She would sigh and say her husband's name once or twice and then talk about something else.

For years after she had first come from Norway she had worked as a servant girl, as so many young Scandinavian women have done. She migrated to the Midwest to be with her brothers and sisters, and, I think mainly, to catch some young strong, unsuspecting Norwegian immigrant. Andrew must have been all of that. We children knew him only as a faded photograph, their wedding picture. He looked strong, and must have been, but if there was any brain inside that sloping head, I don't know where God could have found room to put it. He worked on a section crew in a small Iowa town. He probably would have been foreman too, except for his untimely death, Aunt Bertha always said.

After Andrew was dead and buried, Aunt Bertha lived with her sister in the house Andrew had built. They had some money, they certainly never spent any, and they watched for thieves night and day. When their vigil was finally rewarded by a thief, after five years or so of watching, they gave him a stinging dressing down. They still weren't too good at speaking English so the worst thing they told him was "go to grass," a fierce expression they had picked up from Andrew, the robust section hand. It must have shocked the thief a good deal to be told to go to grass by two middle-aged foreign ladies. They were both somewhere around fifty years old then.

Finally, at the ripe age of sixty, her sister tired of living with her and joined Andrew. Aunt Bertha spent some of her sister's money for more plots in the cemetery and came to live with my grandfather. In another ten years she had salted him away with the sister and Andrew. This left her, the oldest, with nobody to outlive, so she made her deal with my father.

My mother, a gullible soul who knew nothing of the record Aunt Bertha had piled up in her years here, thought it was a way to solve the depression. Father had been forced out of the garage because he could no longer sell new cars, even Fords. Things were getting pretty well stretched—to the point where we didn't get up from the dinner table with full stomachs any more. At that we were better off than most of the families in our town; we still ate three meals a day. A chance to take care of the old lady, then well into her seventies, and to get what she left us when she died, looked like the best thing that could happen to us.

In five years her money was gone, father had been forced to almost everything but stealing to feed us all, and she was still going strong. I had been born during this interim to further complicate things. She hobbled around the house whenever she thought we weren't home, snooping into all our secrets. Once my sister buried a pirate treasure, a dime in a tobacco can, and Aunt Bertha dug it up and kept it. We got back on her by stealing from her though. At eighty-two she broke her hip showing us how to ski. It healed as well as if she had been only twenty and we still had to put up with her hobbling around after us. I think she got a few more years to live during the weeks that her hip was broken, by sucking them from my mother. I will always believe that my mother gave, or was forced to part with, part of her very life during that time to care for that old vampire.

Then the REA began to build lines and Dad got his job. He soon had a car, an old one because he couldn't afford better and still keep Aunt Bertha, and we used to get mother out from under the old lady's thumb once in a while. That's what really gave us our chance to get rid of her.

About this time my sister realized she wanted to go to college. When spring came that year, I needed a baseball glove, and that was practically her death warrant. We had enough reasons to get rid of her, and she herself gave us the chance we had wanted for years.

When we began to take mother for rides once in a while, the old lady was afraid that mother's life might be taken away so that she couldn't suck on it. She said she was sick, to keep mother home, safely within reach. And she could make it pretty convincing. She had never been pretty and she had worked up a skin cancer on her temple by this time. She looked like a witch, and she soon developed a moan good enough to scare my sister and me anytime, and we were used to her.

When she pulled her sickness on us we decided it was time for her to go. We knew, and she knew too, that if she ever got out of reach of tender young people to draw life from and into the hands of professionals at killing, she would die. We called the county home and made an appointment for them to send their ambulance the next day. My mother bathed her the next morning, without

telling her why. Aunt Bertha was getting such tender consideration that she smelled a rat. She was too mean to be fooled for
long. Mother told her why she was being bathed and she began to
moan and yell for father. Father went in, chased out my sister and
me and closed the door. We heard father talking quietly whenever
she paused in her moaning and screaming to catch her breath. She
shut up pretty soon and father came out.

The ambulance came, and they rolled her out to it on a litter.
My sister and I stood by, watching with savage satisfaction. She
did one last venomous thing before I saw the last of her. She
called me over to the litter and asked if I were sorry to see her go.
I said no and she spit on me. Later, father told me that the last
day there in the room she had tried to spit on both him and
mother. But she hadn't hit them. It's pretty hard to spit very high
lying down.

Four days later mother answered the phone, listened a minute,
and then told all of us standing around, "She's dead." Nobody
said anything.

MRS. MATHER [1]

Sophie Kerr

It was a fine morning and Mrs. Mather had a great deal to do.
First, she must make the rounds of certain pay-telephone stations
where no attendants or other tiresome people were likely to be
near, and slip a quick finger into each coin-return box. Sometimes,
indeed, far more often than you'd think, hurried folk made a call,
didn't get their party, and didn't wait for their money back. One
day Mrs. Mather had found thirty cents, but that was a gala event.
Generally a nickel or a dime was all her booty, but these were
frequent enough to be worth while.

By the time Mrs. Mather had finished with the pay-telephones
the grocer and butcher boys would be making their rounds in the
residence streets, and, as the stupidest person knows, many such
boys have carts filled with the orders for delivery, each in a box or
a package. Now, while such a boy is taking an order into a house,

[1] Sophie Kerr, "Mrs. Mather," *Century Magazine*, June, 1927. Reprinted by
permission of the author.

the cart stands unattended, and if you are casual in manner and careful in action you can usually pick up something, an orange, an apple, a couple of bananas—Mrs. Mather was fond of fruit—an onion and a few potatoes, or tomatoes, a dinner roll, even a chop or a link of sausage sometimes. Never take large unruly articles, such as bunches of celery, or a steak, or a roast, however much your mouth may water for such delicacies, because if you do inquiry will be made at the store, and the cop on the beat will be notified. Little pilferings are not missed; most cooks do not check up their orders, and if there should be a bit of a shortage it is set down to carelessness on the part of the order-clerk.

In Mrs. Mather's decent black skirt, made long and full as befitted her age and respectable expression, there was a slit which effected entrance to a pouch pocket as big as a flour-sack. This slit was strategically placed to come under Mrs. Mather's decent black shawl. There were few days indeed in Mrs. Mather's life when her pouch pocket came home empty, though the shameful practice of many grocers and butchers of putting strong iron network over their delivery-carts was not helpful to filling it. Trust and honor, and belief in one's fellow-creatures, reflected Mrs. Mather observing these safeguards, are rapidly leaving this world. Happily, the carelessness of delivery-boys admits of no known remedy, and just as often as not, perhaps oftener than not, they left the iron network tilted open when they ran into the back doors of the big apartment-houses, or the basements of fine residences.

Mrs. Mather did not know whether to be sorry for the passing of the fine residences and the building of big apartments or not. There was a decided pro and con to it, as she saw it. Apartment-house dwellers bought small orders from small markets whose owners were far more likely to use hand-carts than motors for delivery. That was pro. But the old residences had a grand manner, an aristocratic feeling of conservatism, long established, invulnerable. Mrs. Mather was a conservative and, in her way, an aristocrat, so that she felt at one with the owners of these haughty old brownstone fronts. That was con. Besides, the servants in these old houses were liberal and kind when an old white-haired woman rang the basement bell and quaveringly asked for a cup of coffee and a slice of bread and may the God of the starving reward ye fer y'r

ginerosity. That was con too. Many a savory half-chicken or hunk
of ham, left-overs of pies and puddings and cakes, many a dish of
elegant soup and grand coffee had been acquired by Mrs. Mather
in this way. Coffee! The only thing she whole-heartedly envied the
rich was their coffee.

In her meditations on this world Mrs. Mather included many
concerning the rich. She was intensely curious about them. Their
houses had so many rooms, the ceilings were so high, the curtains
so fine. Looking into basement windows she could see many maids
at work, maids who wore dresses quite good enough for church,
who washed and ironed with machinery, or who mixed rich complicated foods on clean white tables, and later cooked them on
stoves eight feet long. The kitchen, the laundries, the servants' din-
ing-rooms—into all these Mrs. Mather peered, at dusk when lights
were lit and carelessness had forgotten the curtains. And all this
cleanliness and order and paraphernalia, which were seemingly concerned only with the (to Mrs. Mather) exceedingly primitive arts
of washing and eating, fired her with wonder as to the beings for
whose ultimate good it must be intended. What shiny tables and
chairs and chests they must have, and painted pictures in gold
frames, maybe solid gold, and china plates with flowers on, and carpets to sink your tired old feet into, and soft beds, too, with blankets
white as the foam on a tub of suds, silver spoons for supping up
their coffee—and plenty of servants to order round, quick and sharp
to do this and do that! A splendid life. Only, somehow, it seemed
to have no bite in it! No tang of matching wits, no savor of artful
conniving and clever, apt pulling the wool over people's eyes to
charm the pence from their pockets. Mrs. Mather had done this so
long and so well, she had developed a quite natural pride in her
resourcefulness.

There were so many good ways! Stand on a street-corner, in a
swell part of the city where there were not too many passers, and
hold a slip of paper in your hand with an address, oh, many blocks
away, written on it. Look bewildered and scared, shrink timidly
toward a lady or a gentleman and in a sad old voice, tuned to
pathos, offer the slip, and will they in their kindness of heart tell
you how to get there, for you've seemingly walked the town over.
Ninety-nine times out of a hundred the lady or the gentleman gives

you a quarter for carfare. The hundredth person knows that game and tells you to ask a policeman.

And if you want to go somewhere, get on the street-car, and you've lost your purse! Oh, woe and misery! It had thirty cents in it (don't make the sum too high) and your handkerchief and a blessed prayer, and the picture of your darling boy who was kilt in the war, and what are you to do, for you're an old woman and poor, and there's half a day's work waiting for you if you can but get to the place. If the car is not too crowded you'll collect fifty cents to a dollar in small change by this story, and sympathy besides, and go to wherever you want to go at the expense of the conductor.

Mrs. Mather would have scorned to do anything so crude as walk the streets with a piece of raw turnip in her hand, as one of her neighbors did, squeezing out tears and saying it was all she'd had to eat the day! That was plain dumb, especially as the woman was a big fat lummox who'd clearly never starved herself an hour! No—but if you strolled in the park and saw a young mother out with her baby, and you stopped and said if you ever saw a child marked for good fortune it was this one, and went on and told of grand things to come for the brat, you mostly won a piece of silver. If it was a nurse-maid, now, with the child, tell her fortune, and don't bother about the little one.

Yes, Mrs. Mather enjoyed making her living, and a rainy day was a real cross to her, for it made her stay in the dingy little room which she called her home. She liked it well enough at night, for then she could light the gas and be cozy with a cup of coffee and the evening picture paper all full of lovely scandals, but in daytime it was too dark, too circumscribed to suit her. She had little domesticity in her make-up. Out in the street for her, where there was something to see, something to do.

She had a regular route—several of them, in fact—for it was foolish to let any one set of people get too familiar with your appearance, but it was her weakness that all of these routes converged at one particular house, a beautiful stately mansion dating from Mrs. Mather's earliest recollections, a house which was her passion and delight. It was through the basement windows of this house that she liked most to watch the servants at work. And she often stood and stared into the upper stories, so bedraped and becurtained, and speculated on the life above stairs. It was, in fact, her ideal home for the rich! And it was the house where the coffee was most superlative in quality of all the places she knew, though she had tasted it but once. Some queer quirk of feeling kept her from asking again. She often imagined herself living in that house, and, of course, when you live in a house you don't ask for victuals at that house's basement door.

In the summer-time, when the residents were away and the place was boarded up, Mrs. Mather used to come of a summer evening and perch on the steps and fan herself, and think of walking up and entering the great front door, and taking off her bonnet and going into the parlor and sitting in the fine chairs they must have there, red satin or maybe red velvet, as soft and as smooth! And a servant-girl would come, and you'd say, "Bring me my coffee!" and she'd fetch you a pink cup on a silver tray and cream too thick to pour, and sugar lumps in a silver dish, and a white linen napkin to lay in your lap—eh, my dear, that'd be the way to live in a house like this one! Just when she was enjoying herself so well, along would come the mean policeman with the fat stomach and order her off. Mrs. Mather hated that policeman. She often wished for him the curse of boils.

PORTRAIT OF MY MOTHER [2]

Rollo Walter Brown

1

Strangely I did not come to know the quality of my mother until I was a great overgrown boy larger than most men. She and my father were out of the same world—the world of vanishing forests—and he was austere, and I was "mother's boy"; yet early I knew him better. There was in him a pronounced trace of the poet that a child was sure to appreciate on sight. My mother was the battler of the two, the one who accepted life where she was and settled down to the unpoetic business of making ends meet. Anyone was in danger of assuming—as I did at first—that her end-

[2] Rollo Walter Brown, "Portrait of My Mother," *The Hills Are Strong*, The Beacon Press. Reprinted by permission of the author and publisher.

less concern with everyday matters indicated content with everyday satisfactions. And that was to misunderstand her entire life.

She spent her early childhood—at the very middle of the nineteenth century—in a clearing that overlooked a modest rapids in an Ohio hill river when the sight of people moving westward, always moving westward, was something to be expected every day. She was the eldest child in a family of an even dozen—every one of whom lived to be old.

All this army of brothers and sisters except one were born before my mother was married, and of the first nine only one was a boy. The mother of all these looked upon a household as something vital and florid right out of the magnificence of a stirring cosmos. There was something of freedom and expansiveness even in the names she gave them. When everybody round about was naming children Isaiah, Ebenezer, Rebecca, or Leah, she named hers Roselba (my mother), Sylvester Byron, Lucinda, Elizabeth Alverta, Cora Ellen. Her family was a tribe pushing up into full life. It called for the ministrations of more than one mother, and the eldest daughter became a kind of associate mother entrusted with keeping track of as many as possible.

Something of this long childhood experience of being always entrusted with life, of being always thoughtful about someone other than herself, was in everything she later did in her own household. She had three sons. Out of the depths of her dark eyes —that with her cheerful countenance made her a woman of unpretentious beauty—she expressed her constant preoccupation with giving these sons more of a push into the world than she herself had known.

It was not easy. For she had become a bride in the devastating years of President Grant's administration when the country seemed to be in the numbness of final death. Everybody needed the fruit jars, milk crocks, and butter jars that her husband turned in his bluebird potshop, but nobody possessed money.

And if the general atmosphere was dispiriting, the specific little world in which she put in her days could scarcely be regarded as a luxurious center of life. The log house in which she lived for many years had a great fireplace in which either coal or wood could be burned, a wide flagstone hearth, an oak floor of boards

of enormous width covered with a rag carpet woven at a neighbor's house, side walls covered with flowered paper that went in
and out in waves over the logs to the wide border of flowers of
deeper color at the top, and a ceiling of neatly hewn whitewashed
beams and whitewashed rough boards—the under side of the upstairs floor.

Beside a bright blue batten door that led to the kitchen was
a shelf on which a Waterbury clock announced the hours with
whirring bangs, and the seconds with ticktocks that could be
heard upstairs through the cracks. And opposite the fireplace by a
window where the sun shone in, there was a triangular flower stand
that rose in terraced shelves to make a kind of half-pyramid four
or five feet high of fuchsias and bleeding heart and geraniums and
begonias and night-blooming cereus and ferns and other plants
grown for their foliage alone.

In this world she moved energetically and always with an awareness that said, "Of course, we are hoping for something better."
Her young life had been nourished on the stories of neighbor boys
who had marched away and done great things on the battlefield,
and she saw no reason why a woman might not proceed as if there
were still important concerns to be occupied with. Occasionally
she did one thing that gave her a look of importance in my eyes,
she took her place in a sidesaddle decorated with red and tan
needlepoint—or something of the sort—high on a somewhat
angular horse, and with a long loose riding-skirt covering even the
toe of her one foot that was in the stirrup, rode away to a meeting
of some kind. My notions of great personages come from the Bible,
or the pictures in the back of it, and when I saw her high on the
tall horse I always thought of some beautiful queen on a camel.

2

Since her sons were going to be living where there would be
persons of gentility, she thought they ought to be well grounded
in essentials. If one of them slammed a door, or let it slam, he
went immediately back and opened it and then closed it appropriately. When a son was ready to go to a neighbor's house to carry
a message, he had to repeat to his mother what he was going to
say when he got there. And when he returned he did not report

approximately what the neighbor said, but gave it precisely, and in the neighbor's exact words—an experience that was almost more than the equivalent of a college education.

Where she got her understandings of how people in other and greater places surely must act, I was never able to learn. But she said she wanted her sons to have "behavior" that would stand them in good stead anywhere, and on the assumption that she knew something of what that would be, she proceeded. She had a backlog in etiquette that if we thought enough about other people, we'd probably do about the right thing ourselves.

We bounced up from our chairs when older people came into the room, and begged them to sit. We spoke with respectfulness to every adult human being. And we were expected to appear in clean clothes and with what she called "becomingness" when we went where other people were assembled. When we were in our Sunday best and there had been heavy summer rains that had left the hill and hollow roads gutters and loblolly, she insisted that we pick our way along the roadside so that our shoes would not be all mud when we reached the church. Although I hit upon the less genteel way of carrying my shoes and socks and enjoying the elemental feel of the soft mud squashing up between my toes, and then washing my feet in the cool water below a spring within sight of the church, putting on my shoes, and appearing as mudless as if I had walked all the way on Fifth Avenue, I did accept her principle of making as decent an appearance as circumstances would allow.

Nor would she permit waste. When school might be had for the going, it was unpardonable to miss a day unnecessarily. Clothes were to be worn with care for their natural life. And food was to be eaten. If we did not eat all that was in our dinner buckets at school, we carried the scraps home for the dog or the chickens. It was a depravity not to be thought of to throw away the tiniest morsel of bread. And of course nobody had to be cautioned about throwing away cake.

We heard her admonitions, saw the reasonableness of them, and usually accepted them without so much as a question. But there was one that I could never accept even in the abstract. Since I was much younger than my two brothers, I required special cautioning. She told me not to fight. To pick trouble, she said, was very low-grade. But I could never see why these two were always mentioned together. I never picked trouble; but I had to fight. In the oncoming world of Coal in which I was obliged to operate, either a boy fought or he did not survive.

When a blustering ruffian of my own years hurried ahead to a level spot, turned to block my way, and said, "Here's where we find out whether I'm good, or you," there was such a healthy satisfaction in bloodying his nose, knocking him down, and sitting astride him and cuffing him with energy until he begged for mercy, that I always had to go through with it. "I hear you were in a fight again," she would say, looking at me with penetrable sternness out of her dark brown eyes; and I would answer "But I didn't start it." And there the matter would rest.

From somewhere she had gained the sure belief, too, that people's lives should include music. A piano was out of the question, but an organ was not. She succeeded well enough with my two brothers. Eventually they played two or three different instruments in public, and one of them directed a stirring military band in college. For seventeen weeks the same teacher who had taught them struggled with me, and my mother daily released me from all other duties for a time in order that I might practice. Eventually she heard me floundering through the easy parts of "The Beautiful Blue Danube Waltzes" with long clumsy fingers—while the birds sang alluringly everywhere outside, or the Plymouth Rock and Brown Leghorn roosters met at their boundary line within full view of where I labored, and waged one of the decisive battles of the world. I worked conscientiously, but rebelliously.

I never knew where my mother learned of my true state of mind, for I was careful not to tell her. But one day when I had poison ivy on the back of my neck and she was bathing it in cool water and sugar of lead she said, "Son, you don't have to take the organ lessons if you don't want to." I was so overjoyed that I generously volunteered to take up the fife instead. With the money for three organ lessons, I could get a fife in rosewood.

The whole of her sense of entrustment was revealed when she sat in the crackling midwinter firelight. The light spread out and upward from the fireplace and made the beams and ceiling boards very white over her head, and touched the great semi-pyramid of blooming flowers behind her with brightness out of a spring dawn. While she sat erect and contemplative, everybody—including my father, who at other times seemed more or less her equal—shrank into subordination.

She could never remain inactive long, and while my father sat with his page twisted round to catch the light and read with great concentration, and the others of us cracked nuts or popped corn or hung apples from the enormous hewn log that supported the chimney above the fireplace so that they would come down just close enough to sizzle and roast without burning—or burning the string—she knitted away at a mitten or crocheted a shawl or did other "easy" work that she left for evenings. But there in the firelight, even while she worked, she was the custodian and guarantor of life—there in a room where most things were either her blood or her handiwork.

3

Just as sure, too, as her feeling of entrustment was her sense of practical adequacy. Her world was not a world of gadgets; there was little "to do with." But a part of the business of being intelligent, she supposed, was to make much of little. When she and her father-in-law philosophized together, she always approved his remark that the true pioneer could go into the woods with an axe, horse, and a plow shovel, and proceed to the growing of a crop and the establishment of a farm. She thought a woman likewise should be resourceful.

So she made any garment worn by a man or a woman—including a man's cap and a woman's hat. She knitted or crocheted mittens, mufflers, socks and stockings, shawls, wristlets, fascinators, earmuffs, and lace of amazing beauty. She made, too, all kinds of woven or hooked or plaited rugs, quilts of the most complicated design and recurrences of color, crazy-quilts of ingenious variations in fancy stitching, stand covers, table covers. When a boy needed a suit of clothes, she carefully studied an old suit and then made the new one. Her aptitude seemed most startling, though, when she saw casually at church a new style of hood which she liked, and went home and proceeded to make one.

In addition to the everyday cooking done in a household, she made all sorts of jellies of the clearest colors and the most trembling consistency, grape marmalade, blackberry and raspberry jam, strawberry preserve, peach butter, the special Ohio kind of apple butter, melting yellow cakes with deep icing, mincemeat of her own proportioning that all the neighbors bought ravenously from her as long as she would sell, butter with such a distinct tastiness that an important industrialist who had known her when he was a boy had her—through some arrangement that he was able to make— provide him with a pound every week until she was eighty-five years old. But the dish which she herself professed greatest pride in was a strangely pungent pie made of green tomatoes and half-ripened grapes, and spices, including nutmeg.

Her day began at four-thirty in the morning, summer and winter, and ended whenever there was a stopping place in her work. Yet she never worked at anything as if it were the only thing she had in mind. She would pick up a volume from the table when she was tidying the living room, see something that interested her, drop into a chair, read the shortest possible section that would enable her to understand, and then go on with her work. But there was a cheeriness in her face which told that something out of the book had contributed to the encompassing enterprise of her life.

After she had taken a nap on a couch at noon—and there was no noise—she would sit up with startling suddenness and move off vivaciously into her work as if the nap had only given her a little clearer view of what she must always be about. She was quick-tempered, but always after the flash of hotness over the immediately vexing matter, she seemed more than ever a contemplative person occupied with inclusive concerns.

In her capacity to hurry and to think at the same time she equaled any commanding general. If a family came just at meal-time, she revealed a kind of magical dexterity in bringing a meal together for extra people in the twinkling of an eye. Nor was she flustered by people who were supposed to be important. A Governor of Ohio walked through the mud before daylight one morning to see her. He was a big boyish person who knew country life and country people, and was known to her somewhat through her sons. He went to the back door in the foggy half-light, and when she answered his knock he asked her if it would be possible for a hungry man to get a handout of some kind. "I guess it will," she replied; "so come on in." And then as he stood like a giant chuckling affectionately over her she added, "But for a half cent I'd box your ears for coming to the back door." Whereupon he became for the rest of his life a kind of fourth son in his devotion to her.

4

Since I was the youngest I was in time much in her immediate world after my brothers had more or less left it. It was then that I began to see the importance of the contemplative and less obvious side of her life. In solitude she considered the place that such a humble life as hers held in the world. The best she could do was to send emissaries out. That was what she had been busy doing. She said little, but sometimes she said enough to reveal her true intent. In a letter that through all the years escaped destruction she once wrote, "Now it affords me great pleasure to deny myself for my sons."

And once when we were alone and I had fallen full length and had struck my head with a terrific jolt and she thought I was at the end of my life, though I was only dazed, I heard her say, when she thought she spoke alone to the Infinite out of her heartbreak, what she thought of me, and of my brothers, and of the purpose of living.

But when the emissaries had gone, here she would be still— probably, for she as well as my father was of a tough breed. She would have to know how to live in solitude. And it was her adequacy in solitude that became more and more noticeable. It was in her manner while she worked; it was in her face when she reflected; it was in her eyes when she turned to you with a look that seemed to come from the experience of a thousand centuries.

I first noticed this depth from which she looked when we one morning picked berries together in the late dewiness down by the deep woods below the locust thicket where the sun scarcely entered. We had filled one large bucket and I took it to the house to empty it. When I returned, the birds were singing in every tree-top, the crows scolded in the locusts, and two great turkey buzzards sat on the leaning steeple of white oak so near that I could study their bare red vulture heads. My mother stood obliviously with one arm outstretched to a briar bending with berries, intent in reflection. Suddenly I was seized by a strange conviction that I had never seen her before; that she was a woman out of the Bible; that she was neither young nor old, but only representative and timeless. But when she saw me there in the edge of the walnut-tree shade, and asked me what time it was up at the house, we were both back where obviously we belonged.

There was nothing morbid in her solitude. It was only that she did not always feel sure of herself in the noisiness of big gatherings, and she did feel sure of herself when she could work things out alone. In consequence, she let her husband represent her more and more at gatherings, until in the end she quit going altogether. She had to write at least three letters every Sunday, anyhow. Thus it came logically that for twenty-one years in her late life she was never off the Ridge where she lived.

In these years she developed a great serenity. She was a part of something expressed everywhere about her. She would stop when she walked, look about in content at the clouds, and the wind in the trees, and the sun on the hillsides, and then stand contemplatively for minutes. She would put her hand against the stout trunk of a pushing young shellbark hickory, look at it as if she and the tree were on very good terms, and then walk on without a word.

She became, too, without any noticeable effort on her part, a special friend of creatures—a custodian of good relations between them and the representatives of mankind round about. Cows thrust their heads through the bars to have her—and no one else—soothingly rub their faces. When she started on one of her afternoon or Sunday morning walks out to the woods pasture, where there was a long vista through the hills, her hens would come running, sometimes half flying, until they were a great accompanying body. They were not hungry; they were expecting no feed; they only chose to go along. In winter she hung ears of yellow corn in an apple tree by the front porch and tacked strips of suet to the body of the tree and had several pairs of cardinals for company throughout the season.

And the environs of the house every spring and summer became a bustling wren sanctuary. If she hung her raincoat on the out-kitchen porch and left it there for a few days, there was certain to be a wren's nest in one of the pockets. When she put a cracked old-style iron teakettle on a low shelf in the coal house, she discovered within a day or two that a wren was using the wide spout as an entrance and was building a nest. She could lift the lid later and exhibit the wren family.

Once when she was eighty she said a bit proudly to one of her sons, "Come out here to the milk bench and I'll show you something." She had turned a milk crock upside down and one edge of it extended an inch or two over the end of the bench. Within twenty-four hours a wren was building a nest under the crock. And now when she unhesitantly turned the crock up, seven lively-looking young wrens, about ready to fly, watched her intently, but did not move. She had been turning the crock up for a look at least once every day.

She knew, too, where to find every beautiful thing that existed in her world. She knew which redbuds in the thicket always bloomed a little ahead of the others, which dogwoods first began to lose their greenish cast and become pure white, where to find the prize patch of sweet williams, when to look for the blackhaw bush in full bloom, when to expect the first odor of locust blossom, when in July to watch for an unfailing field lily on the hillside, where always to find the softest and greenest moss, where to look for the first maple branch that bespoke autumn, where to go for flint stones that had the most interesting spiral markings on them.

Whenever her friends from town came to see her—and they were always coming, as many as fifteen or twenty on one Sunday afternoon—she reverted to her more customary role of giver. They walked out to the locust trees, on out to the woods pasture, down to a romantic old orchard close in the hollow where one could still find fragments of Staffordshire blue tableware by the site of an early house, back up the hill to sit for a time in a clean pasture field and enjoy such quiet as they did not know existed. And when they were ready to go she placed something in their hands to be carried away—some fruit, some bittersweet, some slips of ruddier begonia, something out of the vegetable garden, some flowers from the profusion in which they grew from the first peonies to the last chrysanthemums.

To give—was not that what life was? That was the easy summary; twenty years or so given to younger sisters and the like; two thirds of a century and a little more given to her own family. She had given.

But what she had achieved within herself seemed more. In a world where life was always hard and often cruel, she met the requirements without ever flinching, without ever thinking of running away to some remote place in pursuit of an evasive happiness. Just to have remained steadfast in itself would have been much. But she persisted until she made a greater usefulness of the hard conditions. She persisted until she saw herself in relation to things, to all things, and, right where she stayed, came to know the deeps of a serenity from which she could look out on whatsoever and be undismayed.

QUESTIONS

Does the writer of "Aunt Bertha" express sympathy, humor, sardonic realism, or does he use a combination of these attitudes? Does he have a central idea? If so, what is it? What fact or event serves as the beginning for his sketch? For the end? What is the difference between the beginning and the end? To what extent does he use the past life of his character? Does he use it in logical or chronological order? Has he analyzed his character thoroughly, or as much as he needed to do for his aim? What effect does he have on you as an individual reader— amusement, sympathy, shock, or some other reaction? Is the unit individual, or imitative and conventional?

In "Mrs. Mather" what is the writer's attitude to her subject? Is she amused, indignant, admiring, or does some other word describe her attitude better? Does she use satire, either for occasional small details or through the whole unit? What contrasts does she imply between conventional views and Mrs. Mather's views of her actions? Between conventional views about respectable-looking old ladies and the reality of Mrs. Mather? What is Mrs. Mather's chief trait, or what are her chief traits? How is the article organized? Is generalized narrative used? Where? How? Where and for what purpose are Mrs. Mather's thoughts used? Are they used effectively? What is the artistic aim of the whole unit? Is the aim achieved?

Can you phrase a central idea for the "Portrait of My Mother"? A smaller central idea for each of the four sections? Are the sections well arranged? What principles guide the arrangement? What is the author's attitude to his mother? How important is this attitude in establishing the tone and meaning of the whole unit? How much analysis seems to lie back of the article? Where and how does the author use incidents or vivid pictures? What is the effect of these? Do you have a complete or an incomplete idea of the mother when you have finished a careful reading of the article? Does the author communicate his own attitude to you as a reader? Why does he fail or succeed?

22

Explaining Yourself

In this chapter you are working toward one of three different composition assignments, all of them closely related. You may analyze and explain either a personal problem, your personal philosophy, or your own character. Each of these topics is a real problem in analysis, but the personal problem is probably the simplest of the three; and if you begin with it, you may be preparing indirectly to write a composition on one of the other subjects. Perhaps you made some indirect preparation for this chapter when you were working on autobiographical sketches in Chapter 18; rechecking your notes there may save time in getting your thinking started. Though you were using time patterns there and are using logical organization here, you had to do some analyzing before you could plan narrative.

A PERSONAL PROBLEM

What is a personal problem? When you have to choose one of two courses of action, when you are in a distasteful situation and would like to find a way out, when you have an important need without any apparent way of filling it, when you have a desire which leads to frustration instead of fulfillment, you have a personal problem. In any problem worth using in composition, you have something at stake besides material issues. You are concerned also with hopes, fears, desires, and with inner satisfaction or dissatisfaction. For example, budgeting your income is a personal problem. Stated without qualifications it is only a material problem; but if your attempts to budget your income threaten your relationships to other people, your subject is worth while. If you need to choose between two jobs and the only difference is the salary, try another topic. But if one job is dull with good pay and the other is a challenge with small pay, you may need to sort out your values, and thus you have a significant subject.

If you can find a solution for your personal problem as you analyze it, you have an extra dividend. But even if you cannot resolve it you may be laying a foundation for a future solution or at least coming to terms with it and learning to live with it. Your analysis, too, may lead you to significant subjects for other compositions or give you background for them.

These subjects may help suggest to you some of your own problems: adjusting to reasonable or unreasonable discipline, wherever it appears; choosing breadth or narrowness in education; wanting adventure in travel or in a new kind of life; meeting new ideas or new standards of conduct; having ambitions without the talent for realizing them; adjusting to inevitable events like a hopeless illness, accident, or death; choosing freedom or restraint; dealing with parents who dominate without reason; deciding whether to marry a person of a different religion or cultural background; balancing the claims of a sorority or fraternity against individual desires; learning to live with all kinds of people after spending your first twenty-two years with thoroughly controlled and apparently normal people.

Besides these subjects which mainly concern you, or you and one or two other people, you may find other subjects by considering your attitudes to whole groups or to racial, religious, social, or economic forces. If you belong to a majority group, you may find something to say by considering your attitude to the minority group; if you belong to a minority group, you may be concerned with the way you are treated by the majority.

When you find a personal problem, ask yourself questions as you did in Chapter 21. Who has helped cause the problem? What environment or training in the past? What new environment? When did the problem develop? Where? What are its results, its effects now? What will its effects be in the future? What do you experience in specific situations? What are your physical and sensory reactions? Why do you wish some solution? What possible solutions can you think of? Why do you accept or reject each of these solutions? When you have put the problem on paper by means of an honest, thorough search for the answers to these and similar questions you can develop it by following some of the suggestions made later in this chapter.

A PERSONAL PHILOSOPHY

When you consider your personal philosophy, your biggest problem, perhaps, is to find what you *do* believe, that is, to analyze your ideas. Read Chapter 21 again, with its discussion of analyzing by asking questions, organizing, arranging, and outlining, unless its ideas have become part of your thinking. Try various approaches. For example, ask yourself the questions which follow and jot down both the answers and all the incidents and sensory details that come into your mind.

1. What is your attitude to yourself, to other individuals, to inanimate and animate nature, to social institutions, and to good and evil (or to God and the devil if you prefer the concrete terms)?

2. What is your attitude to work, play, love, and worship? (One writer uses these four terms as a plan for his book on a personal philosophy.)

3. What do you believe so deeply that you would act on it in a crisis almost instinctively?

4. What do you say at times that you believe without really believing it? Does this area include political ideas, love of country, religion, personal morals, attitudes to minority groups or to other groups or individuals?

5. Where did you get your opinions on some of the important questions mentioned above? Who is chiefly responsible? Are many people responsible—parents, brothers and sisters, other relatives, teachers, ministers, organizations to which you have belonged, your whole community? When? Where? What were causes? Results? What do these opinions lead you to do? Whole-heartedly? Reluctantly?

6. Are you conscious of any conflicts between your views and

the views of some of the people mentioned in the preceding question? Spoken conflicts? Unspoken ones?

7. What is your philosophy of a good family life? Do you wish to repeat the pattern of your own childhood? Why or why not? If you would change it, in what ways? What is your theory about your responsibility to your father, mother, brothers, sisters? Their relationship or responsibility to you? Is there any difference between your theory and your practice in these relationships? In your future family do you wish to create an autocratic or a democratic group? What kind of relationship do you hope to have between you and the person you marry? What standards do you have for the person you marry? Do you wish your children to share decisions and take responbilities, or to be given orders, to be sheltered, and to have life made easy for them? Do you hope that they will be individuals or conformists? That they will be creative, adventurous, independent, or noncreative, cautious, dependent?

8. What theory do you hold about your relation to groups, either those in which you have chosen membership or those to which you belong by birth and residence? Your church? Fraternity? Another club? Your community? What is your attitude toward the recreational facilities, educational facilities, government, and moral tone of your community?

9. What views do you hold about God or about the mystery of the universe? About a future life?

10. What do you believe about education and personal development? Is a technical training enough? Should all human powers be developed? Should moral and ethical ideas be cultivated? If so, how? Should latent talent be brought out? Should creative and imaginative powers be developed?

11. What are your ideas about work? Is it merely a means of making a living, a police power to keep people out of trouble, or a chief satisfaction in a good life? Should work be creative? A means of continuing one's education? A contribution to general human life? Do you wish to see something tangible or to believe that something valuable but intangible is growing from your work?

12. What are your ideas on recreation, amusements, and pleasure? Do you value books and reading? Music? Crafts? Arts? Theater? Movies? Hunting and fishing? Other outdoor life? How

do you regard alcoholic drinks? Do you believe in absolute pro-
hibition or in temperance, for yourself? What is your theory about
others, to let them take care of themselves or give them rigid
controls?

13. How do you define the word "sin"?

14. What is your idea of honesty, not the conventional platitudes from your training, but the views you have wrested from
living?

15. What is your general code of personal conduct?

16. What things do you laugh at—what jokes, what people, what
situations?

17. What things make you angry? Sad? Discouraged?

18. Are you egocentric or not egocentric?

19. Are you an individualist or a conformist, or do you take a
position between the two attitudes?

20. How do you treat your equals, your superiors, your inferiors,
children, members of the opposite sex, the helpless, animals?

21. Do you believe in a creative or in a routine existence for
yourself?

22. Do you believe that you have complete freedom of the will?
No freedom at all? Or do you believe that, whatever philosophers
conclude, you have limited freedom and that you must act as if
you believed in free will? Can you lay out a plan for the future and
then move consciously toward that plan?

23. What is your definition or your description of success? Do
you accept or reject this idea: "He succeeds who makes it possible
for others to succeed"?

24. What is your definition or your description of happiness?

25. What is your best character trait? Your worst one? The one
that will contribute most to your real happiness? To your material
success? To the happiness of others?

The answers to the preceding questions, if they are honest and
searching, will furnish you the raw material for either a character
sketch or an account of your personal philosophy. In fact, they
would probably provide material for a dozen good sketches or a
whole book of analytical autobiography. For of course you have a
character, whether it is good or bad, developed or neglected. And
you have a personal philosophy.

Besides, do what we will, we cannot get away from ideas. We cannot speak or act without being conscious of a kind of intellectual tribunal within us ready to sanction or redress what we say or do. This system of notions constantly appealed to may be inherited through education, or it may have been taught us by our successes or failures; it may be conscious or unconscious, but it rules our existence. We call it sometimes our principles, sometimes our philosophy.

We are also aware that any man who possesses a talent or an influence possesses what we call a technique as well. The politician has his technique and the business man has his, both based on a knowledge of psychology. Lawyers and magistrates all systematize a body of practical rules. So do artists. . . .

But this is not all. Behind the technique is something much more general, that is to say applicable to more than one realm: that is the politician's, the business man's, the artist's philosophy. The politician has gathered his from history or from lectures on constitutional law; the business man has risen from economics or publicity to superior notions; all artists are ready to expatiate on the strange relation between lines or colors and the human emotions. Facts have been summed up in conclusions and the conclusions have led to a philosophy, or, as often as not, to philosophy.[1]

There are certain cautions to be observed if you plan to write about your philosophy. Do not undertake too much. Limit, and then cultivate your small area intensively. As it is living material, let it have an organic growth from within. Suppose, for example, that you are interested in your philosophy of a creative rather than a routine existence. Again ask yourself questions: Who is responsible for your having this philosophy? Who will be affected by it? When did it originate in your life? Why? What results? What causes? How is it related to your past, your present, your future? Does it influence your education? The kind of job you will choose? Your recreations and hobbies? How do you behave in a routine job? What is your outer behavior? Your inner experience? How do you behave in creative work? What is the relation of this behavior to your choice of a future job? Your future success? Your future happiness? As you ask yourself such questions and add more questions of your own, jot down ideas, incidents, pictures, conversations, and any other vivid details. Any one of the twenty-five questions listed above can be developed in the same way.

[1] Ernest Dimnet, *What We Live By*, Simon and Schuster, New York, 1932.

A CHARACTER ANALYSIS

Many of the preceding questions will help you also in a character analysis. Here again, do not undertake too much; do not try to make a complete balance sheet of your character unless you have much time and perseverance. Suppose instead that you are interested in your tendencies toward individualism or conformity, and you decide that you are a conformist. What is a conformist? What does he do? What does he refuse to do? When? Where? Who has influenced you in this direction? What other causes, not people? When and where have they influenced you? What are the present results of your conformity? When and where do they show themselves? In what areas of your life? In your amusements, dress, friends, the organizations you join? Will your conformity affect your future? Your choice of a job, a place to live, the kind of person to marry, the way to train your children? Will your conformity lead to happiness? If you consider yourself an individualist you can apply similar questions and get much raw material for a composition.

ARRANGING, ORGANIZING

Suppose you have the raw material collected for one of the three topics which have been discussed. Then organize, arrange, work toward a central idea, rearrange, restate the central idea at need, according to the suggestions in Chapter 21. Know your attitude to the material as soon as you can; estimate the kind of reader you wish to reach and your effect on him; using this information, rework your plan as many times as you need to before you are satisfied.

Of course you can use a humorous or a satirical tone for a character analysis or an explanation of your philosophy; you might even do so for a personal problem. In any of the three, perhaps you may try to achieve the light touch with the serious intention.

Be sure that you have plenty of supporting material, such as incidents, bits of talk, vivid details, and pictures of past, present, or future. If you wish, jot these down on the spaces in your outline. Plan a method of personalizing. The first person seems the natural approach for these topics; but use the third person to represent yourself if you feel that you can manage it better.

WRITING YOUR COMPOSITION

A. Explain a significant personal problem, with or without a solution. If you have no solution, make your readers understand your inability to find one. Personalize, using your attitude freely, to give emotional unity to your whole composition, and try to be clear, interesting, and vivid.

B. Explain your philosophy of life or some limited phase of it, such as your views of family life, theories of work, attitude to religion and the unknown, or any other significant part of the whole. Again personalize, use your attitude freely, and try to be clear, interesting, and vivid.

C. Explain something about your own character, preferably limiting your scope to certain related traits, a conflict in traits, one trait that seems of paramount importance, or some other small part of the whole. Again personalize, use your attitude freely, and make your composition clear, vivid, and interesting.

READING

I AM AFRAID *

Robert Harvey

Sitting here at my desk, typing this, I am afraid. Yesterday I was afraid, and the day before that. I have been afraid for several years; I expect to be afraid for years to come. Not every second of course, not consciously. My fear is not powerful enough for that. I forget about it for days at a time, maybe even weeks. But it is still there, snuggled deep in some dark corner of my mind, waiting until all is quiet to creep out and whisper to me, and titter to itself because I cannot sleep. It is not the sudden sharp shock of physical fear that dries your mouth, and makes your hands clammy with sudden sweat. It is no fear of anything I can reach out and touch with my hands. It is a shifting, formless fear that takes a hundred different shapes, and forms and vanishes and forms again.

Why am I afraid? While I cannot make myself believe the little preachers yelping down from their tall pulpits, I have found nothing to take their place. And though I cannot believe them as they prate on about the glories of eternity reserved for their particular sect, I cannot rid myself of an inborn, almost instinctive fear that the punishments they tell of may be true. I wish I could believe them entirely. It would be comforting to have your way of life ordered for you in advance, with the results clearly tabulated, so that you know if you do the one thing you will be granted eternal happiness, but if you do the other you will be eternally damned and suffer forever. It would simplify life, and banish all doubts and contradictions.

I am afraid because so far I have found nothing that I can entirely believe in, not even myself. Everyone has to believe in something, true or false, important or unimportant. So far I have not found that thing.

I am afraid because I can see no purpose in life. If life has no ultimate design, if there is no high goal toward which all mankind is gradually striving, then what is the use of it all? A game with no rules and no winner is a poor game.

If only I felt no need to believe in something greater than myself I would be happier. Then I could sit back and take a morbid pleasure in the spectacle of mass futility which is our present-day life. But I do feel the need to believe in something, some power greater than I—a Cosmic Plan, a Life-Force, call it what you will. Yet I can find nothing to believe.

What can I do? I can't talk to other people about it. That sort of topic doesn't come up in casual conversation. What do we talk about to the people we meet? The weather? What we did today? What they did today? How hard the last test was? Dozens of subjects will do, just so they don't require any thought from either of us. But what would the average person's reactions be if I went up to him and said, "I'm afraid. Are you afraid?" No, I can't talk to other people about it. For all I actually know I may be the only person with this fear. Other people show no signs of it. The vast majority seem content with religion. Others have thrown out religion and are happily prostrating themselves before the whirling atoms of science. Some have disposed of everything and are basking in a lovely nothingness. None seem dissatisfied or troubled with any serious doubts. I wish I knew if they really believe, and are as content as they seem, or if they are merely paying lip service and are inwardly as confused as I.

I am like a man lost in some dark corridor that endlessly twists and turns and doubles back on itself. I grope my way along, my only light a flickering match. The old myths tell of the corridor as being lighted by the tall, ever-burning candles of religion. But the candles have long since gone out. I cannot find them, nor do I really believe that they are there. But though I do not believe in the candles, I still fear the pitfalls mentioned in the myths. So I go slowly, fearfully, at any moment expecting the floor to tilt beneath my feet and plunge me down into unimaginable depths. It is dark, and cold, and my match is fast burning out. I have no more matches.

I think of these things and once again I am afraid.

STRAIGHT AHEAD *

Anonymous

Do you think I am taking the easy way out? Do you think it is hard to follow the same pattern I have followed from infancy, the same pattern my parents have always followed? Do you think it is easy for me to look for the first time at Darwin and evolution, at Protozoa and *Homo sapiens*, at atoms and molecules and run right back to the church without thinking, without reasoning?

I cannot read Robinson Jeffers and automatically repeat, "Peace and good will . . . faith, hope, love. . . ." I cannot do anything until I find a solution, not your solution, not the preacher's solution, not my next-door neighbor's, not my professor's, but MY solution.

Maybe I'll reach the same conclusion that you have. Maybe I'll come stumbling back . . . maybe I already suspect that you're right, but first, first, I must search it out for myself. I must let my spirit catapult through the darkness until it trips and falls at your feet or goes rocketing into emptiness.

I cannot accept what was good enough for my grandparents;

my world is different, my problems different. What did they know of bombs and atoms and communism? They only knew the soil and the sun and the stars. It fit; it was logic; it was perpetuity. And I stare at my world. Headlines and babies, Bibles and test tubes. They are like magnetized poles, only all the poles are north. I move them, I juggle them, I throw them, and they always repel each other. . . .
Help me now, not in your way but in your understanding. Don't shake your head and give me up as lost and evil. I'm trying . . . and bit by bit my feet will ooze out of the quicksands and I will be free.

EVERYTHING POTENT IS DANGEROUS [2]

Wallace Stegner

It is terribly difficult to say honestly, without posing or faking, what one truly and fundamentally believes. Reticence or an itch to make public confession may distort or dramatize what is really there to be said, and public expressions of belief are so closely associated with inspirational activity, and in fact so often stem from someone's desire to buck up the downhearted and raise the general morale, that belief becomes an evangelical matter.

In all honesty, what I believe is neither inspirational nor evangelical. Passionate faith I am suspicious of because it hangs witches and burns heretics, and generally I am more in sympathy with the witches and heretics than with the sectarians who hang and burn them. I fear immoderate zeal, Christian, Moslem, Communist, or whatever, because it restricts the range of human understanding and the wise reconciliation of human differences, and creates an orthodoxy with a sword in its hand.

I cannot say that I am even a sound Christian, though the code of conduct to which I subscribe was preached more eloquently by Jesus Christ than by any other. About God I simply do not know; I don't think I can know.

However far I have missed achieving it, I know that moderation is one of the virtues I most believe in. But I believe as well in a

[2] Edward R. Murrow and Edward P. Morgan, *This I Believe*, First Series, Simon and Schuster, 1952.

whole catalogue of Christian and classical virtues: in kindness and generosity, in steadfastness and courage and much else. I believe further that good depends not on things but on the use we make of things. Everything potent, from human love to atomic energy, is dangerous; it produces ill about as readily as good; it becomes good only through the control, the discipline, the wisdom with which we use it. Much of this control is social, a thing which laws and institutions and uniforms enforce, but much of it must be personal, and I do not see how we can evade the obligation to take full responsibility for what we individually do. Our reward for self-control and the acceptance of private responsibility is not necessarily money or power. Self-respect and the respect of others are quite enough.

All this is to say that I believe in conscience, not as something implanted by divine act, but as something learned from infancy from the tradition and society which has bred us. The outward forms of virtue will vary greatly from nation to nation; a Chinese scholar of the old school, or an Indian raised on the *Vedas* and the *Bhagavad Gita*, has a conscience that will differ from mine. But in the essential outlines of what constitutes human decency we vary amazingly little. The Chinese and the Indian know as well as I do what kindness is, what generosity is, what fortitude is. They can define justice quite as accurately. It is only when they and I are blinded by tribal and denominational narrowness that we insist upon our differences and can recognize goodness only in the robes of our own crowd.

Man is a great enough creature and a great enough enigma to deserve both our pride and our compassion, and engage our fullest sense of mystery. I shall certainly never do as much with my life as I want to, and I shall sometimes fail miserably to live up to my conscience, whose word I do not distrust even when I can't obey it. But I am terribly glad to be alive; and when I have wit enough to think about it, terribly proud to be a man and an American, with all the rights and privileges that those words connote; and most of all I am humble before the responsibilities that are also mine. For no right comes without a responsibility, and being born luckier than most of the world's millions, I am also born more obligated.

QUESTIONS

What specific problem is the central idea of "I Am Afraid"? Does the writer offer a solution, either whole or partial, to his problem? What is the aim or the topic of his first paragraph? Of his last paragraph? What kind of transitions does he use? Is his organization as a whole effective or ineffective? What comparisons or figures of speech does he use? Do you agree or disagree with the point of view he expresses? Does his sketch have power? What reasons can you give for thinking that it does or does not have power?

Whom is the writer of "Straight Ahead" addressing? Or at least, what type of person is being addressed? What is the writer's central idea, or what is the problem? Is it stated or implied? Is any solution suggested? What is the effect of the sketch on you as a reader? Does it have power? Give reasons for your answer.

What does the title "Everything Potent Is Dangerous" really mean as the author applies it in his article? Which paragraph relates directly to the title? What does the writer say about the ease or difficulty of setting down honest beliefs? Does your experience lead you to the same conclusion or a different one? What is his important statement about the Christian religion? About God? What virtue does he name as an outstanding one? What other virtues does he value? How does he measure the "good" in things? What does he say about the social or the personal control of potent things? What are and what are not necessarily the rewards of personal control? How does he define conscience? Do you agree or disagree with his definition? What value judgment does he express about conscience? What does he say about the universality of the "outward forms of virtue"? The universality of the "essential outlines" of human decency?

23

Criticism [1]

Your composition at the end of this chapter is the writing of a criticism, probably of literature, since the discussion which follows is pointed toward it. Since criticism includes praise and condemnation you may evaluate any type, good or bad, that interests you. You may criticize an individual movie or a type of movie, either seriously or satirically. You may evaluate the comments on people in the work of a great cartoonist, as John Mason Brown estimated the work of Helen Hokinson. If you have the background, you may discuss a piece of music, a painting, a school of painters, a specific performance by a jazz band, an orchestra, a ballet dancer, or a program given by musicians or ballet dancers. As you read this chapter you can be making up your mind about your subject and your point of view.

THE MEANING OF CRITICISM

What is criticism? It is an evaluation which brings out merits or defects or a blend of them, depending on the critic and the subject. It is not limited to literature or the fine arts; it is part of your daily life. If you leave half a piece of pie because the crust is tough though the filling is good, you have a set of standards for pies. If you reject your pie because the crust is not salty enough, though it is just right for your friends, you are still applying standards but

[1] Some of these ideas were used in an appendix to *Interpreting Experience*, Pearl Hogrefe and W. Paul Jones (eds.), Ginn and Company, 1935.

450

personal ones. Every day, you accept or reject people as friends, as fraternity or sorority members; your decision is based on conscious or unconscious criticism. Choosing and buying an article of clothing is a critical process. Testing an engine is a critical process carried out best by those who have exact knowledge about what to expect of the best engines under certain conditions. Though you may also be concerned about some quality which you value in an engine, universal standards (a *norm* for engine efficiency) are more important than personal taste.

Your criticism of food, clothing, machinery, or people in daily life may sometimes be superficial, like some literary criticism; but good criticism of life or of literature is thoughtful and based on knowledge. At some stage you need to be cool, impersonal, and detached, not biased and irrational; but after you have found that something is worthy, your criticism may become emotional, warm, personal, sympathetic. Sound criticism is never all prejudice; it is based on a sense of values; it combines emotion and intellect.

Criticism, then, is an evaluation which may bring out merits or defects, a process which one applies to something almost every moment of his waking life, as well as to life and literature, a judgment influenced by emotion but based on values and knowledge.

THE MEANING OF LITERATURE

Before you criticize literature, perhaps you need to review briefly its nature and purpose. In this discussion *literature* is used to mean reading that has human values, not trivial or superficial reading. "Light reading" that rests the mind without weakening or degrading it may be harmless, but it is not literature as the term is used here. Literature is not intended primarily to give a reader facts above geography, or history, or economics, or strange climates, to confirm a reader in a view of life which he already holds, or to teach a moral by direct methods, though it is seldom great literature unless it has ethical implications. It does not exist in order to make a reader forget reality. Indirectly it may do one or more of these things, but it cannot truly be called literature for these things alone. The main purpose of literature, perhaps, is to enlarge, clarify, and enrich human experience; to "reach the secret spring of responsive emotions"; to clarify for a reader his attitudes to himself, his own experience, other people, and the problems of his world; and thus to develop a sense of values.

Great literature has genuineness and depth of feeling; it often presents a writer's profound beliefs about human life. It may set forth artistically all that the sciences have been able to discover about people, as well as the writer's observations of life. It is free from sentimentality, from exaggerated, superficial, insincere feeling, free from shoddiness in form and content.

Great literature has imagination. To bring out his personal truth the writer usually creates something that has not existed in the exact form of his creation. He may bring out the inner meaning of a situation, an action, or a character; thus he uses interpretative imagination. He may even use fantasy to interpret his truth.

Great literature, it has been said, usually has ethical or moral implications. Perhaps the statement needs some qualification, whether the literature is "a criticism of life," as Mathew Arnold maintained, or "an enlargement of experience." Sometimes an enlargement of experience may be amoral. Sometimes the most profound truths about human life (its transitory quality, its blend of joy and sorrow, its flashes of beauty, its ugliness) have little direct relation to precepts about human conduct; and yet they interpret life. And neither the evil character nor the evil deed alone makes literature immoral; the test is the writer's attitude. When a writer presents unsocial or perverted actions as if they are desirable or weaves a covering of beauty to make them attractive, his work is immoral. Great literature, then, may perhaps be amoral occasionally but not immoral.

Great literature usually has a twofold claim to greatness: form and content. Its form makes its content effective without waste of space; its wording, though it may be simple, bears rereading and conveys to thoughtful readers what the writer thinks and feels. (Of course it does not convey its meaning to every superficial reader without any effort on his part.) Content is more important than form; words without meaning are "sounding brass or a tinkling cymbal." Great literature has both form and content.

THE POSSIBLE EFFECTS OF LITERATURE

The effects of literature are likely to be important when you try to estimate your reading. First, from thoughtful reading you may gain a better understanding of other people. The writer who creates a flesh-and-blood character, like Hamlet, Lord Jim, or Soames Forsyte, knows human nature and gives a complete view of his character through talk, action, and even analysis. Unaided by reading, you might spend years getting less knowledge about one person, although you need also to supplement your reading by observing life. Such reading, then, is vicarious experience in human emotions and values. Second, if "to know all is to forgive all" or even to forgive much, such reading will develop your sympathy and tolerance. Third, you may also learn to understand, develop, and control yourself. As a thoughtful reader, you tend to estimate yourself in relation to the situations, characters, and emotions you meet in reading. Thus you may realize your weakness and your strength. Since emotion is the basis of nearly all human action, especially in crises, most of us need to train our emotions toward socialized action, control, and wise enjoyment. You may derive even these values best from literature that does not stress direct lessons in morals but presents truth as the writer sees it. Fourth, as a thoughtful reader you may learn also that your inner experiences are not isolated but universal. You may endure sorrows which others have met bravely, avoid errors which others have regretted, and come to feel a little less lonely in a vast universe, one in which man seems a late accident, not the center and the cause of all creation. Fifth, in thoughtful reading you may find some outlet for your own emotions and a vacation from yourself, a vacation surpassing one you could find in drink, in drugs, or in other people.

THE APPROACH TO CRITICISM

If literature has these qualities and effects, how can you begin to criticize it? You may be aided in a fair-minded approach by asking yourself these questions: First, just what has the writer tried to do? What is his artistic aim? Second, has he succeeded or failed in his aim? Where and when? By what methods and techniques? Third, was his aim worth while? You may need to summon all your breadth and tolerance for the third question. If you prefer beauty in literature, can you admit possible values in pain and ugliness?

If you can answer the third question well, the three will give you a basic approach to all literature.

You may need to recall that there are three kinds of criticism: historical criticism, criticism by the use of standards you assume to be somewhat universal, and impressionistic or personal criticism. If you estimate the influence of a writer or a single work of his upon writers who followed him, you use historical criticism. If you use standards, you assume that certain qualities tend to appear in all great literature or at least in certain types of it. The attempt to define or explain great literature earlier in the chapter made use of such standards as universality, power and genuineness of feeling, ethical implications, and freedom from direct moralizing. If you use impressionistic or personal criticism, you tell us what you think and feel. Personal criticism, unchecked by more objective standards, may be narrow or superficial; but when your opinions are carefully chosen and based upon some knowledge of literary history and of universal standards, they are the heart of your criticism.

PRACTICAL SUGGESTIONS FOR YOUR CRITICISM

The first essential in making any judgment on literature is knowledge. You cannot criticize until you understand *as a unit* the piece of literature before you, even if you must give it several readings and look up some key words in the dictionary. You will not achieve this understanding by hasty, uneven reading. Since the last part of any unit is likely to be the most important, you will give it special attention but will relate it to the whole. To understand the full meaning of most literature you must use your senses; you must see, hear, touch, taste, or smell as the writer wishes. You must hear the words, not merely see symbols on a page. You must hear poetry especially; but much great prose will give up its full meaning in thought and in emotional values when you hear the words, even when you read them aloud several times. The writer has used creative imagination; try to meet him halfway; re-create his thought with your mind, your senses, and your emotions. Be a creative reader.

The second essential is fairness. As a human being you have prejudices from training and environment, from race, religion, politics, and occupations, and from your locality. Try to recognize these attitudes and to detect good qualities in spite of your prejudices. Try to reach the stage of saying, "That writer contradicts one of my cherished and fundamental beliefs, but he achieves his aim with vividness and power."

The third essential is the ability to analyze a piece of writing, just as you analyzed other people and yourself. Again, analysis is hard because thinking is hard for nearly all of us. Other people cannot teach you to think; they can sometimes help you a little. The initiative must come from yourself. The three major questions in the preceding section are a beginning. If you are dealing with fiction, you may analyze the theme or meaning, the conflict or plot, the characters, and the setting (the time, place, atmosphere, social conditions), and then try to determine which of these elements are important. You may break each of these down into other questions: What action predominates? Physical, emotional, or intellectual action? What are the opposing forces in the conflict? Which wins? Is suspense maintained? Is the ending happy or sad? Is the ending justified? Who is the principal character? What functions do the minor characters serve? Are the characters types or individuals? What methods of character portrayal does the author use? Do the situations or conflicts grow out of character? If you are trying to write criticism of poetry, you need some knowledge of form (rhythm, meter, rhyme, stanzas, assonance, alliteration and other elements of tone color). Unless you have this background from previous study, consult books on poetry, or confine your writing of criticism to prose. Any type of prose has its own special problems, its own approaches that are best for analysis, whether you are dealing with biography, autobiography, essays, or discussions of world problems. Perhaps the only sound advice that can be given you here is not to choose areas in which you lack background unless you have the time to get more knowledge.

The fourth essential is to choose something near your own interests as well as your own knowledge. If you like drama but do not understand poetry yet, you will write a better paper on drama. If you like *The Devil's Disciple* by Shaw, and dislike *The Admirable Crichton* and all of Barrie's work, you might do better on Shaw, unless your dislike of Barrie moves you to satire.

The fifth essential is to select a definite, limited central idea, probably by the same methods recommended in Chapter 21. Jot down your ideas, arrange, eliminate, make a tentative outline, and restate your central idea until a useful plan finally emerges. Early in this process, understand your own attitude to your material, estimate your reader and know the effect you would like your work to have on him, and then find supporting details. When you limit your central idea to something you know and are interested in and when you acknowledge your limitations, you have laid the foundation for work that your reader can respect. When you begin with a central idea like this one, you have given yourself a large and vague order: *John Doe does good character work in his novels.* When you limit yourself to this idea you have a better chance of succeeding: *In John Doe's story called "The Wanderings of James Elton" the main character is as real to me as the members of my own family.* Then start asking yourself why, when, where he is real, how the writer makes him real, what *reality* means—and you are off to a good start.

The sixth essential is to test your opinions carefully, instead of jumping at hasty conclusions. Consider them in relation to the writer's main purpose and to each other; test your own supporting ideas in relation to the central idea.

WRITING YOUR COMPOSITION

A. Write a criticism of a story, a poem, a personal essay, or some other single piece of literature. Use historical and personal criticism, and also evaluation by general standards, as you and your subject require them. Limit your central idea. Do not attempt too much in mere quantity and do not be a fence-straddler who says "I like some things about this poem and I do not like some other things." Of course you may concede in your introduction that there are some things you dislike in a good poem and some things you like in a bad poem; but do not write on a poem or any other piece of literature until your central idea is definite enough to control your organization.

B. Write an impressionistic or a personal criticism of some piece of literature. Before you plan your work, examine your prejudices to see if they are completely out of hand and check yourself carefully by some universal standards. But when you know your attitude and your central idea, when you are ready to write, state your opinions firmly without undue apology for them.

C. Write a satirical criticism of a specific piece of literature.

D. Write a satirical criticism of some type of literature.

E. Write a criticism of one of the other arts: a Beethoven symphony or sonata, a Gershwin composition, a performance by an orchestra or an individual musician, a painting or a type of painting, a ballet performance, a movie, the performance of one actor in a play or a movie, etc. Limit carefully by phrasing your central idea to indicate your attitude and your scope.

READING

A RECURRING BLIGHT: THE WASTELAND *

Wayne Billings

The Wasteland by T. S. Eliot is a cold catalog of the diseases and symptoms of the time following the Great War, of the peculiar and deadly changes that occurred in people then. These changes are—or were—in the reactions of the human mind to common situations. And if the things that scuttle through that postwar desolation of humanity typify these changes, the times were enough to make the skin crawl. For the characters are spectral, insubstantial, like the phantoms one sometimes imagines in the darkness. And their emotions are undisguised and tangled. I think Eliot wanted it so. To him London was the unreal city, the mirror in which the reflections of hollow people drifted and changed.

What people?

There is Stetson, whose wife has decomposed in his garden this past year.

There is the couple playing chess:

"My nerves are bad tonight. Yes, bad. Stay with me.

"Speak to me. Why do you never speak? Speak.

"What are you thinking of? What thinking? What?

"I never know what you are thinking. Think."

And he thought:

I think we are in rat's alley.

Where the dead men lose their bones.

Narrating all this is the Theban seer, Tiresias, fatalistically foreseeing, somberly telling. Tiresias is gripped by a paralysis of will. He sees, sees clearly; he cannot act, just as a spectator at a play doesn't act. I believe Eliot identifies himself with the Theban. Eliot sees the barrenness, but can only suggest its cure.

Sometimes the people were to me inscrutable in their relation to the scenes depicted. I would cite Mr. Eugenides, the Smyrna merchant (selling currants) who, between an observation of a city-riverbank and an illegitimate love-passion, invites Tiresias (Eliot) for a weekend. Eugenides supposedly merges into a drowned Phoenician after an interval of 100 lines. This connection is arbitrary and explained in a note at the poem's end. Here *Wasteland's* thought was broken for me.

The collection of notes attached to the work points out the derivation from certain books of particular ideas, the melting of one character into another. In general, I believe this is distracting and needless. Poetry is a form of emotion and thought communication. If a writer cannot express his perceptions without five pages of notation, his creation is incomplete. Eliot occasionally perplexes me by inserting German, French, Latin and Greek into his lines. Perhaps what I missed thus was fairly unimportant, but the human mind is just inquiring enough to be perturbed. A refined form of torment. Certainly I didn't—and don't—understand the significance of each English word. Yet enough was retained that I am not sorry I read and re-read *The Wasteland*.

Perhaps because of Eliot's repeated settings in stony worn-down voids, this work carries a menace of something terrible having happened from a remote, undetermined time down to the present. And the present is desiccated and pointless, like a cat skeleton in anatomy class. A war has ended. Many wars have ended before; this has been one muddled era too many. Man the social animal is becoming man the calculating animal. It is a cannibal's disease, this slickness, this preying on each other. We shall all die in Bedlam, biting each other's jugular veins.

"We who were living are now dying.

With a little patience."

Somewhat similar conditions exist now as in 1922. A state of caution exists. We seem to hang in a transition from one war to another. And the personal problem is to preserve our native enterprise and natural inquiry among the caution. Those of us who cannot retain a certain daring almost certainly fall into apathy. The virtue of *Wasteland* is its pitiless catalog of subverted, twisted human beings. Maybe in time it will become a bit of historical insight, provided the thought police haven't censored it.

OBJECTION SUSTAINED! [2]

Newman Levy

I was born and reared in the practice of law. While other boys frivoled away their time with air rifles, slingshots, baseball bats, and similar lethal weapons of youth, I used to sit indoors playing contentedly with a demurrer or a subpoena duces tecum that had been given to me by my doting parents. Demurrers have been abolished in New York State, but I still remember with affection those cherished playthings of my childhood.

These early habits still cling to me. When I go to the movies I like to see a picture about law and lawyers. This is not a busman's holiday; rather it is a pleasant escape from the realities of my daily occupation.

For the practice of law, as it is revealed upon the screen, bears about as much resemblance to the real thing as Walter Huston does, let us say, to Ambassador Davies. Motion-picture law is a rare and beautiful thing, and if lawyers and judges were not so tied down to crusty tradition they might learn some useful lessons, and the world would be a sweeter and better place.

Judges in the movies are invariably dignified, courteous, and handsome. This is not an important departure from realism, although it is one that will immediately be observed by any experienced lawyer. The judicial charm and urbanity are compensated for, however, by a serene ignorance of the elementary rules of law, a condition that happily does not exist in real life. These judges never fail to sustain the bad objections and overrule the good ones, and their comments from the bench must undoubtedly cause the

[2] *Atlantic Monthly*, January, 1944.

late lamented Chancellor Kent to spin dizzily in his grave. Their record of reversals on appeal I am sure is staggering.

A few years ago I made a discovery that throws some light upon the eccentricities of Hollywood law. I was visiting a studio where a courtroom scene was being shot. I walked over to the judge's bench during a lull in the proceedings to examine the ponderous tomes that he was studying so learnedly. One was the Los Angeles Directory for 1932, one was the Motion Picture Register, and there were three novels of Bulwer-Lytton. How can you expect legal erudition from that kind of library? I knew that judge was a fraud the moment I saw how polite he was.

The most fascinating thing to me about a motion-picture trial is its gay, unrestrained informality. Everybody takes part just as in the Town Hall Meeting of the Air, and if Lionel Barrymore is in the courtroom he answers the judge back and calls him Henry.

It's all nice and friendly. Spectators keep bobbing up from all parts of the courtroom to prompt the witnesses and interject unsolicited remarks into the record. The defense lawyer, who, judging from the way he tries his case, seems to have gone to the same law school as the judge, never bothers to object to the unorthodox procedure. Perhaps he has a premonition that the missing witness, who is speeding along the highway at ninety miles an hour, will arrive just in time to dash into the courtroom, upsetting court officers and spectators, rush into the witness box, and exonerate the defendant by confessing that he did the murder himself. So why should the lawyer worry about an occasional procedural irregularity?

I wonder if the jolly, carefree atmosphere of these trials may not be due to the fact that they generally turn out to be family affairs. It is astonishing how everybody is related. I remember one case in which the defendant was the young lawyer's long-lost mother, one in which the district attorney was engaged to the defendant's daughter, and one in which the judge was found to be the childhood sweetheart of the murderer's mother. It has been revealing to observe how often the judiciary is romantically involved in these cases. Many times in the midst of a discouraging litigation I have wished that the judges before whom I practice had not lived such impeccable sex lives. It would be comforting to know that even though my adversary had me licked on the law and facts, the sour-faced judge on the bench was nursing a secret passion for my client's aunt.

2

The busy lawyer who spends his days tangled up in the intricacies of legal procedure must be filled with envy at the charming simplicity of the Hollywood system. Take the foreclosure of a mortgage, for instance. Ordinarily this is a job that involves a considerable amount of work, delay, and red tape. In Hollywood, however, all that is needed is to walk into the premises and wave a document with a large seal on it in the face of the frightened victim. Fortunately the method of canceling a mortgage is equally simple. Someone, generally the missing son, dashes in from Alaska, South America, or somewhere, snatches the document, and tears it into fragments. That is all there is to it. No fuss, no red tape, no filing fees.

There is one curious misapprehension I have met repeatedly in motion pictures, and that is that a wife may not be a witness against her husband. I cannot recall how many beautiful girls I have seen cajoled or coerced into unwilling matrimony to seal their lips. Of course, the opposite is the fact. A wife may testify against her husband—which Hollywood could have discovered by the simple device of asking some lawyer. Maybe they found this statement of law in the Los Angeles Directory.

There are dangers in the practice of motion-picture law that might well terrify the genuine practitioner whose greatest occupational hazards are nervous indigestion and disbarment. I do not refer to such elementary risks as drinking poison in the courtroom, which, I am informed, was a customary practice of those real-life mouthpieces, Earl Rogers and Bill Fallon. Any lawyer worthy of the name will take a dose of cyanide in his stride.

No, practicing law on the screen is a man's job, and the successful practitioner has to combine the qualities of a Demosthenes and a commando. I have in mind as an illustration a masterpiece in technicolor that I saw recently (the name escapes me), in which the guilt or innocence of the defendant depended upon whether the body of the alleged victim was at the bottom of the sea in a shipwrecked vessel. Most of my cowardly associates would have hired a professional diver to go down and find out. Possibly I might have done so myself. But not the lawyer in this case. He said he was going down in a diver's suit and find out himself if the girl was there.

It was what the Lord Chancellor in *Iolanthe* would have described as "a nice point." The judge pleaded with him and tried to dissuade him. There was nothing in Pollock on Torts on the subject, nor in Chitty on Pleading. It was doubtful whether even Clarence Darrow had ever donned a diver's outfit. But this young lawyer was determined, and down he went. After battling with an octopus and also with the real murderer—who happened to be in the neighborhood also in a diving outfit—and after the air tube became hopelessly clogged up, he emerged at length, breathless, but triumphantly clutching a fragment of the corpus delicti. It was the sort of thing that made me proud of my profession and glad that I had not taken up undertaking or plumbing instead.

Sometimes when the daily grind becomes particularly vexatious I wish rather wistfully that I had been admitted to practice at the Motion Picture Bar. It might be disconcerting to discover that the client I was defending for felonious assault was none other than my little sister who had run away to sea in her infancy, and that the judge who looked so stern and imposing in his silken robe was still cherishing a sprig of mignonette that my mother had given him fifty years ago. But it would be consoling to know that, after I had acquitted my client, Paulette Goddard, Rita Hayworth, and Lana Turner would be waiting in the courtroom to fold me in their arms and tell me what a great guy I was.

LOGICAL PATTERN IN SHELLEY'S LYRICS [3]

Stopford A. Brooke

Finally, I should like to dwell on the unconscious logic in arrangement of some of Shelley's lyrics. I have said of a certain class of them that they have little clearness or method, or continuity of thought or emotion. They wander and drift, as it were, without

[3] *Studies in Poetry*, Stopford A. Brooke, G. P. Putnam's Sons, 1907.

an aim. But with others, and those the best, it is not so, but the very contrary. They have a logical arrangement of their own. This is not so uncommon a thing in poetry as those imagine who think that the poet, driven by a kind of divine mania beyond himself, works without knowing where he is going or how he will get to the end. There is a logic of emotion as well as of thought, and though it does produce itself without a previous scheme, it appears when the lyric is done, and, if the poet have great genius, in a clear order which may be subjected by those who are not the poet himself to an analysis as rigid as that to which we can subject a great musical composition. The poet himself is indeed swept away, but all throughout his torrent movement he follows a course which is obedient to a development of his emotion as natural and as orderly as a process of nature. I think this is true with regard to all the great lyrics of the world; and it is true especially of Shelley, because his intellect played so large a part in the whole of his work. It was accustomed to do close work, and when the emotion was first, as it is in poetry, and carried him away, his intellect, in rejoicing subordination, went with the emotion, working in harmony with it and working as a willing servant, so that the result, which was fully emotional, possessed also an intellectual order. I suggest one example in the little lyric—*When the Lamp Is Shattered*. The first verse uses four comparisons to illustrate the passing of love. These are taken up and re-used in different ways throughout the rest of the poem, as if they were four themes which a musician brings in, at intervals, into the main idea, in order to emphasize various forms of its passion. It is a subtle weaving, but a reader, similarly emotionalised as the poet, may pass easily and clearly through its labyrinth. Such a logic of emotion may be found throughout *Epipsychidion*, where metaphors seem to run riot. They are all really held in hand. I give another instance from *Alastor*, where Shelley is describing the dying frame of the wanderer:

> A fragile lute, on whose harmonious strings
> The breath of heaven did wander—a bright stream
> Once fed with many-voiced waves—a dream
> Of youth, which night and time have quenched for ever,
> Still, dark, and dry, and unremembered now.

The last line takes up in its adjectives the three illustrations. The lute is still, the stream is dark and dry, the dream is unremembered. But the finest example of this characteristic quality is the *Ode to the West Wind*, and though I do not like analyzing a poem any more than I care to dissect a flower, yet for once, and to see Shelley's way, and as conclusion and illustration of this essay, it may be permitted.

He has been walking by the Arno, in the wood which skirts it, among the fallen leaves, and has seen the congregated clouds rising from the south-west to usher in the yearly storm with which the autumnal rains begin in October in Italy; and the tempestuous motion of the trees and the clouds awakens the tempestuous passion of his heart, so easily raised, so stormily uplifted, so transient when its power was spent. Then the impulse from without and the awakened impulse within, mingling in passionate embrace, brought forth the poem. I can well imagine the first lines leaping from his lips in a moment—thought, emotion, metre, movement—all rushing together into a self-creation.

It begins with the West Wind rushing through the wood like a living river, and bearing with it the dead leaves—yellow and black and hectic red—the Destroyer, the wild spirit who buries the dead. But with the dead leaves are also the winged seeds which the wind too bears to their rest, where they may quicken when Spring blows her clarion—Preserver, then, as well as Destroyer.

I

O wild West Wind, thou breath of Autumn's being,
Thou, from whose unseen presence the leaves dead
Are driven, like ghosts from an enchanter fleeing,

Yellow, and black, and pale, and hectic red,
Pestilence-stricken multitudes; O thou
Who chariotest to their dark wintry bed

The wingèd seeds, where they lie cold and low,
Each like a corpse within its grave, until
Thine azure sister of the Spring shall blow

Her clarion o'er the dreaming earth, and fill
(Driving sweet buds like flocks to feed in air)
With living hues and odours plain and hill:

Wild Spirit, which art moving everywhere;
Destroyer and Preserver: hear, oh, hear!

The same theme is repeated, with clear strange changes, in the sky, then in the ocean, then in Shelley's own heart, and then for the whole of man. Nothing can be intellectually clearer than the order, and yet the emotion is always the master, the lord of the poem. Nay more, the images used in these several repetitions are similar, though fresh images are continually added.

He sees in the sky, where the storm is beginning, the same things he has seen in the wood. Heaven, and ocean from whose bosom all the waters came, are now the great forest through which the wind is sweeping like a broad and surging river. The sky, before the huge mass of cloud brings with it the steady wind, is full of rushing and separate avant-couriers of small dark clouds, red and pale and black, that fly over the sky. These are the leaves of this forest of the sky, and are shaken down upon the stream and surge of the wind. That image then, and daring it is, is bound up with and repeats the first verse. But Shelley, thrilled, as he looked, by the splendour of the tempest, and driven by his emotion to change the image that he might better feel the passion of the hour and represent it better, now sees the coming clouds like the pageant of the burial of the year; a vast and congregated procession, to which night is the sepulchral dome, and out of which black rain and fire and hail will burst—new images of that which he originally imagined as the black and red leaves of the wood. Before this the loose clouds fly like Maenads, their locks blown forward by the wind, and the wind itself is the dirge of the year, the impersonated sorrow of all that has been, but which it now destroys. For in this verse that side of the West Wind which makes it the Destroyer, and not the Preserver, the God that slays rather than saves, is given.

II

Thou on whose stream, 'mid the steep sky's commotion,
Loose clouds like earth's decaying leaves are shed,
Shook from the tangled boughs of Heaven and Ocean,

Angels of rain and lightning: there are spread
On the blue surface of thine aery surge,
Like the bright hair uplifted from the head

Of some fierce Maenad, even from the dim verge
Of the horizon to the zenith's height,
The locks of the approaching storm.   Thou dirge

Of the dying year, to which this closing night
Will be the dome of a vast sepulchre,
Vaulted with all thy congregated might

Of vapours, from whose solid atmosphere
Black rain and fire and hail will burst: oh, hear!

But the next verse shows the West Wind as the kindlier impetuosity of the universe. The theme in the first verse of the wind
as the Preserver, as the giver of life, as life itself, is taken up. The
wind wakens now the blue Mediterranean, for we have passed
from the forest, from the wind on the earth, from the wind in the
sky, to the wind upon the sea. He wakens the loveliness of the
isles in Baiae's bay; he disturbs the sleep of the waters in which
lay the old palaces and towers—freshly, brightly disturbs them.
Then the theme changes as before: one picture is not enough for
Shelley, nor one aspect of his theme. We are swept back again into
the thought of the wind as Destroyer. From the Mediterranean
we are borne into the Atlantic, and again the original image recurs.
The sea itself is like the forest. It cleaves itself into chasms before
the fierce stream of the wind. The woods of ocean, the sea-blooms,
and the sapless foliage grow gray with fear, and tremble and
despoil themselves.

III

Thou who didst waken from his summer dreams
The blue Mediterranean, where he lay,
Lulled by the coil of his crystalline streams,

Beside a pumice isle in Baiae's bay;
And saw in sleep old palaces and towers
Quivering within the wave's intenser day,

All overgrown with azure moss and flowers
So sweet, the sense faints picturing them! Thou
For whose path the Atlantic's level powers

Cleave themselves into chasms, while far below
The sea-blooms and the oozy woods which wear
The sapless foliage of the ocean, know

Thy voice, and suddenly grow gray with fear,
And tremble and despoil themselves: Oh, hear!

Then in the next verse, having finished with earth and sky and
sea, he takes up a side issue of emotion, which has reference to
himself—he who is earth and sky and sea in one. Enthralled by the
swiftness and strength of the wind, he wishes to be lifted and
borne on the river of its strength. But even then he does not forget
to link this new issue to the original theme. He takes up forest and
sky and ocean in his repeating way: If I were a dead leaf thou
mightest bear—If I were a swift cloud to fly with thee—If I were
a wave to share the impulse of thy strength—If I were even what
I was when young I seemed thy equal, scarce less swift than thou
—I would not be so full of prayer to thee; but I am as weak as thou
art strong. O lift me—and again knitting his thought into his
emotion, not letting us loose from the first theme, he repeats in
change the images: "O lift me as a wave, a leaf, a cloud."

I know nothing of music, but if this is not like the way a musician works his changes, I should be surprised.

Then, lastly, he returns from this side issue to the main emotion
and the main image. He himself is now the forest, his leaves are
falling. They are his thoughts, multitudes of which have withered
and died. Through him the wind is passing, the wind of the universe, and it drives his thoughts along. But as it passes it makes harmonies in him. He is the lyre on which the wind plays. In that way
he describes how the poem arose, how all poems about nature are
born. There is nothing about destruction in this verse, but there
is of waking and kindling. The impetuosity and strength of the
wind—it is now a spiritual power of the universe—has entirely
since the last stanza quenched in Shelley's mind the thought of
the wind as a Destroyer. That part of the theme is exhausted, but
the thought of the wind as the Preserver, which was barely touched
before, is dominant in the last; and Shelley, now at the very height
of passion and in full union with the tempest, which is about
to burst in rain and splendour, calls on the wind to be himself, to
drive with it his dead thoughts—the winged seeds which are in
them, as germs are in the flying leaves of the wood, thus recalling
again the original image—to quicken a new life in mankind.

V

Make me thy lyre, even as the forest is:
What if my leaves are falling like its own!
The tumult of thy mighty harmonies

Will take from both a deep, autumnal tone,
Sweet though in sadness. Be thou, Spirit fierce,
My Spirit! Be thou me, impetuous one!

Drive my dead thoughts over the Universe
Like withered leaves to quicken a new birth!

But as before, uncontent with a single image, he repeats the same thought in another image, still, however, clinging close to the wind, and images an unextinguished fire in his heart, each spark of which is a thought. Over this fire the rushing wind is blowing, and bears on its wings the living embers to kindle fire in the souls of men.

And, by the incantation of this verse,

Scatter, as from an unextinguished hearth
Ashes and sparks, my words among mankind!
Be through my lips to unawakened earth

The trumpet of a prophecy!

The last thought has now been reached, the last realm over which the wind is sweeping. It has passed through the forests of earth, through the clouds of the sky, into the depths of ocean, through the woods and sky and ocean of Shelley's heart; and then, at the very point and climax of emotion, it leaves himself and sweeps through all mankind, bearing away with it dead things and the seeds of new. Out of the personal Shelley passes into the universal, and at that moment the future opened to him. Beyond the storm, beyond the winter it ushers in, he sees the new-awakened world, the birth of all the seeds, the outburst as of a spring in humanity:

O, Wind,
If Winter comes, can Spring be far behind?

This is the lyric of lyrics. It is the hymn of our own world. It ought to be set to music by a great musician, but he should have the genius of Beethoven. "Ineffectual Angel!" indeed; nay rather, impassionating Angel!

QUESTIONS

Does the writer of "A Recurring Blight: The Wasteland," use personal criticism, historical criticism, criticism by standards, or a blend of the three? What specific examples do you find of these kinds of criticism? Does he understand the main aim of the writer's work? What admissions does he make about details he does not understand? What is the effect of these admissions on you as a reader? What praise, if any, does he give to the work? What condemnation, if any? Does he arrange his ideas well? Does he use any effective comparisons? Any outstanding diction for his aim? Is his title effective? What is his central idea? Is it implied or directly stated?

In "Objection Sustained!" what is the controlling idea? What is the writer criticizing and what is his real opinion? Is his method satirical, humorous, or an effective combination of the two? Does the division of his article into two parts help you as a reader? Can you apply some of his methods to your own criticism? Which ones, if any?

The "Logical Pattern in Shelley's Lyrics" is part of a longer work. What evidence of this fact do you find in the wording? In the opening paragraph, what is the largest statement of the central idea? Then how does the writer limit it to one poet? To one poem? The writer gradually quotes verbatim four of the five sections of the poem, and he summarizes most of the other section, the fourth; he uses them in the same order Shelley used them. Does this quoting make his criticism more or less effective for you? As he limits to one poem, could you write better criticism by limiting to one poem, one essay, one story? Could you also use some quotations and mention many specific details to support your ideas?

24

Persuasion:

INDIVIDUAL OR SOCIAL PROBLEMS

When you finish reading this chapter, it is assumed, you will write a persuasive composition, either on some significant problem of personal conduct or on some problem of your community—a situation, a custom, a condition, a kind of behavior which is desirable or undesirable for group life. You may interpret *community* as a small or large group, so long as your topic does not require you to do extended research or to give your reader pages of facts and figures before he can understand the problem. Probably your best topics are concerned with your code of personal conduct, your treatment of other people, your beliefs about the world in which you live—all the questions which you must answer before you can live well in your personal world—not problems of the state and nation.

WHAT PERSUASION IS

In the larger sense, of course, all significant fiction is persuasion. If a writer is effective he draws his reader into emotional agreement; he uses "a semblance of truth sufficient to procure . . . that willing suspension of disbelief for the moment, which constitutes poetic faith"; he wins sympathy so that his reader follows him or his character in authentic experience.

But in this chapter you are writing a type of personalized exposition. The term *persuasion* is used here in its smaller or customary meaning; you are trying to get your reader to accept a point of view, to believe something or to do something. Many times, if you accomplish your aim, you must bring about some inner change in him. That, of course, is difficult. If you succeed, you will probably have to appeal to his emotions and satisfy his mind at the same time. Why? First, if your reader is a reasonable creature you probably cannot take his emotions by storm without building upon reason. Second, whether he is rational or not, you have no ethical right to make irrational appeals. Also it is possible that you have no ethical right to conceal from him vital information which would destroy your case, or to persuade him to accept opinions which you do not accept, or to move him to action against his own genuine interests. But you do have every right to urge upon him information he has overlooked, to appeal to his emotions when they are based on reason, to show him broad instead of self-centered interests, long-range instead of immediate and short-sighted interests, and intangible satisfactions rather than material gains. It might be said that the democratic process at its best is merely honest and effective persuasion.

When you use ethical persuasion it is possible that there are four kinds of changes or effects which you may at some time wish to bring about in your reader. First, you wish him to accept facts. Unless he is already hostile, this should be easy. You assemble sound facts and use them in an effective order. Second, you wish him to accept your value judgments. If he is neutral or uninformed (and tractable) your task may be easy; if he is hostile because of deep convictions you may not move him at all or you may merely make him a little more tolerant of your views. Third, you wish your reader to agree that a certain course of action is desirable or practicable or at least to cease his opposition to it. Here your task will vary greatly, depending on him, his reasons for his attitudes, and the possible results so far as he is concerned. It may be easy to secure his passive assent if he fears no personal consequences; if you propose to increase his taxes or to take his home from him by the right of eminent domain, you may have a hopeless battle. Fourth, you wish your reader to take some action himself. Your task here may be rather difficult, unless your reader is already friendly or informed, because you need to bring about some inner change in his attitude and, in addition, overcome his share of human inertia.

BASES OF PERSUASION

How can you plan and write effective persuasion? First, analyze three things: your reader, your own ideas and attitudes as the writer, and your subject.

How can you learn to know the mind of your reader or your potential audience? Listen, if possible, to some person who takes a view opposed to yours; listen to a public address by him, his remarks in a circle of your acquaintances, or have a personal talk with him. Inquire further after you have listened; let him tell you the *why* about every small point, give you examples, and define phrases or terms. Try to keep yourself in the position of a humble inquirer, instead of answering back; this may be harder than you think. Notice especially any objections he is making to what you are going to propose; then plan to meet these objections as you arrange and write your paper. To answer possible objections almost before your reader has thought of them himself may keep him from building a thick wall of hostility and putting himself beyond your power. Know also, in a general way, what your potential reader needs or desires, and what his values are, both his obvious material values and his less tangible inactive desires which might be stirred to life. Know the degree of his hostility or friendliness to your idea; if he is neutral but uninformed, discover that too. When you understand his views and attitudes, you can prepare yourself better to treat him with respect, tolerance, fairness, and courtesy, as well as understanding. You can avoid the overstatements, exaggerations, and assumptions which would alienate him.

There is one other important thing to be recognized about your readers. Do not try to persuade them to some view if they already agree with you one hundred per cent or if they are completely powerless to bring about change. For example, don't try to persuade your classmates that a difficult examination, which they have all resented, should be eliminated. If they resent it, they do not need persuasion. You might try persuading the teacher in charge to eliminate it; if the teacher is a person of integrity and high standards, you have a real problem. Or you might try persuading your classmates that they are getting from that examination values which they really desire when they think honestly about the problem. Here again your audience would furnish a real challenge.

How can you learn your own views and attitudes on your topic? If you really listened to a potential reader, as suggested above, you probably learned much about your own views. You may also have learned much about your attitudes. Did you really succeed in remaining an inquirer? If not, where, on what points did you boil over and start arguing? Why did these points or remarks move you? Can you examine and relieve the pressure at these boiling points? What do you now know about your own prejudices? You might at this stage try to jot down on paper all your beliefs and attitudes, with all the examples, incidents, and specific details which come into your consciousness as you think of them.

The third essential is to know your subject. If you have gone through the processes, described above, of learning an opponent's views and your own reactions, you may think that you already know your subject. But ask yourself now what the real issues are or what the one real issue is. Word the issue or issues as concisely as you can. Do you have your central idea now, or do you still need to shape and reshape your ideas? In either case, examine your wording. Are there loaded words which must be eliminated? A loaded word suggests an emotional bias; usually it is a word that you have no right to use until you have given your reader some reason to agree with you. Are there terms which need to be defined? For example, a group of amatuer writers were in hot disagreement over the question whether they should try to *communicate* in creative writing; they finally discovered that they had entirely different meanings for the word itself. Some assumed that communicating meant expressing everything in simple, matter-of-fact words that a normal child could understand; they refused to be guilty of communicating. Others assumed that communicating meant having an artistic aim, expressing that aim without willful obscurity, and using language appropriate for the writer, for the implications of his subject, and for his chosen and perhaps limited audience. Careful defining might have prevented much waste of emotional words. In the same way, your use of obscure or loaded words will block effective persuasion.

ELIMINATING, ARRANGING

After you have done what you can to know your potential reader, yourself, and your subject, and have stated your central idea in a concise sentence, you are ready to think about eliminating unessential ideas and arranging essential ones. Perhaps you should throw away half or three-fourths of the ideas you have already jotted down. Try to use only essential ideas and the fewest possible number of them. Do not cover in detail ideas on which your opponents agree; do not use dozens of facts if a few will serve your purpose; and do not think that there is virtue in using many arguments if one will serve to persuade. Spend your time and space in making a few ideas vivid and convincing.

Arrangement is extremely important in persuasion; use it to win over your reader. Sometimes you can win him by using a concise, vivid picture in your opening sentences and then saying in persuasive words, "Here is what we need and what we can have if you wish," or "Here is the blight on your community, and it is within your power to remove it." With some subjects you may need to make concessions if you can honestly do so, and to make them as soon as you can. Thus you will please, soothe, and disarm your reader; and you will make your own task easier by getting rid of excess baggage. If you need to define key words you will probably do so in this beginning. When you start arranging main ideas to win your reader, use the simple ideas first and then go on to the difficult and the complex. Or start with what your reader already accepts or with the familiar; lead him gradually to unfamiliar or less acceptable ideas, or show him that your proposal is really part of what is already acceptable to him, although it does not seem so on the surface. Plan to meet his possible objections as you proceed; consider his needs and desires; appeal to them wherever you can. Next, try to show him that what he now understands and finds desirable is also practical. Show him, if you can, that his acceptance will help. Show him what he can do and inspire him to act. But, especially at the end, do not tell him what he should do; avoid that touch of authority. Let him feel that he is deciding. Rhetorical questions, skillfully used, are often effective in the conclusion.

As your aim is not merely to be clear but to influence attitudes or beliefs, use details which appeal to the senses and the emotions all through your composition. These may occasionally come from authority, preferably neutral authority, but they will more often come from your experience. You may use illustrations or examples, figures of speech, extended literal comparisons, and extended similes which are analogies. If you were speaking, you could use gesture and voice for persuasion. In writing you may use repetition, parallel structure, euphony, rhythm, and connotation. You will find rhetorical questions extremely effective, not only in the conclusion but at other strategic places, especially those which impel your reader to make the kind of answer you wish him to make. The reason for the effectiveness of a question is simple. Human beings do not like to be told what they should do; they prefer to be asked, and left to respond with their own answers.

PLANS FOR PERSUASION

Here are some plans for use in persuasion. They have some overlapping which is essential to bring out certain differences.

A. 1. Describe a desirable situation, condition, way of acting, or way of life which now exists.
   2. Explain vividly the forces which threaten destruction.
   3. Show how these forces can be removed or controlled.
   4. Show the reader that he can do something to help.
   5. Give him a final impetus to act.
B. 1. Describe a desirable situation, condition, way of acting, or way of life which does *not* now exist.
   2. Explain vividly the actions which will bring it into existence.
   3. Show that these actions are practical.
   4. Show the reader that he can help.
   5. Give him a final impetus to act.
C. 1. Describe an undesirable situation, condition, way of acting, or way of life which now exists.

2. Show the causes.
3. Show how the causes can be removed, or what the cures are.
4. Show the reader that he can help.
5. Give him a final impetus to act.
D. 1. Describe and explain a problem.
2. Describe vividly a solution.
3. Show the reader how he can help in the solution.
4. Give him an impetus to act.

Here are other specific ways of developing persuasion. Some of them are like specific narrative. Again they show a basic truth, that there is no rigid separation between narration and exposition.

1. A personalized exposition, using *you* and *your*, and addressing the reader directly. This type is a little like a debate speech but is less combative perhaps. It uses connotation, specific details, examples freely.

2. A single specific narrative, well developed to stress the essential ideas without seeming to do so. This might be combined with a conclusion which raises some rhetorical questions; it might also have a similar beginning.

3. A personalized exposition in which the writer uses mainly *I* and *my*, with little or no address to the reader. But he hopes to win the reader's assent to the principles he believes in or upon which he bases action.

4. Two specific narratives or specific pictures, one presenting a desirable and the other an undesirable situation, with brief transitions between and a brief conclusion with rhetorical questions. The aim, of course, is to get the reader to ally himself with the desirable situation.

5. Narrative with talk and action but with typical characters who point out an undesirable course of action unconsciously through what they have or haven't done. For example, two parents discuss with each other the problem of the crowded schools and their four children. They can't understand why "they" voted down the bonds for a new building last year. Quite incidentally they bring out the fact that they themselves did not vote.

6. A monologue in which a speaker is trying to persuade a listener— and incidentally the reader—to a belief or an action. Though this has been used satirically, it may also be used seriously.

WRITING YOUR COMPOSITION

A. Write a persuasive paper on some problem related to individual conduct or individual lives.

B. Write a persuasive paper on some problem larger than individual conduct, one which concerns a community or a large group in the community.

C. Write a persuasive paper, using a satirical style consistently through the whole unit. That is, seem to say literally the opposite of your real belief. Perhaps a problem related to individual conduct will be more desirable to choose for this method.

D. Write a persuasive paper using either a narrative style or a monologue as your method.

READING

FINANCIAL REPORT *

Donna Rae Danielson

Our church's annual financial report—or as it is more commonly known, the "scandal sheet"—arrived a few weeks ago. As usual, it carried the official inscription of our church in precise, Roman lettering, together with the adage "Come unto me, all ye who labor and are heavy laden, and I will give you rest." The incongruity of these words with the contents and purpose of the little pamphlet made me add mentally—"for a price."

There is nothing wrong with a church issuing a financial report, but this one is a good deal more complete than most. Not only does it give the balance in various funds, but it lists each member of the church together with the exact amount he contributed during the preceding year to local funds, missions, and assorted special funds, which include such items as a new furnace, carpet for the parish house, or a remodelling job on the parsonage.

There is a general procedure most members of the congregation follow in absorbing the information contained within the booklet. The first step consists of scanning the column at the far right of each page where the total contributions of each person is listed.

Quite a few "ones" extend beyond the two-digit numbers in the column. This denotes the $100 totals. Several "twos" also are evident. Only two "threes" appear, and by the process of elimination the identity of the year's highest contributor is known. It was a close race this year, but Mr. Martin won out over the wealthiest of the numerous Larson families. This was an unprecedented result, but my father assured my mother this was due to the large amount of money the Martins inherited when Mrs. Martin's Uncle Elmer died. The next step can be accomplished rather quickly. It consists of comparing your own contribution with that of the highest contributor. The speed with which this step is completed depends to a large extent upon the ratio of the two totals. The next step is more tedious. It entails going down the column of names and stopping at those of close friends or relatives. A discussion on why this or that person should or should not have given more or less invariably follows.

It is evident that this financial report makes interesting reading material as well as conversational topics. Too, it serves the purpose for which it was created—a purpose which does not seem definable in any way other than blackmail in dilute form. It is not peculiar that our church, although relatively small, never lacks for money. How many of those two-hundred or one-hundred totals would be cut at least by half if the contributions were not going to be made public? This can be illustrated by an incident involving the previously mentioned new furnace for the church. When one Sunday's offering provided only a small fraction of the amount needed, the minister remarked casually, "Each person's contribution will be published in the financial report." Next Sunday the quota was reached.

The financial report is not used solely for monetary purposes. The authors of the report have a "sly" way of continuing to include the names of people who have married out of the church. Across from their names are conspicuous rows of large black zeros.

Yes, the financial report seems to accomplish its purpose. Our church is economically secure. People give freely—sometimes more freely than they can afford. People have to keep up appearances and on this principle "doth our church flourish." However, I often wonder if the end result is worth the questionable means used to obtain it. Blackmail does not become the church.

WHAT AM I? *

Rosemary Moody

1. I Am a Seeker

Mister, can you tell me? What am I? Where am I going? The man in the black suit says, "You are a child of God. Cast aside worldly things, believe in Him, obey His commandments, and thank Him daily. If you do all this, He will let you into His heavenly city to spend eternity. Now we will pass the collection plate."

The man on the street-corner says, "Yer a fool. Goin' to get licked by the world, kid, that's where yer goin'. Wanta buy a pencil?"

The navigator of a B-29 says, "I dunno. I dunno. It's the good guys that get it. And the world is lousier than before."

Mister, I can't base my life on intuition and folk tales and rose-colored glasses; I won't be sent fleeing to the minister by fear of hell and fear of despair. I shall go to the scientists, to the men who peer through the telescopes and microscopes, who chart and calculate, who doubt until they can doubt no longer. I shall go to the truth-seekers.

2. I Am a Pinpoint

The sun is a gaseous mass 860,000 miles in diameter, premiere danseuse of a troupe of planets, satellites and planetoids, all twirling on their axes and circling about it.

The Earth is a tiny cold ball in black immensity, a speck in the sky which would hardly be missed even by Mars if it suddenly disappeared.

The sun-mother we trail through space has at least a hundred billion star-sisters. We call her family the universe. Beyond it swirl other universes in an endless sky.

Who am I? Why do I crawl microscopic on this cold pellet, with space swishing past my ears at twelve miles a second?

3. My Home Was Sun-Spawned

Two billion years ago the sun spat out a bolt of gas. Gas eddied and merged, liquefied into a molten ball bouncing through sun-nights and days, cloaked in an atmosphere of gases. As it cooled to rock, the gas condensed; rain fell. Rivers cut furrows in the rock, began battering it into soil. The water danced itself into seas. Through the broken clouds knifed the sun-rays.

Life was possible.

Who am I? Why did my home shoot from the sun two billion years ago? Where was I then?

4. My Mother Is a Starfish

Who was my mother? I know only that she rose from the sea. Amoeba . . . sponge . . . seaweed. From her veiled form the centuries dragged life. First tiny crustaceans and sand-burrowing worms. Later armored fishes, fishes with teeth and spines and lungs. Life wriggled up from the sea, grew legs from paddle-fins, conquered the swampy land. Growing and lifting its belly from the ground, it became a dinosaur. It spread out wings and flew. It became a tiny mammal, creeping through time toward higher forms of life, snatching the land from reptiles. Small apes bore larger apes, and then almost imperceptibly the larger apes merged into man. Man—a youngster now just over a million years, a youngster who has been writing himself down only seven thousand years—in a home two billion years old!

I am a newcomer. It took a billion nine hundred million years to bring me forth—and then a million more to bring me even this far. I am a baby in the world.

5. Tomorrow Is My Child

Shall I tell you who I am? I am a creature rising. I am a creature growing now, just as I grew to reach my present stature. I am being shaped by the same mysterious forces that have pushed me this far up the ladder.

As an individual I parallel species-evolution, developing from conception as a one-celled animal to adulthood. Once in a while

I rise above myself—rise to life a hundred thousand years from now. Is it any wonder that sometimes I sink to myself a hundred thousand years ago? Disorder is but a phase in my growth as a species, as ice ages and the crumbling of mountains were phases in my previous development.

I am a humble creature who has learned very little, who tries again and again to revise the process of evolution. I am a sex pervert, a killer, a sadist; I mimic the monkeys and mock the truth-seekers; I challenge the stars and curse them; I try to destroy this world.

The minister says that sin is doing "Thou shalt nots"; but the truth-seeker says that the only wrong I can do is that of scrambling back toward the ape, the dinosaur, the amoeba.

Where I am going, I don't know. At the end of my own life I may sing in a heavenly city or crumble into soil or merge with the wind and stars. Why should I ponder the end of "I"? "I" is a word, a chicken-track in spinning dust; "I" is a balloon pin-pricked by death.

But I am the first paragraph of a story. I cannot believe that only by chance the sun bore a world, that only by chance I inched out of an amoeba. I am a pinpoint, but I am the mother of tomorrow.

This, then, may well be the purpose of my wandering, painful years: to live for the child tomorrow. I sought an ultimate value; I can find it in her glory.

A QUESTION OF VALUES [1]

Paul L. Errington

Over and over again, practitioners in the professional field of wildlife management are asked, and ask themselves, exactly what they work for. To increase game, to make hunting easier, to control pests, to hold their jobs, or what?

Among other things, I suppose that I may be classed as a wildlife manager, having made a living for nearly twenty years by doing research on game birds and fur-bearers and having published find-

[1] Paul L. Errington, "A Question of Values," *Journal of Wildlife Management*, July, 1947. Used by courtesy of the author and the *Journal*.

ings that presumably apply to what is known as management of those species. Like my co-workers in the field, I have been asked, and have asked myself, basic questions.

I am pleased when good use is made of my research by conservation commissions and other practical agencies. Yet, if I felt that I merely worked for a salary and to provide more game for hunters to shoot or more fur for trappers to catch, I probably would not want to remain in the profession. If I didn't feel that I might be working for something more important than my own or any other person's selfish advantage, a drudgery and strain that I have come to accept as an unavoidable accompaniment of my life-work would be burdensome, indeed.

I am in no position to undertake here a comprehensive discussion of human motivations, in the field of wildlife management or out of it. I had even better leave out of consideration some very strong scientific and sociological motivations and restrict this essay in scope to a few aspects suggesting denominators common to wildlife managers and, let us say, the hunters and trappers.

From early youth to mid-twenties, or up to the beginning of my graduate training, I earned my living largely by fur-trapping. This was my recognized vocation, and it usually paid off in cash as well as any other that I could have had at the time. But some of the trapping seasons that I enjoy recalling were among the less profitable economically. My two most ambitious expeditions (which in the end perhaps yielded me as much enduring satisfaction as anything I ever did as a young man) were business failures. Moreover, the drawbacks of a trapper's life as I lived it ruled out money as a full explanation for the attraction trapping may hold for civilized men. Nor am I convinced that prospects for adventure are any more of an explanation. Part of the answer lies in intangibles, in chickadees fluffing themselves into feathery balls and tree trunks popping in the north-woods cold, in grouse budding in aspen thickets at dusk, in sun dogs hanging over the western plains, in clean air and freedom, and in the sweet loneliness expressed by passages in Sibelius' "Finlandia."

I was also a hunter during my trapping years. I won't lay claim to having been the idealized sportsman of whom I read in outdoor magazines. I wasn't, and I shot more for meat than for sport, but, at any rate, I know the hunter's side of hunting.

In the eastern South Dakota of my upbringing were chain after chain of glacial lakes, marshes, and potholes, with ducks in variety and numbers possibly not found anywhere on earth since the decade following the first World War. Like other hunters, I have my memories of the folding of birds singled out of flocks whipping over the rushes, of the impacts of falling bodies on the water, of drifting feathers and the smell of powder smoke.

For all of that, I must confess that my hunting memories are not as a rule memories of shooting or of bag limits.

One October afternoon, I sat on a ridge between two of the Tetonkeha Lakes adjoining our family's home farm. The day was warm and still, and I saw only scattered, high-flying ducks until sundown. Then, a redhead flight started from the west. The birds were flying out of shotgun range, so I just continued to sit. Flock following flock, the sound of their passage roared over land and water like the sound of an express train crossing a trestle. I doubt not that I was disappointed to go home without any of those ducks, but the vision that stays with me is one of the color and power of the redheads pouring down onto the lake.

Another occasion on which there was more shooting comes to mind. The numbers of waterfowl I saw on a raw, windy day at Lake Albert in 1927 hardly compared with those to be seen when my grandparents lived in their sod shanty in the Tetonkeha hills, nor with the numbers existing in my childhood when men would come home with all of the ducks they could carry and guns would flash on the marshes late into the evening. Nevertheless, on this day, there were in view on the horizon mallards in flocks of hundreds and thousands, and these were interspersed by an unending succession of smaller flocks and stragglers. The ducks that furnished our shooting were mainly lesser scaups.

The scaups were high, wide, and fast; they were low, close, and fast; they came tumbling and zigzagging down from the heights on slanted wings to skim over the water; they swept by in compact bunches or in open arcs or in irregular formation. The shooting was extremely "sporty," though attended by exasperating losses of dead and crippled birds because of the roughness of the water. Now, I find that day most pleasing in retrospect if I simply think of ducks in the air.

Nor do all of my hunting memories relate to panoramic spectacles. I recall a day spent along the Sioux River, west of Brookings, South Dakota. I don't know what my bag was but it wasn't large—a mallard brought down by a lucky snapshot through an opening in the tree tops, a green-winged teal, and maybe a couple of cottontail rabbits. I don't remember what else, if anything, I may have shot and don't care to. What I do remember was the contrast of the white wedge on the dark head of a hooded merganser swimming in a patch of open water. I stood watching it from the underbrush until it saw me and took wing, to disappear around the bend and to leave to me the empty setting of water and wet snow.

Memories arise that are still more gunless, of the slow wing beats and sailing of white pelicans; of curlews, avocets and hosts of smaller shorebirds; of muskrats floating on the marshes at sunset, their tails crooked in the air. There are memories of spawning pickerel in the shallows and herons standing along the lake shores and ground squirrels in the pastures. There are memories of ordinary and trivial things.

Ordinary or trivial as may be the substance of these memories, they are my prize trophies from the out-of-doors. How much the values underlying them may be identified with James Norman Hall's "spirit of place" I am not sure, but unquestionably they are of it. One spring day long after my trapping years, I walked the banks of a creek familiar to my youth and was depressed because of having seen no mink tracks on mud bars where I knew there should have been some. Those mink tracks, in my mind, were integral to the "spirit of place" of that creek, and no amount of the crowing of introduced pheasants could compensate for their lack.

Nostalgia doubtless enters into the equation, but again I can not say how much. The pronghorn antelope, the anhinga, the limpkin, the sage grouse, and the woodland caribou were not creatures of my early background; and I have never seen living in the wild a musk-ox, polar bear, black-footed ferret, or ptarmigan. Even so, I don't believe that I fail to appreciate how unmistakably they may belong in their respective habitats. One may easily go on and list at random almost any number of organisms, plants and animals, similarly belonging in their own biotic communities: flying squirrels in aspen stubs, white-footed mice climbing in the underbrush, cypress draped with long moss, ant lions under sandstone bluffs, fungi and crawling life under dead leaves.

Whether or not I ever again do any fur-trapping, I am still a hunter and dream of spending my declining days amid an abundance of game sufficient for me to shoot some of it without feeling ashamed of myself. As a hunter, I am interested in management programs having promise for increasing the game I like to hunt. That can be acknowledged without implying that my enthusiasm for a given program is proportional to the success with which it may increase the game, irrespective of damage to other outdoor values resulting from the means employed.

To me, with gun in hand or without, the appeal of the out-of-doors seems chiefly conditioned by the relative diversity and completeness of its native fauna and flora and the naturalness of its topography.

Although we may not anticipate a general return of bison herds to the central plains of North America as long as we retain our present social and economic system, the perpetuation of much of our natural out-of-doors is not incompatible with modernity. The growing literature on integration of ends for sound and permanent land use contradicts the thesis that "progress" must inevitably be accompanied by what we have been pleased to call the "conquest of nature," with its top-heavy artificialities and its wastefulness.

Many of the problems of conservation and management are vexatious and appallingly involved. It is not hard to understand why conservation or management practice (or policy) has not been free from confusion and cross purposes or how it may be guided less by long-time than by immediate objectives. In common with other human endeavors, conservation or management probably always will be attended by its share of futility and short-sightedness. Regrettable though this may be, worse still is the outright destruction of the values needing most to be preserved—especially in management programs sponsored by agencies subject to public pressure or catering to circumscribed groups.

It is fitting to strive for "businesslike" efficiency in wildlife management and to take aggressive action to stay or reverse the forces that impoverish the continent. Management, in the sense of judicious manipulation both of organisms and of their environment, should be legitimate and desirable as long as the price is not too great.

The chief mistakes in management practice that I have seen in my professional experience fall in two categories. The writings of Aldo Leopold and O. J. Murie have dealt with the first—the "cleaning up" and "doctoring" of places that should be left alone. The opening of roads, the cutting of grass, brush, and dead trees, the thinning of timber, the planting of exotic vegetation, the building of feeding stations, shelter, and bird houses, the breeding of wild animals in pens, are proper activities of man but they should not be carried on everywhere; and, whenever man's ancient weakness for painting lilies becomes translated into artificializing in the name of wildlife management the remnants of natural out-of-doors that some regions have left, we need to take our collective bearings. What if a wilderness be comparatively unproductive in game yields or commercial assets if its own intrinsic values outweigh the ones it might conceivably gain through artificial changes?

Not many years ago, I visited an island in a marsh, and my first impression was one of exceptional solitude and wild beauty, of a place where, despite the surrounding farm lands, a person wanting relief from human banalities might enjoy an illusion of remoteness. The illusion, however, could not withstand the reality of the series of game shelters that had been cut out of the island's trees.

In the second category of mistakes falls a vast amount of the "control" of native vertebrates advocated or conducted by this or that faction.

The traditional emphasis placed by sportsmen upon campaigning against the predatory or competitive species they designate as "vermin" is seldom based on adequate studies. In too many instances, it betrays the confusion introduced by mixed variables and cherished "fallacies of misplaced concreteness." Predation and competition being manifestations of life are, like life, phenomena of multitudinous complexities that do not always work out as it may be taken for granted that they should. Suppression of predators or of competitors does not necessarily mean benefit to the game or more game to shoot; it is not a panacea and on the whole —not entirely—shows less promise with investigation.

If, however, "vermin control" had many times over the effectiveness ascribed by its proponents, its use as an instrument of game or wildlife management would be no less in need of tempering with moderation and discrimination. Let it be understood that among the so-called vermin are some of our most beautiful and valuable of wild creatures. They comprise a resource demanding sane administration as much as any class of wildlife.

At its worst, "vermin control" may be carried on with an almost unbelievable pointlessness and intolerance. One may scarcely bring to mind a living thing larger than a tree frog that is not "vermin" to someone—including game species in alleged behalf of which someone else may be shooting up the out-of-doors. I have seen hunters deliberately trying to shoot every shoveller—an easily killed duck and one greatly reduced a few years back—that came within gunshot, to leave the carcasses where they fell, with remarks that the birds weren't fit to eat and ought to be cleaned out.

The coyote, the crow, and other adaptable and widely distributed predators are not the ones that are endangered by the anti-"vermin" crusades and the ceaseless killing as opportunities offer. It is the irresponsible harassment of species that "can't take it" that should cause us the most concern—the raptorial and fish-eating birds of restricted geographic range or of strikingly diminished numbers, the predatory fur-bearers that are gravely enough depleted by over-trapping and shrinkage of habitats, the slow-breeding, the unwary, the bizarre, the big and tempting targets. Luckless may be the rare or waning species that concentrates conspicuously in localities where it is vulnerable to raiding by man, notably if it be charged with "harmful" habits.

In my opinion, it is highly dubious strategy to propagandize in favor of mass action for the "control" of native predators, to accelerate wholesale persecution by contest awards, bounties, and the sanction of influential organizations. The prejudices against wild flesh-eaters are so entrenched in people's minds that encouragement may invite excesses and further squandering of what we may not have to spare. When even school children are urged to go out and kill an interminable variety of wild animals as "vermin," we should not be surprised at the peculiar turns that love of the out-of-doors may take.

Writing as a hunter, I would say that sport purchased at disproportionate cost to other outdoor values is not worth having. Wildlife management will be found very much wanting if it fails to safeguard any but popular game species and, incidentally, the song birds and unnoticed forms that are likely to thrive, anyway.

Hunter though I am, why should I have to be one to gain caste, to be entitled to more than outdoor left-overs that may escape gun or pole-trap? Why should I not dawdle on a hill top in the hazy autumn sunshine if I would rather do that than go hunting, and, if I choose not to hunt, why should it follow that I automatically relinquish to hunters all of my rights in game or in wild animals associated with game? To the extent that I as a citizen am mindful of the courtesies due others, I think that I should be entitled to a certain freedom in my choice of outdoor pleasures, without carrying the insignia of gun any more than of rod or field glass or camera or hiking kit. If management itself is to be in analysis anything except exploitation, it must guard against the fundamental wrongness of giving me, upon payment of a piddling license fee, more shooting privileges than I deserve, at the same time shortchanging me as a citizen.

Herein lies a most serious obstacle to harmonious cooperation of outdoor groups in matters that should be to their mutual interest. The harvesting of a seasonal game crop through hunting isn't always the bitterest source of dissension between sportsman and "protectionist." Far more may be attributed to the blindness and selfishness of too many of the sportsmen and their leaders and their assurance that not only is the game theirs to shoot if they want to but also that theirs is the prerogative of doing about whatever they may wish with wildlife in general.

Flatly, I would say that it is time for hunters to reappraise their position in terms other than what they can get by with. I regard hunting logically justifiable only in so far as it may be done without real detriment to both game and non-game species, which means in short that the hunting toll (bagged and lost) of a given species be pretty well confined to biological surpluses. If I were to continue to hunt a severely declining species—though the primary cause of the decline be something besides shooting—I would consider myself justly entitled to less rights than the non-shooters. It is perfectly fair to expect me as a hunter to make concessions when that is the decent thing to do, as during emergency crises, the depressed phases of periodic cycles, years of overshooting, etc.

Of course, this, too, reflects in part my philosophy as a wildlife manager. It may or may not be that of others, but at least the profession could rightly accept something of the broader responsibilities implied by the leadership it exerts and the degree of custody it in effect holds over outdoor values that are not to be reckoned as material harvests. The issue is not one of management versus no management, but rather of what management should be and where it should be done; the criteria of accomplishment may be conformity to good taste as well as statistical impressiveness.

Within reason, we and our editorialized but cheated posterity should be able to think of wildernesses extending beyond highways, of barren grounds and ice-fields and deserts and unlogged forests and untampered lakes and streams. We should know of marshes with sandhill cranes and the more retiring of water birds, of rivers where otters live, of mountains where martens, fishers, wolverines, cougars, wolves, grizzly bears, and native sheep and goats exist in some security. Close to home, we should be able to find natural retreats in appropriate places, to see an eagle, osprey, loon, or one of the larger falcons on occasion; still to watch, among the sights that belong, the red-tailed hawk in the sky; still to hear, among the night sounds, the hooting of the horned owl in the woods.

QUESTIONS

Is "Financial Report" best described as opposition to the church, opposition to one practice of the church, opposition to a practice because it violates the true Christian spirit, or would some other wording describe its aim more accurately? Is the opening paragraph effective or ineffective? Why? What paragraphs make clear what the report is? What ones show the effects of the report? Why does the church publish the report in the form it uses? Does the writer justify her use of the term *blackmail*? Is the unit persuasive for you as a reader? That is, does it bring about any change of attitude in you or deepen an attitude, either positive or negative, that you already had? If it makes any change in you, does it move you to believe, to take action, or does it have some other effect?

In the article with the title "What Am I?" what is the main idea of section one, or what adjustment to the world is the writer rejecting? What is the main idea of section two? Of three? Of four? Of five? What is the writer's ultimate value? Where and why does the writer use questions? Are they effective? Is the article persuasive? Does the persuasive aim stand out at the beginning, or does it appear later? Does it come only from a cumulative effect? Is the writer dealing with a personal problem or one which is universal?

What is the central idea of "A Question of Values"? (Try to phrase it precisely in your own words.) What is the writer's purpose: to inform, to stimulate, to persuade? Does the writer gain by being able to speak as former trapper, hunter, professional wildlife manager, and citizen? If so, how and why? Does he also imply an interest in aesthetic values? If so, where and why? When he says in paragraph eight that his hunting memories are not limited to "memories of shooting or of bag limits," how many paragraphs does he use in supporting and developing this idea and what kind of supporting material does he use? Where else does he use specific details or examples to good advantage? What does he name as the two chief mistakes in management practice? What does he say is the real issue: management versus no management or some other question? What important statement does he make about his rights as hunter and as citizen? Is his conclusion effective? Why? Judging from the magazine in which the article was published, what sort of reader did the author intend to reach? Assuming that you have understood the article, what is its effect on you? Do you reject his ideas, give assent, or do you wish to take action?

25

Personalized Essays

What is a *personal* essay, or an *informal* or a *familiar* essay, since all three terms are used in the same way? The personal essay has a basis of generalizations that tend to be reflective, philosophical, and often subjective; it expresses the writer's attitudes and emotions even more than his intellectual ideas; it is highly personal in style. An impersonal or formal essay is also based on generalizations, but it deals mainly with the writer's intellectual ideas and it tends to be impersonal in style. Again the difference is not rigid. Certain essays wander along the border between the two; one reader might call one of them a personal essay and another might call it a formal essay.

All through Part II you have been writing compositions that might be called personal essays by some people, or at least some of them might be so called. There are some exceptions. The satirical comment in Chapter 20 is more like an editorial; and the persuasive paper, especially when it is aimed at definite action, would not usually be called a personal essay. But the persuasive paper often tends to lead its readers into emotional agreement with attitudes or beliefs of the writer; and there seems to be no difference between this type of persuasion and the personal essay. Again you are confronted with the truth that it is impossible to separate human expression rigidly into narrative and exposition or into any other types.

Certain compositions by professional writers belong in a borderland between short story and personal essay. Galsworthy's "Quality" is one example. Galsworthy uses a specific bootmaker, a conflict (largely unconscious and unplanned by the opposing forces) between an idealist and people who are more and more inclined to accept shoddy work, and a climax—the death of the idealist from slow starvation. But the narrative qualities are less important than the writer's attitudes and general comments on quality; these comments are reflective, philosophical, subjective, and highly personal in style.

SUBJECTS

What subjects will you use for personal essays? It is often said that you can write about any trivial topic, such as wrapping paper or shoestrings. So you can. But the term personal essay seems to have fallen into disrepute because too many writers discussed trivial things in superficial and trivial ways. You may write about trifles if you wish, but try to write about them in a manner which is not trivial. Satirize them, expose their smallness, or make us laugh at people who take them seriously.

You might use as a subject almost any topic which you have considered for a writing assignment in any chapter of either Part I or Part II. You might write about some activity or hobby: a type of creative work such as painting in oils or water colors; a kind of labor; unorganized outdoor sports such as hunting, fishing, trapping, canoeing, skating, skiing; organized sports like football, baseball, basketball, polo; other sports such as golfing, bowling, table tennis. You might write a dozen essays on environment, and in them range from generalizations giving the feel of an environment to an analysis of its causes and effects. You might write about human relations—about family, community, individual friends, minority groups, or your relation to superiors, inferiors, and equals. You could write about people or about the moods and ideas you considered but did not use for stories. If some of these subjects were significant but you did not know how to use them in specific narrative, you may find them well adapted to the generalizations of the personal essay.

As for the preceding chapters in Part II, you may become reflective and philosophical about scientific, technical, or psychological processes, ways of life, nature, animate or inanimate, and autobiographical experiences. You may write about objects, mechanisms, places. You may find a dozen good subjects as you explain other people. You may analyze personal problems, your own character, or your personal philosophy. You may criticize or evaluate the food you eat, the clothing you buy, the training your family or your community gave you, the education offered in one of your courses or by your whole college, the books you read, the paintings you see, the movies or theaters you attend. The more impressionistic your criticism becomes, if you have first considered general standards, the more it will be like the tone of a personal essay.

Why should you need any further suggestions about subjects? But if you do feel a need, consider types of people. What types amuse you? What types do you admire? What types make your fur rise when you see them, hear their voices and their comments, or watch their actions? Consider the subject of food, which is seldom written about by people who really enjoy it. Do you remember the typical Christmas dinner of your childhood? Of a family reunion? Do you enjoy outdoor cooking or cooking with herbs? Can you tell us how to enjoy preparing a certain kind of dinner, or how to enjoy eating it? Consider travel experiences if you remember enough to organize and unify them and to write with richness of detail—a bicycle tour, hitchhiking, canoeing, a walking tour, mountain climbing, going home for vacations. Consider the customs of your family, your community, your church, or your college. Which ones are different, amusing, or endeared to you by association? Consider the views and attitudes which seem conventional because nearly everybody accepts them—honesty is the best policy; punctuality or hard work or thrift is desirable; virtue is its own reward. Has your experience taught you to be skeptical of one of these views? If it has, and if you are not merely assuming a point of view, you have a good subject.

Yes, you can write a personal essay on almost any subject if you are willing to think, to discover your attitudes, and perhaps to analyze your subject.

ORGANIZING AND ARRANGING

In organizing a personal essay you will be able to choose time patterns, space patterns, logical patterns, or any combination of them. Sometimes your plan will be simple, though not sloppy or careless. Sometimes your subject will require careful analysis.

The time pattern is effectively illustrated by an essay called "Annie"; in the 1945–1946 contests for college students conducted by *The Atlantic Monthly* it was given first prize as *an essay*. It is the sketch of a "hired girl" who adopted the family she worked for because she loved the children. Thus it has unity from an idea; it also has unity of attitude, because the writer, one of the children Annie loved, was fond of Annie and communicates to the reader a share of that fondness. The plan can be outlined so as to make the whole unit seem like a narrative:

I. Annie arrives.
  A. Her shyness disappears when she sees the children.
  B. She asks to put them to bed—as she had done at her own home.
II. She becomes important in the lives of the children.
  A. She works for them.
  B. She plays games with them of evenings and tells them stories.
  C. She takes them to her own home each year for Butchering Day.
  D. She gets a tent for herself and the children, to sleep outside in summer.
  E. One dry fall, the tent catches fire from a neighbor's field.
    1. She rescues Bob at the risk of her life.
    2. They recover together.
III. Now she is beginning to look after the children of these children.

Some of these points, I (A, B), E (1), seem to be specific narrative. Others, II (A, B, C, D), are generalized narrative; they tell us what often or usually happened. All of them, whether specific or generalized, are arranged in a time order. But though the writer uses this time order, she also weaves the whole unit together with much explaining. Thus the unit is personalized exposition. It has some right to be called an essay.

You might also use generalized narrative, with some generalized description, for an entire unit, perhaps for a type character. Suppose you wish to explain the type of student who takes an abnormal delight in being busy, and, like Chaucer's Sergeant of the Law, has the ability to seem busier than he is. You might show us what he usually does in a day—how he gets up, eats breakfast, goes to class, what he does between classes, at evening meetings, at his study, and so to bed. You could use the present tense throughout, to indicate customary action.

If you write about a place or about some kinds of environment, you may choose generalized description, with the present tense and with time and space patterns. It can be effective in expressing your attitude about a house, a school, or a playground which has many memories for you. But you may need to combine with it flashbacks in the past tense, and these flashbacks may sometimes be specific and sometimes general.

For some subjects, space patterns combined with simple action in time may be useful. The writer of "Fireside" (at the end of this discussion) uses a contrast between details inside and outside, with active but generalized description to communicate her usual enjoyment of the fire.

An imaginary talk between two typical characters, one of them the writer, may be used to express personal opinions. For example, a student who wishes to express opinions about certain types of teachers might use his own hypothetical interviews with them. Anyone might give his views on any subject through an interview by an inquiring reporter. This method lends itself readily to humor or satire.

A kind of soliloquy might be possible or even a part soliloquy, with some talk by another person, and with action. Steinbeck uses such a pattern in one chapter of *The Grapes of Wrath* to explain the cottonpicker's life, work, and wages. Though this sketch is not exactly a personal essay because the center is probably not Steinbeck himself, the method might be adapted to give a writer's own view.

If you need, at this stage, an example of logical analysis, consider this plan for an essay which was called "Closed Doors": [1]

I. I dislike closed doors.
II. Many others, like me, have tried to open them.

[1] Helen L. Coffin, "Closed Doors," *Harper's Magazine*, March, 1923.

A. Some found tragedy when the door opened.

B. Many found new worlds or great discoveries—Columbus, Franklin.

C. Some try and some oppose opening the doors of psychical research.

III. Many would like to forget the closed doors in their past.

IV. Some doors cannot be opened by force—the doors into other's hearts.

V. Perhaps a Divine Keeper of the Doors exercises some control over the doors we open.

When you need to make an analysis of a subject for a personal essay, ask yourself questions—who, what, when, where, why, what causes, what results—following the suggestions in Chapter 21. Find your important ideas; eliminate, arrange, shape your controlling idea; become conscious of your attitude; know your potential reader and your intended effect on him. As you write, use plenty of narrative and descriptive detail, partly to clarify but mostly to add vividness and interest.

STYLE

Personalize freely and frankly as you write. Probably you will use *I*, *my*, *me*, because it is natural; if you can be consistent you may use *you* with a suggestion of universal experience. Unless you wish to make an individual experiment with colloquial language, try to use the language of your own best conversation—spontaneous, natural, communicative, rich in connotations—or come as near it as you can. Use examples, incidents, and specific details; bring to life the dry bones of your plan.

WRITING YOUR COMPOSITION

A. Plan and write a personal essay on some activity—labor; creative work such as music, dancing, or painting; organized or unorganized sports or such individual sports as hunting, fishing, mountain climbing, etc.

B. Plan and write a personal essay on some phase of nature, animate or inanimate—dogs, horses, or any other animals; stars, mountains, prairies, the ocean, etc. If you use inanimate nature, find ways to make your unit active and to use narrative and vivid description.

C. Plan and write a personal essay on human relations, either group or individual.

D. Plan and write a personal essay on some type of person, using generalized narrative and perhaps generalized description.

E. Plan and write a personal essay that is an evaluation of your home training, or your community background, or your high-school education, or your college training—*one* of these only, not all of them.

F. Plan and write a personal essay on some unconventional or highly individual view—one which makes you feel that you are out of step with everyone you know. Or write on some phase of your personal philosophy.

G. Plan and write a personal essay which is impressionistic criticism (checked by some universal principles). Use a piece of literature, a painting, music, a dramatic performance, a movie, radio or TV drama, etc.

READING

FIRESIDE *

Doris Plagge

I like the quiet of autumn evenings; I like lying before the open fire, stretched out long and lazy. Eyelids grow heavy and fall, but I can see the fire. . . .

Grey wisps of smoke slide through the crevices between the newly split logs, and I hear the crackle of yesterday's crumpled newspaper as it unfolds in the heat of the growing flame. An orange tongue of fire works its way up and catches hungrily to the logs' splintered surfaces. The grate begins to hum, and the blackened brick becomes alive and glowing; the dark, sober parlor is friendly and warmed. Across from me the curving side of the ebony piano glistens in the dappling light.

Outside, the rising harvest moon shines eerily on the mist hanging low over the fields; drying leaves rustle thinly in the wind which makes the passerby glad for his warm topcoat. He lifts his head and breathes deeply as he smells wood smoke; he sees the flickering reflection of my fire on the window pane and wishes he were home. . . .

Inside with me my fire snaps . . . spits . . . settles . . . showers sparks dangerously close to, but never quite reaching, the worn rug on which I lie. Idly, I toss a spiny pine cone into the grate, where it lies in a chink between two logs. I see the orange and yellow tongues of fire dart out, igniting the horned tips. Explosively they blaze in a white dart of heat, swirling madly around and around the cone, adding a low humming note to the staccato cracking of the logs. When they die out, the tips are left a glowing red, then they whiten and softly drop off, one by one. I see the top-most point, though, where a constant and clear blue flame still burns, fed by the firm heart of the cone; it sparkles and dips for a long time. . . .

Chilled, I wake to find the last red embers slowly blackening and greying into ashes. More newspaper, more logs . . . warmth and comfort . . . sleep . . . sleep. . . .

HONOR *

Donald W. Hendrickson

I have known a number of men, some called honorable and others dishonorable. Most of them were somewhere between. Some of them said that they were honorable but were not. Some of them said they had little honor and yet had a great deal. I have known men that were destroyed by honor and some that were destroyed by dishonor.

Honor is an ideal, a truth, a lie, or an illusion. It is many things with many shades of meaning. Life and men and honor are complex. They mean many things to many people. Each man has his unique definition for the three of them.

Remember Falstaff's discourse on honor?

. . . honour pricks me on. Yea, but how if honour prick me off when I come on? How then? Can honour set to a leg? No. Or an arm? No. Or take away the grief of a wound? No. Honour hath no skill in surgery, then? No. What is honour? A word. What is in that word honour? What is that honour? Air. A trim reckoning! Who hath it? He that died o' Wednesday. Doth he feel it? No. Doth he hear it? No. 'T is insensible, then? Yea, to the dead. But will it not live with the living? No. Why? Detraction will not suffer it. Therefore I'll none of it. Honour is a mere scutcheon; and so ends my catechism.

I think that Falstaff's words were true, but there's more to tell about honor. Honor is a word and yet more than a word. We can put any name to any thing and yet not change a particle the thing we're naming. A thing is real if its results are real. A lie can be a real lie and generally is. There is reality about the results of honor. It may not heal but it can kill. The graveyards of the world are thick with the graves of men who died for honor.

I knew a man once who lived almost without honor. He was a bootlegger. Unlike most bootleggers, he was a coward. He was afraid of everything. He was afraid, at first of the law, later of himself, and at last, of life, itself. He had a wife. It's hard to say for certain, but I don't think he loved her. He might have loved her, once, but he became too afraid to love anyone or like anyone or even know anyone. She must not have loved him. She cheated him constantly with other men. She did it obviously. He didn't seem to care. He was too afraid. Fear was all he had or cared about.

One night she came home with another man. It wasn't an un-usual thing at all. This man was a big man and a tough one who had hurt a lot of other men in fights. The bootlegger met them at the door and stretched the big man unconscious on the sidewalk with a single blow. The incident was noticed in passing and then forgotten, for men ignore the things that they can't explain.

There was another man, a banker. He was brave, wise, and highly respected. He had many friends. He loaned them money, a lot of it, but always wisely and logically. He became successful. He was honorable both in his business dealings and in his personal life.

When the depression came, his friends couldn't pay. A syndicate took over the bank. The syndicate had no friends and didn't care for any. They insisted that he foreclose on his friends' property. He shot himself. His friends still lost their property. His death was senseless and useless. It was soon forgotten. But he had acted on his code of honor.

I once had a friend who made no compromise with his honor.

He endured no insult. He fought men and broke their bones. He fought often and with all his strength because it might have been a little dishonorable not to. According to his own code, he was completely honest, and yet he broke many laws in fulfilling the demands of that code.

Men hated him, but he was a man. He was as good a man as he knew how to be. He was more of a man than many men are. He never compromised and he had a savage strength and fanatic bravery. He betrayed women because a man takes women, and not to do so was slightly dishonorable.

They called him a criminal after awhile, and perhaps they were right, but he defended his own code of life, fanatically. There wasn't anything in his beliefs that anyone could call wrong. The sin was in his inflexibility.

He went to prison, at last, and was soon forgotten.

I don't pretend to know the exact definition of honor. I think I'd be a fool if I thought I did. It's a lot of things. It's a kind of integrity in living. It's a payment to life for life. It's honesty toward yourself as a living being and honesty toward others. We have to live together on earth. If we were predatory to an unlimited degree then none of us could live. Each of us would kill the other. We make standards whereby we can live and have time to work without having to watch each other so much that we starve. This is called honorable conduct.

Bravery is another facet of honor. No man or animal can live passively. He must move or fight or, no matter how friendly it may be, his environment will kill him. Men are carnivorous by nature and by necessity. To live, we must destroy. We have to be dangerous. When something threatens this dangerousness, no matter how shaded it may be in connotation, we must resist it. Nothing can live without a sort of respect from its environment. This respect comes from fear. In order to live, we must make our environment, in some way, afraid to kill us. All the world must live by killing. There are excellent reasons for killing, and they must be nullified by better ones for not killing. If we destroy to live, then the only reason we won't destroy must be the fear of death.

We must either be strong or have the appearance of strength. A man must resist any threat to either the actuality of his strength or to its façade. This is sometimes called bravery and sometimes called honor and the meanings are identical.

Honor is more than a word. It is closely connected with the survival urge. It is intimately related to the simpler facts of our existence. In the beginning, it was a simple primitive concept. As time passes, it becomes more and more complex, shaded with different meanings, some of them false. I think, though, if we ever lose sight of the simple outline among its cloak of mistakes, lies and hypocrisies, we shall surely die.

THE TRUE PURPOSE OF PHILOSOPHY *

William Blanchard

Since the first stirrings of human thought, man has sought something in life beyond pleasure and the satisfaction of his biological needs. When man has reached the highest stage of pdeasure, he still retains the impression that somehow this is not enough. He has an inner feeling that the top of one stage of development (the enlargement of physical and mechanical progress) is only the groundwork for a higher and greater stage.

Spinoza expounded this desire to look beyond everyday existence as follows: "After experience had taught me that all the usual surroundings of social life are vain and futile, I finally resolved to inquire whether there might be some real good having power to communicate itself which would affect the mind singly, to the exclusion of all else, of which the discovery and attainment would enable me to enjoy continuous, supreme, and unending happiness."

This development of learning began with solitary thinkers such as Socrates and Plato who first began to seek knowledge in a different manner than by a mere collection of facts. They refused to accept the doctrines of their fathers and sought concepts of virtue and immortality which penetrated beyond the fanatical dogmatism of their contemporaries. Spinoza says in his "Ethics," "Blessedness is not the reward of virtue, but virtue itself. . . . And perhaps . . . immortality is not the reward of clear thinking, but clear thought itself; such thought is immortal because every truth is a permanent creation, part of the eternal acquisition of man."

Slowly this new kind of knowledge called philosophy began to develop, taking more men into its scope, until it branched out into mathematics, chemistry, biology, physics, and the related fields. The various branches became too much to keep in one brain, and scholars began to specialize. They began gradually to perfect their particular field until many of them regarded philosophy as the dried and empty ovary from which the newer and more important seeds of civilized thought had sprung.

The universities and colleges, taking the cue, began to polish their education in the same manner: throwing out what was "not strictly necessary" until we have that triumph of education, the modern industrial college, which promises jobs instead of knowledge and trains men for the position of Chief Cog (or Chief Subordinate Assistant Cog) in the mammoth industrial machine.

The individual is taught to specialize, taught that he cannot make a living in a world of competition unless he devotes himself to one line of work. His sense of the eternal is frustrated by too great a demand for the immediate. If he makes any contact with philosophy, he usually finds that it is taught in the same manner as chemistry and physics: memorization of theories and men's names, concentration upon the logical steps to proving a theory instead of consideration of the worth of the theory from an objective viewpoint. A study of formal logic can teach a person of high I.Q. how to prove almost any theory in a most admirable manner— with words. But what relation has high I.Q. and clever word manipulation to good judgment?

When the normal individual feels the desire to expand, he is confused by the attitudes of those about him. Confused at first, perhaps, but as he is subject more and more to the ideas of those around him, his imagination loses its impetus and he takes refuge in religion or the banalities of human society.

The aim of philosophy, then, is to establish a sound foundation upon which the individual can build. The essential unity of the once formed philosophical mind is not easily scattered or confused. This unity, however, is usually difficult to achieve. The world has pounced upon the average individual before he recognizes a need for philosophy.

As a rule the individual is born into a world of creatures who insist upon talking babytalk to him and reserving their own language for each other. He begins his life by living and loving honestly and thinking (whatever tiny stirrings of thought he may have) clearly. Slowly the world begins to weave a net around him and draw him closer to the bosom of its conformity. He is told that there are rules by which he must govern his life and that people do not always mean what they say. When he tries to disregard the rules or simplify them according to his own needs he is either laughed at for a fool or frowned upon as a villain. The net tightens. He is told that he must grow up, learn a vocation, earn money, get married, have children, and die. All with as little fuss as possible so that his children may grow up and do the same thing. At first he is resentful. He struggles violently, but the net is strong. Sometimes he rebels and leads a life of crime. Sometimes, as the net threatens to close in upon him, he finds his escape in the cool waters of a river at night, and those who would have wrapped him in the net mourn his death and weep for him.

Most of the time, however, he never escapes, but is taught to accept the net as the horse accepts his halter. Once in a while, perhaps, he finds an opening in the top of it and looks out. "Why should I obey the rules?" he says. "The worst that can come is death and that will come anyway. Is there a purpose in life and a mind behind the universe? Why not live my life the way I want to and hang the consequences?"

But soon his friends see him and notice the "bad" signs. Perhaps he has been working too hard. He is lonely, poor fellow. They slap him on the back, get out a deck of cards, look in the paper for the latest movie, turn on the radio in his ear, and laugh and shake his hand. Soon he is laughing, too, but when he goes back to look for the opening in the net, it is gone.

When man refuses to smile and shrug his shoulders at the net of human complexity he has made the first step towards philosophy. By obtaining a philosophical outlook the individual reaches that broadness of vision that carries him beyond the mere acceptance of circumstances. Nirvana is not the end of philosophy, but it is the basis upon which philosophy works and moves. Not that man may reduce his desires to nothing, but that he may regard his desires at their true worth. That he may use his desires and ambitions and not let *them* use *him*. That he may see clearly his own position with respect to human society and the material universe instead of fighting with pieces of it separately. That he may integrate science, music, literature, mathematics, history, and art, and see beyond them without leaping ahead into the aimless ramblings of wild speculation. That he may live, in short, as an integrated human being who understands the universe as much as it will yield itself to understanding and not as a mass of restless somatic cells tossed about by his immediate environment.

Few men have reached such a goal, it is true, but those who have managed to remain individuals despite the dissolving in- fluence of the environment have gone on to build and shape the destiny of men. The peoples of the earth have destroyed beasts of prey, built cities, produced clothing and food, and provided com- forts for themselves; but men like Spinoza, Christ, and Leonardo have looked beyond Homo sapiens as he appears to his fellows, with the idea that this simple, fumbling creature called man might have divine possibilities. All the real progress of civilization has been made by such men, though we all bask in its glory. Many have provided the pericarp, but the seed of civilized thought is small and fine.

THE ASS OF CHARTRES [2]

Ernest Sutherland Bates

What are you doing, Ass of Chartres? Poor foolish ass, ineffably dull, are you still trying to learn to play the lyre? Don't you know that it is quite hopeless? For six hundred years you have tried, in season and out of season, through rain and sleet and snow, and you are now no nearer than at the beginning. Nay, further—for your hoofless leg cannot even reach the lyre that you still hold—rather uselessly it seems.

What are you waiting for, Ass of Chartres, that you keep your bleared eyes turned so steadily toward the square? Do you think to see Thibault the Good, or stout Count Henry, or perchance King Louis the Saint, come riding up once more to the doors of your

[2] By courtesy of Mrs. Gladys Graham Bates and the *Saturday Review of Literature*. "The Ass of Chartres" was first published in the February 20, 1926, issue of *SRL*.

cathedral? They have all gone on crusade—on the last crusade. They will not return.

Or do you watch for the coming of the pilgrims, the cripples and the sick, to lie for nine days in the crypt of Notre-Dame-de-Sous-Terre and then go away—some to live and some to die? Are you expecting new miracles, that the blind will see and the dumb open their lips and praise the Virgin, and men from all France come again to build the Church of God? Poor stupid ass, today the pilgrims go elsewhere, and after miracles they raise no cathedral but cheap hotels, trinket shops, and booths of picture postcards— picture postcards printed for the glory of the Lord.

For what are you listening, Ass of Chartres, with your long ears turned back so wistfully? For Gabriel and Marie in the Old Tower to ring out the tidings that the Prince of Peace is risen? Do you not know that Gabriel and Marie were melted down by the Terrorists and made into leaden bullets to carry different tidings? Poor foolish ass.

Or is it indeed the Prince of Peace himself that you await, and do you think to be able to join in his praise on the great day? Thrice foolish ass—are you so proud because he rode upon the back of your brother into Jerusalem long ago? He did not die for you—you are but a dull beast without a soul. And it is more than doubtful whether He will ever come. Even we, who have immortal souls, have grown weary of waiting. Cease to cling to the walls of the church, Ass of Chartres, come down among us, your betters, eat hay with us and bray with us. For we, we too once thought to play the lyre, but we have learned long since to prefer braying. Then do you, who were made for braying, come down—O Ass of Chartres, come down and be our King.

FREEDOM [3]

E. B. White

I have often noticed on my trips up to the city that people have recut their clothes to follow the fashion. On my last trip, however, it seemed to me that people had remodeled their ideas too—taken

[3] E. B. White, *One Man's Meat*, Harper & Brothers, 1944. Copyright, 1940, by E. B. White.

in their convictions a little at the waist, shortened the sleeves of their resolve, and fitted themselves out in a new intellectual ensemble copied from a smart design out of the very latest page of history. It seemed to me they had strung along with Paris a little too long.

I confess to a disturbed stomach. I feel sick when I find anyone adjusting his mind to the new tyranny which is succeeding abroad. Because of its fundamental strictures, fascism does not seem to me to admit of any compromise or any rationalization, and I resent the patronizing air of persons who find in my plain belief in freedom a sign of immaturity. If it is boyish to believe that a human being should live free, then I'll gladly arrest my development and let the rest of the world grow up.

I shall report some of the strange remarks I heard in New York. One man told me that he thought perhaps the Nazi ideal was a sounder ideal than our constitutional system "because have you ever noticed what fine alert young faces the young German soldiers have in the newsreel?" He added: "Our American youngsters spend all their time at the movies—they're a mess." That was his summation of the case, his interpretation of the new Europe. Such a remark leaves me pale and shaken. If it represents the peak of our intelligence, then the steady march of despotism will not receive any considerable setback at our shores.

Another man informed me that our democratic notion of popular government was decadent and not worth bothering about—"because England is really rotten and the industrial towns there are a disgrace." That was the only reason he gave for the hopelessness of democracy; and he seemed mightily pleased with himself, as though he were more familiar than most with the anatomy of decadence, and had detected subtler aspects of the situation than were discernible to the rest of us.

Another man assured me that anyone who took *any* kind of government seriously was a gullible fool. You could be sure, he said, that there is nothing but corruption "because of the way Clemenceau acted at Versailles." He said it didn't make any difference really about this war. It was just another war. Having relieved himself of this majestic bit of reasoning, he subsided.

Another individual, discovering signs of zeal creeping into my blood, berated me for having lost my detachment, my pure skeptical point of view. He announced that he wasn't going to be swept away by all this nonsense, but would prefer to remain in the role of innocent bystander, which he said was the duty of any intelligent person. (I noticed, however, that he phoned later to qualify his remark, as though he had lost some of his innocence in the cab on the way home.)

Those are just a few samples of the sort of talk that seemed to be going round—talk which was full of defeatism and disillusion and sometimes of a too studied innocence. Men are not merely annihilating themselves at a great rate these days, but they are telling one another enormous lies, grandiose fibs. Such remarks as I heard are fearfully disturbing in their cumulative effect. They are more destructive than dive bombers and mine fields, for they challenge not merely one's immediate position but one's main defenses. They seemed to me to issue either from persons who could never have really come to grips with freedom, so as to understand her, or from renegades. Where I expected to find indignation, I found paralysis, or a sort of dim acquiescence, as in a child who is dully swallowing a distasteful pill. I was advised of the growing anti-Jewish sentiment by a man who seemed to be watching the phenomenon of intolerance not through tears of shame but with a clear intellectual gaze, as through a well-ground lens.

The least a man can do at such a time is to declare himself and tell where he stands. I believe in freedom with the same burning delight, the same faith, the same intense abandon which attended its birth on this continent more than a century and a half ago. I am writing my declaration rapidly, much as though I were shaving to catch a train. Events abroad give a man a feeling of being pressed for time. Actually I do not believe I am pressed for time, and I apologize to the reader for a false impression that may be created. I just want to tell, before I get slowed down, that I am in love with freedom and that it is an affair of long standing and that it is a fine state to be in, and that I am deeply suspicious of people who are beginning to adjust to fascism and dictators merely because they are succeeding in war. From such adaptable natures a smell rises. I pinch my nose.

For as long as I can remember I have had a sense of living somewhat freely in a natural world. I don't mean I enjoyed freedom of action, but my existence seemed to have the quality of free-ness. I traveled with secret papers pertaining to a divine conspiracy. Intuitively I've always been aware of the vitally important pact which a man has with himself, to be all things to himself, and to be identified with all things, to stand self-reliant, taking advantage of his haphazard connection with a planet, riding his luck, and following his bent with the tenacity of a hound. My first and greatest love affair was with this thing we call freedom, this lady of infinite allure, this dangerous and beautiful and sublime being who restores and supplies us all.

It began with the haunting intimation (which I presume every child receives) of his mystical inner life; of God in man; of nature publishing herself through the "I." This elusive sensation is moving and memorable. It comes early in life: a boy, we'll say, sitting on the front steps on a summer night, thinking of nothing in particular, suddenly hearing as with a new perception and as though for the first time the pulsing sound of crickets, overwhelmed with the novel sense of identification with the natural company of insects and grass and night, conscious of a faint answering cry to the universal perplexing question: "What is 'I'?" Or a little girl, returning from the grave of a pet bird leaning with her elbows on the windowsill, inhaling the unfamiliar draught of death, suddenly seeing herself as part of the complete story. Or to an older youth, encountering for the first time a great teacher who by some chance word or mood awakens something and the youth beginning to breathe as an individual and conscious of strength in his vitals. I think the sensation must develop in many men as a feeling of identity with God—an eruption of the spirit caused by allergies and the sense of divine existence as distinct from mere animal existence. This is the beginning of the affair with freedom.

But a man's free condition is of two parts: the instinctive free-ness he experiences as an animal dweller on a planet, and the practical liberties he enjoys as a privileged member of human society. The latter is, of the two, more generally understood, more widely admitted, more violently challenged and discussed. It is the practical and apparent side of freedom. The United States, almost alone today, offers the liberties and the privileges and the tools of freedom. In this land the citizens are still invited to write their plays and books, to paint their pictures, to meet for discussion, to dissent as well as to agree, to mount soapboxes in the public square, to enjoy education in all subjects without censorship, to hold court and judge one another, to compose music, to talk politics with their neighbors without wondering whether the secret police are listening, to exchange ideas as well as goods, to kid the government when it needs kidding, and to read real news of real events instead of phony news manufactured by a paid agent of the state. This is a fact and should give every person pause.

To be free, in a planetary sense, is to feel that you belong to earth. To be free, in a social sense, is to feel at home in a democratic framework. In Adolf Hitler, although he is a freely flowering individual, we do not detect either type of sensibility. From reading his book I gather that his feeling for earth is not a sense of communion but a driving urge to prevail. His feeling for men is not that they co-exist, but that they are capable of being arranged and standardized by a superior intellect—that their existence suggests not a fulfillment of their personalities but a submersion of their personalities in the common racial destiny. His very great absorption in the destiny of the German people somehow loses some of its effect when you discover, from his writings, in what vast contempt he holds *all* people. "I learned," he wrote, ". . . to gain an insight into the unbelievably primitive opinions and arguments of the people." To him the ordinary man is a primitive, capable only of being used and led. He speaks continually of people as sheep, halfwits, and impudent fools—the same people from whom he asks the utmost in loyalty, and to whom he promises the ultimate in prizes.

Here in America, where our society is based on belief in the individual, not contempt for him, the free principle of life has a chance of surviving. I believe that it must and will survive. To understand freedom is an accomplishment which all men may acquire who set their minds in that direction; and to love freedom is a tendency which many Americans are born with. To live in the same room with freedom, or in the same hemisphere, is still a profoundly shaking experience for me.

One of the earliest truths (and to him most valuable) that the author of *Mein Kampf* discovered was that it is not the written word, but the spoken word, which in heated moments moves great masses of people to noble or ignoble action. The written word, unlike the spoken word, is something which every person examines privately and judges calmly by his own intellectual standards, not by what the man standing next to him thinks. "I know," wrote Hitler, "that one is able to win people far more by the spoken than by the written word. . . ." Later he adds contemptuously: "For let it be said to all knights of the pen and to all the political dandies, especially of today: the greatest changes in this world have never yet been brought about by a goose quill! No, the pen has always been reserved to motivate these changes theoretically."

Luckily I am not out to change the world—that's being done for me, and at a great clip. But I know that the free spirit of man is persistent in nature; it recurs, and has never successfully been wiped out, by fire or flood. I set down the above remarks merely (in the words of Mr. Hitler) to motive that spirit, theoretically. Being myself a knight of the goose quill, I am under no misapprehension about "winning people"; but I am inordinately proud these days of the quill, for it has shown itself, historically, to be the hypodermic which inoculates men and keeps the germ of freedom always in circulation, so that there are individuals in every time in every land who are the carriers, the Typhoid Marys, capable of infecting others by mere contact and example. These persons are feared by every tyrant—who shows his fear by burning the books and destroying the individuals. A writer goes about his task today with the extra satisfaction which comes from knowing that he will be the first to have his head lopped off—even before the political dandies. In my own case this is a double satisfaction, for if freedom were denied me by force of earthly circumstance, I am the same as dead and would infinitely prefer to go into fascism without my head than with it, having no use for it any more and not wishing to be saddled with so heavy an encumbrance.

QUESTIONS

What qualities in "Fireside" might give some reason for calling it a personal essay? Is it an intellectual or an emotional expression of the writer? Does it deal with one time only or with customary attitudes? What kind of sensory details does the writer use best? How does she use comparison or contrast? Does she give the feel of experience? Is the end effective? What reason can you give for your answer?

In "Honor" what is the relation of the first paragraph to the whole article? Is the entire essay developed as an extended definition? What methods of developing a definition are used? How many developed examples does the writer use? Are any of his ideas objective rather than subjective? Does he back up his ideas with thinking and experience, so that he commands the respect of his reader? What are his final conclusions about honor?

What is the topic of paragraphs one to three in "The True Purpose of Philosophy"? What is the topic of paragraph four? What comment on contemporary education does the writer make in paragraphs five and six? In his opinion, what is the true purpose of philosophy? What does he mean by the "net"? Who uses it? What is its effect on the individual who is trying to think? What types of people escape it by violence? What happens to most people who try to escape it? When a man escapes it by individual thought what attitudes does he have to philosophy, to his own desires and ambitions, to society? What does the writer mean by the "integrated" human being? How does he estimate the influence on the world of the few integrated men who have best understood the universe?

How clearly does the writer of "The Ass of Chartres" describe the object he uses as a center for his ideas? Is it effective even for the person who has not seen the cathedral at Chartres? Is the essay more effective because the writer uses this object? How and where does he use questions? Are they effective? Are the paragraphs unified? Are they in a carefully planned order, or could they easily be rearranged? What comparisons does he use in the last paragraph? Are they effective? What comment on human beings, or even upon civilizations, does he imply by these comparisons? What is the central idea of the article? What is the writer's chief attitude? Is "The Ass of Chartres" a personal essay?

In "Freedom," what general state of mind is E. B. White explaining in paragraphs one and two? What comparison does he use for his idea and how does he word the comparison? What is his reaction to this state of mind? How are paragraphs three through seven each related to this state of mind? What is the topic of paragraph eight? How do paragraphs nine to twelve define or describe freedom? What methods of an extended definition does he use—origins, description, comparison, contrast, division? If he uses any of these, how and where does he do so? In paragraph fourteen what does he say about the survival of freedom? What discovery did Hitler make that helped him destroy freedom? How does the author progress from this statement to his conclusion? Is the article universal, or did it apply only to the situation in 1940? Is American freedom in any danger now? What methods if any are being used against it? What kinds of attacks are made upon it? If you are a college student, are you interested in intellectual freedom, that is, in your right to examine all sides of questions?

Appendix

HELP IN FINDING MATERIAL

PERSONAL EXPERIENCES

1. What are your earliest memories? After you think that you have found the earliest ones, let your senses explore further. Can you discover any that have been buried? What sounds, odors, touch sensations, and pictures are associated with these memories?

2. What sensory details have been most vivid in your experience the last few weeks—details that you have enjoyed, details that have bored or disgusted you?

3. What did you like most to do in your childhood before you entered school? In the elementary grades? In high school? What do you like most to do at the present time?

4. What did you dislike most to do at the same stages? What do you dislike most heartily at the present time?

5. What sports or physical activities have you enjoyed at some time? Skating, skiing, learning to control a car, a motorcycle, a plane? Hunting, fishing, hiking? Basketball, baseball, football, hockey, polo?

6. Have you preferred organized or unorganized physical activities?

7. Do you remember moments of tense experience centered around mere physical achievement in sports?

8. Do you remember moments of tense experience centered around psychological conflicts—hate, rivalry, fair play, approval of others, conflicts with other members of your own team?

513

9. Do you remember moments of experience when you enjoyed handling a good rifle, using sharp tools, hearing and seeing powerful machinery?

10. What labor have you tried and enjoyed or hated? Factory work, typing, digging ditches, detasseling hybrid corn, harvesting crops—cranberries, potatoes, oranges, sugar beets, corn—making model planes, furniture; cleaning house, making a birthday cake, designing dresses?

11. Did any of these labor processes have psychological meaning, because you conquered, or discovered tastes and interests, or wished to please another person?

12. What troubles and fears did you have at different stages of your development in the past?

13. What troubles and fears do you have now?

14. What experience in your life has made you most sad?

15. Whom did you admire most in your childhood before you entered school? In the grades? In high school? Whom do you admire most at present?

16. Whom did you dislike most at the same stages? Whom do you dislike most at present?

17. With whom did you get along better in the past—father or mother?

18. With what sort of person do you get along best? With what types are you usually at ease?

19. What persons have had a definite influence on you?

20. What is the greatest personal problem that you have ever had to decide? What is the greatest one that you foresee in the future?

21. What is the most difficult new situation that you have ever faced?

22. Did you ever hide a real feeling or opinion? When? Why?

23. Did you ever meet anyone who forced you to feel inferior? To feel important?

24. Did you ever feel thoroughly ashamed of yourself? Why?

25. Do you have clear impressions of the dominating interests and motives of the people you know well?

26. Did you ever feel group disapproval? Did you ever feel yourself one with a group?

27. Do you remember being happy because you did something well and received approval or praise? Did you ever suffer because you did something badly? Were you ever disappointed because you did something well and failed to receive praise or approval?

28. Did you ever experience a feeling of responsibility or duty? Did you ever develop under new responsibility?

29. Did you ever realize suddenly that you had developed a new skill or power?
30. Are you self-sufficient? Have you lost a former feeling of self-sufficiency?
31. What is the real basis of your liking for someone you know? Of your dislike for someone you know?
32. Did you ever hold an unpopular opinion or belief? With what result? Did you ever court favor?
33. Did you ever break the code of behavior accepted by your associates or your community? With what result?
34. What are the hardest things that you have ever done?
    a. The heaviest physical labor?
    b. The most exacting task or skill?
    c. The most difficult interview or conversation?
    d. The most depressing or discouraging task?
    e. The severest effort of your will or perseverance?
35. Have you ever defended yourself from an accusation by another person? From an accusation by yourself?
36. Created ideal versions of a situation-to-be and then bungled the same situation when it became real?
37. Bungled a situation and then created ideal versions of it afterward?
38. Talked to a person when you felt superior but reproached yourself for it?
39. Tried to conceal your triumph over a rival?
40. Tried to persuade a person to do something against his disposition? His convenience? His principles?
41. Tried to find out something that was none of your business?
42. Known a very painful moment of misunderstanding, hurt feelings, failure, fear, envy, hate?
43. Given yourself discipline? In what? Why? With what result?
44. Tried to lead other people, instead of driving them?
45. Discovered that your mind and emotions were in agreement? Were not in agreement at first but were brought closer together? Could not be harmonized?
46. Discovered an inferiority complex or any other defense mechanism in yourself?
47. On what subjects do you "rationalize" and why? What opinions or beliefs of yours are really irrational prejudices?
48. How do you react to small annoyances or irritations?
49. In serious crises, do you become helpless or do you rise to meet difficult situations?

50. Are you afraid of being alone? Afraid of thinking? Afraid, in irrational ways, of other people?

51. What educational background have you had at different stages of your life? What influences in it have been good? What influences have been bad?

52. What informal education has been most important in your life? What people, events, environment, reading, sports, recreations have influenced you? Were the influences desirable or undesirable? What traits or interests do you have as a result of informal education?

ENVIRONMENT

1. Have you ever been miserable in a house because it was too clean and too neat?

2. Been suddenly and completely happy in a place because it was restful and you were very tired?

3. Hated a place because it was too quiet or too noisy?

4. Become tired of a place because it restricted your desire to grow and develop?

5. What house, yard, city, farm, scene do you love most at present, or hate most at present?

6. What place which you are not seeing now would you like most, in all the world, to see at present?

7. What place or places are you seeing now but wishing that you might never see again?

8. Have you ever seen a thoroughly beautiful building? A lonely place? A house that you will long remember for its ugliness?

9. What place do you remember because it is associated with former carefree days, with some other form of past happiness, with past sorrow, with a grandeur or mystery which is now gone?

10. What is the ugliest landscape you know? The most beautiful landscape you know?

11. Do you remember vividly a place where you struggled to defeat or victory?

12. A school which is closely connected with your development—either a building or a single school room?

13. A church which is closely connected with your community or family life?

14. Is there a chest, vase, picture, brooch, necklace which you value because it is a family heirloom?

15. Do you remember some historical spot or house clearly because you learned something significant from it?

16. How does your city street or a corner in your small town look in summer on a Sunday morning, a Saturday morning, a Monday morning, a Saturday afternoon, a Saturday night? On a cold winter night, on a morning in early spring, on a raw November afternoon?

17. How does a farm look in the opulence of midsummer, in a dry season, in heavy rains; at morning, noon, and evening in the same season and weather; in spring, summer, autumn, winter?

18. How does a summer cottage, on the lake or the ocean, look as you see it on your arrival for vacation, on your departure at the end of the season; at morning, noon, evening; on a moonless night; by moonlight?

19. What surroundings stimulate you? Depress or annoy you? Why?

20. What physical environments do you know well—what regions of the United States, what foreign places? Oceans, lakes, prairies, mountains?

21. What moral, ethical, or religious environment are you most familiar with? Is it tolerant or intolerant, social or self-centered?

22. Have you had some contact with an entirely different moral and ethical environment? What was the result of this contact?

23. What social class do you know best? What other social class do you know well enough to contrast with it?

24. What occupational or professional backgrounds do you know best?

25. Have the environments mentioned in questions 20–24 affected the people living in them? In desirable ways? In undesirable ways?

26. Have these same environments grown up without much conscious effort? Have they been created by the conscious effort of many people? By the conscious effort of one person?

27. In the homes you know best, is the prevailing atmosphere the conscious or the unconscious result of one person's effort? Of group effort?

28. Of your environments—physical, ethical, psychological, social, educational, economic—which have had the greatest influence on you? Desirable? Undesirable?

29. What sort of environment do you prefer to help create in the future? In business or professional work? In your community? In your social group? Among your intimate friends? In your family?

PERSONAL PHILOSOPHY

1. When you face crises, what principles are you ready to act upon spontaneously? What principles would you act upon after careful thinking?

2. Do these principles concern your relation to your father and mother? Your brothers and sisters? Your community? Your choice of friends? Your attitude to young women if you are a young man, to young men if you are a young woman? To marriage?

3. Do these principles concern your reasons for pursuing an education? Your aims in your education? Your attitude to work? To money? To honesty? To amusement and recreation? To reading? To writing? To religion? To morals in general?

4. Are there important questions on which you have not yet developed a philosophy? If so, what are these questions?

5. Are there important questions on which you have changed, even reversed, your basic principles? If so, when, under what circumstances, and why did you change?

6. What basic attitude to religion or morals has been the prevailing one in your own family? What attitude to work? To money? To the different attitudes of some other family? In what situations have you seen these attitudes appear?

7. Do you differ with your parents on any important questions? With your brothers and sisters? With relatives? With your friends? With other associates?

8. Do you disagree on any important questions with the leaders in your community? With the majority opinion in your community?

9. What things in the past have given you the greatest personal satisfaction? What things could give you the greatest personal satisfaction in the future?

10. What beliefs, notions, or preferences of yours are really irrational prejudices, instead of basic principles? What or whom do you dislike for no sound reason? On what subjects do you rationalize, and by what processes?

11. Do you know well any person whose ideas—religious, moral, political, social—differ sharply from your own? Or any person whose artistic and intellectual attitudes differ sharply from your own? How well do you understand the views of this person? Do you know what he thinks of you and your opinions?

12. What specific hopes and fears do you have for the future?

13. Will what you hope or fear for the future differ from what you will probably get? If so, will you make an adequate adjustment?

DISCOVERING MOODS

1. Have you ever been lonely at home, in a strange place, in a foreign country? What is the loneliest moment you have ever known?

2. Have you ever left a country, a town, or a house, hating to leave but knowing that you would never return?
3. Discovered from specific experience that friends change? That the home town doesn't stay the same? That a time comes when you wait between two worlds, the past and the future?
4. Known a fear that troubled you for days or weeks? Thought you had an incurable disease or a social stigma that you could never live down?
5. Known insecurity? What kind of insecurity—economic or social insecurity, loss of personal relationships, loss of belief in civilization or in religion?
6. Discovered that you were inadequate when you wished to be adequate?
7. Tried to appear self-reliant and sophisticated when you did not feel so?
8. Enjoyed giving your best to a cause or an undertaking?
9. Discovered an undesirable character trait in yourself?
10. Discovered an undesirable trait in another person whom you valued, so that you lost confidence in that person?
11. Discovered a racial prejudice or some other prejudice which you felt against another person? Discovered another's prejudice toward you?
12. Felt helpless because you couldn't make another person understand a moral or social principle which you had taken for granted, or your reason for having another person as a friend?
13. Suffered because of a wound or some physical condition which made you conspicuous?
14. Tried to protect a sensitive person?
15. Discovered that you can never understand another person completely?
16. Suffered because you were misunderstood?
17. Suffered because you misunderstood a situation or another person, or because you were too sensitive?
18. Watched a sensitive person suffer when you could do nothing?
19. Watched an imaginative individualist try to adjust to mechanical work?
20. Suffered through the lack of sensitivity in another person?
21. Developed under responsibility?
22. Recognized your own gain in maturity—when you assumed leadership, kept your self-control, learned to understand parental feelings, began to think of giving rather than getting at Christmas time?

23. Harmed yourself by your own stubbornness?
24. Watched an adventure seeker who overlooked the chances nearest him?
25. Changed your attitude to death, to immortality, or to some religious belief?
26. Realized the smallness of the individual in contrast to eternity, infinity, perfect beauty?
27. Felt the transient quality of human life?
28. Tried to understand how an old man or an old woman, past the age of activity, feels?
29. Found satisfaction because you dared to be yourself instead of following custom, convention?
30. Felt hate, envy, regret, triumph?
31. Delighted in physical activity—swimming, diving, horseback riding, tennis, wrestling?
32. Tried to borrow something, to persuade someone to vote for you, or to ask some other help or support—when you were in conflict about your action?
33. Tried to persuade another person to do something against his convenience, or his principles?
34. Enjoyed victory in a physical contest?
35. Felt helpless against someone at a later stage of development than your own—as a child when you tried to make grown-ups understand; when you tried to understand their attitudes to sex, love, death; when your older brother began going with girls and scorned playing with you?
36. Fought against dust storms? Drought?
37. Fought against a fear of darkness?
38. Been completely happy without being able to find out why? Been completely happy, knowing why?

PEOPLE

1. What kind of person amuses you? Antagonizes you? Disgusts you? Stirs your sympathy? Rouses your admiration?
2. What individual person amuses you? Antagonizes you? Disgusts you? Stirs your sympathy? Rouses your admiration? (Try to find the person who is perhaps your best answer to each, and to find out *why* he has this effect.)
3. What kind of person do you dislike for no sound reason? What individual?
4. With what kind of person do you get along best? Why?
5. With what kind are you least at ease?

6. What people have had the greatest influence on you? Undesirable influence? Desirable influence? Considered undesirable at the time but desirable later?

7. Are you able to understand people whose religious, moral, political, or social ideas differ from yours? Whose artistic or intellectual tastes differ from yours?

8. Have you watched a person talking to another and feeling superior about some specific thing—knowledge of baseball or chemistry, family, taste in dress, ability to get dates and to manage men (if a girl) or to manage girls (if a man).

9. Have you ever watched a girl becoming a woman? A boy becoming a man as he assumes responsibility or realizes a new attitude?

10. Watched a girl becoming a sorority sister? A boy becoming a fraternity man?

11. Watched a student being turned into an economist, a chemist, a historian, an engineer, a dietitian?

12. Which of your acquaintances seem to you to be the most popular? What is the reason for the popularity of each one?

13. Do you know any person who has at some time shown one of these traits: courage, cowardice, stubbornness, greed, patience, loyalty, dishonesty, stinginess, determination, stupidity, superstition, provincialism, pride? In what situation was the trait brought out?

14. Listened to a person reporting on an offer made to him of a position when you knew that he was modest? Boastful? Unhappy about it but attempting to conceal his unhappiness?

15. What individuals have you seen in conflict with physical environment? With social environment?

16. Where—at what time, place, or situation—could you best reveal to someone else your friend, your roommate, your brother, sister, father, mother, grandfather, grandmother? Your worst enemy? Your favorite instructor?

IDEAS

1. What principles would you really act on in a crisis spontaneously? After thinking?

2. How do these principles differ from those you used to act on, those of your friends, your family, your community?

3. Have you ever clashed with your parents over dancing, late hours, religion, your future occupation?

4. Have you clashed with authority of another kind, over these same principles or similar ones?

5. Have you watched others as they clashed with family authority or other authority?
6. Do you have a sharply defined sense of integrity? Do you admire others who have personal integrity or do you prefer conformity in others?
7. What are desirable results of conformity? Undesirable results of conformity on the people you know?
8. What are your real beliefs about religion?
9. What are your real beliefs about death? About immortality? Have these beliefs changed?
10. Do you believe in coöperation or in unrestrained individualism?
11. Do you think that happiness or love or friendship comes more certainly from self-centeredness or from unselfishness?
12. Do you have any other real belief (not conventional platitudes) about happiness?
13. Do you have a philosophy about your place in your community, your state, your nation, the world?
14. Do you have a basic philosophy about family relationships—about the equality or inequality of husband and wife? About responsibility for the children? About their discipline?
15. How has the desire for perfection, in some form, affected the people you know?
16. Do you believe that a person can change his emotional patterns or his behavior patterns? How? Why?
17. Do you believe that human beings have some freedom to shape themselves and their own futures? Or do you believe that they must act as if they had freedom to shape their own destinies?
18. What forces may limit one's freedom to shape himself and his future?
19. What forces may we use as individuals to shape ourselves and our futures?
20. What forces may we use in social groups to help others shape desirable futures?
21. Have you known insecurity, from outer circumstances—illness, death, drought, depression, war?

INDEX

Student writers and the titles of their compositions are starred

Additional helps, 25–26, 142–143, 167–168, 180–181, 207–208, 235–236, 257
Aiken, Conrad, quoted, 93
Allegory, 241
Anderson, Sherwood, "Reverie," 350
Angoff, Charles, "Where Did Yesterday Go?," 105
*"Anne," Dick Campbell, 116
Arabian Nights, quoted, 49
Archer Pilgrim, Don Jackson, 41
"Ass of Chartres, The," Ernest Sutherland Bates, 504
Assumptions, 6
Attitudes, as basis of creative work, 8–9
  how to express, 9–10
*"Aunt Bertha," Tom Olsen, 418
*Austin, Jean, "Fourteen," 219
Autobiographical material, 358
  results of using, 359
  narrative plan for, 359
*Avey, Robert J., "Purgatory," 102

"Bach," Frank Lloyd Wright, 372
"Ballet Meister, The," Margaret Mattison, 159
Behrman, S. N., quoted, 314
  "A Sale to John R. Thompson," 322
*"Benediction," Maurice Kirby, 384
Berge, Bill, quoted, 56
*"Best Concrete in the Dam, The," Tom Vernon, 61
*Billings, Wayne, "A Recurring Blight: The Wasteland," 457
"Biography of a Dancing Ground," F. N. and Frances Hamerstrom, 335
"Birth of A Foal, The," T. H. White, 333
"Black Water Blues," Montgomery Culver, 195

*Blanchard, William, "The True Purpose of Philosophy," 501
"Bloodhound," James Boyd, 298
Boyd, James, "Bloodhound," 298
Brooke, Stopford A., "Logical Pattern in Shelley's Lyrics," 462
*"Brotherhood," 401
*"Brown Boxes," Pat Minear, 38
Brown, Rollo Walter, "Portrait of My Mother," 425
Browning, Robert, "My Last Duchess," 178
Buck, Pearl S., introduction to "The Frill," 162

*Campbell, Dick, "Anne," 116
Character, analysis of, 443
  bringing to life, 123
  characterizing of, 110–111
  choice of, 127
  knowledge of, 124–126
  specific detail for, 128
Clark, Walter Van Tilburg, quoted, 97–98
*Clure, Miriam, "Send Me Orchids," 191
*"Coming Home," Gertrude Richards, 362
Comparisons, literal and figurative, 15–16
*Cowgill, George, "Some Catoidoid Breed," 248
Criticism, definition of, 450–451
  essentials in, 454–455
  questions as an approach to, 453
Culver, Montgomery, "Black Water Blues," 195

*Danielson, Donna Rae, "Financial Report," 477
Diary, creative, 5
*Dunkelberg, Dorothy, "Nurses' Home," 60

525